The Death of Hitler's War Machine

THE DEATH OF HITLER'S
War Machine

The Final Destruction of the Wehrmacht

SAMUEL W. MITCHAM JR.

REGNERY
HISTORY

Regnery History™ is a trademark of Salem Communications Holding
Corporation
Regnery® is a registered trademark of Salem Communications Holding
Corporation

ISBN 978-1-68451-138-9
eISBN 978-1-68451-184-6

Library of Congress Control Number: 2020949471

Published in the United States by
Regnery History
An imprint of Regnery Publishing
A division of Salem Media Group
Washington, D.C.
www.RegneryHistory.com

Manufactured in the United States of America

10 9 8 7 6 5 4 3 2 1

Books are available in quantity for promotional or premium use.
For information on discounts and terms, please visit our website:
www.RegneryHistory.com.

Contents

INTRODUCTION

The purpose of this book is to write the military history of Nazi Germany from the latter part of 1944 until May 23, 1945—the period in which Hitler's empire was finally and totally destroyed.

From June 6, 1944, until early September 1944, Hitler's Wehrmacht was smashed on both the Eastern and Western Fronts. It nevertheless made a desperate last stand and checked the Anglo-American armies in a series of battles along the Siegfried Line while simultaneously administering a stinging defeat to the British Army at the Battle of Arnhem. At the same time, it almost miraculously created an entire new panzer army, which it unleashed in the Ardennes on December 16, 1944. It was Germany's "last chance" offensive, and it gave the Americans, in particular, some very bad moments.

On the Eastern Front, the main focus was on Poland and Hungary. In August 1944, Romania defected from the Axis, and Germany lost most of its 6th and 8th Armies. Hungary was wavering and in September was invaded by the Soviet Union. Against seemingly overwhelming odds, Hitler's generals desperately tried to prevent the collapse of their southern flank. That they succeeded was one of the minor miracles of the war. This is where our story begins.

Since 1960, there have arisen in the Western world what might be termed "social military historians." They deal with war from a sociological (or in some cases pseudo-sociological) point of view without discussing battles and campaigns, which are dismissed with a wave of the hand, if they are mentioned at all. I believe war has its sociological and philosophical elements, but it also involves strategy, operations, and tactics, as well as logistics, training, the inclination of a people to wage war, and the warrior himself, be he general or private. In other words, this book will follow a more "nuts and bolts" approach in which strategy, battles, and campaigns are emphasized rather than sociological motivations.

I wish to thank all those who helped in the researching, writing, and producing of this book, especially my wife, Donna. Thanks also go to the archivists and other employees at the National Archives, Washington, D.C., the Bundesarchiv, the War College, the Center of Military History, and the Imperial War Museum, as well as the late Friedrich von Stauffenberg and anyone else who shared information, advice, photographs, or memoirs with me.

Dr. Samuel W. Mitcham Jr.
Monroe, Louisiana
February 2020

CHAPTER I

SETTING THE STAGE

The Nazis came to power on January 30, 1933. At that time, Germany lived under the restrictions imposed by the Treaty of Versailles, which ended World War I. Its military force (the *Reichswehr* or armed forces) was limited to 115,000 men—100,000 in the army (*Reichsheer*) and 15,000 in the navy (*Reichsmarine*)—which left Germany unable to defend itself or threaten its neighbors.

Adolf Hitler changed all that, and he had an excellent foundation upon which to build. The notoriously efficient General Staff was officially abolished in 1919, but its de facto replacement, the *Truppenamt* (Troop Office), secretly continued to train top-level General Staff officers. Germany also continued to maintain its *Wehrkreise* (sometimes spelled *Wehrkreisen*) or German military districts, which were the heart of the German Army.

Each Wehrkreis was a corps-level, territorial command responsible for recruiting, mobilization, supply, administration, logistical support, and all military-political and military-civilian matters within its area. After Hitler renounced the Treaty of Versailles, the Wehrkreise were responsible for implementing conscription for the German Army. When the war began in September 1939, they were placed under the Home Army (also known as the Replacement Army). Their field components were designated corps headquarters and sent to combat zones. Their territorial elements remained in Germany, where older officers, often extremely capable administrators, focused on keeping the badly outnumbered German Army well-trained and in the field for the duration of the war.

Initially, there were seven Wehrkreise. By 1939, there were fifteen, numbered I through XIII, and XVII and XVIII. The Wehrkreise and their headquarters are shown on Map 1.1. Later, Wehrkreise XX, XXI, and General Gouvernement were added in the occupied territories. They never approached the importance of the earlier (German) Wehrkreise.

In February 1938, Hitler set up the machinery for running his war. It consisted of the High Command of the Armed Forces (*Oberkommando der Wehrmacht* or OKW), the High Command of the Army (*Oberkommando des Heeres* or OKH), the High Command of the Luftwaffe (*Oberkommando der Luftwaffe* or OKL), and the High Command of the Navy (*Oberkommando der Kriegsmarine* or OKM). The military SS (*Waffen-SS*) was also important by 1944, but its combat divisions remained under the operational control of the army, and there was never an *Oberkommando der Waffen-SS* per se.

Field Marshal Wilhelm Keitel, commander-in-chief of OKW, late 1941. *Bundesarchiv Bild 183-H30220 CC BY-SA 3.0*

OKW was headed by Colonel General (later Field Marshal) Wilhelm Keitel, whom Hitler once declared had the brains of a cinema usher.[1] That was precisely what Hitler wanted: a mindless yes-man who would relay his orders to the forces without too much thought. Keitel initially tried to establish an actual high command, but OKL and OKM refused to cooperate with him, and Hitler (who practiced the political principle of "divide and rule") was fine with that. By 1941, an unofficial dual command of the German ground forces had evolved. OKH directed the Eastern Front. OKW directed everything else.

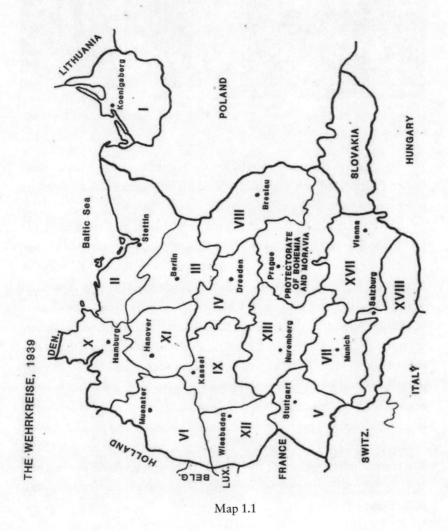

Map 1.1

Hitler reviews marching infantry, Poland, 1939. *Bundesarchiv Bild 183-S55480 CC BY-SA 3.0*

The real military brains at OKW was its chief of operations, Colonel General Albert Jodl. He often suppressed his intelligence and knowledge, however, to remain "loyal" to the Fuehrer.[2]

The chief of OKH was Field Marshal Walther von Brauchitsch. He had made a deal with Hitler in 1938. Brauchitsch was allowed to quietly divorce his wife and marry his mistress. The wife was paid off with Nazi Party funds. In exchange, Brauchitsch accepted the new command structure with the Army High Command subordinate to OKW (that is, Hitler). As part of the bargain, he also forced nineteen senior generals into retirement and transferred other anti-Nazi or non–Nazi sympathizers to less important posts. In this manner, the Fuehrer basically gained control of the army. Needless to say, he did not have much respect for Brauchitsch. When the German offensive of 1941 stalled in front of Moscow, Hitler blamed Brauchitsch for it and sacked him on December 19, 1941. The Fuehrer then appointed himself head of OKH and commander-in-chief of the army. OKH was directed by the chief of General Staff, although Hitler interfered with its operations on a daily basis.[3]

OKL was directed by Hermann Goering, a former World War I flying ace and an early Nazi. He had some military talent but not much. By 1944, he was in deep disgrace for his mishandling of the Luftwaffe.

Grand Admiral Karl Doenitz was the commander-in-chief of the Navy (OKM). He experienced less interference than any of the other service heads. Hitler, a former corporal, was less inclined to interfere in naval matters about which he knew nothing. Doenitz was also a loyal Nazi supporter, so Hitler generally left him alone.

After rebuilding the German *Wehrmacht* (armed forces) and winning a series of bloodless victories, Adolf Hitler ignited World War II by invading Poland on September 1, 1939. At first, there were only victories. The Wehrmacht overran Poland, Denmark, Norway, Luxembourg, the Netherlands, Belgium, France, Yugoslavia, Greece, Crete, and most of North Africa. Only over the skies of Great Britain were the Germans checked, and that was a close-run thing.

The war reached a turning point on June 22, 1941, when Germany invaded the Soviet Union. Although it won some spectacular victories, the Wehrmacht could not conquer Stalin's empire. The German armies were severely damaged in the Soviet Winter Offensive of 1941–42 and suffered decisive defeats at Stalingrad (1942–43) and Kursk (1943). Meanwhile, the United Kingdom recovered and defeated the Afrika Korps in Egypt and Tunisia. The United States entered the war following the Japanese attack on Pearl Harbor on December 7, 1941. The Western Allies destroyed two German armies in Tunisia (May 1943), defeated the German U-boats in the Battle of the Atlantic (May 1943), conquered Sicily (July 1943), and invaded Italy, knocking her out of the war (September 1943). By the spring of 1944, the Allies had defeated the Luftwaffe over the skies of France and Germany and were reducing the cities of the Third Reich to rubble. The stage was set for another decisive battle: the invasion of western Europe.

In late 1943, the war was going badly for Nazi Germany, but an unbiased observer could still come up with a plausible scenario in which the Third Reich could, if not win the war, at least survive it. This strategy was adopted *de facto* by the German High Command and by the German people simply because it was based on common sense. It would involve: 1) delaying the Red Army and avoiding defeat in the East; 2) obstructing the Anglo-Americans in Italy and holding them south of Rome; and 3) defeating the Allied D-Day invasion.

If Germany could repulse the British–American cross-Channel invasion, the Allies would not be able to mount another one for a year. This would free more than thirty divisions for employment in the East—including Germany's entire armored strategic reserve in the West. These forces amounted to ten panzer and SS panzer divisions. With such a powerful command, Germany could conceivably force Stalin back to the negotiating table. He had already shown a willingness to negotiate behind the backs of his Anglo-American partners in 1943, but these talks broke down because Hitler had insisted upon territorial concessions. Stalin might have changed his mind in 1944 if the cross-Channel invasion had failed. It is even possible that Hitler might have mitigated his demands in 1944, though this is much less likely. In any case, German scientists would have been given another year to perfect Hitler's "wonder weapons": new and improved tanks, anti-tank weapons, U-boats, and jet airplanes. We know that the improved U-boats could have reopened the Battle of the Atlantic, and the jets—in sufficient numbers—would have fundamentally shifted the air war in Germany's favor. It is even conceivable that German scientists might have invented a workable atomic bomb, though this too seems less likely. It is reasonably certain, however, that a few hundred jet fighters would have swept the Royal and U.S. Air Forces from the skies, and the new U-boats would likely have reimposed an economic blockade on the United Kingdom. At that point, anything would have been possible.

But Germany was able to do none of the three things mentioned above. Rome fell on June 4, 1944, and the Allies landed in Normandy on June 6. By mid-June, Anglo-Americans had a secure foothold in Europe and were reinforcing it at an incredible rate. The German mobile strategic reserve was committed to battle in Normandy, where it was being ground to bits. The German field commander, Field Marshal

Erwin Rommel, was able to check the Anglo-Americans but not defeat them in the hedgerow country of Normandy. The "Desert Fox" begged Hitler for infantry divisions, but Hitler would only send him panzer and SS panzer divisions. By the time the Allies finally broke out of the hedgerow country at the end of July 1944, the German panzer divisions had lost more than 80 percent of their armor.

On the left, Colonel Count Claus von Stauffenberg, would-be assassin of Adolf Hitler, looking at his target. This photo was taken on July 15, 1944, five days before the attempt. *U.S. National Archives*

Normandy was excellent terrain for infantry; most of the rest of France was exceptionally good terrain for armor. When the Allies broke out of Normandy, Hitler had little left with which to defend France but non-motorized infantry. These forces (called "marching infantry" by the Germans) were quickly swamped by the highly mobile British and American forces, especially those under the command of General Patton.

The war was going so badly for the Third Reich that a segment of the German Officer Corps, led by Colonel Count Claus von Stauffenberg, the chief of staff of the Replacement Army, launched a coup against the Nazi government on July 20, 1944.

Although Hitler was wounded in an assassination attempt, the plot failed, and Stauffenberg and several hundred others paid for the failure with their lives. Colonel General Friedrich Fromm, the commander-in-chief of the Home Army, was fired on July 21 and replaced by Reichsfuehrer-SS Heinrich Himmler, so the army came even more under the control of the Nazis, and Hitler's already rampant paranoia grew by leaps and bounds. Fromm was eventually executed for cowardice.

Once Stalin was sure the panzer divisions were committed in the West, he launched Operation "Bagration," a massive offensive in White Russia, on June 22. By the beginning of August, he had virtually destroyed the German Army Group Centre. The German Army was being pushed back on all active fronts with no prospect of reversing the situation. By this time, there was little hope for the Third Reich.

August 1944 was the month of victory for the Allied armies. The German Army Group B (5th Panzer and 7th Armies) was largely destroyed in the Falaise sector, and the British advance cut off the 15th Army in the coastal sectors of France and the Low Countries. The other German Armies in France (1st and 19th) were reduced to remnants by the Allied invasion of southern France. (The Headquarters, 1st Parachute Army, was also in the west, but it was nothing but a training command at this time.) The Allies seemed on the verge of crossing into Germany and seizing the Ruhr Industrial Area without which the Third Reich could not wage war. There was widespread talk among the Allies of ending the war by Christmas.

The Allies' strategy of isolating the Normandy battlefield by destroying the French highway and rail networks was a good one; however, it proved to be a double-edged sword. The Allies were unable to supply all their divisions and maintain their momentum. Meanwhile, the German Army rallied. The Anglo-Americans were engaged in what they later called "pursuit thinking." They were, however, facing an opponent who had a remarkable talent for staging swift recoveries. The German *Landser* (the companion in misfortune to the English Tommy and American G.I.) had not lost his will to resist and was on the fringe of his own territory, which further encouraged him to hold on.

Montgomery came up with a rather brilliant—but risky—plan to finish off the German Wehrmacht. Dubbed Operation "Market Garden," it called for the Allies to lay down an airborne carpet and seize the bridge at Arnhem. It failed—mainly because luck was on the side of the Germans during the Battle of Arnhem. Market Garden depended upon the Germans' reacting with average speed. The British did not know that

Field Marshal Walter Model, the new commander-in-chief of Army Group B, had established his headquarters only two miles from the easternmost British drop zone. He reacted with lightning speed—far more quickly than the Allies anticipated—and wiped out the Allied airborne bridgehead at Arnhem.[4]

Because Model was a Nazi sympathizer, Western historians tend not to give him credit for the German victory at Arnhem. While it is true that Model almost certainly would have been hanged as a war criminal (and deservedly so) had he not committed suicide in 1945, he was primarily responsible for checking Montgomery at Arnhem and deserves credit for it.

While Montgomery and his generals were trying to "bounce the Rhine," they failed to finish off the 15th Army. On September 4, 1944, when the British captured Antwerp, the 15th Army had only one escape route left—and it was unguarded and within fifteen miles of the spearheads of the British Guards Armoured Division. The British, however, were engaged in "pursuit thinking" and did not cut off the 15th Army or clear the Scheldt River when it was theirs for the taking. By the time they decided to turn their attention to the west three weeks later, it was too late.

Antwerp, located seventy miles up the Scheldt River, is one of the best ports in the world, and the British had captured it intact. Not even its giant cranes were destroyed. That port alone could supply all of Eisenhower's divisions. Without control of the Scheldt, however, it was utterly useless—a fact that the German General Staff grasped several weeks before Eisenhower and Montgomery. In September, the Germans reinforced their positions along the Scheldt, and it would take the British and Canadians months to clear them.

Walter Model, 1944. *U.S. Army War College*

Meanwhile, in early September 1944, Hitler had one of his flashes of military inspiration. He would check the Allies at the Siegfried Line, hold the Scheldt, and marshal his reserves for a major offensive through the Ardennes to Antwerp with the objective of destroying Montgomery's armies and much of the U.S. 1st Army. Such a decisive blow might end the war in Germany's favor.

In August 1944, as the Wehrmacht streamed back to the German border, the Home Army (*Ersatzheer*, also known as the Replacement Army) faced the task of reforming smashed divisions and creating new ones. They no longer had the manpower or equipment to create the standard Type 1939 units or even the Type 1944 Divisions, which were reduced in size, so they began turning out *Volksgrenadier* (People's Infantry) divisions.

The 1939 infantry division consisted of three infantry regiments, a reconnaissance battalion (three companies), an artillery regiment (three medium artillery battalions of a dozen 105mm guns each), one heavy artillery battalion (of nine 150mm guns), and a motorized forward observer battalion (*Beobachtungs-Abteilung*), an anti-tank battalion (four companies), an engineer battalion (three companies and a bridging column), a signal battalion, a field replacement battalion, and assorted service support elements, including medical, ambulance, workshop, anti-aircraft, veterinary, military police, bakery, and other units. Each infantry regiment had three battalions, an infantry gun company, and an anti-tank (*Panzerabwehr*) company. In all, the standard authorized strength of an infantry division in 1939 was 17,734.

The Volksgrenadier division was much smaller. It included three grenadier regiments of two battalions each. The regiment also had an infantry gun company (equipped with a dozen 75mm guns) and a tank destroyer (*Panzerzerstoerer*) company, giving the division six infantry battalions, as opposed to the nine of most earlier infantry divisions. Its artillery regiment was also smaller. Most artillery regiments in Volksgrenadier divisions had two medium battalions instead of three, and each battalion had two gun batteries instead of three. (Both the Type 39 and

Volksgrenadier battalions had a staff battery.) The Volksgrenadier unit also had a Fuesilier company instead of a reconnaissance battalion, and it was usually mounted on bicycles instead of trucks or armored reconnaissance vehicles. The anti-tank, signal, and other units were also smaller.

A Volksgrenadier division could theoretically be produced from scratch in three months, but this process was often speeded up, and a decent division could be put together in eight weeks. A battered and depleted veteran infantry division could be ready for action as a Volksgrenadier division in six weeks.

A Sturmgewehr 44 with scope. Most StG 44s were not equipped with scopes. The AK47 used in the Vietnam War is a modified copy of the StG 44. *Bundesarchiv Bild 146-1979-118-55/ CC BY-SA 3.0*

The people's infantry divisions were well-equipped with automatic weapons, shoulder-fired anti-tank weapons, and mortars, but they lacked motorized vehicles, horses, and heavy equipment (including artillery, assault guns, and crew-served heavy machine guns). Almost all of them suffered from equipment deficiencies, many lacked trained personnel, and their effectiveness was mostly as defensive units.

The theoretical strength of a Volksgrenadier division was around 11,250 men, but most of them weighed in well short of this figure. Some of them were barely half that, even before they met the enemy.

To compensate for a lack of manpower, the Home Army relied on increasing the number of automatic weapons given to the troops. Each

Volkssturm (Home Guard) soldiers equipped with Panzerfausten (disposable anti-tank weapons), Berlin, March 10, 1945. *Bundesarchiv Bild 183-J31320/CC-BY-SA 3.0*

grenadier company contained three platoons—one equipped with Mauser rifles and two with machine pistols. The *Maschinenpistole 44* (MP 44) was gas operated and fired a short 7.92 x 33mm "Kurz" cartridge. It was excellent close-up, but its maximum effective range was only 400 meters when in single-shot mode and only 150 meters at full automatic. It featured a curved, 30-round magazine.

Adolf Hitler initially opposed the serial production of this weapon because, he believed, it would lead to a wasteful expenditure of ammunition. Some major manufacturers produced them anyway. Hitler reportedly discovered this during an inspection tour that fall. He was so impressed by the weapon that he ignored the fact that the manufacturers had disobeyed his orders, and made only one alteration to the weapon—he changed its name to *Sturmgewehr 44* (StG 44).

The trademark weapon of the Volksgrenadier and the entire Wehrmacht in late 1944 was the Panzerfaust. It was a shoulder-fired, single-shot, disposable anti-tank weapon. It weighed about eleven pounds and could penetrate any tank armor. Many new recruits and Home Guard (*Volkssturm*) troops were issued Panzerfaust as their only weapon. After they fired it, they were unarmed on a battlefield, which prompted some German generals to jokingly recommend using the disposable firing tube as a club.

Another relatively new, deadly weapon then in mass production and issued to both the new and veteran divisions was the *Panzerschreck* anti-tank gun. It was an enlarged copy of the American bazooka, and it fired a deadly 88mm rocket.

Soldiers of the Grossdeutschland Panzer Grenadier Division prepare to fire a Panzer-schreck, Eastern Front, May 1944. *Bundesarchiv Bild 183-J27051/CC-BY-SA 3.0*

From July to September 1944, the Home Army and its subordinate Wehrkreise (military districts) cranked out or were in the process of completing the formation of eighty-two Volksgrenadier divisions and one *Volkssturm* (People's Storm) division.[5] This was the equivalent of around ten armies.

CHAPTER II

DEFEAT IN THE ARDENNES

On December 16, 1944, Hitler launched the Battle of the Bulge and caught the Western Allies—especially the Americans—flat-footed. The U.S. Army was staggered, but it was not the knock-out blow upon which Hitler was counting. By December 20, the veteran 2nd Panzer Division had, as usual, outdistanced every other unit and gone to the forefront of the German Army, just as it had during the Battle of Moscow three years before. After winning a vicious little battle at Noville, it had pushed on to the Ourthe River and seized a bridgehead at Ortheuville. Fuel shortages and troop exhaustion kept it stalled on December 21, but early on December 22 it started moving again, driving north toward Namur. Led by Colonel Meinrad von Lauchert, it continued heading for the Meuse, pressing through a seven-mile gap between the U.S. 84th Infantry Division at Marche to the north and the U.S. 335th Infantry Regiment at Rochefort to the south.[1] General of Panzer Troops Baron Hasso von Manteuffel, the commander of the 5th Panzer Army, of which the division was a part, energetically did what he could to support his spearhead. He ordered Lieutenant General Fritz Bayerlein, the commander of the Panzer Lehr Division, to capture

Rochefort in order to widen the gap, and commanded Major General Siegfried Waldenburg's 116th Panzer Division to siege Marche for the same reason; meanwhile, the 2nd Panzer Reconnaissance Battalion of the 2nd Panzer Division pushed to within four miles of the Meuse River. There it ran into increasingly heavy resistance from the American armored cavalry, so Lauchert ordered a halt. Part of the division was at Foy-Notre Dame, and the rest was between Celles and Conjoux. More than 40 percent of the division would be killed within the next seventy-two hours.

SS men advancing past abandoned U.S. equipment, Ardennes, December 18, 1944. *U.S. National Archives*

On December 23, Bayerlein attacked Rochefort but could not clear it until the following day. At the same time, Waldenburg's division was stopped cold near Marche, and the leading elements of the 2nd Panzer were running into American armor at Foy-Notre Dame. General of Panzer Troops Baron Heinrich von Luettwitz asked Manteuffel to withdraw the division, but Manteuffel—knowing what Hitler's reaction would be—refused.[2] By the end of the day on December 24, the 2nd

Panzer Division was increasingly isolated, practically out of gas, and in a situation even more serious than Lauchert realized.

At Havelange, just ten miles north of his division, lay Major General Ernest N. Harmon's fresh U.S. 2nd Armored Division. Belgian civilians informed the aggressive American commander that the panzers were out of fuel. At 8:00 on Christmas morning, Combat Command B (CCB) of the U.S. 2nd Armored Division struck southwest to Celles, intent on destroying the German tank concentration at the western tip of the bulge. He was joined in this effort by the British 29th Armoured Brigade.[3] At the same time, Combat Command A of the U.S. 2nd Armored Division drove southeast toward Rochefort to stop any further German units from advancing toward the Meuse and perhaps rescuing the 2nd Panzer Division.

The slaughter lasted three days. Second Panzer was pounded by colossal artillery concentrations and attacked repeatedly by rocket-firing British Typhoons and American fighter-bombers—not to mention American tanks. To the east, Panzer Lehr was unable to fight its way through Combat Command A and swarms of Typhoons and *Jabos* (as the Germans called Allied fighter-bombers), while the 116th Panzer Division suffered heavy losses in failed attempts to break through the U.S. 84th Infantry Division. Meanwhile, at Celles and Foy-Notre Dame, the 2nd Panzer Division was annihilated. The 304th Panzer Grenadier Regiment, the II/3rd Panzer Regiment, the 74th Panzer Artillery Regiment, and two-thirds of the 273rd Panzer Anti-Aircraft Battalion were wiped out. About 2,500 German soldiers were killed or wounded, and 1,200 more were captured. Some 82 tanks, 81 artillery pieces, and 450 trucks and other motorized vehicles were lost in the carnage. At the same time, less than two miles to the northeast, the British 29th Armoured Brigade and the U.S. 82nd Reconnaissance Battalion struck the 2nd Panzer Reconnaissance Battalion at Foy-Notre Dame. It was also destroyed. From the main body of the 2nd Panzer Division, only about 600 men, led by the indomitable Major Ernst von Cochenhausen, managed to break out of the pocket and eventually reach German lines—on foot.[4] Not a single vehicle or tank escaped the American encirclement. Colonel von Lauchert did escape, but he no longer had a division to command.

After Celles, all roads led backward for the German Army in the West.

CLEARING THE BULGE

With the destruction of the 2nd Panzer Division, Hitler's last great offensive in the west failed. The Fuehrer, as usual, refused to recognize this fact; he ordered that Bastogne be captured at all costs despite the fact that Lieutenant General George S. Patton Jr., the commander of the U.S. 3rd Army, had attacked from the south, pushed through the German 7th Army, established a corridor to the town on December 26, and reinforced it. On December 28, the 26th Volksgrenadier Division, the Fuehrer Begleit Brigade, and the 115th and 901st Panzer Grenadier Regiments attacked Bastogne. Before the day was out, the 1st SS Panzer Division, the 3rd Panzer Grenadier Division (just released from OKW Reserve), and the Fuehrer Grenadier Brigade began arriving in the Bastogne sector. Patton reinforced the garrison with the U.S. 6th Armored Division, and Eisenhower released the U.S. 87th Infantry and 11th Armored Divisions from Supreme Headquarters Allied Expeditionary Force (SHAEF) reserve and committed them to the Battle of Bastogne.[5] Before the siege was over, the 9th and 12th SS Panzer and the 340th and 167th Volksgrenadier Divisions also joined the fighting, but they could neither cut the corridor nor take the town.[6]

On December 30, the newly arrived U.S. 87th Infantry and 11th Armored joined the battle and ran straight into an attack by the veteran, but depleted and exhausted, Panzer Lehr and 26th Volksgrenadier west of Bastogne. At the same time, the 1st SS Panzer and 167th Volksgrenadier Divisions struck the U.S. 35th and 26th Infantry Divisions which were supported by elements of the U.S. 4th Armored. They were beaten back, thanks in large part to the efforts of the Allied fighter-bombers. Nazi Germany lost another fifty-five tanks that day plus hundreds of men it could no longer replace. The German divisions in the Bulge were now used-up formations without any hope of trained replacements—the 26th Volksgrenadier, for example, had lost about three-quarters of its authorized strength and numbered fewer than 2,000 combat effectives— and the Allies were coming after them.[7] Eisenhower assigned the fresh and exceptionally well-trained U.S. 17th Airborne Division to Patton on December 25, and after being delayed by weather, it was able to reinforce the Bastogne Corridor by the end of the year.

Like a gambler who does not know when to quit, Hitler committed the last of General of Fighter Pilots Adolf Galland's fighter reserve to the battle early on the morning of New Year's Day, 1945. Flying at treetop level, all available units attacked Allied ground targets and airfields in the Netherlands, Belgium, and Luxembourg. The Germans destroyed or severely damaged 800 Allied airplanes (most of them on the ground) but lost 150 themselves, as well as some of the Luftwaffe's best surviving pilots. With their vast reserves of air power, the Allies could absorb the blow, but Germany could not. "The Luftwaffe received its death blow in the Ardennes," Galland said later.[8]

On January 3, 1945, the U.S. 1st Army launched a major offensive from the north into the bulge. The attack was spearheaded by Lieutenant

U.S. General Eisenhower inspecting a destroyed Tiger II tank, 1944. *U.S. Army*

General J. Lawton Collins's U.S. VII Corps, which included four divisions (two of them armored)—100,000 men in all. SS Colonel General Sepp Dietrich's 6th Panzer Army met the attack with Colonel Rudolf Langhaeuser's 12th Volksgrenadier Division, Major General Rudolf Bader's 560th Volksgrenadier Division, and SS Lieutenant General Heinz Lammerding's 2nd SS Panzer Division: a formidable force—on paper.[9] Actually, the 560th Volksgrenadier Division had only 2,500 men remaining, and the 2nd SS Panzer Division had only 6,000. All totaled, the forces facing Collins numbered fewer than 15,000 men.

The entire Ardennes sector was controlled by Field Marshal Walter Model's Army Group B, which directed the 6th Panzer, 5th Panzer, and 7th Armies (north to south respectively). Since his attention was focused on Bastogne, this offensive took Model by surprise. The following day, Hitler ordered Dietrich reinforced, but the American advance was slowed as much by the terrain and the freezing cold weather as by the Germans, though they resisted fiercely. (The winter of 1944–45 was one of the coldest on record.) Baron Hasso von Manteuffel was ready to retreat, but the tough, profane, and hard-drinking Model would not hear of it. On January 2, 1945, he ordered SS General Hermann Preiss's I SS Panzer Corps to attack Bastogne again on January 3, this time with the 9th SS Panzer Division, most of the 340th Volksgrenadier Division, and part of the 12th SS Panzer Division "Hitler Jugend." SS Major General Sylvester Stadler, the commander of the 9th SS, however, refused to attack in daylight hours because of the Jabos. Model insisted. The result was a screaming contest. Remarkably enough, Stadler won. The field marshal stalked off in a rage, but the SS Gruppenfuehrer got his way. The officers present were amazed that Model did not relieve Stadler of his command on the spot.[10]

Preiss's attack achieved little. On January 4, the Germans finally admitted defeat and went over to the defensive. To the north, the U.S. 18th Airborne Corps joined the offensive, and village after village fell to the Americans. On January 7, the critical Baraque-de-Fraiture crossroads (Parker's Crossroads) was lost, and the German generals were acutely concerned that the U.S. 1st and 3rd Armies might soon link up and sever the bulge near its base, trapping much of the 5th and 6th Panzer Armies. Even Hitler recognized the danger. On January 8, he gave Model a rare authorization to withdraw. The next day, the Fuehrer tacitly admitted defeat by ordering Dietrich's 6th Panzer Army out of the Ardennes. He also issued an order to withdraw the General of Waffen-SS Willi Bittrich's 2nd SS Panzer Corps (including the 1st SS, 2nd SS, 9th SS, and 12th SS Panzer Divisions plus the two Fuehrer brigades and two *Werfer* [rocket launcher] brigades) to the rear of Army Group G for rehabilitation.

Hitler was not the only one to recognize that the German armies in the Ardennes were defeated; George S. Patton realized it too. On January 9, he struck the 5th Panzer Army with a massive offensive, employing all eight of his available divisions in the attack. Again, German resistance was determined, and American progress was slow. A gain of two miles a day was considered a good advance. But the German soldiers were no longer fighting for victory or for a cause they believed in; they were fighting desperately just to keep their escape routes open.

Hasso von Manteuffel and Sepp Dietrich extricated their forces as rapidly as they could but not as quickly as they would have liked. The lack of fuel, the Jabos, and the constant rearguard actions delayed them considerably. They nevertheless managed to get almost all their formations out of the trap before General Courtney Hodges's First Army and General Patton's Third Army linked up at Houffalize on January 16. Map 2.1 shows this battle.

By this time, the German officers were facing a heretofore almost unheard of difficulty: low troop morale. It had occasionally surfaced in green, hastily formed units, but now it was affecting the veteran divisions as well. Physical and mental exhaustion set in. To make matters worse, OKW had to reduce their rations. Because most units needed every man, home leaves were cut, causing further drops in morale. Mail services were thoroughly disrupted, and the lack of news from home caused consequential mental anguish. When letters did arrive, the news they contained was usually bad. Leaves to East Prussia and some of the other frontier provinces were no longer allowed—they were in the combat zone. Those who got leaves often wished they had not. They spent much of their time searching for their families and relatives who were evacuated from bombed-out cities. Many men had the heartbreaking experience of returning home only to find their neighborhoods reduced to fields of ruin and their homes destroyed. Others, unable to find their loved ones, spent their furloughs in the local barracks. "By now," John Eisenhower wrote, the German

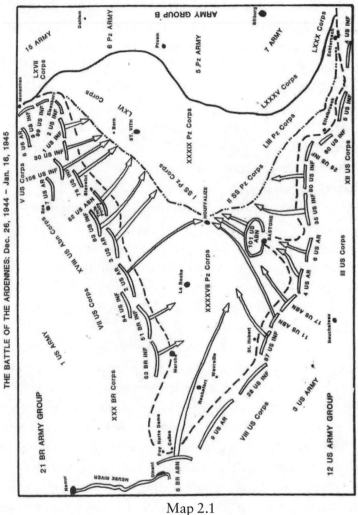

Map 2.1

troops were tired from long commitments without breaks. Replacements were of low quality and lacked training; forces were poorly supplied, and rations were being cut. The news from the Eastern Front and home had reached them. The American forces were far superior on the ground, and every clear day Allied planes were supreme in the skies. After the high hopes at the beginning of the offensive, failure now stared every soldier in the face."[11]

Not even the SS divisions fought with their previous elan. The 12th SS Panzer Division "Hitler Youth" is a good example. Arguably, no division on either side fought as well as it did during the Normandy campaign, but it was smashed in the process. The replacements it received were mainly former Luftwaffe ground crewmen and excess naval personnel—and all too few of the young volunteers who had been its trademark a year before. The 12th SS Panzer was no longer an elite unit; it had suffered too many casualties and accepted too many inferior replacements. In the Battle of the Bulge, 9,870 of its men were captured, including 328 officers and 1,698 NCOs.[12] Such a statistic would have been unheard of even six months before.

On January 14, Hitler announced his decision to transfer Dietrich's 6th Panzer Army from the Western Front to the East; he was planning yet another offensive, this one in Hungary. The following day, he gave Field Marshal Gerd von Rundstedt, the western commander-in-chief (OB West), permission to withdraw the German forces in the Ardennes salient back as far east as Cherain (seven miles northeast of Houffalize).[13] It was January 22, however, before the 6th Panzer Army could completely extricate itself from the Ardennes; it handed over its few units remaining in the bulge to Manteuffel. The next day, Sunday, January 23, the U.S. 7th Armored Division retook St. Vith. Only three houses in the town were still inhabitable. The Battle of the Bulge was over.

During the Ardennes Offensive, the American forces suffered 80,987 casualties, including 10,276 killed, 47,493 wounded, and 23,218 missing.[14] German losses are not known so precisely. German sources place their casualties at more than 76,000 men as a minimum figure. Most

Western sources generally estimate German casualties at 103,000.[15] They also lost 600 tanks and assault guns. The American victory in the Ardennes Offensive was not tactically decisive (when the battle ended, both sides were back roughly where they started), but psychologically, it was. As General von Manteuffel pointed out, "For a while, the spirit of duty, self-sacrifice, and comradeship made it possible to carry on, but then the will to resist finally collapsed. Helplessly, the man at the front was forced to recognize that the superiority of the enemy on land, in the air, and at sea was now so great that there was no longer any chance whatever of putting up a successful resistance."[16]

• • •

As the Allies approached the borders of the Reich, the Home Army also churned out new panzer divisions. In terms of size, they did not resemble the original panzer divisions of 1935.

When Germany invaded Poland on September 1, 1939, the German Army had seven panzer divisions: the 1st Panzer (309 tanks); the 2nd Panzer (322 tanks); the 3rd Panzer (391 tanks); the 4th Panzer (341 tanks); the 5th Panzer (335 tanks); the 10th Panzer (150 tanks); and the ad hoc Panzer Division Kempf (164 tanks).[17] Except for Panzer Division Kempf, they had an authorized strength of more than 17,000 men. From that point, they were steadily downgraded in strength, to produce more tank and motorized infantry divisions.[18] By 1944, the Type 44 had an authorized strength of fewer than 12,000 men and 168 tanks. Most of them had about half that many or fewer.

After the Battle of the Bulge, the Replacement Army created the Type 45 panzer division. It had three regiments: a panzer regiment, a panzer grenadier regiment, and a panzer artillery regiment. The tank regiment consisted of a staff and staff company, a panzer battalion, and a panzer grenadier battalion. It had an authorized strength of fifty-four tanks—a far cry from the force that so confidently overran Poland and western Europe in 1939 and 1940. Some of the divisions did not even have that.

These new divisions also had fewer than half the mobile infantrymen as their predecessors. Their tanks, especially the Panthers (Panzerkampfwagen V or PzKw V) and Tigers (Panzerkampfwagen VI or PzKw VI) were considerably better than the 1939 tanks; on the other hand, the enemy's tanks were also much improved, although they were generally inferior to both the Panther and Tiger.[19]

CHAPTER III

OPERATION NORTHWIND
AND THE BATTLE OF
THE COLMAR POCKET

As strange as it may seem, the Battle of the Bulge only whetted Hitler's appetite for further attacks. The Americans, he told his generals, had been "forced to withdraw something like 50 percent of the forces" from their other sectors to save their divisions in the Ardennes; therefore, he declared, their line in Alsace must be "extraordinarily thin" and there "we shall find a situation which we could not wish to be better."[1] Near the end of December 1944, he ordered an entire new offensive to be made ready in the south. Its objectives would be to capture the Saverne Gap, cut the U.S. 7th Army in two, and destroy half of it in the Strasbourg-Bitche-Lauterbourg triangle.

The Allies were, in fact, vulnerable in Alsace, but Hitler picked the wrong man to command the offensive when he named *Reichsfuehrer-SS* Heinrich Himmler commander-in-chief of the newly created OB Upper Rhine (*Oberbefehlshaber Oberrheim*, also called Army Group Upper Rhine).[2]

Why was Himmler appointed to the army group command? Heinz Guderian and SS Colonel General Paul Hausser said that Martin

Reichsfuehrer Heinrich Himmler, commander-in-chief of OB Upper Rhine. Himmler directed the Strasbourg Offensive. *Bundesarchiv Bild 183-S72707/CC-BY-SA 3.0*

Bormann (Hitler's secretary and the chief of the Nazi Party) arranged Himmler's appointment in order to ruin him (or more accurately, to help him ruin himself). Others thought Hitler was letting his generals know that he could get along without them. Both are probably right. To Himmler, on the other hand, it represented the achievement of one of his military ambitions, and he had been lobbying Hitler for such an appointment for months. On December 10, the Fuehrer gave it to him.

As soon as he took up his position, Himmler began organizing two new corps in his sector: the XIV SS and the XVIII SS. They were led respectively by the "heroes" of the Warsaw Uprising, Police General Erich von dem Bach-Zelewski and Police Lieutenant General Heinz-Friedrich Reinefarth.[3] It included frontier guards, battalions of Eastern and German workers, Volkssturm, police, and other miscellaneous units. The only unit in OB Oberrhein with any muscle, however, was the 19th Army.

The 19th was well led by General of Infantry Friedrich Wiese, who exhibited considerable skill in extracting it from the south of France in August and September 1944.[4] After his army lost the Bedfort Gap and Strasbourg to the Anglo-French forces in November, Wiese fell back a short distance to positions along the Rhine River where his forces linked up with Hans von Obstfelder's 1st Army to the north. From north to south, Wiese deployed Lieutenant General Hellmuth Thumm's LXIV Corps (two static infantry divisions and two assault gun brigades), Lieutenant General Werner von Erdmannsdorff's LXXXX Corps (two infantry divisions) and Lieutenant General Erich Abraham's

LXIII Corps (106th Panzer Brigade "Feldherrnhalle" and five infantry divisions).[5] All of these units were badly understrength, and many of the infantry divisions had only two infantry regiments. In addition, they were short on artillery, ammunition, and equipment of every kind. Even so, Heinrich Himmler was soon looking for an excuse to assume the offensive. There was, after all, no glory in holding a quiet sector with a ragtag collection of units.

Himmler's murderous tendencies disguised that he was basically a colorless technocrat with little military training and no combat experience. He joined the Imperial Army in 1918 (at the age of eighteen) but never rose beyond the rank of *Fahnenjunker* (officer-cadet) and could not abide the sight of blood. As a commander-in-chief, he set up his headquarters near the former tourist resort of Triberg in the Black Forest, where he kept his special train near a railroad tunnel in case of air raids. Here he held dinners as if he were on peacetime maneuvers and bothered Wiese and his corps and divisional commanders with trifles.[6] According to Rundstedt's chief of staff, General Westphal, Himmler issued "a deluge of absolutely puerile orders." He was "hag-ridden by a pathological distrust" and never hesitated to saddle army officers with the blame for his own impractical schemes.

Among the officers sacked by Himmler was Friedrich Wiese, who was relieved of his command on December 15, 1944, and never reemployed.[7] Wiese was replaced by Siegfried Rasp, an officer who had been promoted to general of infantry only two weeks before. Rasp was a surprise choice. He was known to have a drinking problem and had never commanded a corps—much less an army—but he led the 3rd Mountain Division, the 335th Infantry Division, and elite 78th Assault Division on the Eastern Front with considerable success, sober or not. A surprise choice is not necessarily a bad one, as Rasp was to prove in the weeks ahead.[8]

Wiese's capable chief of staff, Walter Botsch, was also transferred to "Fuehrer Reserve" (that is, was without an assignment) on January 1, 1945, despite the fact that he had been promoted to lieutenant general

General of Infantry Friedrich Wiese from a Nazi era postcard. *Library of Congress*

only four months before. Botsch had been chief of staff of the army since it was created and no one knew more about the strengths and limitations of the 19th than did he; yet, he was relieved the very day a major offensive began—not exactly a recommended procedure for a successful army group commander.[9]

General Westphal also charged that Himmler was wasteful of the supplies sent to him and was in any case receiving greater quantities than were allotted to other sections of the front because, otherwise, it was feared he would ring up Hitler and have all munitions trains diverted to his sector. "Yet he fired off every shell that was sent to him and then simply asked for more. . . . It is almost superfluous to mention that Himmler never visited the front himself, but issued his orders from the safety of the rear."[10]

Himmler's chief of staff, SS Major General Werner Ostendorff, an East Prussian who served in the Reichsheer and the Luftwaffe before joining the Waffen-SS in 1935, partially made up for the deficiencies of his commander-in-chief.[11]

Himmler got his chance to launch his offensive during the latter stages of the Battle of the Bulge when Field Marshal von Rundstedt tried to obtain Hitler's permission to launch a diversionary attack south toward the Moder, using the 10th SS Panzer Division.

The Reichsfuehrer-SS seized upon this request to persuade the Fuehrer to expand the diversion into a major offensive against the 1st French Army, aimed at recapturing Strasbourg and Alsace. It was code-named Operation *Nordwind* (Northwind) and was under the general command of Himmler himself.

The northern wing of the attack—against the right flank of the U.S. 7th Army—came under the direction of General of Infantry Hans von Obstfelder's 1st Army, which was part of Colonel General Johannes Blaskowitz's Army Group G. Table 3.1 shows the Order of Battle of the German forces involved in Operation Northwind.

SS General Werner Ostendorff, chief of staff of OB Upper Rhine and former commander of the 17th SS Panzer Grenadier Division. Ostendorff was one of the more capable SS generals. *Bundesarchiv Bild 101III-Zschaeckel-149-16/Zschaeckel, Friedrich/ CC-BY-SA 3.0*

The operation was indeed a rushed affair; in fact, due to the sorry state of the heavily bombed German transportation system, three of the main divisions earmarked for the attack—the 10th SS Panzer, 6th SS Mountain, and 7th Parachute—had not arrived when the offensive began.

Operation Northwind began on New Year's Eve night when Blaskowitz attacked the U.S. 7th Army's 79th Infantry, 12th Armored, and 36th Infantry Divisions with the 36th Volksgrenadier, 47th Volksgrenadier, 1st Parachute, 21st Panzer, 25th Panzer Grenadier, and 17th SS Panzer Grenadier Divisions.[12] SS Colonel Hans Lingner's 17th SS Division, which spearheaded the attack, was specially reinforced with the 653rd Heavy *Panzerjaeger* (Anti-Tank) Battalion, which was equipped with twenty *Jadgtigern* and two companies of special flame-throwing assault guns. The Jadgtiger was armed with very heavy 128mm main battle guns mounted on a Panther chassis and was perhaps the best anti-tank assault weapon produced in the Second World War. Unfortunately for Nazi Germany, it was only just now going into series production and only 400 were ever manufactured. They operated very effectively in

Operation Northwind, however, and the Germans were soon pushing the Americans back through the Haguenau Forest in the direction of the Moder River. Several American units were overrun, and the U.S. 70th Infantry Division suffered especially heavy losses. We "feasted on captured U.S. rations, resupplying our losses in clothing and taking American rifles to supplement our weapons," one SS man recalled. "We were astonished to see how well American soldiers lived."[11]

Order of Battle of the German Forces Involved in Operation Northwind		
Army Group G: Colonel General Johannes Blaskowitz		
1st Army: General of Infantry Hans Obstfelder		
LXXXIX Corps:		
		256th Volksgrenadier Division 245th Infantry Division 361st Volksgrenadier Division
LXXXX Corps:		
		257th Volksgrenadier Division
XIII SS Corps:		
		19th Volksgrenadier Division 347th Infantry Division
LXXXII Corps:		
		416th Infantry Division
XXXIX Panzer Corps:		
		526th Reserve Division
		559th Volksgrenadier Division
		17th SS Panzer Grenadier Division
		25th Panzer Grenadier Division
		21st Panzer Division

Army Group Reserve:	
	10th SS Panzer Division (in transit from Bonn)
	6th SS Mountain Division (in transit from Denmark)
	7th Parachute Division (in transit from Denmark)
Army Group Upper Rhine: Reichsfuehrer-SS Heinrich Himmler	
19th Army: General of Infantry Siegfried Rasp	
LXIII Corps:	
	338th Infantry Division
	159th Infantry Division
	269th Infantry Division
LXIV Corps:	
	16th Volksgrenadier Division
	106th Panzer Brigade
	189th Infantry Division
	716th Infantry Division
	708th Volksgrenadier Division
	198th Infantry Division
XIV SS Corps:	
	no divisions attached
XVIII SS Corps:	
	405th Replacement Division
Army Group Reserve:	
	553rd Volksgrenadier Division
SOURCES: Tessin, Volumes 2, 5, and 14.	

Table 3.1

U.S. Lieutenant General Jacob L. Devers, the commander of the Allied 6th Army Group, was a good commander, and his troops were not taken by surprise. Unlike in the Ardennes, the American retreat was an orderly one. Devers nevertheless considered Strasbourg as good as lost, and on the afternoon of January 1, 1945, he telephoned Eisenhower to ask permission to fall back to the eastern slopes of the Vosges Mountains and to the Belfort Gap, abandoning the plain of Alsace. Eisenhower approved but General Charles de Gaulle, who was now premier of France, strongly objected and ordered General Jean de Lattre de Tassigny, the commander of the French 1st Army, to defend Strasbourg to the utmost even if the Americans withdrew toward the Vosges.[14] He did not intend to risk subjecting the 150,000 inhabitants of Strasbourg to Nazi reprisals.

General de Lattre also had no intention of abandoning Strasbourg. During the night of January 2/3, he reinforced the city with the 3rd Algerian Division, a solid unit under the command of General Augustin-Leon Guillaume.[15] The following night, Eisenhower yielded to political considerations and instructed Devers not to fall back beyond the Moder. The U.S. VI Corps was digging in at the Haguenau Forest north of this river on January 5 when Rasp's 19th Army suddenly went over to the offensive to the southeast. General Thumm's LXIV Corps attacked across the Rhine at the junction of the American and French armies, and the 553rd Volksgrenadier Division soon had a sizable bridgehead over the Rhine at Gambsheim, north of Strasbourg. Meanwhile, Abraham's LXIII Corps, spearheaded by the 198th Infantry Division and the 106th Panzer Brigade "Feldherrnhalle," attacked the 1st French Army south of Strasbourg and pushed the 1st Free French Division northward between the Ill River and the Rhone-Rhine Canal in the direction of the city.

The situation became critical for the 1st French Army as the 553rd Volksgrenadier captured the village of Killstett (twenty miles north of Strasbourg), while the "Feldherrnhalle" and the 198th Infantry attacked out of the northern edge of the Colmar perimeter and drove as far as the Erstein Heights (less than thirteen miles south of Strasbourg), and

Erdmannsdorff's LXXXX Corps threatened to take the city by frontal assault. During a blizzard on January 4, the 17th SS struck at the junction of the U.S. 44th and 100th Infantry Divisions, using captured Sherman tanks at the point of their assault. They captured the village of Gros Rederching before the Americans rallied and contained the assault. Fortunately for the Allies, the U.S. VI Corps was able to hold most of its positions north of the Moder, while Himmler wasted the strength of his divisions in a series of uncoordinated, piecemeal attacks.

To the north, Blaskowitz's Army Group G fared little better. Despite continuing his attack for days, he was unable to break the American line north of the Moser. SS Colonel Lingner, the commander of the 17th SS Panzer Grenadier, was captured by the U.S. 44th Infantry Division on January 9. He was replaced by SS Colonel Fritz Klingenberg.

On January 13, Blaskowitz tried again. The 10th SS Panzer, 25th Panzer Grenadier, and 7th Parachute Divisions struck the newly arrived U.S. 12th Armored Division in the Hagenau sector, while Himmler struck out of the Gambsheim bridgehead with the 553rd Volksgrenadier and 21st Panzer Divisions. (The corrupt and incompetent Lieutenant General Edgar Feuchtinger, who had commanded the 21st Panzer since the summer of 1943, was at last arrested for dereliction of duty in late December 1944 and replaced by Major General Werner Marcks, a brutal Nazi.) Despite repeated Jabo strikes, the Germans were able to knock out seventy American tanks in a single day and virtually wiped out the U.S. 43rd Tank Battalion. Devers, commander of the Allied 6th Army Group, and Lieutenant General Sandy Patch, the commander of the U.S. 7th Army, fell back to the Moser on January 21 and reinforced their sagging front with three fresh American infantry divisions. Here they made their last stand and brought the German offensive to a halt. Blaskowitz continued to attack until January 25 but was not able to break the American line. Meanwhile to the south, Himmler pushed to within eight miles of Strasbourg but failed to dislodge the French 1st Army, which tenaciously defended the capital of Alsace. For the Wehrmacht, Operation Northwind was an expensive failure, and Hellmuth Thumm, the commander of the LXIV Corps, was made the scapegoat. He was relieved of his command on January 20 (less than three weeks after he had been promoted to general of infantry) and never reemployed.[16]

Himmler was not long for the Western Front. On January 21, despite his failure in the West, he was promoted to commander-in-chief of Army Group Vistula on the Eastern Front, where his task was defending Berlin from the Russians. He was replaced as commander-in-chief of Army Group Upper Rhine by SS Colonel General Paul Hausser, who had just recovered from the wounds he suffered in Normandy. The next day, however, Army Group Oberrheim was dissolved, and its units were absorbed by Army Group G, which was now also commanded by Hausser. Its former commander-in-chief, Colonel General Blaskowitz, was on his way to Holland to replace Colonel General Kurt Student (an officer in whom the Fuehrer had little confidence) as commander-in-chief of Army Group H, which was activated on November 11, 1944.

Under Hitler, it seemed at times as if the Wehrmacht was playing a game called "musical commanders." The dance would get even faster in the next four months.

THE BATTLE OF THE COLMAR POCKET

Insofar as possible, General Eisenhower wanted to eliminate all German strongpoints west of the Rhine before crossing that river in strength. The largest position was the German 19th Army's zone south of Strasbourg, in the area known as the Colmar Pocket. Eisenhower reinforced the French 1st Army with two of his best American divisions, as well as the fresh but inexperienced 12th Armored Division. De Gaulle also reinforced de Lattre with the French 2nd Armored Division under General Philippe Leclerc.[17] This gave de Lattre a strength of twelve divisions, four of which were armored. General Rasp faced them with seven infantry divisions (none of which had 7,000 men) and the depleted 106th Panzer Brigade, which had only four companies of tanks at its maximum strength. Unlike Himmler, Rasp suffered a severe supply shortage, and as of the eighth day of the battle, he was strictly limiting his artillery gunners to fifteen 105mm shells per day per gun, while his heavy batteries were limited to a dozen 150mm shells per gun per day. On the other side of the line, de Lattre protested when he was limited to 120 105mm shells and 90 155mm shells per gun per day.

For the main attack, de Lattre concentrated four divisions along a fourteen-mile front between Thann and the Nuenenbruck Forest on the southern side of the pocket. His advance began at 7:00 a.m. on January 20, but the drive progressed slowly because of tough German resistance, well-positioned minefields, and snowstorms that eliminated Allied air support and limited the visibility of artillery battalion forward observers.

Despite continued snowstorms on January 21 and 22, the French attack made progress. General of Infantry Erich Abraham launched a counterattack with his LXIII Corps on January 22, and in the muddy terrain the German Panther tanks and newly manufactured Jadgpanther and Nashorn tank destroyers outmaneuvered the French Shermans and M-10 tank destroyers because the German armor had wider tracks. In addition, the German PzKv Vs (Panthers) and tank destroyers were equipped with long range 88mm guns, which blew apart the American-made Shermans before they could even get within range of the Panthers. (See Appendix 4 for the characteristics of selected German and Allied tanks.) Emil Bethouart's I French Corps suffered severe casualties and, on January 22, Bethouart wanted to call off the offensive. Lattre ordered him to continue the attack.[18] The next day he threw General de Monsabert's II French Corps (U.S. 3rd Infantry and 1st Free French Divisions) into the battle on the northern face of the pocket. The Anglo-French offensive gained ground at first, but Lieutenant General Max Grimmeiss counterattacked with his LXIV Corps reserves and prevented de Monsabert from outflanking Colmar to the north.

As the Allies slugged their way forward through the snow, their overwhelming numerical superiority finally began to tell. Hitler, however, would not authorize a general withdrawal, so the battle continued

Siegfried Rasp. *Wikimedia Commons*

in the increasingly constricted pocket. Meanwhile, at de Lattre's request, Devers sent him the U.S. XXI Corps and the fresh U.S. 75th Infantry Division.

On January 30, the Allies fired 16,438 105mm and 155mm shells in support of the U.S. 3rd Infantry, which managed to cross the Colmar Canal. The U.S. 28th Infantry then pushed into the suburbs of Colmar, where Major General Norman D. Cota halted and diplomatically gave the honor of liberating the city to elements of the French 5th Armored. The U.S. 1st Armored Division was then thrown into the pursuit and, on February 5, linked up with the French I Corps at Rouffach and Sainte Croix-en-Plaine. Several thousand Germans—more victims of Hitler's "hold at all costs" orders—were thus encircled in the western half of the Colmar Pocket.

After the latest disaster, General Rasp was at last given permission to fight a delaying action across the Rhine. At 8:00 a.m. on February 9, his engineers blew up the Rhine River bridge at Chalampe, on the Mulhouse-Freiburg road, leaving behind only a few rearguards, trapped in the la Hardt Forest. These were mopped up the following day. The Battle of the Colmar Pocket was over. It had lasted twenty days. General Rasp inflicted 20,505 casualties on the 420,000 Franco-Americans engaged in the battle. In the process, he lost 22,010 men (mostly prisoners), 80 guns, and 70 tanks, assault guns, and tank destroyers, but he succeeded in escaping across the Rhine with roughly 50,000 men, 7,000 motorized vehicles, 1,500 guns, and 60 armored vehicles. The fact that the 19th Army still existed as an effective combat force is a testimony to the outstanding generalship of Siegfried Rasp. Hitler, of course, did not see things that way, and another scapegoat was needed to explain away his latest defeat. Rasp was relieved of his command on February 15 and replaced by General of Infantry Hermann Foertsch.[19] Germany had lost another excellent commander.

CHAPTER IV

THE BATTLE FOR HUNGARY

With some brief exceptions, the German armies in the East had been in retreat since the original 6th Army was destroyed in Stalingrad in February 1943. On August 20, 1944, Romania defected from the Axis, and the Red Army launched a massive offensive against the German Army Group South Ukraine, pouring through gaps left by the 3rd and 4th Romanian Armies. As a result, the reconstituted German 6th Army and much of the German 8th Army were trapped in two huge pockets on the Prut River. By August 29, the pockets had been cleared, and 180,000 Germans had been captured. Constanta, the Romanian Black Sea port, fell that same day, Ploesti and its vital oil fields were lost on August 30, and Bucharest fell the next day, as the remnants of the German Army fell back into Hungary. The Sixth Army had only two intact divisions left.

Colonel General Johannes Friessner, the commander-in-chief of Army Group South Ukraine, was given a respite of several weeks as the Soviet armies overran Bulgaria, and Tito's Communist guerillas captured most of, and the Soviet Union invaded part of, Yugoslavia. Sofia fell on September 16, and Belgrade was taken on October 20. Meanwhile, Army

A Panther transmission is repaired behind the Eastern Front. *Bundesarchiv Bild 101I-280-10965-33/ Jacob/CC-BY-SA 3.0*

Group South Ukraine was redesignated Army Group South on September 23 and was reinforced with a few new formations, including the 23rd and 24th Panzer Divisions, the mediocre 4th SS Panzer Grenadier Division "Police," and the Headquarters, LVII Panzer Corps under General of Panzer Troops Friedrich Kirchner. By the end of the month, General of Infantry Otto Woehler's 8th Army had three German and three Hungarian divisions, while General of Artillery Maximilian Fretter-Pico's 6th Army had four German and six Hungarian divisions.

On October 6, the Soviets launched a massive offensive against Army Group South. They planned a giant envelopment, aimed at encircling and destroying the army group and *Armeegruppe* Heinrici (1st Panzer and 1st Hungarian Armies) on its left flank. (An *armeegruppe* was a temporary formation, as opposed an army group [*Heeresgruppe*], which was a permanent headquarters.) The attacking forces included Rodion Malinovsky's 2nd Ukrainian and General Ivan E. Petrov's 4th Ukrainian Fronts, which were coordinated by Marshal Semen Konstantinovich Timoshenko. Malinovsky alone had 6 Soviet rifle armies, a tank army, and 2 Romanian armies: 42 Russian rifle divisions, 22 Romanian divisions, 500 tanks and 1,100 airplanes.[1]

Although the Germans were badly outnumbered, the Soviet plan was far too ambitious for its logistical abilities. Because of the differences in gauges, the Romanian railroads were of little use to the Soviets, and everything had to be brought up by truck from west of the Dnestr River. The overextended Soviet supply lines simply were not able to properly

LEFT: General of Infantry Otto Woehler (1894–1987). After the war, Woehler was convicted of war crimes in connection with Einsatzgruppe actions against Slavs and Jews when he was chief of staff of the 11th Army and was sentenced to eight years imprisonment. He was released in 1951; RIGHT: Colonel General Johannes Friesnner (1892–1971). *Bundesarchiv Bild 183-2007-0313-500; Bundesarchiv Bild 146-1984-018-27A/CC-BY-SA 30*

supply an offensive of this scale. On the first day of the offensive, the 4th Ukrainian Front on the Soviet right routed the 3rd Hungarian Army. After that, however, Petrov had to deal with Germans. Performing with his usual brilliance, Colonel General Gotthard Heinrici took maximum advantage of the excellent defensive possibilities in the Carpathians and quickly checked the 4th Ukrainian Front in the mountains. Friessner, however, had less suitable defensive terrain and less reliable troops; he was soon in serious trouble. On his left, the Russian 53rd Army and General Issa Pliev's Mechanized Cavalry Group broke through the 3rd Hungarian Army and gained fifty miles in three days. Fortunately for him, Major General Josef von Radowitz's 23rd Panzer Division put up a magnificent defense at Oradea, on the northern shoulder of the 3rd Hungarian, and stopped the entire 6th Guards Tank Army cold, forcing the Pliev Group to come back to assist it. Even so, Friessner realized that his front could not hold indefinitely and, on October 8, warned Colonel General Heinz Guderian, the chief of the Army General Staff, that it would take Woehler's 8th Army six days to withdraw behind the Theiss River. Hitler, however, would not allow a timely retreat. When Radowitz finally lost Oradea on October 12, most of the 76th Infantry Division was cut off and destroyed. In the meantime, Friessner decided that he could wait no longer and, on October 12, ordered a retreat. Cluj was abandoned, and much of the army group fell back toward the Theiss. Malinovsky was slowed by supply problems but, on October 17, launched an attack aimed at cutting off the retreat of the German 8th and Hungarian 1st and 2nd Armies east of the Theiss. The Germans made their stand at Debrecen, the third largest city in Hungary, which did not fall until October 20. Then the Pliev Group, which included the 1st Tank and 2nd Guards Cavalry Corps, knifed into the rear of the 8th Army and captured Nyiregyhaza on October 22, cutting Woehler's main line of retreat. This time, however, Friessner was ready for them. Acting on a plan originated by Major General Helmuth von Grolman, the army group's chief of staff, General of Panzer Troops Hermann Breith's III Panzer Corps of the 6th Army, spearheaded by the ever-reliable 23rd Panzer Division, struck from the west on October 23 while Woehler attacked from the east with Lieutenant General Kurt Roepke's XXIX Corps and part of General of Mountain Troops Hans Kreysing's XVII Corps. The 4th Ukrainian Front tried to break up the impending encirclement by launching heavy counterattacks against Woehler, but without success. Woehler recaptured Nyiregyhaza on October 29 and linked up with Radowitz's 23rd Panzer, cutting off the Pliev Group. Some of the Russians managed to escape in small groups, but by the time the pocket was cleared, the Russians had lost 25,000 men and 600 tanks.[2] The entire operation resembled the "blitzkrieg" operations of old.

When they recaptured Nyiregyhaza and the surrounding villages, the Germans got an ample opportunity to see how the Soviets were going to behave in occupied Axis territory. Hungarian women of all ages had been raped; afterwards, many had been murdered. Mothers and fathers had been nailed to doorposts and forced to watch as their children were raped, mutilated, and murdered.[3] These horrific sights redoubled the determination of German soldiers to prevent the Russians from reaching German territory.

Meanwhile, Hungary's regent, Admiral Miklos (Nicolas) Horthy, was secretly trying to negotiate an armistice with the Soviet Union. The Hungarian cabinet and parliament, on the other hand, were pro-German, as was at least half the army, with many generals wanting to continue fighting as German allies against the Soviets.

Hitler was in a much better position to foil Hungary's attempted defection than he had been Romania's six weeks earlier. The commandant of the Budapest garrison was one of Horthy's leading military supporters. On October 8, the Gestapo arrested him. On October 15, Hitler's most famous commando, SS Major Otto Skorzeny, kidnaped Admiral Horthy's son. (Skorzeny reportedly rolled up the noted playboy—and armistice negotiator—in a carpet and sent him back to Germany.)

That same afternoon, Radio Budapest broadcast Horthy's declaration of an armistice with the Soviet Union, and the cabinet promptly resigned in protest. The next morning Skorzeny seized the royal palace. Apparently hoping to avoid being captured by Skorzeny, Horthy surrendered to General of the Waffen-SS Karl von Pfeffer-Wildenbruch. As his last official act, Horhty was forced to appoint Ferenc Szalasi, the leader of the Arrow-Cross Party (the Hungarian version of the Nazi Party), as his successor and request "asylum" in Germany.[4]

According to military historian Earl Ziemke, Szalasi's chief claim to distinction was "his incoherence both in speech and in writing." He promptly named himself "*Nador*" (Fuehrer), with all the powers of the Prince Regent.[5]

The Wehrmacht's problems in Hungary remained pressing. Its flat terrain made it well-suited for Soviet mobile operations against German Army Group South, which was badly understrength. The 6th Army,

LEFT: Admiral Nikolaus Horthy (1868–1957), Regent of Hungary (1920–1944), and Adolf Hitler in happier times, 1938. Horthy refused to wholeheartedly support the German war effort or the Holocaust and secretly tried to negotiate with the Allies. He was overthrown and arrested. He spent the last years of his life in exile in Portugal. His body was not returned to Hungary until 1993; RIGHT: General of the Waffen-SS Karl von Pfeffer-Wildenbruch, commander of Fortress Budapest, 1944–1945. *Ginzery Sandor, Tomor Laszlo, and Dulovits Jeno; Bundesarchiv Bild 101 III-Ege-237-06A*

for example, had four panzer and two panzer grenadier divisions (the 1st, 13th, 23rd, and 24th Panzers and 4th SS and Feldherrnhalle Panzer Grenadiers), but, all totaled, these divisions had only sixty-seven tanks and fifty-eight assault guns. In short, Friessner's armies now held a continuous front, but it was weak, thinly manned, and could not hold long against a determined attack. Friessner also did not have firm contact with Weichs's Army Group F, since elements of the 2nd Ukrainian Front had already taken advantage of the weak 3rd Hungarian Army, crossed the lower Theiss, and occupied much of the Hungarian Plain between the Theiss and the Danube. Hitler nevertheless commanded

Friessner to fight for every foot of soil and refused to allow voluntary withdrawals.

The fall of Horthy and the advent of Szalasi also hurt Hungarian morale, which was already low. Hungarian soldiers began to desert in large numbers; in some places entire units went over to the Russians. Colonel General Janos Voeroes, the Hungarian chief of staff and minister of war, defected (crossing the lines in a Mercedes Heinz Guderian had given him a few weeks before), as did Colonel General Bela Miklos, the commander of the 1st Hungarian Army. Colonel General Lajos Verres, the leader of the Hungarian 2nd Army, was arrested on Friessner's orders. Of the senior army officers, only General Joseph Heszlenyi, the commander of the 3rd Hungarian Army, remained in office.[6]

On the afternoon of October 29, Malinovsky attacked the Hungarian 3rd Army again. The German elements of this army, under the command of Kirchner's LVII Panzer Corps, held their positions, but the Hungarians scattered almost immediately. The Russians captured Kecskemet on the 31st and were halted only a few miles from the suburbs of Budapest. Meanwhile, German defenders were reinforced by the 8th SS and 22nd SS Cavalry Divisions. Elements of the 8th SS and the Feldherrnhalle Panzer Grenadier Divisions counterattacked and recaptured the town of Vecses, just southeast of the city. The Soviets, mindful of the disaster they had recently suffered at Debrecen, withdrew to the southeast.

During the first week of November, Timoshenko regrouped his forces and prepared for an offensive on a much broader front. On his left, Fedor Tolbukhin's 3rd Ukrainian Front, which had captured the Yugoslav capital on October 19, entered Hungary from the south with three armies and an independent tank corps. East and northeast of the Hungarian capital lay Malinovsky's 2nd Ukrainian Front with six armies. The Axis forces available to meet this threat included the 2nd Panzer Army (of OB Southeast) and Army Group South, which deployed the remnants of the 2nd Hungarian Army, Armeegruppe Fretter-Pico (German 6th Army plus a few Hungarian units) and Armeegruppe Woehler (German 8th and 1st Hungarian Armies).

The Soviet offensive started on November 7, when the 3rd Ukrainian Front attempted to cross to the west bank of the Danube near Mohacs, Batina, and Apatin. Most of this area was flooded and easily defended. For two weeks, the 2nd Panzer Army foiled Tolbukhin's advance until he finally broke through on November 22. The Russians, aided by a miners' revolt, overcame the fierce resistance of SS Major General Gustav Lombard's 31st SS Volunteer Grenadier Division "Bohemia-Moravia" and took Pecs on November 29. The 31st SS Volunteer Grenadier Division was a mixed German/*Volksdeutsch* unit (which had been in the process of forming in southern Hungary when Tolbukhin's offensive struck).[7] It managed to evacuate 80,000 ethnic Germans from southern Hungary and fell back to Lake Balaton to reform.

Friessner met the latest Soviet offensive in a manner that had become standard operating procedure for senior German generals: he rushed his armored and motorized units from crisis point to crisis point, losing ground while valiantly trying to keep his front from collapsing. On December 8, Malinovsky captured the city of Vac on the Danube bend, about ten miles due north of the capital, while Tolbukhin pushed to the Lake Balaton-Lake Velencze line, southwest of the city. Map 4.1 shows the deteriorating situation in Hungary between October 29 and December 30, 1944.

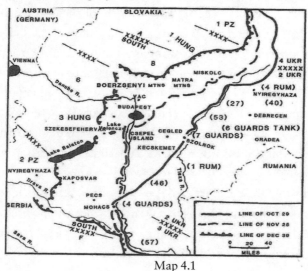

Map 4.1

It was now clear that a Soviet encirclement of Budapest was in the offing. With Hitler's permission, OKH reinforced Friessner with two panzer divisions and three Tiger battalions for a counterattack, but they were slow to arrive because Allied bombers had crippled the German transportation system.

On December 14, after the Russians captured the town of Ipolysag north of Budapest and began working their way through the small Boerzsenyi Mountains northeast of the city, Friessner had no choice but to defend Sahy with the Dirlewanger Brigade, led by the notorious SS Oberführer Oskar Dirlewanger, which had recently come down from Slovakia. This brigade consisted of the scum of the German Army; most of its men were convicted criminals and most of the rest were Communists. The army group commander visited it on the 14th, and what he saw amazed him. Dirlewanger, who was responsible for many of the terrible atrocities committed in putting down the Warsaw uprising a few months before, was sitting calmly at his desk with a monkey on his shoulder. Neither he nor his staff knew anything about the situation in their sector of the front, but Dirlewanger nevertheless wanted to withdraw. Friessner ordered him to stay put. Then Friessner visited the 24th Panzer Division and, returning to his headquarters that evening, passed through the Sahy sector again, where he narrowly avoided being captured by the Russians. Dirlewanger had ignored his orders and pulled out; no one knew where his brigade had gone.

On December 18, the situation deteriorated to the point that Friessner was forced to commit the 8th Panzer Division—part of his counterattack force—to the northern wing, against the Russian 6th Tank Army. Friessner and Guderian, meanwhile, were having another series of arguments because Friessner did not want to use his panzer reserve to attack right away. The weather—rain and above-freezing temperatures—was too bad for the use of armor, and the plain southwest of Budapest was a giant field of mud. On December 14, Friessner categorically refused to assume responsibility for the attack until the ground had frozen, but still Guderian persisted in ordering him to strike. Their arguments became so heated that on December 18 Friessner flew to the headquarters of the High Command of the Army in Zossen, about thirty miles south of Berlin, to straighten out the matter. Friessner discovered that Guderian—and his operations officer Colonel Bogislaw von Bonin—agreed with him but had been repeating Hitler's orders. Friessner argued for Budapest's evacuation. Hitler wanted the city defended house by house even though it was utterly unprepared for a siege. Guderian said that he would relay Friessner's views to the Fuehrer but could promise nothing.[8]

The next day, the Dirlewanger Brigade mutinied and effectively disbanded. Several companies went over to the Reds, while other units merely shot their officers and deserted.

Meanwhile, the III Panzer Corps' counterattack (ordered by Hitler) failed, and the Soviets closed in on Budapest. By December 22, the city was in danger of encirclement. Once again, Friessner called for the abandonment of the Hungarian capital—and he and General Fretter-Pico were subsequently sacked. Woehler was given command of Army Group South, General of Panzer Troops Hermann Balck was transferred from the Western Front to assume command of the 6th Army, and General of Mountain Troops Hans Kreysing succeeded Woehler

A German Tiger II and a column of Arrow Cross soldiers, Budapest, 1944. *Bundesarchiv Bild 101I-680-8283A-12A/Faupel/CC-BY-SA 3.0*

as commander of the 8th Army.[9] Guderian signaled the new commanders that they should have but one battle cry: "Attack!–whether by
patrols, locally, or on a large scale."[10]

Woehler called Guderian and argued that, historically, Budapest
had always been defended from the west bank. Listening to his arguments, Guderian agreed to speak to Hitler about abandoning Budapest.
Three hours later, he relayed the Fuehrer's decision to General Woehler.
The city, including the bridgehead on the eastern side of the Danube,
was to be defended; OKH would launch a rescue attack, using the IV
SS Panzer Corps (3rd SS and 5th SS Panzer Divisions) from Army
Group Center; and Woehler had permission to withdraw two divisions
from the city.

It was already too late even for that; by December 24, Budapest
was encircled.

THE SIEGE OF BUDAPEST

From early November 1944, Budapest was defended by 33,000
Germans and 37,000 Hungarians under the direction of General of
Panzer Troops Hermann Breith's III Panzer Corps.[11] Table 4.1 shows the
Axis Order of Battle during the Siege of Budapest.

The Axis Order of Battle, Siege of Budapest, November 1944–February 1945

III Panzer Corps: General of Panzer Troops Hermann Breith
(replaced by General of SS Karl von Pfeffer-Wildenbruch's IX SS
Mountain Corps on December 4) (1)

(60th) Panzer Division "Feldherrnhalle"(2): Colonel Guenther Page (3)
13th Panzer Division: Major General Gerhard Schmidhuber
8th SS Cavalry Division "Florian Geyer": SS Oberfuehrer Joachim Rumohr (4)
22nd SS Cavalry Division "Maria Theresia": SS Oberfuehrer August Zehender (4)
1st SS Police Regiment (5): SS Oberfuehrer Helmut Doerner
Kampfgruppe, 271st Volksgrenadier Division: Lieutenant Colonel Herbert Kuendiger (6)

I Hungarian Corps: Colonel General Ivan Hindy (7)

10th Hungarian Infantry Division
12th Hungarian Infantry Division
Elements, 1st Hungarian Armored Division
One regiment, 1st Hungarian Cavalry Division
Arrow Cross Party Militia
Several police and auxiliary units

NOTES:

(1) Pfeffer-Wildenbruch was named Wehrmacht Commander Budapest on December 25, 1944.
(2) Parts of the FHH Division, including the 13th Tank Destroyer Battalion, were outside the city when it was surrounded.
(3) Colonel Page was promoted to major general on December 1, 1944. He was on detached duty commanding an ad hoc battle group outside the fortress and was not with the part of the FHH Division that was inside Budapest when it was surrounded.
(4) Promoted to SS major general during the siege.
(5) Part of the 4th SS Panzer Grenadier Division "Police"
(6) *Kampfgruppe* (battle group) denoted a burnt-out division with the combat value of a regiment.
(7) Captured in 1945 and executed in 1946.

Table 4.1

The tone for the battle was set on November 10, when a Russian armored force took the key town of Vecses (Vecsus) from SS Major Walter Drexler's 8th SS Panzer Reconnaissance Battalion. SS Major General Joachim Rumohr, the commander of the 8th SS Cavalry Division "Floyian Geyer," launched an immediate counterattack and retook the town in bitter, house-to-house fighting. They found that most of the citizens of the town had been killed; most of the women had been raped before they were murdered. Survivors cried to the SS cavalrymen: "My God, my God, why did you leave us?" Several Waffen-SS men who had been captured were also found, but their bodies were so badly mutilated that they were difficult to identify.[12] After Vecses, quarter was seldom given or asked for, and the SS men never gave up a position voluntarily. The Soviets were not able to retake Vecsus until the end of December.

The 8th SS and 22nd SS Cavalry Divisions, now fighting as infantry, barred the direct route to Budapest and were subjected to repeated attacks, which they repulsed, except for one.[13] On November 17, the Soviets broke through the German trenches and barreled into the western sector of Vecses but were quickly surrounded by a counterattack. The SS cavalrymen then wiped out the attacking force.

On December 4, 5, and 6, the Soviets penetrated the Hungarian lines in several places. Most of these penetrations were liquidated by counterattacks by Major General Gerhard Schmidhuber's 13th Panzer Division[14] or by Colonel Guenther Pape's 60th (Feldhernnhalle) Panzer Grenadier Division, but the *panzertruppen* lacked the strength to seal the holes in the Hungarian lines and had to fall back into the "Budapest Bridgehead" positions, on the very outskirts of the city.[15] By December 11, the Russians were hammering Budapest with 10,000 artillery pieces that ringed the city north, east, and south.

On December 13, III Panzer Corps withdrew and IX SS Mountain Corps took charge of defending the Hungarian capital. This corps had been formed in the summer of 1944 to oversee the training and operations of the 13th SS and 23rd SS Volunteer Mountain Divisions "Handschar" and "Kama." Most of its troops were Croatian Moslems who were not particularly interested in serving the Greater German Reich. Indiscipline and lack of training time led to the dissolution of the 23rd SS, and the 13th was scaled back to regimental size, which left the IX SS Mountain free for employment at the front. In early December, SS Lieutenant General Karl-Gustav Sauberzweig was replaced by General of SS Karl von Pfeffer-Wildenbruch, who was also a general of police.[16] As commander of the IX SS Mountain Corps, he led the German forces throughout the siege. A tough veteran, he had already lost both of his sons in the war. The oldest was killed in action as a Fahnenjunker in North Africa in 1941, and the youngest, an army second lieutenant, was killed in France in 1944. Despite his SS status, Pfeffer-Wildenbruch was accepted by his army colleagues and was considered competent by the army commanders in Hungary. He was to prove them right during the Siege of Budapest.

Budapest, a city of a million people, tried to treat the siege as a minor inconvenience. The 8th SS Cavalry Medical Battalion, for example, set up its main dressing station in the wine cellar of the elegant Hotel Britania. Affluent Hungarians ate in the dining room and ignored the mud-covered German medics carrying filthy, wounded SS men. The streetcars still operated, Christmas festivities continued, shops were open, and many Hungarian officers spent their nights at home and commuted to the front. There was relatively little fighting in the trenches around Budapest during the week of December 17–23, and the troops tried not to think about the deteriorating strategic situation.

By December 24, however, Budapest was surrounded. Pfeffer-Wildenbruch wanted to launch an immediate breakout and sent the Floyian Geyer SS Cavalry Division to Buda, on the western side of the pocket, to lead the way. Then came the order from Fuehrer Headquarters: "Budapest must be held under all circumstances."[17] Instead of attacking, the 22nd SS Cavalry dug in to defend the western approaches to the "fortress." Unfortunately for the defenders, their supply depots were located to the west of the city, and the staff of the IX SS Mountain Corps did not start moving them east until it was too late. Most of their 450 tons of ammunition and 300,000 rations were lost to the Russians on Christmas Eve. Once again, the Waffen-SS demonstrated its major weaknesses as a combat force: a lack of trained General Staff officers and faulty staff work.

The fighting escalated when the Soviets tried to batter their way into Budapest on December 25. The siege was constant now, and the civilian population was driven to cellars by air and artillery bombardments. In most quarters, the electricity, gas, and water services failed in the first days, and city authorities had made little provision for food or medical supplies, leaving thousands to die of cold and illness.[18]

On Christmas Day the FHH Division held the suburb of Budaors in fierce fighting. The next day the Russians suffered heavy losses at Budakesci, which was held by the 8th SS Recon Battallon. In the Danube, the Soviets managed to capture the main heights on Csepel Island. The Russians were attacking everywhere, and disaster was frequently averted only by counterattacks by the last battalions. All Pfeffer-Wildenbruch had left in reserve was a *kampfgruppe* (battle group) from Oberfuehrer Helmut Doerner's 1st SS Police Regiment (Oberfuehrer was an SS rank between SS colonel and SS major general; it has no direct English translation). He signaled Fuehrer Headquarters that he wanted to evacuate the east (Pest) sector of the pocket, so he could concentrate his forces on the western side of the Danube. Needless to say, permission to retreat was not forthcoming.

The situation deteriorated. On December 27, Drexler's 8th Panzer Reconnaissance Battalion was finally pushed out of Vecses, and the Reds looked to gain further ground. By now, the defenders were outnumbered about 5 to 1 in men and much more than that in guns, tanks, and airplanes—and German supplies were running out. The IX SS Mountain predicted that it would be out of ammunition by January 3 and out of food by January 12. Even so, on December 29, Gerhard Schmidhuber's 13th Panzer Division launched a vicious counterattack and wiped out the Russian penetration from the day before.

The IX SS depended on resupply landings or air drops at the Budapest racetrack. Twenty-seven He-111s and Ju-52s landed during the night of December 29/30 and deposited seventy-five tons of ammunition and ten tons of fuel.[19] Another forty-five tons were airdropped, and another twenty-nine supply planes landed on December 30, during daylight hours, though several were shot down by Soviet fighters.

Near Csomor, Soviet attacks broke though the 10th Hungarian Division, and the 13th Panzer was not able to close the gap completely. The two divisions had to retreat to a shorter defensive line to the west. Soviet Marshals Rodion Malinovsky and Fedor Tolbukhin had been sure that they would capture Budapest within three or four days after completing the encirclement, but the German-Hungarian resistance was stubborn, tying down more than a quarter of a million Soviet troops, including nineteen Soviet and Romanian divisions, three mechanized or tank brigades, and several specialized artillery and assault units. The Russian generals therefore tried diplomacy. On December 29, a team of four "parliamentarians" crossed the line under a flag of truce. They were first taken to the command post of SS Colonel August Zehender, the commander of the 22nd SS Cavalry Division, who contemptuously rejected the very idea of surrender, refused to look at the offered terms, and sent the emissaries packing. What happened next is disputed.

One witness, an SS man, said a Hungarian anti-tank gun, hidden near were the Budaorcsi Road crossed the Hamszabegi railroad line, fired

A 75mm Pak-40 anti-tank gun, manned by a Hungarian crew, Budapest, late 1944. *Bundesarchiv Bild 146-1986-064-15/Keimling/CC-BY-SA 3.0*

on the Soviet jeep, killing all four of its occupants. The Hungarians denied the charge and said the jeep must have struck a mine. The Soviets accused the Waffen-SS of murdering the men. Via loudspeakers and radio broadcasts they swore revenge for this serious war crime, which only stiffened German and Hungarian resistance, and the Siege of Budapest became one of the bitterest battles of the Second World War.

By December 30, the Germans had concentrated their flak guns in the zone of the 13th Panzer Division around Csomor, where the race-track/airfield was located. To the west, the 8th SS Cavalry was hard-pressed by repeated Soviet attacks, and by December 31, the 15th Cavalry Regiment of the 8th SS had been pushed back to within a half a mile of the Margarethen Island bridge on the Danube.

During the night of December 31/January 1, the Soviets launched a massive attack. At many points, the Germans were forced to commit their last reserves, the 13th Panzer near Csomer was forced back, and in several areas the fighting was hand-to-hand. "My wounds are not so bad," a soldier from the 18th SS Cavalry Regiment wrote to his parents in Duesseldorf:

> On the 29th I received a splinter in my left foot, had it bound up and went back on duty. On the 30th I got a shell fragment from a Russian anti-tank gun in my left thigh which was worse. . . . There were five floors in the Hotel Imperial, all full of wounded . . . . The situation in the city is crazy. The Hungarians have really lost their heads. We must fight in the streets . . . the Russians are shooting with their artillery from all sides. . . .
>
> The last days forward at the front were terrible, we never stopped fighting. Three times the Russians broke through a little bit with tanks and each time we had to counterattack with units made out of thin air! My platoon has gone from 42 men to 14. We don't get much food—only a loaf of bread for each 18 men . . . .

> The Russians are coming ever closer . . . the streets are fully blocked up. Dead men, horses, animals and ruined cars are all over. . . .[20]

The man who wrote this letter was more fortunate than most. The next day, he was flown out of the pocket to Papa, Hungary, by a Ju-52. Inside the pocket, however, his comrades continued to fight and die. Of the 33,000 German soldiers trapped in Budapest, approximately 2,000 had been killed and more than 7,000 wounded. The Hungarians had also suffered heavy casualties and about one-third of them deserted to the Soviets by the time the battle was over. The Reds helped speed up this process by promising Hungarian deserters that they could go home if they lived behind Russian lines.

During the night of January 1/2, 56 He-111s dropped 73.5 tons of ammunition and supplies into the garrison, as well as a small quantity of fuel. Then the rescue operation began.

To save the garrison at Budapest, Army Group South was given IV SS Panzer Corps (3rd SS Panzer Division "Totenkopf" and the 5th SS Panzer Division "Viking") commanded by Waffen-SS General Herbert Gille.[21] Map 4.2 shows this offensive. The operation began on January 1, 1945, and the IV SS Panzer (supported by Colonel Hermann Harrendorf's 96th Infantry Division) initially made good progress along the Komarno-Budapest road. The Soviets reacted quickly, however, and prevented a decisive breakthrough. Soviet fighter-bombers were particularly effective in slowing the advance of the panzers. On January 6, the IV SS Panzer was stopped near Perbal, about fifteen miles from the Budapest perimeter, and the 6th Guards Tank and 7th Guards Armies launched a powerful counterattack to the north, threatening its rear (Map 4.3). The next day, General Hermann Balck, the commander of the 6th Army, struck the Russian lines to the south with the I Cavalry Corps and gained several miles, but the Russians again reacted quickly by sending in the 4th Guards Army. By January 7, both attacks were stalled. Balck signaled that he needed to withdraw the 6th Army, but

Hitler refused to allow it. General Woehler, as commander of Army Group South, had no choice but to continue trying to punch through the Russian lines, hoping to relieve the garrison at Budapest though he knew it was probably futile.

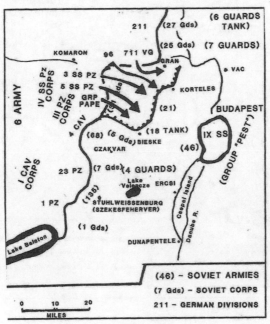

Map 4.2

Meanwhile, inside the pocket, the defenders absorbed blow after blow. As one historian has noted:

> Frontlines as such no longer existed. Machine gun nests and foxholes in the ruins provided the key points of resistance, and wherever they were located, there was the "front" .... House-to-house fighting, with hand grenades, revolvers, machine-pistols, bayonets and spades, was the order of the day. The streets were so shell-cratered and plowed up that tanks and vehicles could no longer move through most of them. Behind the "front," the Russians and their Hungarian communist

counterparts went on a rampage of murder, rape, and plunder. No civilian was safe from their reign of terror.[22]

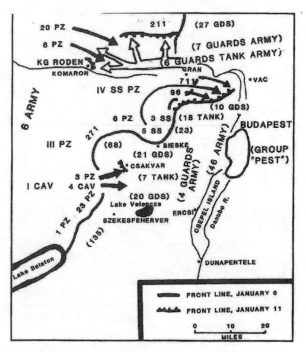

Map 4.3

By January 7, food was in critically short supply, and the garrison's main source of water was melted snow. On January 12, the Russians broke into the eastern parts of the city of Pest but were wiped out in bitter street fighting. The next day, another breakthrough took place to the south at Kispest, but again it was eliminated by a prompt counterattack. On January 15, the Reds launched an all-out attack but only managed to gain a few blocks in eastern Budapest. It was, however, becoming increasingly evident that the German positions east of the Danube were doomed. Most of the bridges across the river had already been destroyed by the Red Air Force. The Germans had lost most of their heavy weapons, were almost out of food and ammunition, and their air squadrons were out of fuel. Pfeffer-Wildenbruch practically begged Army Group

A pair of He-111 bombers. This type of aircraft was used as an emergency transport to convey supplies to Budapest during the siege. This photograph was taken in Romania. *Bundesarchiv Bild 101I-622-2960-35A/Grosse/CC-BY-SA 3.0*

South and Fuehrer Headquarters for permission to pull back across the river. Hitler finally relented at 7:25 p.m. on January 16. The evacuation began at 10:00 p.m. on January 17 and continued until after daylight on January 18. German engineers destroyed the Elisabeth Bridge and the last pontoon bridges at 7:00 a.m. on January 18. The eastern side of the Danube was now clear of Axis forces.

Meanwhile, the IV SS Panzer Corps turned north and advanced up the western bank of the Danube, to a point only a dozen miles south of the Budapest perimeter (Map 4.4). Pfeffer-Wildenbruch would have broken out had he been allowed to, but Hitler's orders were firm. For him, the rescue of the Magyar capital was the only solution to the problem. So, as was the case with Stalingrad, the garrison of Budapest was forced to pass up its last real chance to break out and escape.

By January 19, the Budapest Pocket extended about one mile along the Danube and was no more than a mile in depth. The men were reduced to eating horse meat or cats—when they were available. (Survivors later stated that cats taste better than dogs or horses.) The garrison held no more airfields, which made resupply problematic. Supply canisters, dropped by parachute, frequently landed behind Russian lines or in no-man's land and sometimes provoked savage little battles. On January 27, the Soviets launched a series of counterattacks against the IV Panzer

Corps' salient, using the 26th Army, as well as the 23rd Tank, 1st Guards Mechanized, and 5th Guards Cavalry Corps.[23] Gille was forced to retreat, but Hitler still would not allow a break-out attempt. That day, the last members of the IX SS Mountain Corps staff company were thrown into the battle as infantrymen, fighting to seal off the numerous Russian penetrations. Losses were heavy on both sides. Two days later, the corps reported that it would soon have more wounded than effective combatants. Daily rations were reduced to five grams (1.7 ounces) of lard, a slice of bread, and one piece of horsemeat per man per day. These rations were supplemented by large quantities of Schnapps and wine, of which Budapest had an abundant supply.

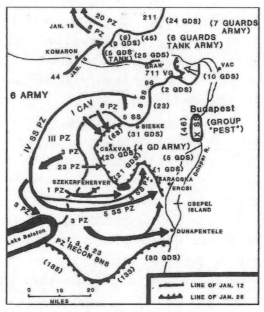

Map 4.4

On January 30, IX SS Corps signaled: "Famine and disease are spreading. The people have lost all faith and hope . . . the situation is very critical. The last battle has begun."[24]

With the garrison nearing the end of its endurance, the house-to-house fighting remained savage. On February 3, for example, the starving defenders destroyed eight Soviet tanks, two anti-tank guns, an anti-aircraft gun, and an armored car. And so it went day after day, as the Russians cleared one block at a time. By February 6, there were 11,000 wounded in the cauldron. Several squadrons of the 8th SS Cavalry Division were surrounded in the area of the Main Railroad Station on February 7, and the 8th SS Flak Battalion (which shot down seventy-five enemy airplanes during the siege and received a special commendation from General Guderian) abandoned its empty guns on the grounds of the university at Castle Hill and went into the battle as infantry.[25]

On February 9, in fierce fighting, the Russians tried and failed to drive a wedge between Castle Hill (the former seat of the Hungarian government) and the Budapest citadel. But the end was obviously not far off. Pfeffer-Wildenbruch again signaled Fuehrer Headquarters for permission to withdraw and planned a break-out for the night of

A Jagdpanzer 38 light tank destroyer. This one was part of the 8th SS Cavalry Division "Florian Geyer," Hungary, 1944. It featured a 75mm gun and a modified Czechoslovakian Panzer 38(t) chassis and was one of the more common late-war tank destroyers. More than 2,500 were built during the conflict. It was mechanically reliable and very successful when the enemy's route of approach could be predicted, as was almost always the case during the Siege of Budapest. It was less successful in a battle of maneuver because of its limited gun traverse and thin side armor. *Bundesarchiv Bild 101I-715-0213A-25/Kreutzer, Wilhelm/CC-BY-SA 3.0*

February 11. As the men prepared, their mood became strangely relaxed, almost carefree. One SS cavalry squadron ate its first hot meal in days—meatballs (made from horsemeat) and gravy; if this was their last meal, the attitude of many was that there was nothing more to worry about. When a dispatch runner from the 8th SS Cavalry entered the command post of SS Major General Rumohr, he saw several high-ranking officers seated around the conference table (the runner recognized General Schmidhuber, the commander of the 13th Panzer, among others), but no serious discussions were going on. The table was piled high with Schnapps bottles. "Come and drink up my boy!" a smiling General Rumohr greeted the runner, "once we leave here we'll be dodging the shit soon enough!"[26]

The break-out attempt began at 8:00 p.m. on February 11. After leaving their wounded with the Papal Nuncio and destroying their heavy equipment and everything else they could not carry, approximately 16,000 soldiers moved out. The Soviets were ready and hit the Germans with every gun in their arsenal, including the dreaded Stalin Organ rockets. Within minutes, the first wave of the infantry assault elements of the 13th Panzer and 8th SS Cavalry Divisions were slaughtered. General Schmidhuber tried to lead the second wave of his division across the open terrain northwest of Vienna-Strasse but ran into a hail of bullets and artillery fire. He was killed, and his troops were dispersed and later captured.

Still, despite heavy resistance, Pfeffer-Wildenbruch's main attempt succeeded in clearing the built-up area of Budapest, which was now a field of ruins. Making surprising progress, they advanced about twelve miles and reached the area of Perbal, near where the IV SS Panzer had been halted a month before. But then, on February 12, they were scattered by Soviet armor, and very few survivors made it back to the German lines.

Budapest has been called "the Stalingrad of the Waffen-SS." Only about 700 Waffen-SS soldiers returned to the Axis front. Most of the rest—at least 25,000 men—were murdered by their Soviet captors or died in "death marches" or in slave labor camps. SS General Pfeffer-Wildenbruch was wounded and kept as a Soviet prisoner until 1955. He died in a traffic accident in Bielefeld, Westphalia (West Germany), on January 29, 1971. Joachim Rumohr, the commander of the 8th SS Cavalry Division "Florian Geyer" and August Zehender, the commander of the 22nd SS Cavalry Division, were both killed in the breakout attempt, although there were unverified reports that Rumohr shot himself to keep from falling into Russian hands. Both had been promoted to *SS-Brigadefuehrer und Generalmajor der Waffen-SS* (SS major general) in the last days of the siege. They and Pfeffer-Wildenbruch were awarded Oak Leaves to their Knight's Crosses.

None of the three of the commanders of the cavalry regiments of the 8th SS Cavalry Division escaped. SS Lieutenant Colonel Oswald Krauss and Major Hans von Schack, the commanders of the 15th and 16th Cavalry Regiments, respectively, were reported as missing in action and never found, and SS Major Hans-Georg von Charpentier, the commander of the 18th Cavalry Regiment, was recorded as killed in action on February 11. But the wounded commanders of the horse regiments of the 22nd Cavalry Division—SS Colonel Karl-Heinz Reitel of the 52nd Cavalry and SS Reserve Lieutenant Colonel Anton Ameiser of the 54th—were flown out of the pocket near the end of the siege. Both were given regimental commands in the new 37th SS Cavalry Division "Luetzow," which was formed using the horses given up by the then-defunct 8th and 22nd SS Cavalry. SS-Oberfuehrer Helmut Doerner, the commander of the 1st SS Police Regiment and a holder of the Knight's Cross with Oak Leaves and Swords, was killed near the Boinay Academy on February 11.

Once again, Adolf Hitler had needlessly sacrificed tens of thousands of desperately needed German soldiers, but their courageous defense of Budapest gave tens of thousands of people the opportunity to escape the Red flood that was about to engulf central Europe. "Finally, on February 12, 1945, the guns ceased firing in Budapest," SS Captain Peter Neumann wrote.

An oppressive silence suddenly hung over the city like a cur-
tain of lead, a silence even more tragic than the deafening roar
of bombs and street fighting.

Budapest had not surrendered.

But there were no men left alive to stop the screaming
hordes who now poured into the city. . . . Drunk with fury
and vodka they murdered, raped, pillaged, and set fire to what
remained of the ruined buildings.[27]

The next battles against the Red Army would be in the Reich itself.
Nazi Germany was entering its death throes.

LEFT: Major General Gerhard Schmidhuber, commander of the 13th Panzer Divi-
sion; RIGHT: SS Oberfuehrer Joachim Rumohr, commander of the 8th SS Cavalry
Division "Florian Geyer." Both were killed in the Budapest break-out attempt.
Rumohr may have committed suicide. *Bundesarchiv, Bild 101I-088-3743-15A /
Fischer / CC-BY-SA 3.0; Bundesarchiv, Bild 183-S73622 / CC-BY-SA 3.0*

CHAPTER V

STALIN'S JANUARY OFFENSIVE

North of the Carparthians, the overall situation on the Eastern Front had not changed significantly since the Soviets isolated Memel in October. On October 19, 1944, the Russians scored a minor breakthrough into East Prussia and captured the districts of Gumbinnen and Goldap. The German 4th Army, under the command of the brilliant but hard-headed General of Infantry Friedrich Hossbach, launched a series of vigorous counterattacks between October 22 and November 5, smashed the Soviet 11th Guards Army, and recaptured most of both districts, including the village of Nemmersdorf.[1] What the Germans found turned their stomachs. All of the inhabitants, including women, children, and babies, had been tortured and murdered in the most bestial manner. Many of them had been crucified; some had been raped, nailed to doors, and left to die. Young girls who had not yet reached their teens had been raped repeatedly, as had women in their seventies. Then they had been murdered. More than fifty French prisoners-of-war, who had been sent to the district to work on the farms, had tried to protect the German families. They were also murdered by the drunken Russians.

Afterwards, the very word "Nemmersdorf" invoked fear in Germany and became shorthand for the Soviet butchery of German villages. General Hossbach was outraged by the Russian atrocities but also livid that he had been forbidden to evacuate civilians from the area; he was told that such proposals smacked of defeatism.

Hitler responded to such proposals as Hossbach's with towering rage and ordered Gauleiters—chiefs of the Nazi Party in the provinces who were, in effect, governors—to keep the civilian populations in place. With the Gauleiters in charge, the German Army had authority only within six miles of the front lines—barely enough depth to deploy a division—and lost its powers of requisition. Hitler's Gauleiter order severely hindered the army and had terrible consequences for German civilians.

In December, Major General Reinhard Gehlen, the chief of the Foreign Armies East Department of OKH, estimated that the Soviet forces opposite East Prussia and the Vistula totaled 225 rifle divisions and more than 22 tank corps. Guderian calculated that the Soviet superiority in this sector was 11 to 1 in infantry, 7 to 1 in tanks, and 20 to 1 in artillery.[2] The 1st Ukrainian and 1st Belorussian Fronts alone had 163 divisions.[3] Hitler, however, refused to believe it. He scoffed at OKH's figures and called the Russian buildup "the greatest bluff since Genghis Khan."[4] But the real bluffer was Hitler who had repeatedly reduced the size of German divisions to create the illusion that there were more of them. Some of his new Volksgrenadier divisions had only four infantry battalions, as opposed to nine in the 1939-type

Major Friedrich Hossbach (center) in 1934, when he was adjutant to the Fuehrer. Later he became a general of infantry and commander of the 4th Army in East Prussia. *Bundesarchiv Bild 183-1988-0107-503/CC-BY-SA 3.0*

divisions. They often had engineer, signal, and anti-tank *companies*, instead of *battalions*, and had fusilier companies instead of reconnaissance battalions. (Fusilier units generally had bicycles instead of motorized vehicles and were sometimes combined reconnaissance/anti-tank units.) Older infantry divisions were frequently reorganized to include a "mobile battalion"—a combination reconnaissance/anti-tank unit—that incorporated old reconnaissance and anti-tank battalions.

The armored divisions were even more drastically reorganized. The 1945-type panzer division had only one panzer regiment with one panzer battalion (sixty-four tanks) and two panzer grenadier battalions, which meant it had approximately one-fourth the combat value of a 1940-type tank division. Hitler assumed that Stalin was engaging in the same type of self-deception, so he angrily rejected Gehlen's estimations. He refused to take units from Norway, Finland, Courland in the Baltic, or from the West, to reinforce the East; the Russian Front, he told Guderian, would have to take care of itself. According to Soviet figures, the Red Army had 55 armies, 6 tank armies, and 13 air armies: 500 rifle divisions, 94 artillery divisions and 149 independent artillery brigades. Their total strength was 15,000 tanks, 15,000 airplanes, and at least 6,800,000 men. These numbers understate their actual strength: they were so abundantly supplied that they mustered additional artillery divisions, anti-aircraft divisions, a rocket launcher division, and a number of independent artillery brigades. Their rifle divisions were motorized, many of their cavalry units were reequipped with American quarter-ton trucks, and roughly half of all motorized vehicles in the Red Army were of American manufacture.[5] (For years after the war, the word "Studebaker" was synonymous with "truck" in the Soviet Union.) Hitler, however, refused to take such facts seriously. At the same time, the German strength on the Eastern Front on October 1, 1944, stood at 1,790,138 men, including about 150,000 Russian auxiliaries (called Hiwis). Equipment was so short that the army was now beginning to outfit panzer grenadier divisions with bicycles.

"As 1945 began, the menacing shadow of Russian domination lay over Germany like an ugly, poisonous cloud, seeping into our minds and

Two members of the 5th SS Panzer Division "Viking" posed in front of a Marder II Tank Destroyer, 1942. This model was discontinued in 1943 but was still in use at the end of the war. *Bundesarchiv Bild 101III-Moebius-117-27/CC_BY_SA 3.0*

clinging there as stubbornly as a wet fog on a gloomy winter morning," Major Siegfried Knappe recalled.[6] On January 1, 1945, the German Army had five army groups on the Eastern Front (Table 5.1). Of these, however, only Army Groups Center and A were located between the Baltic Sea and the Carpathian Mountains, in the path of Stalin's gigantic build-up. Army Group A had the task of blocking the Soviet drive into Germany proper, while Army Group Center had the mission of defending East Prussia.

With its overwhelming forces, Moscow planned nothing less than to capture Berlin and end the war within forty-five days. Specially, Stavka (the Soviet Supreme Command) planned for the main blow to be delivered by Marshal Ivan Konev's 1st Ukrainian and Marshal Georgy Zhukov's 1st Belorussian Fronts against the 9th Army, 4th Panzer Army, and 17th Army of Army Group A. These two Soviet fronts each had 10 armies, including two tank armies each, and several independent tank and mechanized corps, totaling 6,400 tanks, 4,700 aircraft, 46,000 artillery pieces, and 2,200,000 men. Against this massive force, Colonel General Joseph Harpe's Army Group A could muster only 400,000 men, 4,100 guns, and 1,150 tanks.[7] The defense was further handicapped by the fact that the Soviets already had major bridgeheads across the Vistula at Magnuszew, Pulawy, and Baranov (Baranow). In the Magnuszew bridgehead alone, the 1st Belorussian Front deployed 400,000 troops, 8,700 guns, and 1,700 tanks: more than the total strength of Army Group A. At their points of main attack, the 1st Belorussian and 1st Ukrainian Fronts outnumbered the Germans by an average ratio of 9:1 in men, between 9:1 and 10:1 in artillery, and 10:1 in tanks and assault guns. In addition, the Red Air Force had more than 10,000 airplanes ready for employment between the Baltic and the Carpathians. As of January 2, the Luftwaffe had fewer than 3,800 operational airplanes in its entire arsenal. Of these, 1,875 were on the Eastern Front. Fewer than 300 of these were with Ritter von Greim's 6th Air Fleet, which supported Army Groups Center and A.[8]

Order of Battle of the German Army on the Eastern Front, January 1, 1945

Army Group North: Colonel General Ferdinand Schoerner (1)		
	18th Army: General of Infantry Ehrenfried Boege	
	16th Army: General of Infantry Carl Hilpert	
Army Group Center: Colonel General Georg-Hans Reinhardt (2)		
	3rd Panzer Army: Colonel General Erhard Raus	
	4th Army: General of Infantry Friedrich Hossbach (3)	
	2nd Army: Colonel General Walter Weiss	
Army Group A: Colonel General Joseph Harpe (4)		
	9th Army: General of Panzer Troops Baron Smilo von Luettwltz (5)	
	4th Panzer Army: General of Panzer Troops Fritz-Hubert Graeser	
	17th Army: General of Infantry Friedrich Schulz	
	Armeegruppe Heinrich: Colonel General Gotthard Heinrici (6)	
		1st Panzer Army: Heinrici
		1st Hungarian Army
Army Group South: General Otto Woehler		
	8th Army: General of Mountain Troops Hans Kreysing	
	6th Army: General of Panzer Troops Hermann Balck	
Army Group F: Field Marshal Baron Maximilian von Weichs		
	Army Group E: Colonel General Alexander Loehr	
NOTES:		

(1) Succeeded by Colonel General Dr. Lothar Rendulic on January 16; he was, in turn, replaced by Colonel General Heinrich von Vietinghoff on January 26.
(2) Replaced by Colonel General Dr. Rendulic on January 26.
(3) Replaced by General of Infantry Friedrich Wilhelm Mueller on January 26.
(4) Replaced by Colonel General Schoerner on January 16.
(5) Replaced by General of Infantry Theodore Busse on January 18.

Table 5.1

On January 9, General Guderian made one last attempt to persuade Hitler that the Russians were about to launch a major offensive. Before he went to see the Fuehrer, he said to his chief of Foreign Armies East: "Gehlen, today is our last chance. If the panzer divisions from the west are sent on their way to the east not later than tonight they may still get there in time. . . ."[9]

The meeting was held in Colonel General Alfred Jodl's spacious study at the Fuehrer Headquarters of Alderhorst. Present were Jodl; Keitel; Goering; Major General Eckhard Christian, the chief of operations of the Luftwaffe and air force liaison officer to OKW; Rear Admiral Karl-Jesko von Puttkamer, the Fuehrer's naval adjutant; Lieutenant General August Winter, the chief of staff of OB Southeast; Himmler; and General of Infantry Wilhelm Burgdorf, the chief of the Army Personnel Office who was already being called the "gravedigger of the German Officer Corps."

Hitler entered and shook hands with every man in the room. He looked old; his left leg dragged, as if partly crippled; his left hand trembled; his shoulders were stooped; his face was pale. He slumped into his chair like a man who had little control over his body. As Guderian spoke, he turned his left ear toward him, as had been his custom since his right eardrum was punctured during the Stauffenberg assassination attempt of July 20, 1944.

Guderian spoke frankly and cut to the heart of the matter. He stated categorically that the Soviets were going to launch a major offensive on

January 12. To meet this threat to the Fatherland, he proposed that the armies in Courland be withdrawn immediately. (The 16th and 18th Armies had been isolated there, in eastern Latvia, for five months and were accessible only by sea.) He asked that the panzer forces be transferred from the West to the East, beginning that night. He asked that Hossbach's 4th Army be allowed to pull back from its exposed position in East Prussia. Finally, at the very least, he strongly recommended that Army Group A be allowed to withdraw from in front of the Baranov and Pulawy bridgeheads so it would not have to take the full weight of the Soviet blow.

He might as well have been talking to a fence post. Hitler still refused to believe that the Russians were going to launch any kind of attack at all.

/ / /

For the invasion of Germany, the Red High Command recast its entire propaganda and troop indoctrination program. During the first part of the war, the theme had been the defense of Mother Russia; then it had been the liberation of Russian territory; now, the key word was "Revenge!" Major Soviet literary figures, political officers, radio broadcasters, and visiting speakers pounded this theme into the heads of every Russian soldier. The crimes the Germans had committed against Soviet women and children were retold countless times, along with tales of burned villages, slaughtered livestock, ruined cities, and German looting and exploitation. The individual Soviet soldier's hatred for Germans was fanned into a white heat; most Soviet soldiers were poorly educated, illiterate, and highly susceptible to propaganda. "Kill, kill!" was the slogan of Ilya Ehrenburg, the top Soviet propagandist, whose words were disseminated to every Red Army unit, both by broadcast and in leaflet form. "In the German race there is nothing but evil! . . . Stamp out the fascist beast once and for all in its lair! Use force and break the racial pride of these Germanic women. Take them as your lawful booty. Kill! As you storm onward, kill! You gallant soldiers of the Red Army."[10]

"Two eyes for an eye!" and "A pool of blood for a drop of blood!" were favorite Ehrenburg slogans which were constantly drummed into the heads of the unsophisticated Soviet soldiers.[11]

By their behavior in Russia, the Germans had sown the wind. Now they were about to reap the whirlwind.

On cold, snowy January 12, 1945, the western face of the Baranov (Baranow) bridgehead (on the west side of the Vistula, southeast of Warsaw) was defended by General of Panzer Troops Baron Maximilian von Edelsheim's XXXXVIII Panzer Corps, which controlled three infantry divisions. General of Infantry Hermann Recknagel's XXXXII Corps, which had four infantry divisions, held the northern face.[12] All seven were veteran divisions, which meant that they were also severely depleted. The three divisions of the XXXXVIII Panzer, for example, had no tanks, only about twelve assault guns each, and only enough infantry to post one man for every fifteen yards of front. In most places along their thirty miles of front they could not form a continuous line; instead, they formed strongpoints and outposts and covered the intervening terrain with patrols. Opposite them, the 1st Ukrainian Front had five armies, two tank armies, and more than 1,000 tanks. Before dawn, the Russians launched a massive artillery bombardment—an incredible concentration estimated at 420 guns per mile of front. The barrage lasted for three hours before the Russian infantry advanced. The Germans were surprised: they had assumed the Soviet offensive would be delayed for better weather so the Reds could take advantage of their overwhelming air power. By noon, the gaps in the German line were wide enough for the Russians to commit their armor, which advanced rapidly.

About ten miles to the west of the front lay two panzer divisions of Walter Nehring's XXIV Panzer Corps.[13] They were ordered to counterattack, but even before they left their assembly areas, they were under attack themselves. The 17th Panzer Division was slaughtered, as was the elite 424th Heavy Panzer Battalion. Only the legendary Lieutenant Friedrich-Karl Oberbracht really stood tall during the battle. Oberbracht was a veteran panzer officer and a master of his profession despite his

Walter Nehring (far right) in Libya, 1942, when he commanded the Afrika Korps. Left to right are Fritz Bayerlein, who commanded the LIII Corps in the Ruhr Pocket, F. W. von Mellenthin, chief of staff of Army Group G (1944) and later chief of staff of 5th Panzer Army in the Ruhr Pocket; and Erwin Rommel, the "Desert Fox," who was forced to commit suicide on October 14, 1944, for his part in the plot to overthrow Hitler. *Bundesarchiv Bild 101I-784-0203-14A/Moosmueller/CC-BY-SA 3.0*

youth. After his battalion commander was killed in an ambush, Oberbracht led his panzer against the Soviets and personally destroyed eleven of their best Stalin tanks before the tracks of his own vehicle were blown off. Immobilized, he kept fighting and destroyed at least seven more Stalin tanks before he was killed. The rest of the battalion was then overrun and annihilated. The elite 424th Heavy Panzer lost sixty-seven of its seventy modern Tigers and ceased to exist. It was arguably the worst disaster to overtake a Tiger unit during the entire war.

By nightfall, the Russians had reached the Nida River and were a dozen miles into the rear of Fritz-Hubert Graeser's 4th Panzer Army.[14] The XXXXVIII Panzer and XXXXII Corps had been smashed, and Nehring had lost half his tanks.

On January 13, General Nehring, conducting his usual skillful defense, slowed the pace of the Soviet advance. The next day, however, Konev committed his reserves and attacked Nehring with three armies. Under attack by the 4th Tank and 6th Guards Tank Armies, the defense of the XXIV Panzer Corps finally broke on January 15, and Nehring fell back to the west. By now the weather had cleared, and the Red Air Force pelted the Germans with hundreds of fighter-bomber and bomber sorties; the Luftwaffe could mount virtually none. To the north, General Recknagel rallied part of the XXXXII Corps but was soon nearly surrounded. Recknagel was killed by a Soviet tank shell on January 15, and the survivors of his corps fell back in disorder. Everywhere German communications broke down. In four days, the Russians gained sixty miles. By January 17, Konev's spearheads had crossed the Warthe. Six days after the offensive began, he had penetrated 100 miles along a 160-mile front.

Meanwhile, Zhukov's 1st Belorussian Front began its offensive on January 14. General of Panzer Troops Baron Smilo von Luettwitz, the commander of the 9th Army, expected the attack but had little with which to meet it.[15] By January 16, the Soviets had smashed his seven understrength divisions, the city of Radom had fallen, and Warsaw faced a double envelopment. On January 15 alone, the Soviet 16th Air Army flew 3,400 sorties in support of Zhukov's armies against 42 for the Luftwaffe. South of Warsaw, Walter Fries's XXXXVI Panzer Corps, guarding the route to Posen, tried to avoid encirclement, was attacked by the 2nd Guards Tank Army, and pushed north of the Vistula. Recognizing the unfolding disaster on January 16, OKW gave General von Luettwitz freedom to conduct his own battle, including the authority to order the evacuation of Warsaw. Luettwitz issued the order immediately.

Baron Smilo von Luettwitz, circa 1960, in the uniform of a West German lieutenant general (a three-star general in the post-war rank structure). *U.S. Army Military History Institute, S. L. A. Marshall Collection, Document I.D.: 44426*

Hitler returned to Berlin later that day and promptly countermanded Luettwitz's order to abandon the Polish capital. By the time Lieutenant General Friedrich Weber, the commander of Division Warsaw and commandant of the city, received Hitler's order, the evacuation was already well underway. The general, who had commanded the 334th Infantry Division in Tunisia in 1934, let the evacuation proceed. Warsaw was occupied by the 1st Polish Army on January 17.

Hitler was furious over the loss of Warsaw and his (correct) suspicion that his orders were being circumvented. The first scapegoat was Colonel General Joseph Harpe, the commander-in-chief of Army Group A, who was relieved of his command on January 16. Though he was an officer who still believed in the Fuehrer and his destiny, he was sacked because he had failed to stop an offensive that Hitler had denied would ever take place. Harpe was replaced by the brutal Colonel General Ferdinand Schoerner, who was succeeded as commander-in-chief of Army Group North by Colonel General Dr. Lothar Rendulic, a long-time Austrian Nazi. Naturally Baron Smilo von Luettwitz was also sacked.[16] His replacement was General of Infantry Theodor Busse, Manstein's former chief of staff, who had most recently commanded the I Corps on the Eastern Front.[17] (Busse owed his appointment to his connections at Fuehrer Headquarters. He and General of Infantry Wilhelm Burgdorf had married sisters, and Busse spoke to his brother-in-law on the telephone almost every night.) Lieutenant General Friedrich Weber's explanation that he had already destroyed his supplies and was in the process of pulling out of Warsaw when the Fuehrer's last order arrived at least kept him out of prison—which is more than three of Guderian's staff officers could say. On Hitler's orders, Colonel Bogislaw von Bonin and Lieutenant Colonels Klaus von dem Knesebeck and Hans-Hennig von Christen were arrested at gunpoint by Major General Ernst Maisel, the deputy chief of the Army Personnel Office. Guderian tried to intercede on their behalf, pointing out that, as chief of the General Staff, he alone was responsible for the actions of his subordinates and that, if anyone should be arrested, it should be he. "No," said the Fuehrer. "It's not you

I'm after, but the General Staff. It is intolerable to me that a group of intellectuals should presume to press their views on their superiors. But such is the General Staff system, and that system I intend to smash."[18] Hitler ordered that the Warsaw affair be thoroughly investigated, and Guderian himself was subjected to lengthy interrogations by Heinrich Mueller, the chief of the Gestapo, and his boss, Ernst Kaltenbrunner, the chief of the Reich Main Security Office (RSHA). Walter Fries, the one-armed, one-legged commander of the XXXXVI Panzer Corps—who had given Patton so much trouble in northern Sicily a year and a half before—was relieved of his command on January 20 and court-martialled. He was found not guilty but was nevertheless sent into professional exile and was never reemployed. He had been promoted to general of panzer troops less than two months before.[19]

On January 19, while the Soviets advanced into Silesia, Hitler issued a directive that stripped away the last vestiges of his field generals' tactical authority. Henceforth, no commander from division upwards could attack, counterattack, or retreat without the Fuehrer's personal approval.

Of Army Group A's armies, only the 17th Army had managed to retreat in any order, because it was the only one the Soviets had not managed to attack with overwhelming forces. In a single week, the Soviets had smashed the entire 9th Army, and the 4th Panzer Army controlled only VIII Corps (which consisted of the remnants of the 168th Infantry Division and the 408th Replacement Division) and a few odds and ends. The bulk of the army, under General Nehring, was trapped in a pocket, encircled by a dozen Soviet armies, miles to the east.

General Nehring faced a desperate situation, but no field commander had more experience with panzer operations than he did. Nehring formed a "floating pocket" and drove northwest, toward the remnants of the 4th Panzer Army. On January 22, on the Warthe River near Sieradz, he linked up with General of Panzer Troops Dietrich von Saucken's Grossdeutschland Panzer Corps. Saucken was a cavalryman who habitually wore a sword and a monocle. He was openly contemptuous of Hitler's "braune Bande" (brown mob). He was also a superb panzer commander. Saucken promptly put himself under Nehring's command. The veteran panzer leader now controlled the Grossdeutschland Corps, as well as the remnants of his own XXIV Panzer, the LVI Panzer, and the XXXXII Corps: eight infantry and Volksgrenadier divisions, two panzer and two panzer-grenadier divisions. His success in holding his perimeter and cutting a swathe west was an incredible feat of tactical genius. "Generals Nehring and von Saucken performed feats of military virtuosity during these days that only the pen of a new Xenophon could adequately describe," Guderian wrote later.[20]

Nehring and von Saucken finally fought their way through to the Oder and linked up with Army Group A at the end of January. By the time they arrived, they had more refugees than soldiers under their command.

But Nehring's and von Saucken's successes were the exceptions—every other German corps and division was routed.

On January 22, the leading elements of the 1st Ukrainian Front reached the Oder. During the next three days, Konev's forces covered 140 miles to join them. Graeser's 4th Panzer Army held Breslau but lacked sufficient forces to block or counterattack the Reds as they crossed the river unopposed north and south of the city.

Also on January 22, Zhukov reached Posen (Poznan), the capital of the German administrative province of Warthegau, Poland, and head-quarters of Wehrkreis (German military district) XXI. The area's fortress commandant was Major General Ernst Gonell, who had eleven replace-ment-training battalions (mostly made up of raw recruits), seventeen battalions of Volkssturm, and ad hoc units from sundry sources.[21] In all, he had a garrison of 10,000 men, including Luftwaffe ground crewmen, stragglers whose units had been dispersed or overrun, and local police and security personnel. Most of them were of little military value. The muscle of Posen's defense lay in its Officer Training School, where about 2,000 highly motivated *Fahnenjunkern* and well-trained veteran second lieutenants fought fiercely, street by street, delaying the Russian advance by a month. By February 22, however, the garrison's survivors were isolated in the Citadel (Fort Winiary). That night, General Gonell went to his quarters, spread a German battle flag on the floor, stretched out on it, and shot himself in the head. Every German officer who tried to escape was caught by the Soviets and shot.

On February 23, Major General Ernst Mattern, the city commandant, surrendered the remainder of the garrison, including about 2,000 wounded. Those who could walk were relieved of their watches, boots, and, in some cases, even their trousers. The Russians marched them through the city for several days, while Poles pelted them with rocks. Prisoners who could not walk the Soviets incinerated with flamethrowers.[22]

THE ISOLATION OF EAST PRUSSIA

At the beginning of December 1944, Reinhardt's Army Group Center defended East Prussia, holding a 360-mile front, with thirty-three infantry and twelve panzer or panzer grenadier divisions. With a reserve of nine mobile divisions, the average forward division had to hold ten miles of front. From this position of relative strength, Reinhardt was confident he could hold East Prussia. By the beginning of 1945, however, he had fallen victim to Hitler's policy of robbing one front to reinforce another and had lost five panzer divisions and two cavalry brigades to other army groups. OKH ordered him to give up another panzer division, but he balked, and when the Soviet offensive struck Army Group Center he still had it. Map 5.1 shows East Prussia on the eve of its annihilation.

The Battle for East Prussia began on January 13, when four armies and two tank corps from General Ivan Chernyakhovsky's 3rd Belorussian Front attacked the 3rd Panzer Army at Stallupoenen and Pil'kallen in the northern sector of Army Group Center. To the south, General Konstantin Rokossovsky's 2nd Belorussian Front launched the main offensive due north from the Narew bridgehead the next day and struck Colonel General Walter Weiss's 2nd Army with five armies, including a tank army. The Soviets had begun a great pincer movement north and south of the Masurian Lakes (Map 5.2), aimed at enveloping Army Group Center, bypassing at first Hossbach's 4th Army, which was defending the lake district.

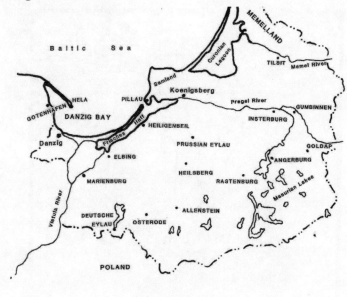

Map 5.1

On January 15, Reinhardt committed the 7th Panzer and Grossdeutschland Panzer Grenadier Divisions (his army group reserves) to the battle. Later that day, however, Hitler transferred Saucken's Grossdeutschland Panzer Corps to Army Group A, significantly weakening the defense. When the weather cleared (allowing the Soviet 4th Air Army to fly 2,500 sorties a day against German positions) and Rokossovsky committed two more tank corps to the battle, the Red Army advanced. By January 19, Rokossovsky had broken through along a seventy-mile front to a depth of up to forty miles and captured the Polish cities of Mlawa and Modlin. He crossed the old Prussian-Polish frontier on January 20. That morning, the wife of the chief of the General Staff of the Army left Deipenhof, her family's estate in the Warthegau, just half an hour before Russian artillery shelled the place. The Guderians lost their remaining possessions (most of which had already been destroyed when Allied bombs struck their Berlin home in September 1943). A homeless refugee, she joined her husband in Zossen and remained with him for the rest of the war.

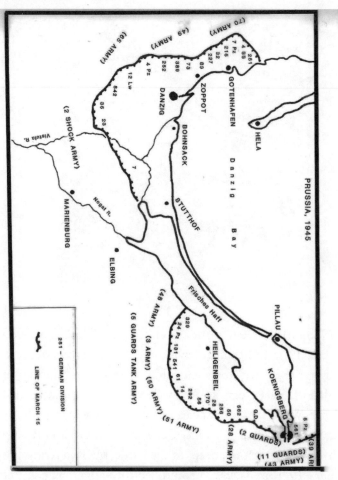

Map 5.2

The German 2nd Army, which lacked the mobility of the Soviets, retreated as rapidly as it could, and there were signs of disorder bordering on disintegration. The roads were clogged with refugees and fleeing soldiers. The XXXXVI Panzer Corps (now under Lieutenant General

Martin Garies) theoretically had four divisions, but all were in remnants, and none amounted to more than a regiment. Lieutenant General Walter Melzer's XXIII Corps consisted of only the 152nd Replacement Division, the understrength 5th Jaeger Division, and the 7th Infantry Division, which was a *kampfgruppe* (a division so reduced by casualties that it had the combat value of a regiment).[23] Supply and fuel depots and other facilities were abandoned without being blown up. On January 21, the Reds reached Tannenberg (now Stebark, Poland), where the Germans had defeated the Czar's forces in 1914. They found that the German engineers had already destroyed the landmark memorial to the great battle and removed the remains of *Generalfeldmarschall* (and former German Chancellor) Paul von Hindenburg and his wife.[24]

By January 22, the 2nd Army was routed. On the evening of January 23, the spearhead of the 5th Guards Tank Army rolled into the town of Elbing (now Elblog, Poland), near the Baltic Sea, and cut the last land route from East Prussia to the rest of the Reich. They found the shops still open and the factory workers still at work. They had advanced 125 miles in 12 days and had trapped the German 3rd Panzer and 4th Armies, as well as part of the 2nd, in East Prussia—along with hundreds of thousands of German civilians.

Meanwhile, the northern Soviet pincer hit Colonel General Erhard Raus's 3rd Panzer Army. When the offensive began, the 3rd Panzer had been reduced to mainly Volksgrenadier divisions and had only two mobile units: the outstanding 5th Panzer Division and the mediocre 10th Bicycle Jaeger Brigade. It also had the excellent East Prussian 1st Infantry Division, which was defending its own soil. Raus's men put up a heroic defense, and the Soviets did not capture Tilsit (now Sovetsk, Russia) until January 18. It would be almost three months before the Red Army was able to enter Koenigsberg, the ancient capital of East Prussia. The Soviet offensive had succeeded in isolating Army Group Center with twenty-seven of its divisions, but not in enveloping and destroying it.

Raus retreated only very slowly, but he was forced to retreat. This endangered the rear of Hossbach's 4th Army, which was still holding the

Masurian Lakes district, but Hitler demanded that the Loetzen line in the Masurian Lakes be held at all costs. Guderian also signaled Reinhardt that there would be no more retreats. Since the Loetzen line was already outflanked, Hossbach ignored the orders of both Hitler and Guderian and continued his evacuation. With the approval of General Reinhardt, he was preparing to launch a breakout attack to the west (into the rear of 2nd Belorussian Front), with the intention of linking up with Weiss's 2nd Army in West Prussia. On January 26, however, Hitler learned what was happening. He flew into a rage and sacked both Reinhardt and Hossbach and their chiefs of staff. (Reinhardt had to be replaced in any case; he had incurred a serious head wound during a Soviet air attack the day before.) Colonel General Rendulic was named commander-in-chief of Army Group North (formerly Center), and Hossbach was replaced as commander of 4th Army by General of Infantry Friedrich-Wilhelm Mueller, a strong Nazi whose great courage far exceeded his intelligence. He had earned a reputation for brutality in the Balkans and would meet his death in 1947 at the hands of a Greek firing squad. Heinrich von Vietinghoff, the acting commander-in-chief of OB Southwest in Italy replaced Rendulic in the Courland Pocket.

These were not the only changes Hitler made on January 26. In a move designed to confuse readers and historians alike, he changed the names of several of his army groups. Army Group North became Army Group Courland; Army Group Center became Army Group North; Army Group A became Army Group Center. Army Groups South and F did not change their names, but a new army group—Vistula—was created from the staff of OB Upper Rhine, at the suggestion of General Guderian. Its missions were to plug the gap between Army Groups North and Center, defend Pomerania and Danzig, and block the Soviets' path to Berlin. For the post of commander-in-chief of Army Group Vistula, Guderian nominated—and thought he had General Jodl's support, as OKW chief of operations—Field Marshal Maximilian von Weichs, the commander-in-chief of Army Group F. Jodl, however, reneged on their agreement and made a sneering remark about Baron von Weichs's deep religious convictions, effectively killing his nomination. Hitler's choice for the post fell to none other than Heinrich Himmler, the Reichsfuehrer-SS, who had done such a poor job on the southern sector of the Western Front. His chief of staff was SS Lieutenant General Heinz Lammerding, a veteran combat officer, but one without General Staff training. Moreover, Lammerding, like many Waffen-SS officers, was contemptuous of Himmler. When Guderian first visited the headquarters of Army Group Vistula, Lammerding greeted him with the words: "Can't you rid us of our commander?"[25] The chief of the General Staff responded evasively, even though behind the scences he was trying to rid the new army group of both Himmler *and* Lammerding.

Himmler's new command consisted of what was left of Busse's 9th Army, the remnant of Weiss's 2nd Army that had not been cut off in East Prussia, and General of Waffen-SS Felix Steiner's 11th SS Army, which was activated on January 26 and did not yet have a single division. (It was formed from part of the Staff, OB Upper Rhine, and was sometimes referred to as the 11th SS Panzer Army.) Table 5.2 shows the Order of Battle of Himmler's Army Group Vistula.

Order of Battle, Army Group Vistula February 1, 1945

9th Army: General of Infantry Theodor Busse		
	XXXX Panzer Corps	
		25th Panzer Division (in Remnants)
	V SS Mountain Corps	
		463rd Replacement Division (1) Panzer Grenadier Division "Kurmark" (1) Division Raegener (formerly 433rd Infantry Division) (1)
	Wehrkreis II	

		Miscellaneous formations (replacement and training battalions, Alarm units, etc.)
	X SS Corps (1)	
		402nd Replacement Division
	9th Army Reserve:	
		608th Special Purposes Division 25th Panzer Grenadier Division (2) Fortress Posen (3) Fortress Schneidemuehl (3)
2nd Army: Colonel General Walter Weiss (4)		
	XVI SS Corps (1)	
		15th SS Grenadier Division (lett. Nr. 1) 32nd Infantry Division 4th Panzer Division
	XXXXIV Panzer Corps	
		1st Sperr Brigade 337th Volksgrenadier Division (in Remnants) 251st Infantry Division (in Remnants)
	XXVII Corps	
		542nd Volksgrenadier Division 252nd Infantry Division (5) 35th Infantry Division 83rd Infantry Division
	XXIII Corps	
		5th Jaeger Division Group Schirmer (Staff, 23rd Infantry Division) 227th Infantry Division

	Wehrkreis XX	
		7th Infantry Division
		7th Panzer Division
	Group Thorn	
		31st Infantry Division
		73rd Infantry Division (in Remnants)
	Fortress Graudenz (3)	
	Fortress Danzig	
11th SS Army (6): General of Waffen-SS Felix Steiner		
	No troop units assigned	
Army Group Reserves:		
	4th SS Panzer Grenadier Division Police" (2)	
	Penal Brigade Dirlewanger (2)	
	604th Special Purposes Division (2)	
	606th Special Purposes Division (2)	
	SS Kampfgruppe "Schill" (2)	
NOTES:		
(1) A newly formed unit		
(2) In transit		
(3) Surrounded by Soviets		
(4) Replaced by General of Panzer Troops Dietrich von Saucken on March 10.		
(5) With the Hermann Goering Parachute Panzer Replacement Training Brigade attached		
(6) Not yet fully operational		

Table 5.2

Himmler came east in his very long and luxuriously outfitted private train, the *Steiermark*, which he parked at the station at Deutsch-Krone. It was totally divorced from the miserable columns of refugees who trekked by the train, heading west. Himmler's only knowledge of the military situation came from occasional outdated situation reports. His

Refugees fleeing East Prussia. *Bundesarchiv, B 285 Bild-S00-00326 / Unknown / CC-BY-SA 3.0*

command was as motley a collection of units as one could imagine, and had they faced an immediate, major Soviet offensive, they would likely have collapsed. But Hitler reinforced Himmler's Army Group Vistula with a panzer division and four infantry divisions, drawn from Army Group Courland. On January 22, Hitler ordered OB West to transfer Headquarters, 6th Panzer Army (soon be to redesignated 6th SS Panzer Army), and the headquarters of the I SS and II SS Panzer Corps, as well as six panzer divisions, a Volksgrenadier division, and several Volks artillery corps, to the Eastern Front. Despite Guderian's heated objections, Hitler sent the bulk of these units to Hungary, where he was planning another offensive.

The Russians, meanwhile, overran East Prussia, subjecting it to unspeakable atrocities. In some districts, every female between the ages of twelve and seventy was raped, some of them by as many as twenty men. Their husbands and parents were often forced to watch; many girls were murdered, followed by the parents. The victims were often tortured to death. Some were even crucified. Other Germans were arrested and shipped off to Siberian slave labor camps, where they would likely die. In the Soviet occupied districts of eastern Germany, 1,300,000 people disappeared.

A refugee "trek," East Prussia, 1945. *Bundesarchiv Bild 146-1976-072-09/CC-BY-SA 3.0*

Word of Soviet behavior spread like wildfire. Many of the citizens of the Eastern districts either fled to the West (toward Germany proper) or to the Reich's northern ports. More by accident than design, they formed huge columns on the roads. Some traveled by cart, some by wagon, and others simply walked. There was very little conversation in these refugee treks; even the children were too tired and hungry to cry or whine. The people trudged along without food, water, or rest, and children and babies died by the score in the bitter East European winter.

The Germans resorted to unusual methods to save their children, many of whom were without shoes. (Adults could wear mended shoes, but children outgrew their shoes; even if a family had enough money and coupons to buy them, the stores rarely had any.) One lady I knew told me that she fled East Prussia in 1945 in shoes her mother had fashioned out of cow manure.

The refugee columns (called "treks") were often strafed by Soviet fighter-bombers, shelled by Russian artillery, or machine-gunned by the Red Army. At least two treks were ground to bits under the treads of Soviet tanks. Still they pushed north, toward the ports. Behind them, the

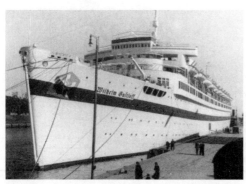

The *Wilhelm Gustloff* in Danzig harbor on September 23, 1939, when it was a hospital ship. Prior to that it had been a "Strength Through Joy" vacation liner. She was a floating barracks for the navy at Gotenhafen (now Gdynia, Poland) from 1940 to January 1945, when she was used to transport refugees. *Bundesarchiv, Bild 183-H27992 / Sönnke, Hans / CC-BY-SA 3.0*

remnants of the German Wehrmacht in East Prussia tried to shield them, while the German navy evacuated them to the West.

Under the overall command of Grand Admiral Karl Doenitz, the task of organizing the evacuation of the refugees fell to *Generaladmiral* Otto Kummetz, the leader of Naval Command East, and his men.[26] Kummetz sent in everything that would float, including more than a dozen liners of 10,000 tons or more. Rear Admiral Bernhard Rogge, the commander of fleet training formations and the former commander of the commerce raider *Atlantis*, particularly distinguished himself during the evacuation.[27]

An estimated 60,000 people were waiting on the docks by late January 1945. Coming to their rescue was the *Wilhelm Gustloff*. In normal times, she was a cruise ship with a crew of 400 and room for 1,465 passengers. During the war, she was converted into a hospital ship and a floating barracks. Now, with a crew of 173, she served as a transport ship, taking aboard 918 sailors from the navy's 2nd U-Boat Training Division, 373 female naval auxiliaries, 162 wounded soldiers, and more than 6,500 refugees. One source puts this total at 8,956 refugees, bringing the total number of passengers to 10,582.

On the night of January 30, 1945, the *Wilhelm Gustloff* heaved into the Baltic Sea, which was crusted with ice flows and peppered by snow flurries. If worse came to worst, there was room for 5,600 people in the lifeboats and rafts.

The senior military commander on the *Wilhelm Gustloff* was a man who had already missed his place in history. On October 30, 1939, just west of the Orkney Islands, Lieutenant Wilhelm Zahn, the commander of *U-56*, had boldly and skillfully evaded a dozen British escort vessels and fired three torpedoes into H.M.S. *Nelson*, the flagship of the British Home Fleet. Two of the torpedoes hit the *Nelson* but did not explode. (Defective torpedoes were a common problem for the German Navy in 1939–40.) The guests on board the *Nelson* that day included Lord of the Admiralty Sir Winston Churchill, Admiral of the Fleet and First Sea Lord Sir Dudley Pound, and Admiral Sir Charles Forbes, the commander-in-chief of the Home Fleet, as well as a dozen other Royal Navy luminaries. The *Nelson* sailed on, and Zahn became known throughout the U-Boat force as "the man who almost killed Churchill." Zahn's failure to achieve this feat sent him into a severe depression, and Admiral Karl Doenitz, the commander-in-chief of the German submarine branch, relieved him of his command.

Zahn was transferred to the training command as an instructor. It took him more than a year to shake his depression, but he did, and Doenitz gave him a new command, *U-69*, in the fall of 1941. Zahn led it on one failed patrol, during which he exhibited a lack of aggression and skill, firing four torpedoes and missing four times. Doenitz relieved him again. He was transferred to the Baltic, then considered a backwater training area, where he languished until 1945. He was nevertheless promoted to lieutenant commander (*Korvttenkapitaen*) in 1943.

Though he was the senior military commander aboard the *Wilhelm Gustloff*, the ship was under the command of a merchant marine captain, Friedrich Petersen. The ship had only one escort vessel, and against Zahn's advice, Petersen decided to put into deep water rather than hug the coast, use his navigation lights rather than run in darkness, and travel at twelve knots rather than push the vessel to its maximum speed of sixteen.[28] The only argument Zahn won was in persuading Petersen to sail in a zigzag rather than linear path.

The outside temperature was negative ten degrees Fahrenheit, with rough seas and high winds. Twenty-five miles offshore, the *Gustloff* was spotted by *S-13*, a Stalinets class submarine, commanded by Captain Third Class Alexander Marinesko.[29]

At 9:08 p.m. on January 30, *S-13* fired four torpedoes at the liner. One hung in the tube. The other three struck the port side of the *Wilhelm Gustloff*. About 300 people were killed in the initial explosion. Water rushed into the engine rooms, and the engines immediately stopped. The internal telephones and public address system also went dead. Officers on the bridge could hear noises below and knew that some of the bulkheads had already collapsed. The ship tried to send an SOS, but the main radio had been knocked out and the emergency sets were not functioning properly. The radio operator grabbed an army transmitter and began sending out SOS signals. Unfortunately, this transmitter only had a range of 2,000 meters—far too short to reach naval headquarters. The signal reached the *Gustloff*'s escort vessel, the *Loewe*, which immediately retransmitted it over its more powerful radio—unfortunately, over the frequency reserved for the U-boat division, not the 9th Escort Division, which was headquartered at Swinemuende and had vessels in the area, within easy sailing distance of the *Gustloff*. The 9th Escort did eventually receive the message and immediately headed for the scene, but it arrived too late to save many from the liner.

The first torpedo had struck the crew's quarters, killing most of the off-duty crew or trapping them behind the bulkheads, which were sealed off to prevent the ship from sinking immediately. There they drowned— and unlike them, the U-boat sailors were not trained in helping passengers board lifeboats.

The second torpedo struck just below the former swimming pool, where the naval auxiliary girls were billeted.

The third torpedo hit amidships, in the forward area of the engine room, ripping open the hull, destroying the engines, and sending the ship sinking.

Gertrude Agnesons, a seventeen-year-old auxiliary, shared a cabin with five other girls. She was in bed when the submarine attacked. Jumping from her bed, she stepped into ankle-deep water. By the time she had grabbed a flashlight, the water was up to her thighs. She vaguely remembered seeing an emergency exit sign and rushed in that direction. Nobody followed her—the surviving girls (most of the auxiliaries were killed in the torpedo blast) ran for the main staircase. She emerged on a deck where thousands of panic-stricken passengers were trying to ascend stairs because the ship was sinking. Small children and anyone who fell were trampled by the mob. Gertrude was very lucky. She had a life jacket on and was one of the 252 survivors the *Loewe* plucked from the freezing Baltic.

By now, the crew had repaired the intercom and the bridge was calling for calm, but it was too late to stem the panic. One officer announced there were enough lifeboats for everybody. There might have been, too, had everyone kept their heads, but even many of the crew did not. A dozen crewmen took a lifeboat for themselves, even though the boat had room for fifty people. A lieutenant opened fire on it. This did no good, since it was already at sea, and his bullets missed the mark, but it probably made him feel better.

Several lifeboats were badly launched and capsized, throwing their passengers into the sea. Courageous orderlies tried to help the badly wounded soldiers and pregnant women in the emergency hospital just forward of the bridge and managed to save a few.

Among those who escaped in a lifeboat was Captain Petersen, who had a well-placed VIP lifeboat available for just such an emergency. Veteran U-boat Commander Zahn then took charge of the ship, sealing the bulkheads, checking the pumps, and trying to buy time. When the ship's list reached 25 degrees and the waves were hitting the windows of the bridge, he ordered that the ship's codes and papers be destroyed.

At that moment, a steward appeared, still wearing his white jacket. "A final cognac, gentlemen!" he exclaimed. The officers and men drank together and then threw their glasses.

Forty-five minutes after the torpedoes hit, Zahn heard the last bulkheads and waterproof doors give way under the pressure of thousands of tons of water. The *Gustloff* shuddered and fell over on her port side, trapping the pumping crews. Only two managed to escape through an air vent. Meanwhile, passengers slid down the enclosed decks, through the glass windows, and into the sea.

The ship's funnels were now parallel to the water and at least 2,000 people were trapped on the lower promenade deck.

For a moment, the window of the bridge cleared, and Zahn saw a mother tossing her baby to two men in a raft. The child fell into the water, and she jumped into the freezing sea. Both disappeared forever.

As the boat went down, shots rang out behind the watertight doors. Men preferred shooting themselves (and in some cases their families) to a more horrifying death by drowning.

Commander Zahn spotted two sailors trying to untie a raft. Holding on to the railing, he moved toward them, but a large wave hit and threw them all into the sea. Zahn went under but was pulled to the surface by his life jacket. He saw hundreds of heads bobbing in the water and between twenty and thirty empty rafts nearby and close together. He boarded one and then hopped to another, trying to get as far away from the *Wilhelm Gustloff* as possible. He finally fell exhausted on the fifth or sixth raft.

Behind him, the *Wilhelm Gustloff* sank. As it went under, the boiler room exploded and the sirens, generators, and lighting system were jolted to life. "Suddenly it seemed that every light in the ship had come on," one survivor recalled. The ship plunged to the depths, its sirens howling.

Men in the lifeboats didn't want them swamped, and clubbed or shot would-be boarders. Even those on the rafts and in the lifeboats were unlikely to survive. Many were up to their knees in freezing water and melted snow; most died of exposure.

Zahn and dozens of others were saved by *T-36*, a torpedo boat commanded by Lieutenant Commander Robert Hering.[30] Though Soviet submarines were in the area, he persisted in his rescue operations. Three pregnant women he rescued gave birth that night. In all, of the 1,239 people rescued from the *Wilhelm Gustloff*, *T-36* rescued 564 of them (and Hering's torpedo boat was already carrying 250 refugees before the liner was hit).[31]

The loss of life from the *Wilhelm Gustloff* disaster was more than that of the sinkings of the *Titanic, Lusitania, Athenia, Andrea Doria,* and *Empress of Ireland* combined. Five times as many people died in the sinking of the *Wilhelm Gustloff* as died in the *Titanic* disaster.

On January 31, after every other German boat had abandoned the search for survivors, *VP-1703,* a worn-out dispatch boat, moved cautiously through the ice flows, and discovered a lifeboat with several people huddled together. They had frozen to death. But hidden beneath the frozen corpses, Petty Officer Werner Fisch found a baby boy, blue with cold but still alive. The petty officer took him to the warm cabin of *VP-1703,* where he slowly revived. Werner Fisch adopted the child and raised him as his own son.

For the next four months, the German navy evacuated refugees despite the constant danger of Soviet submarine or air attack. The news of the *Wilhelm Gustloff* affected the refugees not at all. They still lined up at the docks, preferring to take their chances at sea to falling into the hands of the Red Army. Even when Soviet fighter-bombers attacked the

The *Goya* in Aker Shipyard, Oslo, shortly after it was launched in 1940. It went down in 1945 with almost the entire elite 35th Panzer Regiment aboard. *Wikimedia Commons*

Evacuation boats in the Baltic Sea, 1945. *Bundesarchiv Bild 146-1972-092-05/ CC-BY-SA 3.0*

harbors, they did not move or run for cover because it might cost them their place in line.

Another disaster occurred shortly after midnight on February 10, 1945. The *General Steuben*, a 14,600-ton luxury liner built in 1922, was hit by two Soviet torpedoes. It sank in seven minutes. Aboard were 100 crewmen, 1,000 evacuated wounded, 30 doctors, 320 nurses, and at least 2,000 refugees. Only 300 of them survived.

On April 16, 1945, Germany suffered yet another naval disaster when a Red navy submarine sank the freighter-turned-troop-transport ship, the *Goya*, killing an estimated 7,000, with only 183 survivors. Aboard was the elite 35th Panzer Regiment, perhaps the most heavily decorated tank regiment in the Wehrmacht. It was almost totally wiped out.

The evacuation of East Prussian refugees and military units continued until the second week in May 1945. According to Grand Admiral Doenitz, 2,022,602 refugees were successfully evacuated. This was more than two-thirds of the 1939 population of the province and one of the largest evacuations in human history. More than 98 percent of those picked up by the German navy were successfully transported to northern Germany or Denmark and were behind the Anglo-American Allied lines when the war ended. They were homeless and had lost virtually everything they had—but they were the lucky ones.

By the last week in January 1945, the Soviets had bridgeheads over the Oder north of Kuestrin and south of Frankfurt and were only forty miles from the capital of the Third Reich. Here, however, the massive

Soviet offensive came to a sudden and unexpected halt. On January 27 and 28, a blizzard blew across central Europe. When it stopped, the temperature rose rapidly, the snow melted, and Soviet tanks stalled in the mud. Himmler hailed the warm spell as a gift from fate, but the thaw served Zhukov's interests as well. His troops had advanced 250 miles, and he wanted to regroup and resupply his legions before the final assault on Berlin.

On February 10, after a pause of almost two weeks, the Russians resumed their offensive when the 2nd Belorussian Front attacked Weiss's 2nd Army with hundreds of tanks and about forty rifle divisions. Their objective was to reach the Baltic Sea and isolate the West Prussian ports of Gydnia and Danzig from the Reich. The Soviets pushed forward, but the German resistance was fierce, and after ten days, and having gained nothing of importance, General Rokossovsky called off the battle.

While Zhukov, Konev, and Rokossovsky rested their men and prepared for the next offensive, Guderian and Hitler quarreled over strategy. Guderian wanted to evacuate the Courland pocket, but Hitler refused. Their heated arguments almost became violent. On one occasion, Major General Wolfgang Thomale, the chief of staff of the panzer inspectorate, actually grabbed Guderian and pulled him back because he thought Hitler was going to physically assault him.[32] Another argument threw Hitler into such a hateful frenzy that even Hermann Goering—who was certainly no friend of the Army General Staff—felt compelled to intervene. He took Guderian by the arm and led him into another room, where they had coffee together and the panzer general regained his composure. Army Group Courland (which controlled the 16th and 18th Armies) remained where it was.

Guderian thought he saw an opportunity to strengthen the German hold on Pomerania by cutting off the Russians north of the Warthe. His plan called for a double envelopment east of the Oder. Sepp Dietrich's 6th SS Panzer Army would lead one attack; Erhard Raus's 3rd Panzer Army would lead the other but would first have to be withdrawn from East Prussia.

Hitler liked the idea of resuming the offensive but amended Guderian's plan. He approved a single-pronged attack in the vicinity of Stargard. The 3rd Panzer Army could be recalled from East Prussia to assist, but the 6th SS Panzer would continue to Hungary. Unfortunately for Guderian this meant Himmler's Army Group Vistula would direct the offensive, and Guderian doubted the Reichsfuehrer-SS could handle what would be a difficult assignment for even a well-trained and experienced commander. OKH performed miracles by pulling ten divisions (seven of them panzer) out of the front lines, earmarking them for the offensive, though Allied bombings, fuel shortages, and damaged German railroads slowed their assembly.[33]

OKH forbade Army Group Vistula from using the new assault divisions prior to the offensive, but Himmler felt compelled to commit several of them prematurely to prevent the Soviets from overrunning his assembly areas. On February 9, he told Guderian that he might not be ready to attack on February 16, as originally planned. This merely confirmed Himmler's incompetence in the mind of the strong-willed and opinionated chief of the General Staff. He therefore proposed that Lieutenant General Walter Wenck, the chief of operations and deputy chief of staff of OKH, supercede Lammerding as chief of staff of Army Group Vistula so he could direct the attack.[34]

Adolf Hitler liked this handsome, outspoken young General Staff officer, despite his coming from an officer corps he distrusted as defeatist. (In their first recorded meeting, Wenck told Hitler that the Eastern Front was like Swiss cheese—full of holes.) Hitler did not, however, like Guderian's proposal of appointing Wenck to lead the attack, and this led to another battle royale at the Reich Chancellery on February 13. In Himmler's presence, Guderian told Hitler that if Wenck were not attached to the army group staff, the attack would fail. Hitler denied that Reichsfuehrer-SS Himmler was incapable of carrying out his duties. Guderian nevertheless continued to demand that Wenck be placed in charge of the attack. Hitler trembled with rage. "He was almost screaming, his eyes seemed about to pop out of his head and the veins stood out on his temples,"

Guderian recalled. "I had never seen Hitler rave so violently." At the end of each outburst, the chief of the General Staff retained his icy composure and repeated his demand. Finally, Hitler realized that Guderian was not going to give in, no matter how long and furiously he screamed. Suddenly he stopped and calmly told Himmler that General Wenck would arrive at his headquarters that night to take charge of the attack.

Later, Guderian retired to an anteroom and sat down. Here Field Marshal Keitel, the commander-in-chief of OKW, found him and berated him for causing the Fuehrer to get so excited. What if he had had a stroke? Keitel asked. (Keitel had supported Hitler in the argument.) "A statesman must be prepared to be contradicted and to listen to the truth, for otherwise he is unworthy of the name," Guderian answered coldly.

Wenck inherited an operation that was already going astray. To meet Guderian's deadline, he would have to attack piecemeal, as there was no way he could assemble the attack divisions in time. After he inspected the initial preparations (which were made by General of Waffen-SS Felix Steiner's 11th SS Army), Wenck became even more pessimistic. The staff work had been done badly. The troops were not properly assembled, supplied, or equipped.

Meanwhile, the advanced elements of Erhard Raus's 3rd Panzer Army Headquarters arrived from East Prussia to spearhead the "Stargard counteroffensive," as Wenck's Pomeranian operation was called. Raus had serious reservations about launching the attack and, after inspecting his new divisions, even doubted if Pomerania could be held. Pleading lack of familiarity with the local situation, he opted out of directing the attack; it would be left to Steiner. Raus was further amazed when, on the eve of the attack, Himmler told him that both he and Hitler were convinced that this offensive would decide the entire outcome of the war in favor of Germany.[35]

Unfortunately, Hitler required General Wenck to attend Fuehrer conferences each evening, which meant he had to make a round trip of almost 200 miles every day, after his demanding frontline duties. On the night of February 14/15, on the way back to army group headquarters,

LEFT: General of Panzer Troops Walter Wenck; RIGHT, General of Infantry Wilhelm Burgdorf, the chief of the Army Personnel Office and "the gravedigger of the German Officer Corps." *Bundesarchiv Bild 1011-237-1051-15A/Schneider/Kunath/ CC-BY-SA 3.0; U.S. National Archives*

the exhausted general took the wheel from his driver, Hermann Dorn, who had collapsed from fatigue. Wenck fell asleep at the wheel and crashed into the parapet of a bridge on the Berlin-Stettin autobahn. Dorn dragged the general from the flaming wreck, doused his burning clothes, and got him to a hospital. He had suffered a fractured skull, five broken ribs, and multiple contusions.

The offensive was scheduled to begin in about five hours. Wenck was replaced as deputy chief of the General Staff and acting chief of staff of Army Group Vistula by General of Infantry Hans Krebs, a veteran staff officer who was a close friend of General Burgdorf. He lacked Wenck's talent, was unfamiliar with the local situation, and the attack came to nothing.[36]

Meanwhile, the conquered districts of eastern Germany were subjected to a reign of terror. Refugees from the Baltic States, East and West

Prussia, Pomerania and Upper Silesia told hair-raising tales of rape, pillage, and murder. Historian John Toland wrote:

> The refugees reported that advancing front-line [Soviet] troops were well disciplined and well behaved, but that the secondary units that followed were a disorganized rabble. In wild, drunken orgies these Red Army men had murdered, looted and raped. Many Russian commanders, the refugees claimed, appeared to condone the actions of their men. At least they made no effort to stop them. From peasants to gentry the accounts were the same, and everywhere in the flood of refugees there were women who told chilling stories of brutal assault—of being forced at gunpoint to strip and then submit to repeated rapings.[37]

As the Russian armies neared their homes, thousands of refugees fled on foot or in farm wagons, through blizzards and bitterly cold weather. They suffered from frostbite, died from exposure, were strafed and bombed by the Red Air Force, and were pursued by Red Army tanks. Dozens of babies died because it was too cold for them to nurse.

Those who remained behind were subjected to extreme cruelty. In the past, Red Army officers had kept their soldiers obedient through threats of draconic punishment. Now, however, they were set loose against civilians. Even in friendly Yugoslavia they acted barbarically. The Red Army only crossed the northeast corner of that country, and then only for a short period of time; yet there were 1,200 reported cases of looting and 121 cases of rape. In all but ten of these incidents, the rape victim was also murdered.[38]

The German record in the East was abysmal, especially toward Jews, Poles, Gypsies, and Soviet prisoners-of-war, and nothing can excuse it. This was especially true for the civil administration, the SS, the security police, and the *Einsatzgruppen* (murder squads). The German Army, however, had generally (but not always) behaved correctly and certainly did not engage in the orgy of rape, murder, destruction, and plunder that characterized the Red Army's drive through Eastern Europe. Many Germans, hoping the reports of Soviet atrocities were exaggerated, did not want to leave their homes or farms and fell into the hands of the Soviet Army or the Communist Poles who followed them. They were beaten, robbed, raped, and murdered. Hospitals were frequently attacked. The doctors were murdered, the nurses raped and sometimes murdered, and the patients were either left to starve or were thrown out of upper story windows along with discarded nurses. The lucky ones were shot in the head. In some villages, everyone in uniform was executed, including postmen and foresters. In other towns, all Nazi Party members were hunted down and killed. Men and women were dragged to death behind jeeps or horses. Members of the nobility and the clergy often received the most brutal treatment because they were regarded as Communist "class" enemies. They were blinded, tortured, and mutilated. Communist sadism was rampant.[39]

The Western Allies seemed to have no illusions about their brothers-in-arms. Stalin had told Churchill that, after the war, the Soviet Union would need 4,000,000 German laborers indefinitely, and he spoke, to Churchill's horror, of the liquidation of 50,000 German officer prisoners of war. Before the firebombing of Dresden, Anglo-American pilots were instructed to try to reach Allied lines if they found themselves in trouble. If this was impossible, they were to bail out in German-held territory. Under no circumstances were they to come down behind Soviet lines.[40]

After the initial Red wave of terror, the deportations began, as civilians were rounded up and sent to the Soviet Union to work as slave laborers. Most of these people were never heard from again.

Meanwhile, the loss of some of the Wehrmacht's best and most important officers mounted at an incredible pace. From late December 1944 to mid-February 1945, they included:

- Lieutenant of Reserves Robert Haas, commander, 1st Battery, 244th Assault Gun Brigade, supporting the 18th

Volksgrenadier Division of the 6th Panzer Army, killed in action in the Ardennes, December 23, 1944. He had destroyed fifty-four British and American tanks and a dozen armored cars since June. Awarded the Knight's Cross posthumously.

- Major Baron Dr. Friedrich August von der Heydte, former commander, 6th Parachute Regiment and commander, Battle Group von der Heydte, surrendered near Monschau, Belguim, December 24, 1944.
- Lieutenant of Reserves Bernhard Sowada, platoon leader, 1st Battery, 237th Assault Gun Brigade, killed in action near Kopolnasnyek, Hungary, December 25, 1944. Knight's Cross holder with twenty-one enemy tanks to his credit.
- Major of the General Staff Albrecht Barth, quartermaster (Ib), 5th Jaeger Division, missing in action on the Eastern Front, December 1944.
- Major of the General Staff Dieter Rohlack, chief of operations, 6th Parachute Division, killed in action near Arnhem on the Western Front, December 31, 1944.
- Lieutenant General Wolfgang von Kluge, former division commander and former commander of Fortress Dunkirk, discharged from the army for political reasons, December 31, 1944. He was the brother of the late Field Marshal Guenther von Kluge, who had committed suicide in August for his part in the plot to assassinate Adolf Hitler.
- General of Panzer Troops Adolf Kuntzen, former commander of the LXXXI Corps on the Western Front, discharged/expelled from the service, December 31, 1944.
- General of Engineers Karl Sachs, former commander of the LXIV Corps, discharged/expelled from the service, December 31, 1944.
- Major General Ernst von Poten, former commandant of Metz, discharged/expelled from the service, December 31, 1944.

- Lieutenant General Wilhelm Weidinger, former General of Army Flak Troops, discharged/expelled from the service, December 31, 1944.
- Lieutenant General Adolf von Schell, former commander, 25th Panzer Division, Eastern Front, discharged/expelled from the service.
- Major of the General Staff Hermann Behrens, quartermaster, 716th Infantry Division, killed in action, January 1, 1945.
- Colonel Joseph Rauch, commander, 18th Panzer Grenadier Division, captured, East Prussia, New Year's Day, 1945.
- Colonel General Lothar von Seydlitz-Kurzbach, former commander of the 924th Fortress Regiment, died in January 1945 of wounds received on December 27, 1944. Posthumously promoted to major general.
- General of Infantry Georg Thomas, former chief of the War Economics Branch of the High Command of the Armed Forces, expelled from the service in January 1945, arrested, and sent to a concentration camp.
- Major of the General Staff Hermann Behrens, quartermaster, 716th Infantry Division, killed in action in Alsace, January 1, 1945.
- Peter Koert, commander of the 246th Volksgrenadier Division, hospitalized in the Ardennes (apparently for stress) on January 2, 1945. He had been promoted to major general the day before. Koert was still in the hospital when he was captured by the British on May 5, 1945.
- SS Major Hubert Erwin Meierdress, commander of the I/3rd SS Panzer Regiment "Totenkopf," killed in action, Dunaalmas, Hungary, by a Russian T-34, January 4, 1945.
- Lieutenant General Edgar Feuchtinger, former commanding general, 21st Panzer Division, was arrested for being AWOL on January 5, 1945.

- Lieutenant General Count Georg von Rittberg, commander, 88th Infantry Division, captured, Baranov Bridgehead, January 8, 1945.
- Captain Hans Christian Stock, commandant of the Tank Destroyer School at Neuhammer, killed in action in Hungary, January 12, 1945. He was the former commander of the 152nd Tank Destroyer Battalion and a holder of the Knight's Cross with Oak Leaves.
- Lieutenant General Friedrich von Scotti, leader of the 306th Higher Artillery Command (Harko 306) on the Eastern Front, relieved of his command and placed in Fuehrer Reserve on January 13 for complaining of an ammunition shortage. His promotion to general of artillery was cancelled and he was never reemployed.
- Major of the General Staff Friedrich Hacke, attached to the Army Personnel Office (HPA), missing in action, January 13, 1945.
- Major of the General Staff Fritz Oelrich, quartermaster, 16th Panzer Division, missing in action at Bautzen (near the Baranov Bridgehead), January 15, 1945.
- Major of the General Staff Baron Klaus-Ruediger von und zu Egloffstein, chief of operations, 88th Infantry Division, missing in action near Baranov.
- Colonel General Joseph Harpe, commander-in-chief, Army Group A, relieved of his command, January 16, 1945.
- Colonel Hugo Dempwolff, commander of the 276th Volksgrenadier Division, wounded in action in the Ardennes, January 18.
- Major General Harald von Hirschfeld, commander of the 78th Sturm Division, mortally wounded on January 18, 1945, in an air attack at Dukla Pass in the Tarta Mountains.

- Lieutenant General Harry von Kirchbach und Lauterbach, commanding general, 214th Infantry Division, killed in action in the Pulawy Bridgehead, near Kielce on the Vistula, January 18, 1945.
- Lieutenant General Max Schrank, commander of the 5th Mountain Division, Ligurien Army, Italy, relieved on January 18, 1945.
- Major of the General Staff Friedrich Brandt, quartermaster, 25th Panzer Division, missing in action on the Eastern Front, January 18, 1945.
- General of Panzer Troops Walter Fries, commander of the XXXXVI Panzer Corps, Eastern Front, relieved of his command, January 20, 1945. Fries had already lost an arm and a leg on the Eastern Front. He was subsequently court-martialled and acquitted.
- General of Panzer Troops Smilo von Luettwitz, commander of the 9th Army, sacked. Luettwitz was later given command of the LXXXV Corps on the Western Front—a definite demotion.
- Lieutenant General Siegfried Rein, commander of the 69th Infantry Division, killed in action, East Prussia, January 20, 1945.
- General of Infantry Helmuth Thumm, commander of the LXIV Corps in Himmler's OB Upper Rhine, relieved of his command on January 20 for disobeying the Reichs-fuehrer-SS's orders. Not wishing to sacrifice boys for Hitler and the Nazis, he pulled Hitler Youth units out of the combat zone. Thunn was indicted but the war ended before he was court-martialled. He lived until 1977.
- Major of the General Staff Baron Joachim Maltzahn zu Wartenberg und Penzlin, chief of operations, 25th Panzer Division, wounded in action, Russian Front, January 20, 1945.

- Major of the General Staff Arnold Wentzel, chief of operations, 712th Infantry Division, missing in action in the Netherlands, January 20, 1945.
- Major of the General Staff Berthold Bollack, chief of operations, LVI Panzer Corps, missing in action in the vicinity of Radom, Eastern Front, January 21, 1945.
- Colonel of the General Staff Martin von Graevenitz, chief of staff, LVI Panzer Corps, missing in action in the vicinity of Radom, Eastern Front, January 21, 1945.
- Major General Ulrich Liss, commander of the 304th Infantry Division, wounded and captured on the Baranov Bridgehead, Russian Front, January 22, 1945.
- Captain Reinhold Karl Ertel, assault gun brigade commander, killed when his assault gun hit a mine, January 22, 1945.
- Major of the General Staff Roderich Snowadzki, operations staff, 9th Army, missing in action, Eastern Front, January 22, 1945.
- General of Infantry Hermann Recknagel, commander, XXXXII Corps, killed in action, Baranov Bridgehead, Eastern Front, January 23, 1945.
- Major of the General Staff Schall, chief of operations, 10th Panzer Grenadier Division, captured near Radom, Eastern Front, January 23. Schall later died in a Soviet prison.
- Colonel Ernst Knebel, commandant, 3rd Panzer Army Weapons School, mortally wounded on the Eastern Front, January 24. Knebel died on January 27, 1945. He was posthumously promoted to major general.
- Lieutenant Colonel of the General Staff Karl Krueckeberg, chief of operations, 100th Jaeger Division, killed in action in Silesia, Russian Front, January 24, 1945.
- Colonel General Georg-Hans Reinhardt, commander, 3rd Panzer Army, critically wounded, East Prussia, Eastern Front, January 25, 1945.

- Major of the General Staff Wilhelm Lammert, chief of operations, XX Corps, missing in action, East Prussia, Eastern Front, January 25, 1945.
- General of Infantry Johannes Block, commanding general, LVI Panzer Corps, killed in action near Kielce, Poland, Eastern Front, January 26, 1945.
- Major of the General Staff Hans von Tiesenhausen, chief of operations, 26th Volksgrenadier Division, killed in action, Ardennes/Eifel, Western Front, January 26, 1945.
- Colonel Carl Andre, commander, 88th Infantry Division, captured at Glogau, Baranov Bridgehead, Eastern Front, January 27, 1945. Andre was promoted to major general three days later.
- Major General Arthur Finger, commander, 291st Infantry Division, missing in action, Baranov Bridgehead, January 27, 1945. Officially declared dead, 1946.
- General of Infantry Friedrich Hossbach, commander, 4th Army, Eastern Front, relieved for disobeying Hitler's orders, January 28, 1945.
- General of Infantry Edgar Roehricht, commander, LIX Corps, Upper Silesia, Eastern Front, relieved of his command, January 29, 1945.
- Major General Gerhard Kegler, commander, Division Woldenberg, relieved of his command and arrested for failing to obey Himmler's orders to hold his positions in Pomerania on the Eastern Front. The division was destroyed on January 28, 1945, and Kegler was arrested two days later. He was court-martialed, stripped of his rank, and sentenced to death, but this part of the sentence was suspended. He was sent to the front as a private.[41]
- Major of the General Staff Hans-Hermann Heldt, 61st Volksgrenadier Division, missing in action near Gumbinnen on the Eastern Front on or about January 30, 1945.

- Colonel General Kurt Zeitzler, former chief of the General Staff, discharged (*verabschiedet*) from the service, January 31, 1945.
- Major General Hans-Erich von Schroeter, former commandant of Breslau, discharged from the service, January 31, 1945.
- Lieutenant General Adolf Sinzinger, former commandant of Vienna, discharged/expelled from the service, January 31, 1945.
- Major of the General Staff Semper, Organizations Staff, OKH, missing in action in the Kuestrin sector, Russian Front, January 31, 1945.
- Colonel Adolf-Friedrich von Drabich-Waecter, chief of staff, XXXXII Corps, missing in action, Eastern Front, end of January 1945.
- Lieutenant Colonel of the General Staff Heinrich Gehm, chief of operations, 214th Infantry Division, missing in action, Silesia, Eastern Front, end of January 1945.
- Lieutenant Colonel of the General Staff Konrad von Heu-duck, chief of operations of the XXXXVI Panzer Corps until January 8, 1945, when he was placed in Fuehrer Reserve, went missing at the end of January. Fate unknown.
- Major of the General Staff Kesselheim, chief of operations, 17th Panzer Division, missing in action, Eastern Front, end of January 1945.
- Major of the General Staff Baron Dodo zu Inn und Knyphausen, chief of operations of the 5th Panzer Division, missing in action, Eastern Front.
- Major of the General Staff Franz-Joseph von Loebbecke, chief of operations, 28th Jaeger Division, missing in action, early 1945.
- Major of the General Staff Fritz Roos, chief of operations, Wehrkreis VIII, Breslau, Eastern Front, killed at the beginning of February 1945.

- Lieutenant General Max Lindig, Harko (Higher Artillery Commander) 1st Parachute Army, severely wounded, Western Front, February 1945.
- Major General Helmuth Bechler, commander, 85th Infantry Division, Eifel sector of the Western Front, wounded, February 1945.
- Colonel Eduard Zorn, commander, 189th Infantry Division, killed in action, Colmar Pocket, Alsace, Western Front, February 4, 1945
- Lieutenant General Hans Degen, commander, 2nd Mountain Division, the Saar sector of southwest Germany, seriously wounded, February 6, 1945.
- Major General of Reserves Dr. Ernst Meiners, commander, 547th Volksgrenadier Division, severely wounded in East Prussia, February 8, 1945.
- Major General Rudolf "Rolf" Lippert, commanding general, 5th Panzer Division, Eastern Front, reported himself sick, February 10, 1945. General Lippert died April 1, 1945. He had won a gold medal in the 1936 Olympics.
- Second Lieutenant of Reserves Alfred Regeniter, commander of the 3rd Battery, 276th Assault Gun Brigade, wounded in action at Stenzlau, West Prussia, on the Eastern Front. He had knocked out four Joseph Stalin tanks at a range of 400 meters on February 1. Lieutenant Regeniter was evacuated and survived the war. He was awarded the Knight's Cross but did not receive it until 1974.
- Major General Ludwig Kirschner, commander of the 320th Volksgrenadier Division, killed in action near Saybusch, eastern Upper Silesia, Russian Front, February 11, 1945.
- Major General Gerhard Schmidhuber, commander, 13th Panzer Division, killed in action, Budapest breakout, Eastern Front, February 11.

- Lieutenant Colonel of the General Staff Arthur von Ekesparre, chief of operations, 13th Panzer Division, killed in action, Budapest, February 12, 1945.
- Major of the General Staff Rudolf Schindler, quartermaster, 13th Panzer Division, killed in action, Budapest breakout, February 12, 1945.
- Lieutenant Colonel of the General Staff Daniel Lindenau, chief of operations, IX SS Mountain Corps, killed in action, Budapest sector, Eastern Front, February 12, 1945.
- Major of the General Staff Erhard Mainka, chief of operations, 22nd SS Cavalry Division, killed in action, Budapest breakout, February 12, 1945.
- Major of the General Staff Bodo Schaper, deputy chief of operations, 22nd SS Cavalry Division, killed in action, Budapest, Eastern Front, February 12, 1945.
- Major of the General Staff Willy Schloss, quartermaster, 17th Infantry Division, missing in action in the Oder sector of the Eastern Front, February 13, 1945.
- Major of the General Staff Erich Wulff, Ia, 15th SS Grenadier Division (1st Latvian), killed in action, Eastern Front, mid-February 1945.
- Lieutenant General Ritter Wolfdietrich von Xylander, chief of staff, Army Group Center, killed in an air attack near Struppen, Pirna, Eastern Front, February 15, 1945.
- Colonel Karl Goebel, commander, 299th Infantry Division, Heilgenbeil sector, East Prussia, Eastern Front, mortally wounded, February 16, 1945. Died in the hospital at Adelschlag, March 2, 1945. Posthumously promoted to major general, effective March 1.
- Colonel of the General Staff Peter Pantenius, economics officer attached to the staff of Wehrkreis IV at Dresden, died of an overdose of sleeping pills on February 16, 1945.

And there were many others of less rank or distinction killed, wounded, crippled, mutilated, captured, or missing.

It should be noted that a few of the leaders who were relieved or arrested deserved their fate. Lieutenant General Edgar Feuchtinger, the commander of the 21st Panzer Division, is a prime example. As an artillery major in 1935, he assisted in making the Nuremberg rallies a success. In the process, he befriended several prominent Nazis, who took an interest in his career.

Feuchtinger was born in Metz in 1894 and joined the Kaiser's Army at the outbreak of World War I, beginning as a Fahnenjunker in the Baden 14th Foot Artillery Regiment. Promoted to second lieutenant in 1915, he spent most of the war on the Western Front. Selected for the Reichsheer, he was assigned to the 13th (Wuerttemberger) Infantry Regiment but managed to return to the artillery as a battery officer in October 1921. Undistinguished before the Nuremberg rallies, he advanced rapidly thereafter, from major in 1935 to lieutenant general in 1944. He remained in artillery assignments until 1942, most notably as commander of the horse-drawn 227th Artillery Regiment (September 1, 1939–August 16, 1942), serving in France and in the northern sector of the Eastern Front. Placed in Fuehrer Reserve, he was given command of a kampfgruppe (battle group) of the 10th Panzer Division in November 1942. His mission was to prevent Vichy France from destroying the French Fleet at Toulon. He was unsuccessful but was nevertheless given command of Mobile Brigade West. In July 1943, this ad hoc formation was upgraded to 21st Panzer Division.

Edgar Feuchtinger was in no way qualified to command a tank division. He owed his command solely to his Nazi Party connections. He performed poorly on D-Day and was in fact absent much of the night of June 5/6, when British paratroopers and gliderborne troops were landing in his division's zone of operations. Feuchtinger's staff finally found him—in a sleezy nightcall in Paris.

Feuchtinger's poor performance continued during the Battle of Normandy and in the retreat across France. At the end of 1944, the 21st

Panzer was involved in heavy fighting in the Saar Lautern when a Nazi lawyer turned up a division headquarters. He was investigating what had happened on D-Day. To his shock, Feuchtinger was not be found. Subsequent investigation revealed that he was AWOL (Away Without Leave), in bed with his lover in Celle.[42] He was relieved of his command and arrested on January 5, 1945. Confined to prison at Fortress Torgau, it was soon discovered that he had enriched himself through the illegal seizure and sale of Jewish assets, as well as army property. He had also communicated military secrets to his South American mistress. He was demoted

Lieutenant General (later Private) Edgar Feuchtinger. *Bundesarchiv Bild 1011-300-1865-12*

to *Kanonier* (gunner or private) and sentenced to death. He was reprieved (thanks to his Nazi friends) and assigned to the 20th Panzer Grenadier Division but promptly deserted. He escaped the Nazis and surrendered to the British, whom he hoodwinked, telling them that he had been busted because of his anti-Nazi activities. Later he also fooled the Americans and went to work for them in Krefeld, where he continued his corrupt lifestyle. He died under mysterious circumstances in a Berlin hotel on January 21, 1960.

CHAPTER VI

THE RUSSIANS CLOSE IN

When the competent but brutal General Rendulic took charge of Army Group North at the end of January 1945, the situation in East Prussia was desperate. General of Infantry Hans Gollnick's XXVIII Corps completed the evacuation of Memel by sea on January 27 and abandoned the city to the Russians. To the south, Chernyakhovsky's 3rd Belorussian Front had pushed to the outskirts of Koenigsberg, and south of that, the right flank armies of Rokossovsky's 2nd Belorussian Front had overrun southeastern East Prussia and were approaching Koenigsberg from the south. At the same time, to the west, the Soviet 3rd Shock Army and elements of the 1st Guards Tank Army lay siege to the small Prussian port of Kolberg.

On March 9, the German Wehrmacht suffered yet another command shake-up. Hitler sacked Rundstedt as OB West and replaced him with Albert Kesselring. Colonel General Heinrich von Vietinghoff returned to Italy to succeed Kesselring as OB Southwest, while Rendulic returned to Latvia as commander-in-chief of Army Group Courland. General Weiss, the commander of the 2nd Army, replaced Rendulic as commander of Army Group North in East Prussia, while Dietrich von

East Prussian refugees just after they crossed the frozen Frisches Haff (lagoon).
Bundesarchiv Bild 146-1979-084-05/CC-BY-SA 3.0

Saucken became the commander of the 2nd Army. Hitler met with Weiss later that day, added 2nd Army to his command, and instructed him to hold Koenigsberg and a land corridor to the city, along with the Hela Peninsula, Gdynia, Danzig, Pillau, and the Frische Nehrung (also called the Frische *Haff* or lagoon).

On March 12, Hitler summoned Saucken to Fuehrer HQ to give him instructions—and received a triple insult: Saucken rendered the old army salute, he continued to wear his monocle (a sign of disrespect), and he kept his left hand on his sabre, even though it was forbidden to carry a weapon in Hitler's presence. Hitler ignored the insults, but informed Saucken that he would report to Albert Forster, the Nazi Gauleiter of Danzig.

The panzer general rebelled. Striking the map table with the palm of his hand, he snapped: "I have no intention, Herr Hitler, of placing myself under the orders of a Gauleiter!" This was a fourth and fifth insult: Saucken had refused a direct order and had not used the term "mein Fuehrer."

Hitler repeated his command, and Saucken repeated his rebuttal: "I will not place myself under the orders of a Gauleiter!"

"All right, Saucken," Hitler finally said in a tired voice, "Keep the command yourself." He then dismissed the general. Hitler did not shake Saucken's hand, and Saucken did not salute.

* * *

The Soviets launched their East Prussian offensive on March 13. For ten days Saucken's and Weiss's men fiercely contested the Soviet advance. Elements of Rokossovsky's front finally reached the sea at Sopot on March 23, cutting off Gdynia and Danzig from the rest of the army group. After prolonged house-to-house fighting, Gdynia finally fell on March 28, and Danzig was lost two days later. The survivors of the 2nd Army then retreated east into the delta of the Vistula.

On March 13, the 3rd Belorussian Front launched a series of massive attacks against the 4th Army, holding a twenty-by-six-mile bridgehead west of Heiligenbeil. By March 26, under continuous landward assault and aerial and artillery bombardment, the 4th Army was on the verge of collapse. Hitler finally gave it permission to abandon the Heilgenbeil bridgehead and retreat across the Frisches Haff to Nehrung—provided the army brought with it all of its panzers and artillery, though of course it was too late for that. On April 1, after its retreat, 4th Army had 60,000 effective combatants and 70,000 wounded; the Soviets claimed to have taken 46,000 prisoners.[1]

With the Heiligenbeil bridgehead eliminated, the Soviets turned their attentions to Koenigsberg and Samland.

Koenigsberg, the ancient capital of East Prussia, was defended by General of Infantry Otto Lasch, the commander of Wehrkreis I, who had been selected for the post of commandant of Koenigsberg because he had a large family, and if he surrendered prematurely it would be at risk of Nazi punishment.[2]

To defend the city, Lasch had the remnants of six battered divisions plus eight battalions of Volkssturm: about 35,000 men. For the attack, the Russians massed four armies—more than 130,000 men, backed by 500

East Prussian Volkssturm defending Koenigsberg, March 6, 1945. *Bundesarchiv Bild 183-J28805/CC-BY-SA 3.0*

tanks, several battalions of huge 203mm and 305mm guns, and 2,500 airplanes. The Luftwaffe had fewer than one hundred aircraft inside the fortress, and they were operating off the city's main boulevards.

Army Detachment Samland (formerly HQ, XXVIII Corps) and Fortress Koenigsberg came under the direct command of 4th Army. Its commander, General Mueller, visited the city on April 2 and confidently told the defenders that they would hold Koenigsberg while he, Mueller, counterattacked and threw the Soviets out of East Prussia. To accomplish this task, Mueller took an infantry division from Lasch, as well as his only panzer division. Lasch did not believe for one second that Mueller had the faintest chance of defeating the Soviets, and he needed every unit he had. A heated argument ensued, during which Mueller threatened to report Lasch to the Fuehrer for his lack of faith in final victory and National Socialism. He then left Koenigsberg, never to return.

Hitler did indeed have full confidence in General Mueller. On April 5, he sacked Colonel General Weiss, disbanded Headquarters, Army Group North, and placed Mueller in charge of the defense of East Prussia.[3] The staff officers and GHQ troops of the former Army Group North were evacuated from East Prussia by sea to the Reich proper and were used to form the staff of the 12th Army (see below).

In addition to his military problems, General Lasch was saddled with the needs of 100,000 civilians, who were terrorized by the bombardments and the thought of what lay ahead. Gauleiter Erich Koch, however, refused to allow them to evacuate, so they were trapped in the city when the Soviet offensive began on April 6. By the end of the day, the Red infantry had already reached the outskirts of the urban area. Lasch signaled 4th Army, asking permission to withdraw to Samland, but Mueller refused. The following day, April 7, the road to Samland was cut. Mueller then ordered Lasch to break out, but this was no longer possible. Lasch and his men struggled desperately against the Russian tide, but they never had a chance. Major General Erich Sudau, the commander of the 548th Volksgrenadier Division, was killed in the street fighting, and his division was destroyed. With his defenses collapsing everywhere, a severely wounded General Lasch asked for the authority to surrender on April 9, but permission was denied. He capitulated anyway that same evening. Three days later, Hitler sentenced Lasch to death in absentia and ordered his family arrested by the SS.[4] He also sacked General Mueller and dissolved his HQ. His command was absorbed by the indomitable Dietrich von Saucken, who now had sole responsibility for the defense of East Prussia.

For two days Koenigsberg was a scene of unspeakable atrocities of rape and the murder of about one-fourth of the civilian population and countless German POWs. Gauleiter Erich Koch, however, escaped via icebreaker to Denmark, abandoning his subjects whom he had refused to evacuate, while broadcasting messages to Berlin, giving the impression that he was holding out to the last. Once he disembarked in Denmark, the former Reichskommissar of the Ukraine disappeared.

After a siege of several weeks, the Russians finally captured Kolberg (now Kolobrzeg, Poland) on March 20. Eighty percent of the city had been destroyed. On April 13, the Soviets began their attack on Samland. General Hans Gollnick met them with nine understrength divisions (one of them panzer)—about 65,000 men. Fighting was desperate, but the

Kolberg (now Kolobrzeg, Poland), 1945. Twenty Years of the People's Republic of Poland *(Poland, 1964)*

Germans were forced back, and on April 20, Lieutenant General Kurt Chill was surrounded in Pillau with about 20,000 German soldiers. He managed to hold out for six more days, during which tens of thousands of civilians and a great many soldiers were evacuated by the German navy.

By April 26, Saucken's Army of East Prussia (formerly 2nd Army) was tenaciously holding its last-ditch positions on both sides of the Bay of Danzig and a small beachhead on the Hela Peninsula, north of Gdynia. That it survived at all is a major tribute to the courage, skill, and determination of its officers and men; they suffered huge casualties but inflicted even greater losses on their enemies. Reliable Soviet figures are scarce, but during the four weeks before February 10, the Reds admit that the 2nd Belorussian Front and the 3rd Belorussian Front suffered 15 and 22 percent casualties respectively.[5] These heavy losses and the desperate courage of the German *soldat* left the Russians unable to break Saucken's final defensive line.

DEFEAT IN THE AIR

While General von Saucken and his men clung to their positions, the U.S. Air Force and the R.A.F.'s Bomber Command pounded German cities in the west. During the last three months of 1944, British Bomber Command alone dropped 163,000 tons of bombs, compared with 40,000 tons in the same period the year before. Some 53 percent of this total fell on German cities. Within a hundred-day period, Duisburg, Essen, Cologne, and Duesseldorf were each blasted by 38,000 or more tons of high explosives, and other cities—like Ulm, Stuttgart, Karlsruhe, Bonn, Kolbenz, Bremen, Wilhelmshaven, Brunswick, and Osnabrueck— were devastated by British bombing. The U.S. 8th Air Force dropped an even greater tonnage of bombs on German targets. They concentrated on cities with synthetic oil plants, including Gelsenkirchen, Castrop, Sterkrade, Hanover, Harburg, Hamburg, Bottrop, Bohlen, and Zeitz. The U.S. 15th Air Force, operating out of Italy, annihilated oil plants, including at Floridsdorfs, Vienna, and Linz.

An estimated 500,000 to 600,000 Germans were killed by bombs during the 1940–1945 period—about ten times the number of civilians killed in Great Britain during the entire war. Between February 1 and April 21, 1945, Berlin alone was subject to eighty-three separate air raids involving heavy bombers. By January 1945, the U.S. 8th Air Force alone was sending up 1,500 bombers a day if the weather did not interfere. Magdeburg and Chemnitz were smashed on February 6, but Dresden got the worst of it. Stalin wanted the city bombed because it was a transportation hub for the tens of thousands of German refugees attempting to escape the Red terror. On February 13, the beautiful Saxon capital and cultural center was fire-bombed with 650,000 incendiaries. The fires could be seen 200 miles away, and the city burned for a week. Dresden was packed with refugees, so the death toll can only be guessed, but estimates run from 100,000 to 135,000—all in a single raid. It is probable that twice as many people were killed in this one raid as were killed during the entire Battle of Britain.

Dresden in 1945. More than 90 percent of the city center was destroyed in the raids of February 13–15, 1945. *Bundesarchiv Bild 183-Z0309-310/G. Beyer/CC-BY-SA 3.0*

As one mordant German observer said of the destruction of his country's towns and cities: "The Fuehrer was right when he proclaimed that Berlin would be unrecognized in ten years."[6]

The veteran Luftwaffe fighter pilots flew out day after day, despite overwhelming odds, trying to stop the onslaught. Lieutenant Otto Kittel, a twenty-seven-year-old who had shot down 267 enemy airplanes, was shot down by a Soviet IL-2 on February 14. Rudi Linz, who had seventy kills, was shot down by a Spitfire, as was Wilhelm Mink (seventy-two victories). Friedrich Haas (seventy-four kills) was shot down by a Soviet MIG, while his wing mate, Franz Schall (137 kills) died in a crash landing. Gerhard Hoffmann, 125 kills, went missing in action, presumed dead. Major Heinrich Ehrler, who had shot down 204 enemy airplanes, was killed over the Eastern Front on April 6, 1945, while Colonel Guenther Luetzow (105 aerial victories in World War II and five during the Spanish Civil War) was last seen attacking a B-17 four-engine bomber over Italy on April 24. Colonel Erich Leie, 118 kills, was killed by a Soviet YAK on March 7, while Colonel Kurt Buehlingen, commander of JG 2 (the Richthofen fighter wing) was shot down on the Eastern Front and captured in early 1945 (see Appendix 5 for a hierarchy of Luftwaffe air formations). He had 112 kills. Captain Karl Schnoerrer, who had forty-six victories, was shot down defending Hamburg on March 30 and lost a leg, while Colonel Johannes "Macki" Steinhoff (176 kills) was horribly burned on April 18 when he unsuccessfully tried to take off from a bomb-cratered runway to attack an American bomber formation. The future commander of the West German Air Force spent the next two years in the hospital.[7] Guenther Rall, another future general in the West German Luftwaffe and the number three ace in history with 267 kills, was shot down for the eighth time and received his third severe wound of the war in 1945. He had not recovered when the war ended. Colonel Hans Ulrich Rudel, the leading Stuka ace of the war and a man who personally destroyed more than 750 Soviet tanks and armored vehicles, as well as 150 artillery pieces, 800 soft-skilled vehicles, and a battleship (among other pieces of equipment), suffered his sixth wound of the war when Soviet anti-aircraft fire blew off his leg in 1945.[8]

Luftwaffe losses were staggering, and by March 1945 there simply were not enough German pilots—especially experienced fighter pilots— left to prevent the Allied bomber formations from attacking whenever and wherever they wanted.

Throughout the Army, Senior and General Staff officer losses between February 18 to March 8 included:

- Lieutenant General Ritter Wolfdietrich von Xylander, chief of staff of Army Group A (formerly North Ukraine), died from injuries sustained in an air crash, February 18, 1945.
- Major of the General Staff Reim, Quartermaster, LXXXII Corps, killed in action on the Western Front, February 21, 1945.
- Lieutenant Colonel of the General Staff Werner Voigt-Ruscheweyh, chief of operations, 7th Army, killed by an Alllied fighter-bomber on the Western Front, February 21, 1945.
- Major of the General Staff Baron Leo-Volkhardt von Wittgenstein, chief of operations, LXIII Corps on the Lower Rhine, died from injuries suffered in an accident, February 22, 1945.

- Major of the General Staff Johann-Dietrich von Hassell, discharged from the Wehrmacht on February 28 after he was linked to the July 20 assassination plot against Hitler.
- Lieutenant Colonel of the General Staff Richard Lang, chief of operations, 225th Infantry Division, killed in action, Courland Pocket, March 5, 1945.
- Colonel General Erhard Raus, commander of the 3rd Panzer Army, relieved of his command, March 5.
- Major General Baron von Elverfeldt, commander of the 9th Panzer Division and former chief of staff of the 9th Army and 17th Army, killed in action in Cologne, Western Front, March 6, 1945.
- Lieutenant General Richard Schimpf, commander of the 3rd Parachute Division, captured by the Americans near Bad Godesberg.

HITLER'S LAST OFFENSIVE

By mid-February 1945, the Wehrmacht finally reached strategic bankruptcy. In January and February alone, it had lost 660,000 men. The Home Army lacked the weapons (including small arms) and ammunition to equip new divisions. In January, against a monthly demand for 1,500,000 tank and anti-tanks rounds, production fell to 367,000.

Despite this hopeless position, with Zhukov's spearheads within seventy miles of Berlin, Hitler planned another offensive in Hungary, using Dietrich's battered 6th SS Panzer Army, which had been pulled out of the Ardennes in January. Hitler planned to envelop a large part of the 3rd Ukrainian Front between the Danube and the Drava, sweep across the Danube, recapture Budapest, and overrun eastern Hungary.

Overriding Guderian, who argued against the offensive, Hitler declared that it was necessary because 80 percent of his remaining oil supply came from Hungary and Austria. He ordered General Woehler, the commander-in-chief of Army Group South, to handle the detailed planning.

Woehler's offensive was code-named Operation *Fruehlingser-wachen* ("Awakening of Spring"), and its objectives were to inflict a sharp, local defeat on the Soviets and push them back, in order to establish something of a buffer zone between them and the Zagykanizsa oilfields. Woehler's plan called for a main attack between Lake Balaton and Lake Velencze, to be launched by Balck's 6th Army and Dietrich's 6th

Heinz Guderian, the "father" of the Blitzkrieg and chief of the General Staff, 1944–45. *Bundesarchiv, Bild 101I-139-1112-17 / Knobloch, Ludwig / CC-BY-SA 3.0*

SS Panzer Army. In all, Balck and Dietrich would have ten panzer and five infantry divisions. Meanwhile, south of Lake Balaton, General of Artillery Maximilian de Angelis's 2nd Panzer Army was to launch a secondary attack with four infantry divisions, while Luftwaffe Colonel General Alexander Loehr's Army Group E attacked across the Drava from the south with three infantry divisions. The main attack was to begin at dawn on March 6.

Hitler's goals for this offensive were completely unrealistic. Every German unit earmarked for the attack was seriously depleted. Dietrich joked that *Panzer-Armee 6* was so called because he only had six panzers left. On the other side of the line, Tolbukhin's 3rd Ukrainian Front had five armies with thirty-seven Soviet rifle divisions, six Bulgarian divisions, several Yugoslav divisions, two Soviet tank corps, a mechanized corps, and a cavalry corps—a total of more than 400,000 men, 400 tanks, and 1,000 airplanes. Thanks to Hungarian deserters, Tolbukhin knew that an offensive was imminent and planned a defense in depth.

Luftwaffe Colonel General Alexander Loehr, commander-in-chief of Army Group E. *Bundesarchiv Bild 146-1969-041-30/CC-BY-SA 3.0*

During the night of March 5/6, Loehr struck the 1st Bulgarian and 3rd Yugoslavian Armies and established three bridgeheads across the Drava, while the 2nd Panzer Army attacked the Soviet 57th Army with only SS Lieutenant General Hermann Priess's I SS Panzer Corps (the II SS Panzer Corps wasn't ready until the following morning) and gained ground only slowly, having to advance through deep mud from the melting snow while avoiding hundreds of Soviet mines. By the end of the second day of the attack, the German 6th Army and 6th SS Panzer Army had gained four miles in most sectors, although the I SS Panzer Corps had pushed forward almost twenty miles.

Woehler's drive caused Tolbukhin some bad moments, but by March 15 the Germans had lost its momentum. On March 16, the Soviets counterattacked with the entire 2nd Ukrainian Front to destroy the 6th Army and the 6th SS Panzer Army between Lakes Balaton and Velencze. On March 17, the Hungarian 3rd Army (north of Lake Velencze) collapsed and Woehler's left flank was threatened with envelopment, while both Balck and Dietrich were subjected to a series of very heavy frontal attacks. Some of the hard-pressed SS units retreated without orders, prompting an enraged Fuehrer to demand that SS-Oberstgruppenführer "Sepp" Dietrich—commander of the 1st, 2nd, 3rd, and 9th SS Panzer Divisions—have his men remove their armbands from their uniforms as a mark of his displeasure and their disgrace. Dietrich had been a supporter of Hitler in the early 1920s, and he had commanded Hitler's personal bodyguard in the late 1920s and early 1930s. Dietrich nevertheless refused to issue the order. Instead, he and his staff officers filled a chamber pot with their ribbons and decorations and sent it to the Fuehrer. The pot had a 17th SS Panzer Grenadier Division "Goetz von Berlichingen" cuff ribbon prominently attached to it. (Goetz von Berlichingen was a German knight and mercenary whom Goethe immortalized in a play where he tells the Bishop of Bamberg: "You can kiss my ass!") As historian Louis L. Snyder wrote: "The incident expressed perfectly the personality of Sepp Dietrich."[9] Unfortunately, Hitler's reaction to the chamber pot (if he ever saw it) has not been recorded. He did, however, publicize his order concerning the armbands. The result was predictable: an alarming increase in SS desertions.

On March 18, Malinovsky's 2nd Ukrainian Front turned north behind the 3rd Hungarian Army, and between Mor and Lake Velencze two Soviet armies supported by two air armies attacked the IV SS Panzer Corps, which was covering the northern flank of Woehler's strike forces. They routed it. Woehler reacted by shifting the 6th SS Panzer Army north into the sector between Lake Velencze and the Danube, while 6th Army took charge of the entire sector between Lakes Velencze and Balaton. The SS divisions were able to slow, but not check, the Russian advance south, where the Reds hoped to cut off the 6th Army east of Lake Balaton. Hitler refused to authorize a retreat, and by March 21, the 6th Army was left with one narrow escape corridor along the lake's north shore. Over the next twenty-four hours, Woehler and Balck succeeded in extracting the 6th Army from the Soviet trap—at the cost of much of the Army's heavy equipment, which was abandoned in the thick Hungarian mud.

On March 24, as the Germans retreated, General Balck reported that morale had plummeted among his troops who were unwilling to fight for a lost cause. The Waffen-SS was no longer the elite unit it had once been—casualties and the recruiting policies of Himmler and General of Waffen-SS General Gottlob Berger had seen to that—and Hitler's armband order was the final straw for many.[10] During the retreats of mid-March, about 75 percent of the deserters that the 6th Army's field

Hermann Balck, the son of Lieutenant General William Balck, a Pour le Merite holder, was born in Danzig in 1893. One of his grandfathers was a British lieutenant colonel. He joined the Imperial Army as a Fahnenjunker in 1913 was commissioned in the Hanoverian 10th Rifle Battalion in 1914. He spent the First World War on the Western Front, was wounded seven times, commanded a machine gun company, and was recommended for the Pour le Merite himself in October 1918, but the war ended before it was awarded. Selected for the Reichsheer, he spent twelve years with the 18th Cavalry Regiment. A friend of Guderian's and an early convert to motorized warfare, he successively commanded the 1st Rifle Regiment, 3rd Panzer Regiment, 2nd Panzer Brigade, 11th Panzer Division, the Grossdeutschland Panzer Grenadier Division, the XIV Panzer Corps, XXXX Panzer Corps, XXXXVIII Panzer Corps, 4th Panzer Army, Army Group G, and 6th Army. After the war he was sentenced to three years' imprisonment for ordering the execution of an artillery officer. He served eighteen months. He retired to Stuttgart and died in 1982 at the age of eighty-eight. He is buried in Osnabrueck. *Bundesarchiv Bild 101I-732-0118-03/CC-BY-SA 3.0*

police apprehended came from the ranks of the SS.[11] Such a statistic would have been inconceivable even a year earlier.

On March 25, the vanguard of the Red Army reached the Raab River. General of Infantry Otto Woehler became Hitler's latest scapegoat. He was sacked to be replaced by General Lothar Rendulic. Woehler, however, remained in command of Army Group South until Rendulic arrived from Courland in the second week of April.

Without its heavy equipment, the 6th Army was unable to check the Russian onslaught. On its right and left flanks, the 6th SS and 2nd Panzer Armies were hurled back, and desertions in the few remaining Hungarian divisions meant they soon functionally ceased to exist.[12] By March 30, Russian armies were heading toward Wiener Neustadt and Vienna. Hitler demanded a counterattack. Woehler responded that given the state of his troops, this was out of the question; he needed to marshal what forces he had to block the Soviets at the Austro-Hungarian border.

The situation was also critical on the flanks of Army Group South. By the end of March, the 8th Army (under the command of General of Mountain Troops Hans Kreysing since December 28) was falling back into Austria and southern Czechoslovakia. Bratislava, the capital of Slovakia, fell on April 4, and the 2nd Panzer Army lost the Nagykanizsa oil fields after a bitter fight. In the German center, the Soviets bypassed Wiener Neustadt on April 2 and headed for Vienna. Hitler ordered the city defended to the last man. "He who gives the order to retreat is to be shot on the spot!" the Fuehrer commanded.[13]

To defend the former capital of the Austro-Hungarian Empire and the city of his misspent youth, Hitler reinforced the 6th SS Panzer Army with the 25th Panzer Grenadier and Fuehrer Grenadier Divisions. The Soviets, however, were now moving very rapidly, and the 2nd and 3rd Ukrainian Fronts quickly launched a double envelopment against the city. When Rendulic finally arrived at army group headquarters on the evening of April 7, the Battle of Vienna had been in progress a day and a half, and the Russians were in the streets of Vienna on both sides of the Danube. Elements of the Red Army were already west of the city.

The battle was not destined to be a long one. Sepp Dietrich was hopelessly outnumbered, and Rendulic could not help him; he needed his remaining regiments to cover the Zistersdorf oil region (Germany's last oil fields) in northwestern Austria and the area west of Vienna. As of April 7, the divisions of the 6th SS Panzer Army had the following strengths: 1st SS Panzer, 1,582 men and 16 tanks; 12th SS Panzer, 455 men, 1 tank; 356th Infantry Division, 1,214 men, 3 Jagdpanzer 38s; 2nd

SS Panzer, 1,498 men, 11 tanks; 3rd SS Panzer, 1,004 men, 6 tanks; 6th Panzer, 1,235 men, 8 tanks.[14] Obviously these burned-out and exhausted divisions were no match for Stalin's legions. Rendulic's forces (which were redesignated Army Group Ostmark on April 7) fell back, and Dietrich abandoned the city. (He surrounded his command post with heavily armed SS companies personally loyal to himself, lest Hitler demand he be shot.) The Russians captured the center of the city on April 10, stamped out the last pockets of resistance three days later, and subjected Vienna to an orgy of rape and pillaging.

THE RUSSIANS CLOSE IN ON BERLIN

While Hitler frittered away his last reserves on senseless counterattacks to the south, the Soviets inched ever closer to the German capital. Given their overwhelming superiority in every category of military power, their operations in February and March were strangely slow, hesitant, and focused on their flanks in Pomerania and Silesia. They began their offensive west of the Vistula on February 24, but it was March 4 before they isolated Western Prussia and eastern Pomerania from the Reich.

Hitler responded to the latest crisis by decreeing that fifteen-year-old boys were eligible for frontline combat duty. In Berlin, barricades were erected, policemen were formed into infantry battalions, and people braced for the worst as public utilities broke down. Newspapers, if they published at all, were limited to a single page; even the newspaper of the Reich's minister of propaganda, Joseph Goebbels's *Der Angriff*, was shut down. Members of the Berlin Philharmonic were called up for military duty. They gave their last concert on April 18. Significantly, it was Wagner's "Die Goetterdaemmerung."

On March 5, Hitler sacked the highly competent Colonel General Erhard Raus and replaced him as commander of the 3rd Panzer Army with Baron Hasso von Manteuffel. (Hitler did not like Raus because he was an Austrian. This prejudice was the only reason he ever gave for relieving him of his command. The general was never reemployed.) Colonel General Joseph Harpe, the former commander-in-chief of Army Group A and the principle scapegoat during Stalin's January offensive, replaced Manteuffel as commander of the 5th Panzer Army in the West.

Manteuffel was a capable commander, but he could not prevent the Russians from shattering the left flank of 3rd Panzer Army. On March 19, Hitler was forced to allow him to evacuate the Stettin bridgehead—but Hitler also issued his first "Nero Decree." Every civilian threatened by the Allies' advances was to be evacuated to the interior of Germany; and all bridges, factories, supply facilities, roads, and transportation facilities were to be destroyed; the enemy was to capture nothing but a wasteland. If the war is lost, Hitler said to Albert Speer in his coldest voice, "the people will also be lost. It is not necessary to worry about what the German people will need for elemental survival. On the contrary, it is best for us to destroy even these things. For the nation has proved to be the weaker, and the future belongs solely to the stronger eastern nation. In any case only those who are inferior will remain after this struggle, for the good have already been killed."[15]

Speer was shaken to the core by these words. Both he and Guderian attempted to persuade Hitler to revoke his decree, and even SS Colonel Wilhelm Zander (Martin Bormann's liaison officer at Fuehrer Headquarters) opposed it, but Keitel and Bormann issued it in the form of orders to the generals and Gauleiters the next day. The Fuehrer's orders, however, were no longer being obeyed everywhere—especially in the west, where civilian delegations appealed to German military commanders *not* to defend their towns and villages if it meant they would be destroyed. SS General Paul Hausser, the commander-in-chief of Army Group G, refused to pass Hitler's order to his troops, and Willy Stoehr, the Gauleiter of the Palatinate and the Saar, flatly refused to evacuate civilians and destroy the towns. In other sectors, the front was disintegrating so rapidly that the Nero Decree was irrelevant.

Despite the increasingly catastrophic situation, the Replacement Army continued to function at near full efficiency. Since 1939, it had already activated thirty-two "waves" of divisions. Wave 33 was organized in January and included ten infantry and Volksgrenadier divisions, most of which were rebuilt units. After this the German Order of Battle became increasingly confused. The *Fahnenjunkern* of the Dresden Infantry School were incorporated into six grenadier regiments in February, as were the Fahnenjunkers at Wiener Neustadt (two regiments), Potsdam (seven regiments), and Wetzlar in Bavaria (three regiments). In addition, three new shadow divisions (Hanover, Dresden, and Donau) were dubbed Wave 34. They were used both to reinforce existing divisions and to create new ones. In February, four new infantry divisions (the 63rd, 219th, 249th and 703rd) were created in the Netherlands, mainly from *Osttruppen* (Eastern volunteers) and sailors.

The "named divisions" rolled off the Home Army's assembly lines in February and March 1945. They included the (303rd) Infantry Division Doeberitz (from the infantry school); the (309th) Infantry Division Berlin (from the Berlin and Grossdeutschland guard regiments); the (324th) Infantry Division Hamburg; the (325th) Infantry Division Jutland, and the (328th) Infantry Division Seeland, which was formed in Copenhagen.[16]

The last wave—the 35th—was organized in March and April 1945. It included the 1st RAD (Reich Labor Service) Division "Schlageter" (7,500 men), the 2nd RAD Division "Friedrich Ludwig Jahn" (7,500 men), the 3rd RAD Division "Theodor Koerner" (7,500 men), the 4th RAD Division (8,000 men), Infantry Division "Potsdam," Infantry Division "Scharnhorst," Infantry Division "Ulrich von Hutten" and Infantry Division "Ferdinand von Schill." All of the RAD divisional headquarters were former army HQ units.[17] The Kurmark Panzer Grenadier, the Clausewitz Panzer, 2nd Feldherrnhalle Panzer, 2nd Hermann Goering Panzer Grenadier, Holstein Panzer, Jueterbog Panzer, Muencheberg Panzer, Schleisien [Silesian] Panzer, Tatra Panzer and Norwegen [Norwegian] Panzer Divisions were also created in 1945.

Meanwhile, Reichsfuehrer-SS Heinrich Himmler, the commander-in-chief of Army Group Vistula, checked himself into Professor Gebhardt's sanitarium at Hohenlychen, allegedly suffering from the flu. The operations of Army Group Vistula were left in the hands of Lieutenant General Eberhard Kinzel, the man whom Halder had sacked as chief of the Foreign Armies East section of OKH in 1942. (Kinzel had replaced General of Infantry Hans Krebs as Himmler's "other" chief of staff after the failure of the Stargard offensive, and Krebs had returned to Berlin and replaced Lieutenant General Walter Wenck as chief of operations at OKH. Despite his lack of qualifications for higher General Staff work, SS Lieutenant General Heinz Lammerding was still chief of staff of the army group.)

General Guderian, the man responsible for the Eastern Front, had not received a single report from Himmler since February 14. On March 20, he drove to the sanitarium and found Himmler, apparently in good health. He called upon him to resign his post as commander of Army Group Vistula and reminded the former chicken farmer that he was national police commander, minister of the interior, Reichsfuehrer-SS, and commander-in-chief of the Replacement Army. With uncharacteristic diplomacy, Guderian asked how one man could possibly fill all these posts.

Himmler, who had lost his taste for combat command, liked the notion of resigning, but said he could not approach the Fuehrer with such a suggestion. Guderian volunteered to personally bring the idea to Hitler, and Himmler seemed delighted with the thought—he appeared to be looking for a way out.

Hitler was in a rare rational mood when Guderian brought up the matter; however, he frowned when the chief of the General Staff nominated Colonel General Gotthard Heinrici, the leader of the 1st Panzer Army, to replace Himmler. Perhaps the immensely competent but relatively colorless Heinrici was not charismatic enough for the Fuehrer—or perhaps it was because he was too religious (Heinrici was a devout Evangelical Christian) and a non-Nazi product of the General Staff, which the dictator despised. The fact that Heinrici was related to Field Marshal Gerd von Rundstedt, the epitome of the Prussian officer corps, may have had something to do with it, or perhaps it was just because

Field Marshal von Kluge (left) and Gotthard
Heinrici (right), Eastern Front, mid-1943.
*Bundesarchiv, Bild 146-1977-120-09 / Berg-
mann, Johannes / CC-BY-SA 3.0*

Heinrici was short (5'7''). Most likely it was because his wife was a *Mischling* (half-Jewish). In any case, Hitler mentioned several other possible choices, but Guderian held firm on the idea of Heinrici, and Hitler relented in the end. Heinrici's appointment was promulgated on March 20.[18] Walter Nehring succeeded Heinrici as commander of the 1st Panzer Army. The next day—in what was virtually his first act as army group commander—Heinrici relieved SS General Lammerding of his duties. On March 22, Hitler agreed to let Guderian transfer most of the staff of the now defunct Army Group F to Headquarters, Army Group Vistula, where it was used to replace most of Himmler's incompetent staff. Lammerding's replacement was General of Infantry Kinzel, a veteran General Staff officer and former chief of staff, Army Group North.

Emboldened by his success in getting Himmler to abandon his military ambitions, Guderian quickly overplayed his hand. On March 21, he visited the Reichs Chancellery and saw Hitler and Himmler, strolling through the ruins. Guderian asked to speak to the Reichsfuehrer-SS in private and told him that it was his duty to approach the Fuehrer and ask him to open armistice negotiations. "My dear General, it's too early for that," Himmler replied. He did not tell Guderian (or Hitler) that he had already made contact with the enemy and was attempting to negotiate, but he did tell Hitler what Guderian had said. That evening, the Fuehrer announced to the chief of the General Staff that he had heard that Guderian's heart condition had taken a turn for the worse. He therefore ordered him to take four weeks' leave. Guderian declined on the grounds that he had no deputy. (Wenck was still recovering from his injuries, and Hans Krebs had been wounded in an Allied bombing attack on OKH Headquarters in Zossen on March 15 and had not yet returned to duty.) Hitler accepted this reasoning for the moment, but on March 28, after another acrimonious exchange with Guderian, the dictator sent him on six weeks' sick leave. He had, in reality, been sacked again, and this time he was not reemployed.[19]

Guderian was replaced by General of Infantry Hans Krebs. He was a well-trained staff officer but had spent the entire war in various General Staff appointments and lacked command experience even at the regimental level. He was, however, a close friend of General Burghoff, the chief of the Army Personnel Office. As soon as Guderian named Krebs chief of operations at OKH, Burghoff drew Krebs into the inner circle of radical Nazis at Fuehrer Headquarters, and he was soon rubbing elbows with Bormann and General of Waffen-SS Hermann Fegelein, Himmler's liaison officer at Fuehrer Headquarters. Within a matter of days, Bormann and the radical Nazis were conspiring to permanently remove Guderian and replace him with Krebs, whom they could manipulate more easily. Under Krebs, the General Staff of the Army became even more subject to the Fuehrer.

Meanwhile, the Russians pushed into Silesia. On February 14, they surrounded Breslau, but the 17th and 269th Infantry Divisions broke out, leaving the defense of the city largely in the hands of Major General Siegfried Ruff's recently created 609th Infantry Division. Overall command of the city was placed in the hands of Major General Hans von Ahlfen, the former commander of the 70th Engineer Brigade of Army Group A. Ahlfen conducted a tenacious defense, but, by March 12, there was fighting in the streets of the city. Simultaneously, other Soviet armies pushed Colonel General Ferdinand Schoerner's Army Group Center away from the Oder and back toward the Sudety Mountains. On March 17, they encircled General of Cavalry Rudolf Koch-Erpach's LVI Panzer Corps. The Russians dispersed the headquarters of the 17th Army and narrowly missed capturing its commander, General of Infantry Friedrich

Residents of Lodz greet Soviet tanks entering the city in 1945. The lead vehicle is a ISU-122 self-propelled gun. *Russian Archives*

Wilhelm Schultz. The LVI Panzer eventually managed to break out of the encirclement but only after suffering heavy losses.

The 1st Panzer Army (under Heinrici and then Nehring) generally held its positions, but General of Panzer Troops Fritz-Hubert Graeser's 4th Panzer and Schultz's 17th Armies were unable to cover the great Silesian industrial area, which included the cities of Glogau, Oppeln, and Breslau. By the time Marshal Ivan Konev halted his offensive on March 31, all of Upper Silesia was in Soviet hands except for a few isolated German pockets, the most notable of which was Breslau.

Hitler wrongly assumed that the next Soviet drive would be aimed at Prague, not Berlin. On March 30, he transferred the 10th SS Panzer Division from Army Group Vistula to the Goerlitz sector, guarding Prague. On April 2 and 3, he belatedly transferred the 25th Panzer and Fuehrer Grenadier Divisions from Heinrici to the 6th SS Panzer Army for the defense of Vienna. General Krebs raised no objection, though the Russians were now within fifty miles of Berlin. The loss of these three divisions robbed Army Group Vistula of half its tanks and mobile forces.

The Soviets' next major offensive would be against Army Group Vistula with the goal of capturing Berlin and destroying the Third Reich forever. Stalin ordered a pause because he wanted no mistakes: the Red armies would be properly equipped, extremely well supplied, and reinforced before he began his last campaign in Europe. But while a lull descended on the Eastern Front, Hitler's Western Front collapsed.

CHAPTER VII

BACK ACROSS THE RHINE

In early January 1945—after the failure of the German Ardennes offensive—the U.S. Division of Psychological Warfare surveyed 324 captured German soldiers. Sixty-two percent still expressed faith in Hitler. Forty-four percent still believed in final victory.[1] But the odds were now heavily stacked against them. By February 1945, Germany had lost more than 2,500,000 sons. (By the end of the war, the total was 3,300,000 killed or missing.) But while Hitler had recklessly wasted his troops, the western allies were approaching Germany with formidable strength.

By New Year's Day, 1945, Eisenhower had more than 3,700,000 Allied soldiers on the mainland of Europe, including 73 well-equipped mobile divisions (49 infantry, 20 armored, and 4 airborne). Backing them were more than 17,500 first-line combat airplanes, including thousands of fighter-bombers, medium and heavy bombers, and rocket-firing Typhoons. They outnumbered the Germans at least 2.5 to 1 in troops, 2.5 to 1 in artillery, about 10 to 1 in tanks, and more than 20 to 1 in airplanes.[2] Within three months, Eisenhower's strength would be 90 divisions and 4,000,000 men. To oppose these masses, Gerd von Rundstedt had 29 infantry divisions (including static, ad hoc, and special

A Marder III tank destroyer in a Belgian town, 1944. It featured a 75mm gun on a Panzer 38(t) chassis with an open-air fighting compartment. Germany produced about 1,900 of these dependable weapons despite its thin upper armor, which was a distinct disadvantage. *Bundesarchiv Bild 101I-297-1729-23/Kurth/CC-BY-SA 3.0*

purpose units), 26 Volksgrenadier divisions, 7 panzer divisions, 5 parachute divisions, 4 panzer grenadier divisions, 2 mountain divisions, and 3 motorized or panzer brigades. (These figures include SS units but exclude divisional staffs which had no combat elements attached to them. Table 7.1 shows the Order of Battle of OB West on January 27, 1945.) On paper, Rundstedt outnumbered Eisenhower in terms of divisions and divisional equivalents, 74–73. Unfortunately for OB West, not a single division in the West was at full strength, and most had but a fraction of their authorized manpower. The 26th Volksgrenadier Division, for instance, had an authorized strength of 10,000 men, but only 5,202 were actually present for duty, and only 1,782 of these were classified as "combat effective" (*Kampfstaerke*).[3] Most of the other units were in equally poor condition. For example, the 198th Infantry, the best-equipped division in the 19th Army, had only 6,891 men (or less than half its authorized establishment). In February 1945, after Dietrich's 6th Panzer Army was transferred to the Eastern Front, Rundstedt estimated that he had the equivalent of 6.5 full-strength infantry divisions on the entire Western Front.[4]

Order of Battle, Ob West
January 21, 1945

OB WEST: Field Marshal Gerd von Rundstedt

Army Group H: Luftwaffe Colonel General Kurt Student

25th Army: Luftwaffe General of Fliers Friedrich Christiansen			
		XXX Corps:	
			Kampfgruppe 346 Infantry Division (Static)
		LXXXVIII Corps:	
			6th Parachute Division
			2nd Parachute Division
1st Parachute Army: General of Paratroops Alfred Schlemm			
		LXXXVI Corps:	
			Kampfgruppe 84 Infantry Division
			Kampfgruppe 180 Infantry Division
			II Parachute Corps: 190 Infantry Division 606 Division z.b.V.
Army Group B: Field Marshal Walter Model			
	15th Army: General of Infantry Gustav-Adolf von Zangen		
		XII SS Corps:	
			176 Infantry Division
			183 Volksgrenadier Division
			59 Infantry Division (Static)
		LXXXI Corps:	
			363 Volksgrenadier Division
			353 Infantry Division
			85 Infantry Division
		LXXIV Corps:	
			272 Volksgrenadier Division
			62 Volksgrenadier Division

		In Army Reserve:	
			27th SS Volunteer Grenadier Division "Langemark"
			28th SS Volunteer Grenadier Division "Wallonien"
			12th Volksgrenadier Division
6th Panzer Army: SS Colonel General Sepp Dietrich (1)			
		LXVII Corps:	
			277 Infantry Division
			62 Volksgrenadier Division
		XIII Corps:	
			246 Volksgrenadier Division
			18 Volksgrenadier Division
			326 Volksgrenadier Division
			9th SS Panzer Division (1)
5th Panzer Army: General of Panzer Troops Baron Hasso von Manteuffel			
		LXVI Corps:	
			15 Panzer Grenadier Division
			560 Volksgrenadier Division (Remnants)
		LVIII Panzer Corps:	
			26 Volksgrenadier Division
			Fuehrer Begleit Brigade
			340 Volksgrenadier Division
			167 Volksgrenadier Division
			5 Parachute Division
		In Army Reserve:	
			3 Panzer Grenadier Division
			9th Panzer Division

			Fuehrer Grenadier Brigade
7th Army: General of Panzer Troops Erich Brandenberger			
		LIII Corps:	
			276 Volksgrenadier Division
			79 Volksgrenadier Division
		LXXX Corps:	
			352 Volksgrenadier Division
			2 Panzer
			212 Volksgrenadier Division
		In Army Reserve:	
			9 Volksgrenadier Division
			Panzer Lehr Division
			HQ, XXXXVII Panzer Corps
Army Group G: Colonel General Johannes Blaskowitz			
	1st Army: General of Infantry Hans Obstfelder		
		LXXXII Corps:	
			416 Infantry Division
			11 Panzer Division
			719 Infantry Division (Static)
			347 Infantry Division (Static)
		XIII SS Corps:	
			19 Volksgrenadier Division
			17 SS Panzer Grenadier Division
			559 Volksgrenadier Division
		XC Corps:	
			257 Volksgrenadier Division,
			6 SS Mountain Division
			256 Volksgrenadier Division
			36 Volksgrenadier Division
		LXXXIX Corps:	

			245 Infantry Division (Static)
			Div Raessler
			21 Panzer
			25 Panzer Grenadier Division
			47 Volksgrenadier Division
		In Army Reserve:	
			Division Number 526
	In Army Group Reserve:		
		HQ, LXXXV Corps	
OB Oberrhein: Reichsfuehrer-SS Heinrich Himmler			
19th Army: General of Infantry Siegfried Rasp			
		LXIV Corps:	
			106 Panzer Brigade
			198 Infantry Division
			708 Volksgrenadier Division
			189 Infantry Division
			16 Volksgrenadier Division
		LXIII Corps:	
			338 Infantry Division
			159 Infantry Division
			Kampfgruppe 716 Infantry Division (Static)
		XIV SS Corps (2):	
			Division Hueter
			553 Volksgrenadier Division
			Division Number 405
		XVIII SS Corps (2):	
			Division Breisach
			Staff, 48 Volksgrenadier Division
		XXXIX Pz K (2):	

			7 Parachute Division
			10 SS Panzer Division (1)
		In OB Reserve:	
			2 Mountain Division (3)
Naval High Command West:			
		XXV Corps (Fortress Lorient):	
			Remnants, 265 Infantry Division (Static)
			319 Infantry Division (Static)
			Kampfgruppe, 226th Infantry Division (Static)
In OB West Reserve:			
		Division Staff 604 z.b.V.	
		361 Volksgrenadier Division	
NOTES:			
(1) Already alerted for transfer to the Eastern Front			
(2) Directly under the command of OB Oberrhein			
(3) In transit			
SOURCE: Mehner, *Geheimentagesberichte*, Volume 12, 422–23.			

Table 7.1

THE ROER RIVER DAMS

General Eisenhower's plans to conquer the Rhineland involved five phases. First, the U.S. 1st Army would capture the Roer River Bridges. Second, British Field Marshal Sir Bernard Law Montgomery's 21st Army Group would clear the Lower Rhineland with a converging attack in which the 1st Canadian Army would drive through the Reichswald and the U.S. 9th Army would drive through the Roer River sector. They would then clear the west bank of the Rhine from Nijmegen to Duesseldorf.[5] In the third phase, Montgomery would prepare for a set-piece attack across the Lower Rhine, while General Omar Bradley cleared the

west bank of the Rhine from Duesseldorf to Cologne. During this phase,
the U.S. 1st Army's left wing would push forward to Cologne and then
strike southeast into the flank and rear of the German forces defending
the Eifel, as the German Ardennes is called. At the same time, Patton's
3rd Army would advance east, take Pruem, and drive on to Koblenz. In
the fourth phase, Montgomery would launch the major assault across
the lower Rhine, while the U.S. 3rd and 7th Armies cleared out the
Moselle-Saar-Rhine triangle and secured crossing places along the Rhine
in the Mainz-Karlsruhe sector. Finally, after the Rhineland was cleared,
the Anglo-American forces would launch a double envelopment against
the Ruhr, with Montgomery's forces playing the major role. Map 7.1
shows the Allied drive west of the Rhine.

Map 7.1

General Courtney Hodges, the commander of the U.S. 1st Army, assigned the primary mission of the first phase to Major General C. Ralph Huebner's V Corps on his northern flank: seize the Roer River dams northeast of Monschau. The two most important dams were the Urft and the Schwammenauel. As long as they possessed these two dams, the Germans had the power to flood the Roer Valley, washing out any tactical bridges the Allies might erect and isolating any Allied invasion force on the eastern side of the river.

Huebner's main opposition came from Major General Eugen Koenig's 272nd Volksgrenadier Division, a well-led, veteran unit which had been reduced to 6,000 men by casualties.[6] It conducted a skillful delaying action without becoming decisively engaged, frustrating Hodges and the other American generals because speed was essential: Montgomery was scheduled to launch the major Allied offensive through the Reichswald and against the Rhine on February 8, and the U.S. 9th Army (on his right flank) needed to secure the dams before that time so it also could take part in the drive. Even so, it was February 7 before the first Americans entered the town of Schmidt, two miles north of the Schwammenauel Dam. The next day, the Americans attacked again, this time supported by no fewer than 40 battalions of artillery—780 guns. Once again, however, the 272nd Volksgrenadier turned back every attack. It was not until after nightfall on February 9 that the Americans reached the dam.

They discovered that the German engineers had blown up the discharge valves on both the Schwammenauel and Urft dams, as well as the machinery in the power rooms. There would be no spectacular, crashing flood of water from the Roer Dams, but the demolitions had been well calculated. They would release a steady

The Schwammenauel Dam, November 1944. *U.S. Department of Defense*

flow of water that would keep the Roer Valley flooded for about two weeks and prevent the U.S. 9th Army from supporting Montgomery's push through the Reichswald.

THE BATTLE OF THE REICHSWALD

Monty's build-up for his drive to the Rhine (code-named Operation "Veritable") was the largest Allied logistical operation since D-Day. The main blow would be delivered by the 1st Canadian Army, which was to be spearheaded by Sir Brian Horrocks's XXX British Corps. Horrocks

would advance out of Nijmegen with five divisions (200,000 men), supported by an artillery bombardment of more than 1,000 guns and by a massive aerial bombardment from several thousand airplanes.

The British were experts at disguising where a main attack would fall. But General of Paratroopers Alfred Schlemm, the commander of the 1st Parachute Army, was not deceived. He expected the main attack in the Reichswald and persuaded a skeptical General Johannes Blaskowitz to give him a regiment of the 2nd Parachute Division. He also quietly moved elements of the 7th Parachute Division forward into a second line of defense.

General of Paratroopers Alfred Schlemm (1894–1986), commander of the 1st Parachute Army on the Western Front, 1944–1945. Before that he was chief of staff of the XI Air Corps (Germany's parachute troops), 1st Air Division and II Luftwaffe Field Corps on the Eastern Front, and I Air Corps in Italy. *Bundesarchiv Bild 101I-579-1962-23/CC-BY-SA 3.0*

Horrocks's plan called for the fortified towns of Cleve and Goch to be leveled by Allied bombers the day before he launched a frontal attack. He hoped to penetrate the forest quickly and capture the two bombed-out towns before the Germans could react and commit their reserves.

Because of flood waters on his flanks, Horrocks had to cram 50,000 Allied troops and 500 tanks into a front only five miles wide. They were to be followed by six more divisions. Opposing this huge force was Major General Heinz Fiebig's 84th Infantry Division, which had two infantry regiments (about 7,000 men) on the front line, with a third regiment (about 3,000 men) in the second line. Although the 84th was one of the strongest divisions in the Wehrmacht in terms of numbers, its men were mostly elderly soldiers normally used as security troops, and several of his units were *Magen* (Stomach) battalions, consisting of men with special dietary needs. In addition to his other problems, Fiebig had only 36 assault guns and a few batteries of artillery to face 5,000 Allied tanks. German reserves near this sector of the front included the 7th Parachute Division, a panzer grenadier division, and 2 depleted panzer divisions, which between them could field only 50 tanks.

The Battle of the Reichswald began at 5:00 a.m. on February 8, when the defenders were blasted by the British Army's heaviest artillery barrage of the Second World War. Simultaneously, the medieval town of Cleve was hit by nearly 1,400 tons of bombs, leaving hundreds of civilians dead. The smaller town of Goch was demolished by 500 tons of bombs, and the villages of Calcar, Uedem, and Weeze were also hard hit.

After a barrage of two and a half hours, a strange silence fell on the Reichswald before the British fired smoke rounds, which were normally used as cover for advancing infantry. The surviving German gunners poured shells into the smoke. But the British were not advancing; they had fired the smoke rounds so the German gunners would return fire and give away their positions. When the bombardment resumed at 7:50 a.m., most of the surviving German batteries disappeared in a storm of high explosives, and the 184th Artillery Regiment was annihilated.

At 10:00 a.m., the bombardment shifted to the German rear, and smoke shells again began to fall on the German front and into no-man's-land. Then, at 10:30 a.m., the Allied assault infantry moved out. Despite the overwhelming material superiority of the enemy, the defenders of the Reichswald did have some important natural advantages. Tanks, for the most part, couldn't penetrate the forest; roads were few, narrow, and muddy; and floodwaters and destroyed ditches constricted the British advance. Units became hopelessly intermixed.

By nightfall, the German 84th Infantry Division had lost six of its battalions and was near collapse, but the Anglo-Canadian advance was itself stuck in the forest and thick mud. The next day, around 4:00 p.m., the Allies finally reached the outskirts of Cleve, eleven hours behind schedule. British communications were not functioning properly, traffic jams in the British rear added to the confusion, and when General Horrocks sent in his reserve, the 43rd Wessex Division, he did not realize the poor conditions of the roads around Cleve. There were now some 40,000 Allied trucks and armored vehicles clogged on disintegrating roads, leaving frontline troops running short of food, fuel, and ammunition.

While the Allies stalled, the Germans acted. By late afternoon, lead elements of Lieutenant General Wolfgang Erdmann's 7th Parachute Division began arriving in Cleve, and Lieutenant General Hermann Plocher's 6th Parachute came down from Arnhem and linked up with the 7th Parachute near Materborn, south of Cleve. Field Marshal von Rundstedt ordered Blaskowitz to hold Cleve "at all costs," and he signaled General Baron Heinrich von Luettwitz to move into the Cleve sector with his XXXXVII Panzer Corps (15th Panzer Grenadier and 116th Panzer Divisions). If the town fell before he arrived, he was to counterattack and retake it. Luettwitz would assume leadership of the battle from General of Infantry Erich Straube, commander of the LXXXVI Corps. Luettwitz's two divisions, however, could muster only fifty tanks, and Luettwitz himself was suffering from combat fatigue.[7]

By February 10, the third day of the Battle of the Reichswald, Fiebig's 84th Infantry Division had lost eight battalions and was finished. Cleve, however, was now defended tenaciously by the 7th Parachute Division and the 16th Parachute Regiment of the 6th Parachute Division, which took full advantage of the cover offered by the bomb craters and ruins. The main roads to Cleve were now flooded, which meant the British needed three-ton trucks and amphibious vehicles to bring up supplies and ammunition. Gradually, however, the weight of five Allied divisions and two armoured brigades began to tell, and by February 12, the para-troopers had fallen back.

Luettwitz arrived the next day and delivered his counterattack at dawn on February 14. The battle lasted two days. Although the Germans were outnumbered more than 10 to 1 in tanks, the Allied tanks, narrow-tracked Shermans, often found the mud impassable, and the range of the panzers' main battle gun was far superior to that of the Allied tanks and tank destroyers. In addition, the 15th Panzer Grenadier was equipped with the Jagdpanther tank destroyer, which carried an 88mm high-velocity anti-tank gun on a turretless Panther chassis. In the end, superior numbers did win out, and the XXXXVII Panzer Corps was pushed back to the German border.

Still, it took another week for the floodwaters of the Roer to recede, allowing Lieutenant General William H. Simpson's U.S. 9th Army to deliver what turned out to be the decisive blow.

The highly capable Simpson massed 11 full-strength divisions—more than 300,000 men, backed by 130 battalions of artillery (more than 2,000 guns) and almost 1,400 tanks. At the point of the main attack (in the zones of the U.S. XIII and XIX Corps), the Americans massed one artillery piece for every ten yards of front.[8]

General of Infantry Gustav-Adolf von Zangen's 15th Army faced Simpson. It held a front fifty miles long with six infantry divisions and no reserves.[9] Nearby in Army Group B was Major General Baron Harald von Elverfeldt's 9th Panzer Division (along the Erft River, east of Juelich) and Lieutenant General Wend von Wietersheim's 11th Panzer Division (which had just left the Saar-Moselle triangle to the south and was in the process of assembling near Muenchen-Gladbach), but both were of *kampfgruppe* (regimental battle group) size. There were, in fact, only 276 tanks and assault guns in all of Army Group B (15th Army, 5th Panzer Army, and 7th Army).

Simpson, hoping to attain surprise, struck on the morning of February 23, before the waters of the Roer had fully receded. His timing was perfect, and German resistance was neither determined nor

LEFT: General of Infantry Gustav Adolf von Zangen, commander of the 15th Army; RIGHT: Gerd von Rundstedt, the Supreme Commander, Western Front (OB West). Rundstedt is shown here wearing the uniform of an honorary colonel of the 18th Infantry Regiment, which he wore most of the time. Occasionally someone would mistake him for an actual colonel and address him as such. When this happened, Rundstedt would just laugh. *Bundesarchiv, Bild 183-H28061 / CC-BY-SA 3.0; The Ohio State University*

effective. Not even the 12th Volksgrenadier Division performed well. Crossing the Roer against 6 German divisions, the U.S. 9th Army suffered casualties of fewer than 100 killed, 900 wounded, and 61 missing. Model at once placed the 9th Panzer and 11th Panzer Divisions under von Zangen's control, but most of the 11th had not yet arrived from the Saar-Moselle, and the 9th Panzer had only twenty-nine tanks and sixteen assault guns. Zangen was forced to commit them piecemeal just to hold his lines. Simpson had sixteen infantry battalions across the Roer at the end of the first day of attack, and thirty-eight across by nightfall on February 24.

Simpson paused to consolidate his forces and then resumed the offensive on February 25. Just as Zangen feared, his main effort was to the north, where the XII SS Corps and 338th Infantry Division were easily swept aside. On February 26, the U.S. 102nd Infantry Division entered Erkelenz—and found the town deserted. German resistance was crumbling. Commanders in the 9th U.S. Army noted that German infantrymen were "confused and drained of all enthusiasm for the fight."[10] The only serious threat came from German anti-tank fire.

Recognizing that the left wing of the 1st Parachute Army and the XII SS Corps were in danger of being encircled between the 1st Canadian and 9th U.S. Armies, Field Marshal von Rundstedt begged Hitler to allow them to withdraw. The Fuehrer refused. Lieutenant General August Winter, the deputy chief of the OKW staff, then made a personal appeal to Hitler, who finally agreed to a retreat. By February 28, German columns were fleeing toward the Rhine, pursued by American divisions and their ubiquitous fighter-bombers.

On March 2, an American task force from the U.S. XIX Corps crossed the Rhine River bridge at Oberkassel and had several tanks on the eastern bank before the Germans blew the bridge. That same day, elements of the U.S. 2nd Armored and 95th Infantry Divisions clashed with what was left of the 2nd Parachute Division (approximately four understrength battalions) at the Adolf Hitler Bridge at Krefeld-Uerdingen, north of Neuss. During the night of March 2/3, a U.S. patrol crept onto the bridge and cut every explosive wire it could find, but when the Americans attacked the bridge in strength at 7:00 a.m. on the morning of March 3, the German parachute engineers blew it up in their faces. The two bridges at Rheinhausen and Duisburg were destroyed in less dramatic fashion, before the Americans arrived.

On March 3, the U.S. 9th Army linked up with the 1st Canadian Army, connecting the forces of Operations "Veritable" and "Grenade." Together they went about crushing "the Wesel Pocket" west of the Rhine. There, General Schlemm and more than 50,000 men, including all or part of every division in his army stood before two intact Rhine River bridges that led to the German city of Wesel.

For the next four days, the Americans, British, and Canadians inched their way forward against the German 1st Parachute Army.

Then, during the night of March 9/10, the Germans suddenly broke contact, escaped across the Rhine, and blew up their bridges behind them. But not even General of Paratroopers Alfred Schlemm's skillful retreat could hide the fact that Simpson's 9th Army had driven fifty-three miles, from the Roer at Juelich to the Rhine at Wesel, in less than three weeks, and had cleared thirty-five miles of the west bank of the Rhine, from Wesel to Duesseldorf. In the process, the U.S. 9th and Canadian 1st Armies had taken 52,000 prisoners, at a cost of approximately 24,000 of their own casualties, and these figures exclude large numbers of German killed and wounded, the exact numbers of which are unknown.[11]

While Montgomery and Simpson were engaged in clearing the northern Rhineland, the bulk of Hodges's 1st U.S. Army and Patton's 3rd Army were busy cracking the Siegfried Line. Patton attacked General of Panzer Troops Erich Brandenberger's 7th Army on February 4 and pushed into the Eifel (the German Ardennes) in one of the 3rd Army's most challenging campaigns. The terrain was some of the worst in Germany. The early thaw and rains had swollen the rivers, turning the countryside into rivers of mud. The Siegfried Line was strong here, and there were mines everywhere. Despite their low numbers, the German rearguards fought an annoyingly effective delaying action. But at this crucial moment, Germany lost one of its best remaining commanders, General of Panzer Troops Erich Brandenberger.

Field Marshal Walter Model disliked Erich Brandenberger from the moment he met him. Model was a hot-blooded, profane, pro-Nazi commander with a talent for improvisation. Brandenberger was a non-Nazi, a gentleman, and a cool military professional who believed in planning, not precipitate action. On February 20, Model drove to 7th Army Headquarters, castigated Brandenberger in front of his staff, and relieved him of his command. He appointed General of Infantry Hans Felber, the commander of the XIII Corps, as his successor.

In being relieved at this moment, Brandenberger was lucky. Hardly had he left his former headquarters than it was attacked by

American bombers, and several staff officers were killed or seriously wounded.
General Felber, who had just left the
building for a farewell visit to XIII Corps,
was only slightly wounded. Major General Baron Rudolf-Christoph von Gersdorff, the chief of staff, was also lucky:
he suffered only minor injuries.[12]

Knowing that he could not expect
rational orders from Fuehrer Headquarters, Felber told his subordinates that they
would now receive two sets of orders.
One, for the official record, would direct
them to hold the line at all costs. The
other, to be destroyed after receipt, would
be Felber's actual order. If questioned, the

Baron Rudolf-Christoph von
Gersdorff. *Bundesarchiv, Bild
146-1976-130-51 / Unknown
author / CC-BY-SA 3.0*

pretext for every withdrawal would be that the Americans had attacked
in overwhelming strength.

On February 11, the Americans captured Pruem. On February 18,
they seized Kesfeld. On February 28, Bitburg fell, and the Americans
were in control of the southern Eifel.

To the north, the U.S. 1st and 3rd Armies launched a double envelopment against German forces west of the Rhine. Collins's U.S. VII Corps
spearheaded the 1st Army's drive; his objective was Cologne. Bradley
code-named his offensive Operation "Lumberjack."

Facing Collins were the weak remnants of General of Panzer
Troops Friedrich Krueger's LVIII Panzer Corps, which did not have a
single panzer, as well as the remnants of General of Infantry Friedrich
Koechling's LXXXI Corps and Corps Bayerlein, an ad hoc unit under
the command of Lieutenant General Fritz Bayerlein, which controlled
the 9th and 11th Panzer Divisions. Facing Patton's 3rd Army, behind
the Pruem and Kyll Rivers, were the shattered remnants of General
Felber's 7th Army.

Cologne, April 24, 1945. What was left of the Hohenzollern Bridge can be seen in the Rhine. German engineers destroyed it on March 1. The cathedral is seen on the left. *U.S. Army Signal Corps*

On March 1, Collins attacked across the Erft River and was soon advancing along the highway from Juelich and Dueren to Cologne. By March 2, the LVIII Panzer Corps had been defeated, but Baron von Elverfeldt's 9th Panzer Division kept up a stubborn resistance. By nightfall, however, the Americans had reached the open country three miles from the river. German troops fell back toward Cologne, though Hitler did not authorize their retreat until March 5, the day Collins attacked the city.

General of Infantry Friedrich Koechling defended Cologne's outer ring with the remnants of the 9th Panzer, 363rd Volksgrenadier, and 3rd Panzer Grenadier Divisions—the equivalent of two weak regiments. The inner ring was held by firemen, policemen, and anyone else who could be found and who could fire a rifle or a *Panzerfaust* (the single-shot, disposable anti-tank weapon of which Germany had thousands and manufactured dozens every day). However, of the 1,200 Volkssturm promised by the Gauleiter, only sixty appeared.

Collins struck the city with three divisions. Progress was slow until the morning of March 6, when the gallant and courageous young commander of the 9th Panzer Division, Major General Baron von Elverfeldt, was killed.[13] Then the resistance of the 9th Panzer—one of the best divisions in the history of the Wehrmacht—suddenly collapsed. The U.S. 3rd

Armored quickly pushed into the heart of the city, which had been reduced to a field of ruins by the ceaseless Allied air attacks. Only the stately cathedral, which the airmen had used as a turning marker, still stood. To the surprise of the American tankers, thousands of the city's survivors poured into the streets and greeted them as liberators.[14] By the time the Americans reached the Hohenzollern Bridge on the Rhine, however, 1,200 feet of it was missing.

The scapegoat for the fall of Cologne was General Friedrich Koechling, who was relieved of his command, arrested, and court-martialled for dereliction of duty and possible treason. He was temporarily replaced as commander of the LXXXI Corps by Lieutenant General Ernst-Guenther Baade, the former commander of the 90th Panzer Grenadier Division, who was now recovered from the wounds he had suffered in Italy in December.[15]

The U.S. III Corps under Major General John Millikin (four divisions) began its part of Operation "Lumberjack" on February 25, against General of Infantry Carl Puechler's LXXIV Corps, which was part of von Zangen's 15th Army. The 353rd Infantry Division was quickly smashed, but Richard Schimpf's 3rd Parachute Division, which was understrength but still battle-worthy, and Koenig's 272nd Volksgrenadier Division put up a very effective resistance, and it was March 1 before Millikin could overcome the LXXIV Corps. On March 2, however, the Americans went over to the pursuit, driving south to link up with Patton's 3rd Army.

Field Marshal Model had erroneously concluded that the main effort of the U.S. III Corps was aimed at Bonn. General von Zangen disagreed; he thought the American objective was Remagen because it was the location of an important Rhine River railroad bridge which had been converted into a traffic bridge and was a vital supply artery for 15th Army. Zangen also recognized a developing double envelopment when he saw it, and he saw no way of halting Hodges's twelve full-strength divisions (three of them armored) with his puny forces. He therefore asked permission to withdraw Walter Lucht's LXVI Corps (5th Parachute Division) and General of Infantry Otto Hitzfeld's LXVII Corps (89th Infantry and 277th Volksgrenadier Divisions) to positions east of the Rhine. Model obeyed Hitler's orders and rejected the request; the two corps would continue to hold their West Wall positions despite the evolving encirclement. Map 7.2 shows the American encirclement of the Ruhr.

Meanwhile, to face the next onslaught of the U.S. 3rd Army, General Felber deployed three corps, north to south: General of Cavalry Count Edwin von Rothkirch und Trach's LIII Corps (three Volksgrenadier divisions) near Pruem; Lieutenant General Count Ralph von Oriola's XIII Corps (two Volksgrenadier divisions and the 2nd Panzer Division) opposite Bitburg; and Beyer's LXXX Corps (two Volksgrenadier divisions) between Bitburg and the Moselle. The remnants of the 9th and 276th Volksgrenadier were so small that they were attached to other units. In all, Felber had ten divisions to cover thirty-five miles of front, but all were kampfgruppen and aside from a handful of assault guns only the remnant of Lauchert's 2nd Panzer had some armor and was mobile. General

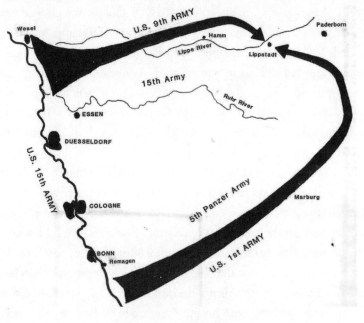

Map 7.2

Felber was under no illusions: his army would not be able to hold its positions if Patton attacked them with significant forces. He recommended 7th Army be allowed to withdraw behind the Moselle prior to Patton's attack, but Hitler would not consider it. Felber then decided to commit his small Tiger reserve to the most threatened sector, which he considered to be Rothkirch's LIII Corps, east of Bitburg, opposite the U.S. 4th Armored Division. He was still trying to find enough gas to move it when the Americans struck.

The U.S. 3rd Army's attack, spearheaded by Lieutenant General Troy Middleton's VIII Corps, began on March 1 and initially met Major General "King Ludwig" Heilmann's tough 5th Parachute Division, a kampfgruppe on the extreme left flank of the 15th Army, near its junction with the 7th Army. Resistance here was so stiff that Middleton considered delaying the commitment of his armor for twenty-four hours, but, in the end, unleased his tanks on March 3, as originally planned. The 5th Parachute fell back skillfully and escaped across the Kyll, where it again held the U.S. VIII Corps to minor gains until March 8. On March 3, Manton Eddy's U.S. XII Corps attacked the LIII Corps and had a sizable bridgehead over the Kyll by nightfall on March 4. Patton committed the U.S. 4th Armored Division to the exploitation the following morning, and the 3rd Army was rolling again. On March 5, Eddy smashed the southern wing of Rothkirch's LIII Corps and the northern wing of Ralph von Oriola's XIII. During the night, General von Rothkirch drained the last drops of fuel out of his command cars and headquarters vehicles and sent it to Weidenbach, where a few Tigers were sitting in a repair shop. They were ordered to rush to the front but were slow to get started and were swamped by the American advance.

Rothkirch also ordered Major General Tolsdorff, whose 340th Volksgrenadier was still holding its positions on the Kyll west of the American penetration, to take his division out of the impending pocket via a secondary road north of Weidenbach. He was then to establish blocking positions near Oberstadtfeld.

Count von Rothkirch's orders to Tolsdorff were based on the assumption that the Americans would continue their usual practice of halting for the night. When Tolsdorff's vanguard arrived near Oberstadtfeld, however, he found that the U.S. 4th Armored Division had already seized the town.

Theodor Tolsdorff was one of the best soldiers in the German Army and a hero of the Third Reich. He had risen from first lieutenant in 1939 to major general in 1944 and was wounded a dozen times in the process. Knowing that an attack on the Americans at Oberstadtfeld was futile (it was held by the equivalent of an armored brigade), Tolsdorff realized that he and his men would have to retreat around the advancing Americans. The daring East Prussian abandoned his vehicles and heavy equipment, including his artillery, and tried to escape by infiltrating to the northeast. Hiding by day and moving by night, Tolsdorff and his men worked their way through woods and open fields, and crossed roads and highways in the intervals between American columns. Remarkably, the young divisional commander made good his escape, taking most of his command with him. On March 18, he became only the 25th German soldier to be decorated with the Knight's Cross with Oak Leaves, Swords, and Diamonds. On April 1, he was promoted again. He had risen from major to lieutenant general in less than a year, and, at the age of thirty-five, was named acting commander of the LXXXII Corps. Despite being wounded fourteen times in six years, Tolsdorff survived the war and died in Wuppertal in 1979.[16]

General of Cavalry Count Edwin von Rothkirch und Trach as a prisoner of war, March 6, 1945. *U.S. Army*

Although Tolsdorff was able to pull off a brilliant escape, he was not able take up the blocking position assigned to him by General Rothkirch. Most of the LIII Corps was unable to escape the trap. The majority of the demoralized men did not try too hard, either—they surrendered in droves. General Rothkirch saw one large mass of German soldiers clustering around what appeared to be tanks. He went to investigate and realized too late that the tanks were American, and the Germans were surrendering.

"Where do you think you're going?" an American lieutenant asked Rothkirch as he tried to sneak away.

"It looks like I'm going to the American rear," the general responded, with a touch of irony.[17]

Army Group B learned of Rothkirch's capture by monitoring an American radio network. Model promptly replaced him with Lieutenant General Walter Botsch, commander of the 18th and 26th Volksgrenadier Divisions, which had been assigned the task of forming a bridgehead from Bonn to Remagen. Botsch wanted to brief his successor on the situation in the Bonn-Remagen bridgehead, but Model considered the situation so desperate that he ordered Botsch to take charge of the LIII Corps at once. Botsch had no choice but to leave for the front and hope that he could find his command post before the Americans found him.

The LIII Corps (now part of 15th Army) was in imminent danger of encirclement, as was Lucht's LXVI and Hitzfeld's LXVII, but still Hitler would not allow a withdrawal. Model ordered Wend von Wietersheim to recross the Rhine at Bonn with what was left of his 11th Panzer Division and counterattack southwest toward Rheimbach, to cut off the spearheads of the U.S. III Corps. This order was, of course, impossible to execute. By the time Wietersheim arrived in Bonn, the bridges were down. All this maneuver accomplished was to waste gasoline that the Germans could not spare.

Zangen also ordered a counterattack, but it failed to materialize. General Botsch located his corps on March 6 and found it was smaller than a peacetime division. The next day it was scattered by the U.S. 11th Armored Division, and separately the LXVI and LXVII Corps began to disintegrate. "Everywhere," U.S. Army historian Charles B. MacDonald wrote later, "irregular columns of foot troops and horse-drawn vehicles toiled toward the Rhine, hoping to find a barge, a ferry, perhaps a bridge still standing. Other Germans gave themselves up by the hundreds . . . while others—some successfully, most not—tried to slip behind the armored spearheads to escape southward across the Moselle. Abandoned equipment, vehicles, anti-tank guns, and field pieces, many of them smoldering, dotted the Eifel in macabre disarray."[18]

General Lucht escaped the debacle with his staff, as did General Hitzfeld, but "King Ludwig" Heilmann, the commander of the 5th Parachute Division, was captured, along with all but a small fragment of his command. Major General Wilhelm Vielig, the commander of the 277th Volksgrenadier Division, received a hold-at-all-costs order from Berlin. He sent the remnants of his combat units back behind the Rhine but did not withdraw his headquarters. He was captured when his command post was overrun on March 9.[19] At last the 15th Army was back on the east bank of the Rhine, but it no longer had enough men left to effectively defend it.

CHAPTER VIII

REMAGEN

THE BRIDGEHEAD

As masses of German troops straggled across the Ludendorff Bridge at Remagen, the German chain of command for defending the bridge was a mess of confusion. The area combat commander, Captain Willi Bratge, lacked authority to destroy the bridge except in an emergency. The bridge was technically under the command of Captain Karl Friesenhahn, an officer of engineers. But neither Bratge nor Friesenhahn commanded the anti-aircraft battery overlooking the bridge, and the local Volkssturm were commanded by the district's Nazi Party officials.

Major General Richard von Bothmer had just replaced Lieutant General Walter Botsch as commander of the Bonn-Remagen bridgehead. Bothmer, the former commandant of Bonn, was unfamiliar with the situation and Botsch did not have time to brief him. General Zangen, as commander of the retreating 15th Army, ordered General Otto Hitzfeld, the commander of the LXVII Corps, to send an officer to check on the situation at Remagen. Hitzfeld sent his adjutant, Major Hans Scheller, telling him to make sure that the bridge was ready for demolition.

Scheller left LXVII Corps Headquarters at 2:00 a.m. on March 7, but the roads were so clogged with retreating troops that he did not reach Remagen until 11:00 a.m. on March 8.[1]

By this time, the U.S. 9th Armored Division was trying to sever the Ahr Valley highway near Bad Neuenahr, to cut off the retreat of Hitzfeld's corps. Shortly before 1:00 p.m., after barreling through minimal opposition, a column from the 9th Armored reached the high bluff overlooking Remagen and, to their surprise, found the Ludendorff Bridge intact.

The bridge at Remagen was a 1,069-foot railroad bridge, wide enough for two train tracks plus footpaths on either side, but by securing planks to the rails it had been converted to allow vehicular traffic. Just beyond the eastern edge of the bridge, the tracks entered a tunnel which ran through a clifflike hill called the Erpeler Ley. It was from here that Captain Friesenhahn planned to blow the bridge. He was, however, operating under a severe handicap. Because the explosives on one of the bridges at Cologne had been prematurely detonated by an American bomb, OKW had decreed that demolitions could not be placed on a bridge until the enemy was within eight kilometers (about five miles) of it, and the igniters were not to be attached until demolition seemed imminent. Finally, the demolition order itself had to be issued in writing by the officer in tactical command of the area. At Remagen on the morning of March 7, this officer was Captain Bratge. He had only his own company (thirty-six men), one hundred twenty engineers under Friesenhahn, and five hundred unreliable Volkssturm, most of whom were looking for the most suitable moment to desert (all but six did). Though the anti-aircraft battery on the western bluff was not under his command, it did provide a measure of comfort—until midmorning, when it was taken down and joined the retreat across the river.

Bratge had tried to contact General Botsch's command post but failed, so he was quite pleased when Major Scheller showed up shortly after 11:15 a.m. and informed him that he had been sent to take command of the bridge.

The Ludendorff Bridge after its capture. *U.S. Army Signal Corps*

Scheller was reluctant to blow the bridge because German combat troops were still making their way across it. When the American tanks finally advanced toward the bridge at 4:00 p.m., Scheller and Bratge were in the tunnel on the east bank; Friesenhahn, however, was on the west side of the river. As he hurried across the bridge, a shell from an American tank knocked him out for several vital minutes. Then he pulled himself from the plank floor and, still dazed, made his way to the tunnel. American tanks were shelling the east bank with white phosphorus rounds, and the tunnel was full of disorganized soldiers, screaming civilians, crying children, terrified Volkssturm, and cowering foreign laborers. Captain Bratge met Friesenhahn at the entrance and yelled at him to blow the bridge. But when Friesenhahn turned the detonator key designed to activate the electric circuit and set off the explosives, nothing happened.

Realizing that the circuit was probably broken, Friesenhahn ordered a repair team to the bridge. The Americans, however, were now too close, and swept the bridge with machine gun and tank fire. Friesenhahn called for a volunteer to go to the bridge and manually ignite the primer cord. A brave sergeant responded, and dodging a hail of American bullets, ignited the primer cord and sprinted back to the tunnel. Then came a deafening roar, flying timbers, and blinding smoke. When the smoke cleared, Friesenhahn could hardly believe his eyes. The bridge was still there.

So were the American infantrymen. They dashed from girder to girder, exchanging fire with the German infantry on the east bank, tearing out packets of explosives and throwing them into the river. As the Americans spread out on the east bank and advanced on the Erpeler Ley, Major Scheller tried to contact higher headquarters, to report that the bridge had not been blown and was about to be captured. When he could not reach anyone, he mounted a bicycle and rode off to give his report in person. Shortly thereafter, Captains Bratge and Friesenhahn surrendered, along with the other Germans in the tunnel.

The Americans, meanwhile, could hardly believe their luck. The news traveled up the U.S. chain of command like an electrical shock. By late afternoon, General Bradley was ordering General Hodges, the 1st Army commander, to shove every unit he could across the river. Within the next twenty-four hours, eight thousand American soldiers crossed the Rhine, and Eisenhower had already given Bradley permission to reinforce the bridgehead with five divisions.

As was his wont, Field Marshal Model was somewhere at the front; while being a frontline officer won him enormous respect, it could also interfere with communications, especially as his headquarters was relocating. When he finally returned on the morning of March 8, and was briefed on events, he ordered the 11th Panzer Division at Bonn to turn south, crush the American bridgehead, and blow up the Remagen bridge. Under his command, General von Wietersheim had four thousand men, twenty-five tanks, and eighteen pieces of artillery—but no gas. By the time he obtained the necessary fuel and pushed to within striking distance of the American perimeter, it was March 10: far too late for the 11th Panzer to be a real threat to the Americans. Model, meanwhile, ordered the recently created and improvised Corps Bayerlein to smash through to the Ludendorff Bridge. He assigned Bayerlein the 11th Panzer, the Panzer Lehr Division (down to a combat strength of about three hundred men and fifteen tanks), the remnants of the 106th Panzer Brigade (five operational tanks) and the 9th Panzer Division (six hundred men and fifteen tanks). Eventually Bayerlein's command would be reinforced to a strength of about 10,000 men under HQ, LIII Corps. (Lieutenant General Walter Botsch gave up this command on March 25 and was given command of the LVIII Panzer Corps, replacing General of Panzer Troops Walter Krueger, who was placed in Fuehrer Reserve.[2] The LIII Corps was given to Bayerlein. It absorbed Corps Bayerlein, which then ceased to exist.)

On March 9, Bayerlein arrived at Model's HQ and outlined a plan to attack the bridgehead, beginning at nightfall on March 10. Model rejected the plan; first, he wanted Bayerlein to cordon off the bridgehead, then to attack it. In adopting this method, Model lost the battle before it began. Due to the speed and strength of the American buildup, Bayerlein would be forced to commit his new units as soon as they arrived and would never be able to do more than launch a few local counterattacks.

On March 8, in reaction to the fall of the Remagen bridge, Hitler summoned Field Marshal Albert Kesselring from Italy to Berlin and, the following day, named him OB West. Field Marshal von Rundstedt was sent into his fourth—and final—retirement.

"I am the new V-3!" Kesselring announced to the command staff of OB West on March 10, referring to the new "reprisal" or "super-weapons" designed by the Germans. By that time, however, Hodges had reinforced General Milliken's U.S. III Corps at Remagen with the 7th Armored Division (March 7–8); Bonn had fallen (March 9); and U.S. heavy artillery could find no suitable targets west of the Rhine. General von Bothmer blew up the Rhine River bridge at Bonn and escaped to the east bank. But because he evacuated Bonn without orders, he was court-martialed, reduced to the ranks, and sentenced to prison. Rather than accept this humiliation he shot himself in the courtroom on March 10.

Field Marshal Albert Kesselring, the last OB West. *Bundesarchiv, Bild 183-R93434 / CC-BY-SA 3.0*

Meanwhile, German troops, abandoning their vehicles and heavy weapons, escaped across the Ahr River via ferries or small river craft. The Americans captured about eighteen thousand prisoners—far fewer than they had hoped, but the German troops who escaped were disorganized and equipped only with what weapons they could carry.

The Germans continued their attempts to destroy the Remagen bridge. They used artillery, including the huge Karl Howitzer (a 540mm gun); eleven V-2s, fired from the Netherlands; and seven underwater divers, all of whom were captured. Nothing worked. Then, shortly before 3:00 p.m. on March 17, the bridge simply collapsed. No one dramatic action caused it to fall, and it was not under attack at the time. About two hundred engineers were working on it when they heard a sharp crack, followed by another. The bridge trembled and the men dropped their tools and ran for the nearest shore. The bridge swayed, twisted, and fell into the Rhine. Of those working on the bridge at the time, twenty-eight were killed and ninety-three were injured.

As the Americans advanced, a raving Hitler looked for more scapegoats for the disaster at Remagen, in addition to von Rundstedt and von Bothmer. A special three-man military tribunal was convened under the direction of SS Lieutenant General Rudolf Huebner and, with no regard for fairness, sentenced to death Lieutenant Karl Heinz Peters, commander of the 44th *Flakwerfer* Battery; Major Scheller, who had taken command at the bridge at Remagen; and Majors Herbert Strobel and August Kraft, who had commanded engineer units nearby. The four officers were

executed by a firing squad. Also sentenced to death was Captain Bratge,
but he survived because he was in
American captivity. Captain Friesenhahn was acquitted.

Hitler's micromanagement of
the war was getting worse—and
even more removed from reality.
Minister of Munitions Albert Speer
remembered visiting Army Group B
Headquarters just after Model had
received orders for attacking the
Remagen bridgehead. The field marshal was "in a state of fury" because
the units Hitler had earmarked for
the attack had no chance of reaching
Remage. They were in tatters and
out of fuel. The attack was never
launched.

By March 17, Model had committed seven Volksgrenadier divi-

Lieutenant General Fritz Bayerlein.
Because of his eager assistance to
them, his reputation among post-war
historians is higher than it was with
his superiors during World War II.
Bundesarchiv Bild 146-1978-033-02/
Dinstuehler/CC-BY-SA 3.0

sions, the 3rd and 5th Parachute Divisions, and the Headquarters of the
LXXIV Corps (General of Infantry Carl Puechler) and LXVII Corps
(Hitzfeld) to containing the bridgehead, as well as the units previously
committed under Corps Bayerlein.[3] Although none of these amounted
to much more than a regiment, they were nevertheless a tremendous
drain on the limited resources of Army Group B and OB West.

Under Model's orders, Bayerlein finally launched his long-delayed
counterattack on March 24. It quickly degenerated into a series of
ill-coordinated, piecemeal efforts that accomplished nothing, except to
deplete the already weak panzer reserves behind the Western Front.
Model was so dissatisfied with Bayerlein's efforts that he reassigned all
of Bayerlein's armored units to Puechler's LXXIV Corps.

A U.S. Army pontoon bridge across the Rhine, downstream from Remagen. *U.S. Army*

Eisenhower had already decided that the main Allied thrust across the Rhine would come farther north, in the zone of Montgomery's 21st Army Group, which meant that German units sent to Remagen were sent to a sideshow. But more serious than the tactical or strategic implications of the Battle of Remagen was the effect the disaster had on German morale, which was already low. With the Allies across the Rhine, German surrenders and desertions multiplied.

The Saar-Palatinate was now the only German-held territory west of the Rhine. It lay south of the Moselle and covered about three thousand square miles, including the Saar industrial area, which produced seven million tons of coal annually. Important cities within the Saar included Homburg, which featured one of the few synthetic oil plants still in production; Ludwigshafen (across the Rhine from Mannheim), home of the I. G. Farben plant, which produced nearly half the Reich's chemicals; Stuttgart, with the Mercedes-Benz facilities; and the minor but important industrial cities of Kaiserslautern, Worms, and Speyer.

On March 13, Dever's 6th Army Group and Patton's 3rd Army launched a major offensive in the Saar-Palatinate. Facing them was Army Group G, which included General of Infantry Hermann Foertsch's 1st Army and Felber's 7th Army, which was already on the point of disintegration. SS Colonel General Paul Hausser, the commander-in-chief of Army Group G, had been begging for permission to fall back behind the Rhine since early March, but the Fuehrer's answer was uncompromising: the Saar-Palatinate would be held.

Meanwhile, Major General Meinrad von Lauchert's greatly reduced 2nd Panzer Division was pushed back against the Rhine. With no bridge, the men's only hope to escape was to swim across the river. Most of the men, including Lauchert, reached the east bank on March 20. The wet general, who was disgusted by Hitler's conduct of the war and the unnecessary slaughter of his division, decided to "quit the war" and walked home to Bamberg, the peacetime base of his old 35th Panzer Regiment, apparently assuming that the Nazis would conclude that he had been killed or captured and would not look for him. He was correct.[4]

Over the next nine days, the American and French forces—aided by their ever-present fighter-bombers—crushed the rag-tag German battalions. On March 23, Hitler finally authorized the 1st Army to retreat across the Rhine. General Foertsch had actually begun the retreat the night before, and many guns and vehicles were already on the west bank, along with thousands of demoralized foot soldiers. Army Group G, however, was smashed, with the 1st and 7th Armies having lost up to 80 percent of their infantry strength in the Saar-Palatinate battles. Total German losses easily exceeded 100,000 men (including 88,000 captured), while the U.S. 7th and 3rd Armies and the attached French units lost roughly 20,000. Army Group G no longer had enough battleworthy units to prevent the Franco-Americans from crossing the Rhine.

THE RHINE CROSSINGS

General Hans Felber, the commander of the 7th Army, had an impossible task: hold more than fifty miles of the Rhine from Wiesbaden (opposite Mainz) to Mannheim with four divisions, three of which were Volksgrenadier: the 246th, 352nd, and 559th. He had one corps head-quarters left (von Oriola's XIII), the 246th and 352nd were *kampfgrup-pen* of only about four hundred men each—smaller than a peacetime battalion—and the 559th was reduced to about 60 percent of its original strength. Felber had no contact with the 1st Army to the south and only one division (the 159th Infantry) in reserve. To hold the northern section of his line, he was forced to resort to using Headquarters, *Wehrkreis XII* (XII Military District), which was located at Wiesbaden and was com-manded by General of Artillery Herbert Osterkamp.[5] (*Wehrkreise* were territorial replacement and training commands. They performed excel-lent service for the Third Reich throughout their existence, but their staffs consisted mainly of older-aged men or wounded veterans who were no longer physically fit for active campaigning.) The *Wehrkreise* had no

General of Infantry Hans Felber (left), SS Major Bernhard Griese, and SS-Brigade-fuehrer Carl Oberg in Marseille, January 24, 1943. Felber cooperated with the SS who were deporting Jews from southern France. Felber (1889–1962) was one of the few German generals who did not serve on the Eastern Front. An Allied POW until 1948, he was never tried for crimes against the Jews. *Bundesarchiv Bild 101I-027-1476-37A/Vennemann, Wolfgang/CC-BY-SA 3.0*

divisions as such and consisted exclusively of security units and replacement-training battalions.

Felber and the other senior German commanders hoped that Generals George S. Patton and Jacob L. Devers would halt and conduct an extensive buildup before attacking across the Rhine. Characteristically, however, Patton crossed the river at high speed. Late on the night of March 22, the U.S. 5th Infantry Division launched an assault crossing at Oppenheim, south of Mainz, taking the defenders completely by surprise. On March 23, the Americans met resistance from an engineer replacement-training battalion, a *Landesschuetzen* replacement-training battalion (made up of men forty-five years of age or older), a handful of Waffen-SS, and some Volkssturm battalions (which were useless and surrendered).

Hans Felber knew he needed to counterattack immediately. He took officer-candidates from the Wiesbaden Officer Training School, formed them into a regimental-size kampfgruppe, and threw them into a night attack on March 23–24. Although they briefly disrupted the American advance, they were easily defeated.

General Patton succeeded in crossing the Rhine before his archrival, Field Marshal Montgomery, if only by a matter of hours. By the afternoon of March 24, the U.S. 4th Armored Division was driving toward Darmstadt. To prevent the encirclement of the few forces he had there, Felber abandoned the city. By March 26, American tanks had reached the southern suburbs of Frankfurt.

At 2:30 a.m. on March 26, Major General Wade Hampton Haislip's XV U.S. Corps of General Alexander Patch's 7th Army launched a deliberate, two-division assault across the Rhine at Worms. Resistance was feeble and before the day was over, the U.S. 7th Army was linked up with the U.S. 3rd Army and had cut the Darmstadt-Mannheim autobahn, eight miles beyond the Rhine, smashing the 246th Volksgrenadier Division in the process. The American forces captured (or accepted the surrender of) more than 2,500 Germans, with a total loss of fewer than 200 men. During the night, Patch sent across the 12th Armored Division and prepared to drive into the rear of the German 1st Army.

Hans Felber was sacked on March 26 and replaced by General of Infantry Hans von Obstfelder, a tough man of Nazi sympathies. Obstfelder was succeeded as commander of the 19th Army by General of Panzer Troops Erich Brandenberger, who had led the 7th Army until he had been unfairly sacked by Model four weeks earlier. With the possible exception of Schlemm, the commander of the 1st Parachute, Brandenberger was the best army commander on the Western Front in 1945 and the Wehrmacht could ill afford to leave him unemployed for long—although there was really very little he or anyone else could do at this stage.

On March 27, the U.S. XX Corps crossed the Rhine-Main arch at Mainz. General of Infantry Baptist Kniess's LXXXV Corps had taken over this sector only two days before from Wehrkreis XII, and the only defensive force available was the 159th Infantry (formerly Reserve) Division, which had practically no combat value. Kniess had been promised that he would be reinforced with the 9th Panzer, 11th Panzer, and 6th SS Mountain, but none of these divisions ever arrived. Unable to hold off an entire American corps with his meager forces, Kniess requested permission to retreat but was curtly turned down by General Obstfelder. Kniess withdrew most of his troops anyway, leaving only a thin screen to face the Americans. Mainz and Wiesbaden fell on March 28, and Obstfelder relieved Kniess of his command the following day. He was replaced by General of Panzer Troops Baron Smilo von Luettwitz, the cousin of Heinrich von Luettwitz, the commander of the XXXXVII Panzer Corps.

Eisenhower made his main effort across the Rhine with the Allied 21st Army Group, which included the 1st Canadian, 2nd British, and U.S. 9th Armies, which brought the overwhelming superiority of 30 divisions, 6 independent brigades, more than 2,000 tanks, and 5,500 pieces of artillery against Colonel General Johannes Blaskowitz's Army Group H.

The focus of the Allied attack was the Wesel sector, which was defended by the 1st Parachute Army (II Parachute, LXXXVI and LXIII Corps, which were led by General of Paratroops Eugen Meindl, General of Infantry Erich Straube, and General of Infantry Erich Abraham, respectively). General Carl Wagener, the chief of staff of Army Group H, called the 1st Parachute a shadow of an army. Its morale, he noted, varied "from suspicion to callous resignation." Its officer corps lacked confidence. The army, he concluded, "could only pretend to resist."[6] General Schlemm, its talented commander, had been seriously wounded on March 21, when an Allied bombing raid demolished his headquarters. He was replaced by the markedly less gifted General of Infantry Guenther Blumentritt, the commander of the newly formed 25th Army, which did not have a single combat division. Blumentritt was succeeded at 25th Army in eastern Holland by General of Cavalry Philipp Kleffel.

Blumentritt's strongest corps was Eugen Meindl's II Parachute, which had only 12,000 men—less than the strength of a peacetime division. First Parachute Army's only reserves were the 130th Infantry Division (a recently upgraded training unit) and the 106th Panzer Brigade, which now had an effective strength of about a battalion. Army Group H main reserve, Heinrich von Luettwitz's XXXXVII Panzer Corps, was near at hand, but only controlled the remnants of the 116th Panzer and 15th Panzer Grenadier Divisions, which could muster thirty-five tanks and assault guns. In all of Army Group H, there were fewer than two hundred panzers and assault guns.

Supported by 3,300 guns, the Anglo-Americans crossed the Rhine on the night of March 23/24 and swept as far as Wesel without meeting much opposition. There they were met by an ad hoc force called Division Wesel. This conglomerate unit put up surprisingly stiff resistance, and the British were unable to declare Wesel secure before March 25.

The American prong of the attack landed along an eight-mile front defended—at least theoretically—by the German 180th Infantry Division and Infantry Division Hamburg.[7] Resistance varied from extremely spotty to non-existent, and two U.S. infantry divisions crossed the Rhine with a combined loss of thirty-one men. The Allies followed up the landing with Operation "Varsity": the largest airborne operation in history, with 21,680 paratroopers and glider soldiers from the U.S. 17th Airborne and British 6th Airborne Divisions delivered behind German lines by

1,696 transport planes and 1,348 gliders, themselves defended by 889 fighters. The Allied airborne troops secured the town of Diersfordt (which yielded 300 prisoners), eliminated most of the German 84th Infantry Division, and captured much of the division's staff and the LXXXVI Corps staff. The 1053rd Grenadier Regiment of the 84th Infantry, however, escaped.

Luettwitz's XXXXVII Panzer Corps arrived south of Lippe but could not stop the U.S. 9th Army's advance any more than the German II Parachute Corps could hold back the British. By nightfall on March 28, the Anglo-Americans had a bridgehead thirty-five miles long and twenty miles deep across the Rhine. At this point, the Allied armies split up. Montgomery sent the British 2nd and Canadian 1st east across the plain of Westphalia, while the U.S. 9th joined Bradley's 12th Army Group to encircle the Ruhr.

On both the Eastern and Western Fronts, casualties and sackings were heavy among German senior officers and General Staff officers. In the last three weeks of March 1945 alone, the losses included:

- Lieutenant General Joseph Kuebler, commander of the 1st Mountain Division in the Balkans, sacked on March 10.
- Major General Richard von Bothmer, commandant of Bonn, committed suicide, March 11.
- General of Infantry Hans Krebs, deputy chief of the General Staff, wounded during a U.S. bombing attack on Zossen, March 15.
- Lieutenant General Baron Siegmund von Schleinitz, commanding general, Division 402, captured on the Eastern Front, March 15.
- Lieutenant Colonel Heinz Huffmann, former commander of the 201st Assault Gun Battalion on the Eastern Front, died of wounds, March 15.

- Major of the General Staff Hans-Joachim Fleeth, 47th Volksgrenadier Division in the Rhine Palatinate, killed in action, mid-March 1945.
- Major of the General Staff Friedrich Flickinger, quartermaster, Panzer Lehr Division, died of wounds, mid-March.
- Major of the General Staff Werner Greten, chief of operations, Division 905, killed in action in the Saar-Palatinate, March.
- Lieutenant General of the General Staff Helmuth Meyer, chief intelligence officer, 15th Army, wounded in action, Western Front, on or about March 15.
- Lieutenant General Guenther Krappe, commanding general, X SS Corps, captured on the Eastern Front, March 16.
- General of Infantry Ernst-Anton von Krosigk, commander, 16th Army, killed in action near Kanden, Kurland (Courland), March 16.
- Lieutenant General Hans von Tettau, commander of Korpsgruppe von Tettau, promoted to general of infantry, placed in Fuehrer Reserve, and never reemployed after March 16.
- Major of the General Staff Joseph Bailer, quartermaster, LVI Panzer Corps, missing in action, Eastern Front, March 17.
- Captain of Reserves Ludwig Knaup, a highly decorated battalion commander in the Grossdeutschland Panzer Grenadier Division, killed in action, Eastern Front, March 18.
- Major of the General Staff Otto Spoerhase, chief of operations, 615th Special Purposes Division, killed in a bombing attack, March 18.
- Major of the General Staff Ernst Wiebecke, chief of operations, LXXXIX Corps, died of wounds received on the Western Front, March 18.

- Colonel General Fritz Fromm, former commander-in-chief of the Replacement Army, shot for cowardice, Berlin, March 19.
- Lieutenant General Erich Schneider, commander, 14th Motorized Division, relieved of his command on March 20 because he objected to Fuehrer Headquarters's interference in his operations. Arrested by the Gestapo.[8]
- Colonel of the General Staff Joseph Selmayr, chief of operations, Army Group F and OB Southeast, missing in action, Balkans, March 20.
- General of Parachute Troops Alfred Schlemm, commander, 1st Parachute Army, wounded in a bombing attack on March 21 and unable to return to duty during World War II.[9]
- Major of the General Staff Heiner Langhans, chief of intelligence, XXVII Corps, missing in action, East Prussia, Eastern Front, March.
- Colonel of General Staff Karl Jessel, former chief of staff to the German Military Representative in Hungary, wounded on the Eastern Front, March 22.
- Major of the General Staff Kurt Misbach, employed as a battalion commander in the 15th Infantry Division, wounded in action in Slovakia, Eastern Front, March 22.
- Lieutenant General Hans-Guenther von Rost, commander, 44th Infantry Division "Hoch und Deutschmeister," killed in action, near Stuhlweissenburg, Hungary, on the Eastern Front, March 23.
- Major General Siegfried Runge, Commandant of Mainz and Wiesbaden and holder of the *Pour le Merite*, killed in action, Western Front, March 24.

- Major Johann-Friedrich Merkatz, commander of the II/ Parachute Panzer Regiment, Hermann Goering Division, wounded in action, March 24.
- General of Infantry Otto Woehler, commander-in-chief, Army Group South, sacked, March 25.
- Major of the General Staff Wolfgang Fiedler, operations staff, VI Corps, killed in action, Eastern Front, March 25.
- Luftwaffe Colonel Kurt Groeschke, Knight of the Iron Cross with Oak Leaves, commander of the 15th Parachute Regiment, missing in action, Western Front, March 26.[10]
- Major of the General Staff Theodor Schmitz, quartermaster, 340th Volksgrenadier Division, missing in action, March 26.
- Lieutenant General Clemens Betzel, commander, 539th Infantry Division, killed in action, Danzig, Eastern Front, March 27.
- Major of the General Staff Eller, chief of operation, 406th Special Purposes Division, killed in a bombing raid, Wehrkreis VI (then on the Western Front), March.[11]
- Major General Gerhard Fischer, Wehrmacht Commandant of Koblenz, captured by the Americans, March 27.
- Colonel Helmuth Hufenbach, commander, 562nd Volksgrenadier Division, killed in action, East Prussia, March 27.
- Major General Hans-Ulrich Back, commanding general, 232nd Panzer Division, badly wounded, March 28.
- Lieutenant General Dr. Hans Boelsen, commander, Division Number 172, captured in the Netherlands, March 29.
- Colonel General Heinz Guderian, chief of the General Staff, sacked, March 28.
- Lieutenant General Rudolf Habenicht, commander, Division 463, captured on the Western Front, March 28.

- Lieutenant General Hans Bergen, commander, Division 476, captured, Western Front, March 29.
- Colonel Dr. Albert Seekirchner, commander, Arko 129 (129th Artillery Command), accidentally killed at the Pillau Airport, Eastern Front, March 30.
- General of Infantry Baptist Kniess, commander, LXXXV Corps on the Western Front, relieved of his command and transferred to Fuehrer Reserve, March 31.
- General of Infantry Otto Schellert, former commander, Wehrkreis IX (Kassel), discharged/expelled from the service, March 31.
- Major General Helmuth Walter, commander, 166th Infantry Division in Denmark, relieved of his command, March 31, and expelled from the service, April 10.

CHAPTER IX

THE BATTLE OF THE RUHR POCKET

The Ruhr had long been Germany's industrial heartland, but by 1945, its factories lacked raw materials, its transportation networks were under attack, and Allied bombing had so completely leveled the Ruhr's big cities that German civilians joked that Allied bombers would soon need to bring their own targets. Nevertheless, the Ruhr still accounted for a large percentage of Germany's war production. The task of defending it fell to Field Marshal Walter Model's Army Group B, which was part of OB West.

Field Marshal Kesselring, Commander-in-Chief of OB West, "felt like a concert pianist who is asked to play a Beethoven sonata...on an ancient, rickety, and out-of-tune instrument." Hitler, he recalled, was "obsessed with the idea of some miraculous salvation" and "clung to it like a drowning man to straw."[1] On all active fronts, but especially in the south and west, the Fuehrer's "hold at all costs" orders had taken the place of sound military strategy. Kesselring dutifully passed on every one of Hitler's orders, even when they were senseless or totally irrational, and insisted that the responsible commander do everything in his power to carry them out. As a result, Army Group G was smashed, and by the end of March, the 1st and 7th Armies were incapable of offering effective resistance.

Army Group B was next in the line of fire. It consisted of the 5th Panzer and 15th Armies, under the command of Colonel General Joseph Harpe and General of Infantry Adolf von Zangen, respectively. Not surprisingly at this stage in the war, its morale was low, it had too few junior officers, and there were only sixty-five tanks left in the entire command.

Leading Army Group B was Field Marshal Walter Model. Born in the Genthin district of Magdeburg on January 24, 1891, his family had no military background but was strongly religious. His father initially wanted to be a priest but became a music teacher at the girls' school at Genthin instead. He advanced in his profession and eventually was named Royal Music Director. Young Walter was educated at the *Buerg-erschule* (public elementary school) at Genthin, the *Gymnasium* at

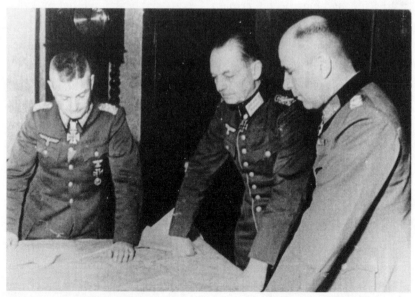

Walter Model (left) with Gerd von Rundstedt and Model's long-time chief of staff, Hans Krebs, who later became chief of the General Staff (OKH). *Bundesarchiv, Bild 146-1978-024-31 / CC-BY-SA 3.0*

Erfurt, and the humanistic *Domgymnasium* in Naumburg. He received his *Abitar* (roughly translated as "school-leaving certificate") on February 14, 1909.[2] Three days later he joined the 52nd Infantry Regiment at Cottbus as a Fahnenjunker.

Model's family was one of modest means and, as General Walter Nehring later declared, a junior officer in the Imperial Army served the Fatherland "pretty much at his own expense." In addition to the financial burden, Model had a difficult time with the harsh training program. One of his sergeants even told him he was not tough enough to become an officer. Cadet Model nevertheless stuck with it, attended the *Kriegschule* (War School) at Neisse (now Nysa, Poland), and was commissioned a second lieutenant in 1910. He was initially assigned as an aide to the battalion adjutant in 1910 and in 1913 became adjutant himself. He was viewed as brilliant, ambitious, and dedicated to mastering his profession—but also as outspoken and undiplomatic, characteristics that only intensified with age.

Physically, Walter Model was considered indefatigable. He spent World War I on the Western Front, where he was highly decorated and wounded several times. One of his superiors, Prince Oskar of Prussia, noted that he was intelligent and always grasped the essentials of every probem, but he was also brusque and not an easy man to have as a subordinate. He was even more uncomfortable to have as a superior. He was regimental adjutant in 1917, when he was transferred to the logistical staff of the 5th Infantry Division. Finally, he was sent to Sedan, where he underwent an abbreviated General Staff training course. (The shortage of General Staff officers was so great that the course was reduced from three years to one month.) Model then became Ib (chief supply officer) of the Guards Replacement Division and finally, in 1918, Ib of the 36th Reserve Division. Here he also briefly served as a company commander.

After the armistice, Captain Model was posted to Danzig and the staff of the XII Corps, but he soon joined Freikorps Hacketau in "the war after the war." In this time of civil unrest, Model considered leaving the army to become a physician and even registered at the University of Halle one semester. During this period, he met Herta Huyssen, the daughter of a wealthy family. They were married in 1921.[3]

He decided to remain in the army. Young Model alternated between General Staff positions and command assignments. In the 1920s and into the 1930s, he often invited junior officers to his home. They were warned, however, not to "talk shop" (discuss military matters) or tell war stories, which Model detested. Political topics were also off-limits.

Model commanded a company in the 14th Infantry Regiment (1919); commanded the machine gun company of the 18th Infantry Regiment (1920) and helped suppress Communist uprisings in the Ruhr; held a General Staff position with the VI Artillery Command (1921); and was a company commander in the 8th (Prussian) Infantry Regiment at Goerlitz. In 1925, he joined the staff of the 3rd Infantry Division in Berlin. From 1928 to 1931, Model (who was promoted to major in 1929) was assigned to the training section (T 4) of the *Truppenamt*, as the clandestine General Staff was called.

As a major, Model wrote an essay on the Prussian Field Marshal August Neithardt Gneisenau, a military reformer and hero of the Napoleonic Wars, which later was included in an anthology on leadership published by General Friedrich von Cochenhausen in 1930. Perhaps as a result, he was given the duty of teaching military history to General Staff officers. Students admired his knowledge, but he talked too fast, could be abrasive and impatient, and had a hot temper. As he rose in rank, Model became ever more demanding of subordinates and intolerant of mistakes.

In 1931, Model was named chief of staff of the Board of Youth Efficiency Training (called the "Kuratorium"), which was designed to help Germany circumvent the Treaty of Versailles, which limited the army to one hundred thousand men. Boys and young men received eight weeks' training. It was theoretically non-military, but it was essentially a basic training course.

Promoted to lieutenant colonel on November 1, 1932, he assumed command of the II Battalion/Infantry Regiment Allenstein in East Prussia in 1933. The following year he was advanced to colonel and took command of the regiment itself. He continued his upward advancement in 1935 when he became head of Department T 8 (technology) of the General Staff in Berlin. His appointment was something of a surprise because while recognized as a forward thinker, he had no particular expertise in technology. The appointment, however, proved inspired, as he helped develop the Wehrmacht's highly effective assault guns.

In 1938 he was promoted to major general and named chief of staff of Wehrkreis IV at Dresden. In 1939, during the Polish campaign, he was chief of staff of the IV Corps. On October 23, 1939, he was named chief of staff of the 16th Army under General Ernst Busch. He was promoted to lieutenant general on April 1, 1940, and performed well during the conquest of France, Belgium, and Luxembourg.

On November 13, 1940, Model succeeded Baron Leo Geyr von Schweppenburg as commanding general of the 3rd Panzer Division. He led it across the Soviet border on June 22, 1941, as part of Guderian's 2nd Panzer Group.

His division crossed the Bug, the Beresina, and the Dnieper, and helped encircle Bialystok, Minsk, and Smolensk. He led the panzer army's spearhead in the battle at Kiev, where 667,000 Soviet soldiers were surrounded and captured. On October 26, he became commander of the XXXXI Motorized (later Panzer) Corps, and was promoted to general of panzer troops, backdated to October 1.

By now, Walter Model was known throughout the Reich as a man of great physical courage, tactical brilliance, single-mindedness of purpose, and, above all, incredible energy. He was always near the front, and his troops loved him. Many of his staff officers and immediate subordinates, however, despised him. It was reported that his behavior was so bad that every member of the staff of the XXXXI Corps requested a transfer. Allegedly, the stress of working with Model drove Colonel Hans Roettiger, the chief of staff, to contemplate suicide.[4]

Model led his corps on Moscow and against Stalin's Winter Offensive, which began on December 16, 1941. The health of Model's army commander, Colonel General Adolf Strauss, gave way under the strain. Model, who had been a divisional commander only three months before, was selected to replace him.

The 9th Army was nearly surrounded by five Soviet armies, but Model repelled every Soviet attack. "It was a strange thing, but the moment Model assumed command of the Army the regiments seemed to gain strength," Paul Carell wrote later. "It was not only the crisp precision of the new C-in-C's orders—but he also turned up everywhere in person.... He would suddenly jump out of his command jeep outside a battalion headquarters, or appear on horseback through the deep snow in the foremost line, encouraging, commending, criticizing and occasionally even charging against the enemy penetrations at the head of a battalion, pistol in hand. The live-wire general was everywhere. And even where he was not his presence was felt."[5]

During this battle, Model had his first confrontation with Hitler—and won. On January 20, 1942, he flew to Fuehrer Headquarters to meet with the dictator. He expected his battered army would soon face another Red offensive, and he wanted an additional corps assigned to his command. Hitler agreed but insisted on placing the unit at Gzhatsk. Model wanted it near Rzhev, almost a hundred miles to the north. What General Friedrich Wilhelm von Mellenthin described as a "acrimonious argument" ensued. It ended when Model stared coldly at the Fuehrer through his monocle and asked: "Who commands the 9th Army, my Fuehrer—you or I?" Hitler, startled, did a double take. Model told the Nazi chieftain that he knew the situation on the ground far better than the dictator and his generals understood it from their maps.

Hitler later said: "Did you see that eye? I trust that man to do it. But I wouldn't want to serve under him."

The Red Army attacked exactly where Model predicted it would—and it was badly beaten by Model's newly arrived corps.

Model surrounded the Soviet 39th Army northwest of Rzhev and by February 24, 1942, he had destroyed it. The Russians lost 187 tanks, 615 guns, and 27,000 men killed. Only 5,000 surrendered. Hitler personally decorated Model with the Oak Leaves on his Knights' Cross.

Stalin launched offensives in March, April, and from late July to mid-October 1942 to obliterate Model's 9th Army—and failed. Model did not abandon Rzhev until after the German defeat at Stalingrad in February 1943. That summer, he commanded the northern wing of Hitler's failed Kursk offensive. During his retreat west, he conducted a "scorched earth" policy against Russian civilians and co-operated with SS murder squads targeting Jews.

Model became Hitler's chief military troubleshooter, commanding 9th Army, Army Group North (January 9–March 31, 1944) and Army Group South, later Army Group North Ukraine (March 31–August 16, 1944). From June 28 to August 16, 1944, he was simultaneously commander-in-chief of Army Group Center. He was promoted to colonel general on February 1, 1942, and field marshal on March 1, 1944.

During the summer of 1944, Model gave up vast tracts of land but sustained the fighting strength of his army groups. When the Soviets finally halted, less than fifteen miles from the East Prussian border, Hitler proclaimed that Model was "the savior of the Eastern Front." Throughout the army he was known as "the Fuehrer's fireman." But an even greater challenge lay ahead. On August 16, 1944, he was sent to the Western Front to replace Guenther von Kluge as OB West and commander-in-chief of Army Group B.[6]

When Model arrived in France, the Western Front was collapsing, and though he ordered an immediate, full retreat, fewer than half his forces escaped behind the German border. Even Hitler finally realized the impossibility of successfully commanding both OB West and Army Group B, and on September 4 he recalled Gerd von Rundstedt to command OB West. As commander of Army Group B, Model defeated Montgomery at Arnhem but was unsuccessful against the Americans in the Battle of the Bulge.

Model discussing the tactical situation with SS Major General Heinz Harmel, the commander of the 10th SS Panzer Division "Frundsberg," during the Battle of Arnhem, September 1944. Arnhem was Model's only major tactical victory on the Western Front. *Bundesarchiv Bild 183-J27784/ Adendorf, Peter/ CC-BY-SA 3.0*

In March and April 1945, Model became uncharacteristically depressed, apathetic, unobservant, and indecisive. He had lost all faith that the Fuehrer's promised "miracle weapons" would save Germany, and with defeat looming—and the prospect that the Soviets would try him as a war criminal—he had taken to the bottle. In the battle of the Ruhr Pocket, the formerly brilliant tactician made mistake after mistake. He committed most of his armor at the wrong place (against the Remagen bridgehead); failed to launch effective counterattacks; improperly sited his headquarters (on the extreme right flank, while his main counterattack was on the extreme left); and became so obsessed with the battle on the northern flank of the Ruhr that he was blinded to his army's falling victim to a classic double envelopment. "Model's proverbial energy let me down; however, to this day even, the operations of Army Group B remain incomprehensible to me," Kesselring declared later.[7]

On March 25, the U.S. 1st Army began its enveloping attack south of the Ruhr with five infantry and two armored divisions. Unlike Model, General von Zangen, the commander of the 15th Army, expected just such an attack and was ready to meet it. German resistance was initially quite stiff, and the Panzer Lehr and the 9th Panzer and 11th Panzer Divisions fought with ferocity, even though all were at kampfgruppe strength. By the end of the day, however, U.S. ground and air power had combined to crush the defenders. The following day, the American 1st Army broke through southeast of Cologne, and the U.S. III Corps roared into the rear of Hitzfeld's LXVII Corps. The U.S. III Corps alone took more than seventeen thousand German prisoners. Map 8.1 shows the Battle of the Ruhr Pocket.

On March 27, Hodges's III, V, and VII Corps barreled through German territory south of the Ruhr at an incredible pace, meeting little or no opposition. On March 27, the U.S. 3rd Armored Division gained twenty-two miles and crossed the Dill River in two places. The next day, American armor gained twenty-one miles and seized the university town of Marburg. The U.S. 3rd Armored Division took more than fifteen thousand prisoners.

General Bradley ordered the 1st Army north to Paderborn, while Patton's 3rd Army protected the right flank of the encirclement by continuing northeast in the general direction of Kassel. To the west a new U.S. army, the 15th under Lieutenant General Leonard Gerow, formed an opposite wing of the impending encirclement.

The spearhead of the U.S. 1st Army was dubbed Task Force Richardson after its commander, Lieutenant Colonel Walter B. Richardson. He pushed his men forward all day and most of the night on March 29, gaining forty-five miles without suffering a single casualty. When he finally halted for the night, he was only fifteen miles from the ruined cathedral city of Paderborn.

The complexion of the battle changed completely the next day. When Task Force Richardson resumed its advance, it almost immediately slammed into an SS panzer reconnaissance training battalion from the SS panzer replacement training center at the Sennelager Maneuver Area, near Paderborn. Soon Richardson was fighting an ad hoc SS *Ersatzbrigade Westfalen* (Replacement Brigade Westphalia), which was led by the camp commandant, SS Lieutenant Colonel Hans Stern, a heavy-set thirty-eight-year-old tanker who had earned the Knight's Cross during his three years' service on the Eastern Front. Stern mustered three thousand young SS men—most of them were seventeen or eighteen. They had no artillery, mortars, or radios and were inexperienced in combat, but they were "true believers" in their Fuehrer and their cause. They also had fifty-seven panzers: thirty-two were mechanically unreliable tanks from the training school, but twenty-five of them were Royal Tigers of the 512th Heavy Panzer Battalion.

The SS Brigade Westfalen stopped the Americans in their tracks. Later that day, the Americans were reinforced and managed to push to within six miles of the town. Here, fanatical young SS men with Panzerfausts checked them again. Major General Maurice Rose, the commander of the U.S. 3rd Armored, hopped in a jeep to head to the front and supervise the final attack on Paderborn. But he, his aide, and his driver suddenly found themselves in the middle of an SS convoy. His driver hit the gas and passed one German vehicle after another until a panzer pivoted and pinned the American jeep against a tree. Confronted by an SS sergeant with a machine pistol, they surrendered. Rose, however, had a pistol in the holster under his left arm. Without thinking, he reached for it with his right hand and began to pull it out. The SS man took this as a threatening gesture, so he shot and killed him. Thus died the highest ranking Jewish general in Eisenhower's army. In the confusion, Rose's aide and driver escaped into the woods. The Germans sent a hail of bullets after them, but the two Americans escaped to Allied lines.[8]

Walter Model finally realized that he was in danger of being encircled. On March 29, he signaled OB West and asked for permission to break out. He noted that he had lost contact with HQ, 15th Army, and his only reserves were two mobile kampfgruppen (the Panzer Lehr and 3rd Panzer Grenadier Divisions), and the 176th Infantry, a partially rebuilt division. He pointed out that, if Army Group B were cut off in the Ruhr, it could hold out until April 15 at the latest.

Kesselring passed Model's request to Fuehrer Headquarters. The response from OKW: Model was to defend the Ruhr as a fortress; he was forbidden to attempt a breakout.

Although he was a Nazi sympathizer and an unimaginative commander, Kesselring was, in his own words, "more than flabbergasted by this decision."[9] Despite his personal views, Kesselring told Model he could counterattack but not retreat. Model tried to counterattack. General von Zangen was missing—his headquarters had been bypassed unwittingly by the rapidly moving Americans, and he was now hiding in the woods behind their spearheads—so Model ordered General of Artillery Karl Thoholte to counterattack on the evening of March 30.[10]

Bayerlein's LIII Corps Headquarters had just arrived, reinforcing Thoholte's two kampfgruppen, which included a dozen tanks from the Panzer Lehr, two mixed battalions of infantry and combat engineers, and a handful of assault guns. He had no artillery. Thoholte placed Bayerlein in charge of the attack. Predictably, it failed and was not even strong enough to throw a single U.S. infantry regiment out of Winterberg. Bayerlein decided to try again after the 176th Infantry Division arrived with reinforcements.

Simpson's U.S. 9th Army drove rapidly toward Hamm, on the northeastern tip of the Ruhr. South of the Lippe River, the U.S. 8th Armored Division was halted by the 116th Panzer Division, but north of the river, resistance was minimal. The Americans crossed the Dortmund-Ems Canal on the afternoon of March 30 and cut the two major railroad lines leading north from Hamm the following day, leaving only one railroad open between the Ruhr and the rest of the Reich.

The rapid American thrust cut the 1st Parachute Army in two. North of the American breakout, it fell back toward the Teutoburger Wald. To the south, Luettwitz's XXXXVII Panzer Corps and Abraham's LXIII Corps appealed to Model for orders. The field marshal placed them under Luettwitz's command (Group von Luettwitz) and gave him responsibility for defending the northeastern section of the Ruhr Pocket.[11]

To the east, the Americans tried to complete their encirclement of the Ruhr. The U.S. 3rd Armored Division, which had been checked by the tough young men of SS Colonel Hans Stern's Ersatzbrigade Westfalen, sidestepped them by sending a task force to the left, in the direction of Lippstadt. This medieval town of twenty thousand was defended by a Volkssturm battalion of a few hundred men under the command of

Captain of Reserves Wilhelm Oberwinter. His soldiers were old men and boys, all poorly armed with foreign equipment, and most of them carried Czech rifles. As was typical for a Volkssturm unit, most of them did not even have uniforms; they wore civilian clothes with an armband bearing the identifier "Volkssturm." The local party boss insisted that they fight, but with the U.S. 2nd Armored Division closing in from one direction and the U.S. 3rd Armored coming up from the other, Captain Oberwinter disbanded his companies and ordered his men to discard their armbands and go home. He did not have to tell them twice. The U.S. 9th and 1st Armies linked up just east of Lippstadt at 1:00 p.m. on Easter Sunday, April 1, 1945. They had trapped the 5th Panzer and 15th Armies of Army Group B—a total of nineteen divisions and seven corps headquarters—in a pocket thirty miles wide and seventy-five miles long. Its total strength was around four hundred thousand men (including one hundred thousand flak troops and Luftwaffe auxiliaries), but they were mostly ill-trained Hitler Youth, old men, Volkssturm, or recent draftees with little training and no stomach for fighting. Many were residents of the Ruhr, which had a long tradition of leftist political leanings and were fed up with this losing war. The towns and cities rolled out the white flags at the first opportunity.

On April 1, Fritz Bayerlein sent his own former division, Panzer Lehr, into the attack at Hallenberg. It collided with the U.S. 9th Infantry Division and fought to a standstill. The next day, Major General Christian-Johannes Landau's relatively fresh 176th Infantry Division and the 3rd Panzer Grenadier Division (Lieutenant General Walter Denkert) reinforced the Panzer Lehr attack. The panzer grenadiers pushed into the town of Medebach but were thrown back in heavy fighting. The following morning, the U.S. 9th Infantry Division took Winterberg, and Bayerlein's LIII Corps had a difficult time holding its positions west of the town.

Hitler named General of Infantry Otto Hitzfeld acting command of the 11th Army (temporarily replacing General Walter Lucht, who was apparently ill), which held positions east of the Ruhr Pocket.[12]

Hitzfeld had under his command his own corps (LXVII Corps), as well as Lieutenant General Hermann Floerke's LXVI Corps, Wehrkreis IX's staff, SS Ersatzbrigade Westfalen, remnants of the 166th Infantry Division, several Volkssturm battalions, a collection of stragglers, recently discharged hospital patients, and Hitler Youths: a total of about 80,000 men.[13] He also had twenty tanks fresh off the assembly line at Kassel. He was told to break through the American armies to the Ruhr—an order that he recognized as pure folly. While Army Group B was essentially a write-off, it was not considered so by Fuehrer Headquarters and OKW. In their unrealistic world, they had "created" another army—or at least another army headquarters, during the first week of April. This one, the 12th, was placed under the command of General Walther Wenck, the forty-five-year-old former deputy chief of the General Staff who, in February, had been injured in an automobile accident on the way to the Eastern Front. Wenck was ordered to form his new command in the Elbe region between Dessau and Wittenberg. Its men came from officer-cadet schools, NCO schools, military training schools, and the Reich Labor Service (RAD). Its tank division, the Clausewitz Panzer, came from tank training schools in central Germany. Its Schageter Panzer Grenadier Division came from motorized and mechanized warfare schools, officer-cadets, and young Labor Service volunteers. Five infantry divisions were created: Potsdam, Scharnhorst, Ulrich von Hutten, Friedrich Ludwig Jahn, and Theodor Koerner. Once formed and organized, the 12th Army was charged with breaking the American encirclement of the Ruhr. The 11th Army's mission was to hold off the Allies until General Wenck was ready to strike. The 12th Army, of course, existed only on paper; it was so scattered that it would have taken weeks to organize.

Model organized the defense of the Ruhr Pocket. The northern half of the perimeter was the responsibility of Colonel General Harpe's 5th Panzer Army, which included (left to right) the LVII Panzer Corps, LXXXI Corps, and XII SS Corps, while Armee-Abteilung von Luettwitz covered the northeast quadrant. The southern half of the pocket was defended by Zangen's 15th Army, which included (west to east) LVIII, LXXIV, and LIII Corps. It was less well organized than the 5th Panzer Army and had three times as much area to defend.

General von Zangen had had an adventure. He and his headquarters had been cut off by the rapidly advancing Americans. In fact, the "Amis" had him surrounded, but they didn't know it. Zangen and his men hid in the woods and filtered out of their mini-pocket between U.S. convoys. Eventually, using back roads or traveling across open fields, they managed to reach friendly lines and reassumed their command functions.

It took one U.S. division four days to clear Hamm, but Duisburg fell in an hour. There was no resistance in western Essen, the home of the Krupp industries, but the fighting at Dortmund was vicious. At Soest the 116th Panzer (*Windhund*, or "Greyhound") Division under General von Waldenburg put up stiff opposition against the U.S. 8th Armored Division, launched a series of local counterattacks, and even forced the Americans to send reinforcements. Then the fighter-bombers of the U.S. XXIX Tactical Air Corps smashed the city, and, by the end of the day, even the "Greyhounds" were beginning to surrender *en masse*.

To the south, the U.S. XVIII Airborne Corps crossed the Sieg River and advanced fifty miles in three days against the remnants of four divisions (including the 11th Panzer Division), which together could muster only 10,000 men. Only at Wuppertal did they meet stiff resistance, but it was overcome within forty-eight hours; then the mass surrenders began there as well.

As the Ruhr Pocket shrank rapidly, OB West hurriedly built up forces in the Teutoburger Wald-Weser River sector, in front of the Harz Mountains and east of the Ruhr, under the command of General of Panzer Troops Karl Decker's XXXIX Panzer Corps of the 12th Army. From this base, Kesselring intended to launch a desperate relief attack to the Ruhr. If, however, the Americans penetrated the Teutoburger Wald and crossed the Weser and the Elbe, there would be no more barriers between them and Berlin. And this was exactly the objective which U.S. Lieutenant General William H. Simpson had in mind. Diverting much of his 9th

Army from the Ruhr Pocket, he placed two armored divisions side by side and swept through the forest as far as the small industrial city of Bielefeld. On the way, the Americans were greeted with white flags and surrender delegations led by the local Burgermeisters. Even where local NSDAP leaders wanted to resist, they were prevented from doing so by the citizens, who dismantled anti-tank barriers, and by the Volkssturm, who simply refused to turn out. Simpson's vanguards reached Bielefeld within forty-eight hours.

Bielefeld was different. Located on the edge of the Teutoburger Wald, it was commanded by Major General Karl Becher, who had joined the Imperial Army as a private and had earned a commission during World War I. After more than thirty years in the German infantry, he led the 574th Infantry Regiment on the Eastern Front and spent several months recuperating from injuries. He had commanded Fortress Koenigsberg (January 4–February 28, 1945) before being sent to Bielefeld. Here he organized a defensive force of seven thousand men; however, it was a motley collection of Volkssturm, training companies, two "ear" battalions (made up of men with hearing disorders who were otherwise fit for duty), the 64th Panzer Grenadier Replacement Training Battalion, and SS men from the nearby infantry training school at Senne—all equipped with captured foreign weapons. Becher had few heavy weapons, no signals equipment, no artillery at all, and a staff that was overage and too small and inexperienced. Becher's mission was to hold his positions against an onslaught of eight to nine U.S. divisions—about one hundred thousand men.

The heart of Becher's defense was the young, tough SS men and the Panzerfaust, Germany's single-shot, disposable anti-tank weapon. The local Nazi Party bosses remained behind, getting drunk in their command bunker; their only acts in the battle were to issue "Fight to the last man" orders and to threaten to have Becher "strung up" as a traitor for asking them to dissolve the Volkssturm battalions.[14]

In the thick forests, Becher's SS men and fanatical Hitler Youths conducted dozens of hit-and-run ambushes; and when cornered, these troops fought to the last man, or, more frequently, to the last teenage boy. The Americans did not succeed in entering Bielefeld until 1:00 p.m. on April 4 and did not reach the eastern edge of the forest until nightfall. Bypassing Becher and his men (who continued to hold out in the Teutoburger Wald), the Americans pushed on in the direction of the Elbe on April 5.[15] German resistance was light thereafter, and, on April 8, the U.S. 9th and 1st Armies were fanning out on either side of the Harz Mountains, driving for the Elbe. Field Marshal Kesselring ordered that "the Leine River line be held under all circumstances," but it had already been breached before he issued the order.[16] The 11th Army (now under General Lucht) was soon isolated in the Harz, with few heavy weapons and little food or ammunition.

With its last, thin hope of relief gone, the resistance of Army Group B weakened with each passing day. Eastern Essen (including the Krupp Works) was captured by the U.S. 17th Airborne Division on April 10, and what was left of Bochum, Oberhausen, and Muelheim were occupied or captured against minimal resistance on April 11. The stubborn 3rd Parachute Division, however, continued to hold the suburbs of Cologne on the east bank. Perhaps overconfident, the U.S. 1st Army sent the 13th Armored Division to finish it off on April 11. The Americans lost thirty tanks and dozens of half-tracks, armored personal carriers, and other vehicles to desperate paratroopers carrying *Panzerfausts*, and had to beat an ignoble retreat. But it was a temporary setback. American infantry arrived later to finish off the 3rd Parachute. Dortmund fell to the Americans on the evening of April 13, and except for a few pockets holding out in Duesseldorf and a handful of other localities, this was the end of the Battle of the Ruhr in the U.S. 9th Army's zone.

By now, even Model was desperate. He had already disobeyed the Fuehrer's orders to lay waste to the Ruhr. (The dictator wanted it destroyed so it would have no value to the Allies. Model was supposed to destroy its bridges, transportation facilities, and industrial plants, but he had not.) Now, on April 13, he disobeyed Hitler again by ordering LIII Corps to attempt a breakout. But it was too late. General Bayerlein

The Krupp factory in Essen, 1945. *U.S. Army Signal Corps*

recognized the situation as hopeless and surrendered that day, along with the remnants of his command.

On Friday, April 13, Hitler summoned Colonel Guenther Reichheim, Model's brilliant young operations officer, to the Reich Chancellery. Colonel Reichheim thought he saw a tear in Model's eye, as the field marshal gave him a letter to deliver to his wife.[17]

Hitler named Reichheim chief of staff of Wenek's 12th Army and ordered a 12th Army counterattack to rescue Army Group B and push on to the Rhine. Berlin sent optimistic messages to Model, but he knew Army Group B's situation was hopeless: he faced overwhelming Allied forces, and his army had food supplies for only three more days. Still, when his chief of staff, Major General Carl Wagener, who had replaced Krebs on February 16, suggested surrendering, Model rejected the suggestion as repugnant. The battle continued.

The U.S. 2nd Armored Division crossed the Elbe at the small town of Westerhusen, south of Magdeburg, during the night of April 12/13. By early morning, there were three American armored infantry battalions across the river. General Wenck, however, acted quickly and threw mobile battle groups from the Scharnhorst, Potsdam, and Ulrich von Hutten Divisions into an immediate counterattack against the bridgehead. The young cadets in these groups were inexperienced but enthusiastic and eager to prove themselves in battle. The Americans were desperately trying to finish a pontoon bridge when German artillery shells slammed into it, isolating the advanced American battalions on the eastern bank. The American commanders tried to call in artillery fire, but it was too late. Striking with an *elan* that the Wehrmacht had not exhibited in many a day, the cadets overran the American positions. More than three hundred Americans were killed, while the rest surrendered or fell back in disarray behind the Elbe. It was the only real defeat the U.S. 2nd Armored Division suffered during the Second World War.

In the Ruhr Pocket, meanwhile, time ran out for the Germans. On April 15, elements of Lieutenant General Matthew Ridgway's U.S. XVIII Airborne Corps pushed to within two miles of Model's headquarters. Ridgway sent a message, asking the trapped field marshal to surrender. Model refused, citing his personal oath of loyalty to Hitler. Ridgway tried again. "Neither history nor the military profession records any nobler character, any more brilliant master of warfare, any more dutiful subordinate of the state, than the American general, Robert E. Lee...." he wrote in a personal letter to Model. Yet even the great Lee had chosen "an honorable capitulation" when finally surrounded by overwhelming forces.

> This same choice is now yours. In the light of a soldier's honor, for the reputation of the German Officer Corps, for the sake of your nation's future lay down your arms at once. The German lives you will save are sorely needed to restore your people to their proper place in society. The German cities you will preserve are irreplaceable necessities for your people's welfare.[18]

Model sent his chief of staff, General Wagener, with his reply: he would not surrender. Ridgway offered Wagener a choice. He could return to Model or become a prisoner of war. Wagener opted for surrender.

From Army Group B Headquarters, Field Marshal Model issued an order, discharging all young boys and old men from the service and instructing them to return to their homes as civilians at once. This order was designed to save their lives or spare them months or years of captivity. Nevertheless, many of these underage or elderly soldiers ended up in POW camps.

That same day, April 15, the Americans split the Ruhr Pocket into several smaller pockets. South of the Ruhr River lay two enclaves, centered around the cities of Duesseldorf and Wuppertal. East of the river there was a floating pocket, which was directed by Zangen and his staff, while a larger pocket (which included the HQ, 5th Panzer Army) held out west of Kassel. All were under attack. Seeing the situation as hopeless, Major General Siegfried von Waldenburg surrendered the remnants of the once proud 116th Panzer Division, and Major General Horst Niemack surrendered the once elite Panzer Lehr Division.

On April 16, Wuppertal, a city of half a million people, finally surrendered. By now, mass surrenders were becoming common. None of Model's divisions had more than 2,000 men, and ammunition supplies were dangerously low. The will to resist was crumbling. At one place, two American military policemen guarded 16,000 German prisoners with a carbine and a machine gun. On April 17, Model admitted defeat. Rather than surrender, however, he dissolved Army Group B, including the Luftwaffe's III Flak Corps. He gave his men 3 choices: make their way home; surrender; or try to break out and join the German armies to the east. Several thousand escaped to the east, though some were too late. Major General Friedrich Wilhelm von Mellenthin, the chief of staff of the 5th Panzer Army, for example, broke out of the pocket with several comrades. Traveling by night and hiding and resting by day, they covered 250 miles on foot. They were finally captured at Hoexter on May 3, after Berlin had fallen and Hitler was already dead. Others escaped to their homes and avoided becoming prisoners of war.

Colonel General Harpe opted for surrender on April 17. Lieutenant General Walter Denkert, the commander of the 3rd Panzer Grenadier

Colonel General Joseph Harpe (1887–1968), the commander of the 5th Panzer Army in the Ruhr Pocket. He had previously commanded 12th Panzer Division, XXXXI Panzer Corps, 9th Army, 4th Panzer Army, and Army Group A on the Eastern Front. He was an Allied POW until 1948. *Bundesarchiv Bild 146-1981-104-30/Hoffmann, Heinrich/ CC-BY-SA 3.0*

Division, also surrendered, as did Baron von Luettwitz, the commander of the XXXXVII Panzer Corps, General of Infantry Erich Abraham, commander of the LXIII Corps, and the commanders of the 9th, 180th, 190th, and 338th Divisions, among others.[19] In all, twenty-nine German generals surrendered or were captured during the Battle of the Ruhr Pocket, along with an admiral. But not Field Marshal Model.

On the morning of April 21, with the Americans only a mile away, he walked into a deep forest near Duisburg, accompanied only by Colonel Theodor Pilling, his intelligence officer. "Anything's better than falling into Russian hands," he said. "You will bury me here."[20] He then shot himself in the head.

The Battle of the Ruhr Pocket was over.

Otto Moritz Walter Model, the youngest field marshal in the German Army, was buried in a secret grave until it was felt safe to reinter his remains in the military cemetery at Vossenack, in the Huertgen Forest, in 1955, not far from the grave of George S. Patton.[21]

Many of the men of his army group also died over the next few months. Some of the POW camps were just fields surrounded by concertina wire, open to the elements, and without medical facilities and even the most primitive shelters or sanitation facilities. At Bad Kreuznach, 56,000 men were crammed into a camp designed for 4,500. One POW later testified before a German investigation committee that for weeks the daily ration in his camp was "three spoonsful of vegetables, a spoonful of fish, two prunes, one spoonful of jam and four biscuits."[22] Many died of malnutrition, sickness, exposure, or collapsed and died in the urine-soaked mud. The death toll climbed into the tens of thousands, and perhaps higher. In his controversial book, *Other Losses*, Canadian writer James Bacque estimated that about 800,000 German POWs died in Western prison camps after the war.[23] Stephen Ambrose, the foremost biographer of Eisenhower, estimated that the number was much lower—50,000 at most. It seems likely that Ambrose's figure is closer to the mark, but this is merely educated guesswork, and it is an open question how readily German soldiers in the Ruhr would have surrendered if they had known what was to follow.

Whatever the "might have beens," German soldiers in the Ruhr did surrender rapidly. At a cost of just over 10,000 casualties, the Americans captured 317,000 German soldiers. For the German army, in terms of pure numbers, it was a disaster larger than Stalingrad. It destroyed the central army group of OB West and tore a gap 200 miles wide in the German line—a gap Kesselring had no means of plugging with his weak reserves (the 11th and 12th Armies).

Defeat was now an accomplished fact on the Western Front. After more than five years of war, the Wehrmacht was disintegrating.

CHAPTER X

DEFEAT IN ITALY

And what was happening in Italy while the German armies in the East and West were being smashed?

After the fall of Rome, Kesselring's Army Group C retreated at a relatively slow pace to the Gothic Line, which it reached during the third week in August 1944. Map 10.1 shows this position, as well as subsequent German main lines of resistance.

Kesselring faced the Allies with two armies: Colonel General Heinrich von Vietinghoff's 10th (now responsible for the Adriatic sector, which was judged more critical at this time) and General of Panzer Troops Joachim Lemelsen's 14th, on the western flank. Since his defeat in front of Rome in June, Kesselring had received five new divisions, plus Infantry Divisions *Ostpreussen* (East Prussia), *Wildflecken,* and *Schlesien* (Silesia). These last three were broken up and their men used as replacements for several divisions in the army group. In exchange, Kesselring had to give up the Hermann Goering Division (sent to the Russian Front in July) and the 3rd and 15th Panzer Grenadier Divisions (sent to the Western Front in August). He had, therefore, gained eight mediocre, non-motorized divisions but lost three good, mobile divisions. This exchange left him with six understrength mobile divisions—the 1st and 4th Parachute, the 26th and 16th SS Panzer, and the 29th and 90th Panzer Grenadier.

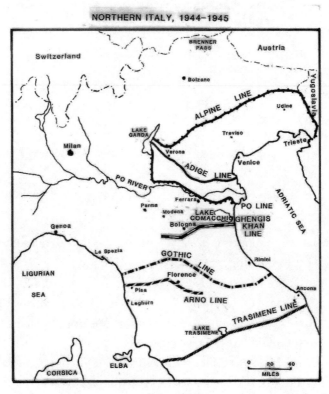

Map 10.1

With his generally unremarkable divisions, Kesselring took maximum advantage of the excellent defensive terrain of Italy to fall back slowly to the north. The British reached the Gothic Line in late August 1944 and launched numerous set-piece attacks on the Coriano Ridge (a key position in the Gothic Line) from September 12 to September 20. The Germans finally withdrew without suffering a decisive defeat, but British losses were heavy. The 8th Army lost 480 tanks destroyed or badly damaged. Almost all of the British infantry battalions had to be reduced from four to three companies for the next six months (in the fifth year of the war, the United Kingdom was finally nearing the end of its manpower reserves), and the famous 1st British Armoured Division had to be disbanded as a combat formation, although its headquarters continued to exist as a staff without combat units.[1]

TO THE GENGHIS KHAN LINE

Now the Germans retreated onto the Plain of Romanga and Kesselring began preparing deep defenses across the Po River Valley. The strongest position was known as the "Genghis Khan Line," which ran from Lake Comacchio to the Apennines, covering Bologna, Modena, and Parma. He also established the shorter and easier to defend (but also weaker) Adige (or Venetian) Line (see Map 10.1).

The German 14th Army still clung tenaciously to the Apennine ridges south of Bologna, and while the U.S. 5th Army chipped away at these defenses, there was no question of a rapid breakthrough. A gain of one mile a day was considered good progress. After three weeks of exhausting climbing and fighting, the Americans took Monte Grande Massif, just five miles from the critical Route 9. By the end of the week they were within ten miles of Bologna. By this time, however, I Parachute Corps had been reinforced to a strength of eleven divisions (none at full strength), including the 16th SS Panzer Grenadier, 1st Parachute, and 29th and 90th Panzer Grenadier. Struggle as they might, the American infantrymen were nearing the end of their endurance, and Bologna remained just beyond their grasp.

On October 23, Kesselring was on the road from 5:00 a.m. until late evening, visiting several headquarters and frontline divisions, as was his habit. In his memories, he recalls how he was greeted with enthusiasm everywhere and how he got the impression that the crisis had passed, as indeed it had. At 7:00 p.m., on his way to visit the last two divisions on his agenda for the day, his driver was passing a column when a long-barreled gun came out of a side road. The field marshal's car was going about forty-five miles per hour when they collided. Kesselring suffered a badly lacerated face, which he later described as "a hideous mess," a severely fractured skull, and had to undergo brain surgery. After it became apparent that he would live, the troops joked that the field marshal was doing well after the accident, but the gun had to be scrapped—a joke that pleased the recovering commander-in-chief immensely.[2] Even so, he was unable to return to duty before 1945. He was temporarily replaced by Colonel General Heinrich von Vietinghoff, who was determined to hold Bologna as stubbornly as he had held Cassino in 1943–44. Vietinghoff was temporarily succeeded as commander of the 10th Army by General of Panzer Troops Traugott Herr. Within a week, however, General of Panzer Troops Joachim Lemelsen moved over from 14th Army to assume command of the 10th, Herr returned to command of the LXXVI Panzer Corps, and General of Panzer Troops Frido von Senger, the commander of the XIV Panzer, became acting commander of the 14th Army for the second time.[3] In December, General of Infantry Kurt von Tippelskirch was named acting commanding general of 14th Army, and General Senger returned to the XIV Panzer.

Colonel General Heinrich von Vietinghoff (1887–1952), at various times commander of the 10th Army, Army Group C, and OB Southwest in Italy. *Bundesarchiv Bild 101I-313-1019-14*

By the time of Kesselring's accident, the Americans were exhausted, and their offensive was suspended on October 27. Except for a minor thrust or two, the Allies, in effect, went into winter quarters, which freed several German divisions to launch a massive attack on Italian partisans, scattering them in the mountains. The U.S. Official History estimated that the number of guerrillas operating against the Germans fell from 130,000 to 50,000.[4] They would remain active for the rest of the war but would not constitute a serious threat to the

German Army in Italy until after Army Group C suffered its decisive defeat in 1945.

THE CANNAE OF ARMY GROUP C

During the winter of 1944–45, Field Marshal Sir Harold Alexander became supreme commander, Mediterranean. U.S. General Mark Clark took command of the 15th Army Group, and Lucian Truscott was recalled from France to take over the 5th Army from Clark. British Lieutenant General Richard L. McCreery commanded the other army in the 15th Army Group—the famous British 8th Army. Both he and Truscott were top-notch commanders. On the German side, Heinrich von Vietinghoff, the OB Southwest and commander-in-chief of Army Group C, made 10th Army responsible for the entire active sector (from about thirty miles west of Bologna to the Adriatic coast), while 14th Army held the inactive Mediterranean coast and western Apennine sectors.[5] Vietinghoff gave the newly arrived LXXIII Corps (commanded by General of Infantry Anton Dostler) control of the sector immediately adjacent to the Adriatic Sea, while at the front General of Panzer Troops Joachim Lemelsen's 10th Army controlled (from left to right) the LXXIII, LXXVI Panzer, XIV Panzer, and I Parachute Corps.[6]

Kesselring returned to command of OB Southwest and Army Group C on January 15, 1945, and Vietinghoff briefly resumed command of 10th Army; then, near the end of January, he was sent to Russia, to command Army Group Courland. Lemelsen returned to the command of 14th Army, General of Infantry Kurt von Tippelskirch went on leave, General of Panzer Troops Traugott Herr again assumed command of 10th Army, and Count Gerhard von Schwerin, the former commander of the 116th Panzer Division, who had friends in the High Command, took over the LXXVI Panzer Corps on April 1 and was immediately promoted to general of panzer troops, in spite of his abysmal record in Normandy and the Siegfried Line battles.[7]

It was fortunate for Army Group C that Kesselring returned when he did, because OKW wanted Hitler to reinforce both the Eastern and Western Fronts at the expensive of the Italian theater. Kesselring deftly negotiated giving up four divisions, only one of which (the 16th SS Panzer Grenadier) was mobile. He rearranged the front he had inherited from Vietinghoff, giving more responsibility to 14th Army and placing the experienced General of Panzer Troops Frido von Senger in command of the Bologna sector. He had to commit three of his five mobile divisions (the 26th Panzer and 1st and 4th Parachute) to the front line because of its length. The mobile divisions left in reserve were the 90th and 29th Panzer Grenadier. Army Group C's order of battle as of March 31, 1945, is shown in Table 9.1.

Lacking fortified positions, Kesselring and Vietinghoff constructed a defense in depth, with delaying positions between several defensive lines. The last, the Adige (or Venetian) Line, ran from Lake Garda eastward through the Alpine foothills to the Adige River, which it followed to the Adriatic. Behind it lay the *Voralpenstellung*—the Forward Alpine Defenses of the National Redoubt, which was being constructed by a special command, Alpine Fortress Command Tyrol, headed by General of Infantry Hans Jordan, the former commander of the 9th Army on the Eastern Front. Kesselring and his generals knew that the best they could do was fight a skillful delaying action to the Adige. The vital question was: Would Hitler approve a withdrawal in time?

Order of Battle, Ob Southwest, March 31, 1945			
14th Army:			
	LI Mountain Corps		
		148th Infantry Division	
		232nd Infantry Division	
	XIV Panzer Corps		

		94th Infantry Division	
		8th Mountain Division	
		65th Infantry Division	
		305th Infantry Division	
	Army Reserves:		
		114th Jaeger Division (1)	
10th Army:			
	I Parachute Corps:		
		1st Parachute Division	
		334th Infantry Division	
		278th Infantry Division	
		4th Parachute Division	
	LXXVI Panzer Corps		
		26th Panzer Division	
		98th Infantry Division	
		362nd Infantry Division	
		42nd Infantry Division	
		162nd Infantry Division	
	LXXXXVII Corps z.b.V.		
		710th Infantry Division	
		188th Mountain Division	
		237th Infantry Division	
	LXXII Corps z.b.V.		
		Alarm units only	
	Army Reserves:		
		90th Panzer Grenadier Division	
Army Group Reserves:			
	155th Infantry Division (1)		
	29th Panzer Grenadier Division		
	715th Infantry Division (1)		

NOTES:
(1) In transit
SOURCE: Mehner, *Geheimentagesberichte*, Volume 12, 434–45.

Table 9.1

Hitler's "strategy" of holding the most forward possible line gave an advantage to Allied commanders Sir Harold Alexander and Mark Clark, who planned to destroy Army Group C south of the Po. If the British could advance as far as Ferrara and Bondeno, they would cut off the bulk of Army Group C. The U.S. 5th Army would attack astride Route 65, in the direction of Bologna. Once the German front broke, the British were to cross the Po and send armored brigades to the north to disrupt any German attempts to man the Adige Line; simultaneously, the Americans would cross the river and drive for Verona, Lake Garda, and ultimately the Brenner Pass.

The Allied attack was preceded by elaborate deception measures, designed to convince von Vietinghoff (who had returned as OB Southwest again, after Kesselring replaced Rundstedt as OB West on March

A German Sturmpanzer infantry support gun in Italy, spring 1945. This gun belonged to Sturmpanzer-Abteilung 216 (the 216th Assault Gun Battalion), which lost all forty-two of its vehicles in the Po Valley campaign. *Bundesarchiv Bild 1011-311-0903-21A/CC-BY-SA 3.0*

9, 1945), that they planned to strike via amphibious landings north of the Po. Vietinghoff fell for the ploy on March 29, when he sent Lieutenant General Doctor Fritz Polack's 29th Panzer Grenadier Division to the Venetian coast, leaving the 90th Panzer Grenadier Division (near Modena) as the army group's only mobile reserve south of the Po. On April 1, the British 2nd Commando Brigade launched a diversionary attack against "The Spit," a narrow strip of coast between the Adriatic and Lake Comacchio. They quickly routed the 162nd (Turkoman) Infantry Division, captured the 142nd Fusilier Battalion (the reconnaissance battalion of the 42nd Jaeger Division), and took 800 prisoners. (Like most German "divisions" at this point, the 42nd Jaeger was no longer the size of a "division," having only 2,600 men when the battle began.) On his own initiative, General Polack sent his 129th Panzer Reconnaissance Battalion to the threatened sector. Vietinghoff was now further convinced that the Allies intended to land north of the Po.

On the other flank, the U.S. 92nd Infantry Division launched another diversionary attack on April 5 and forced General Lemelsen to commit a regiment-sized battle group from the veteran 90th Panzer Grenadier Division to the front. This left the Germans with less than a full mobile division to commit against the Allies when the British 8th Army commenced the long-awaited main offensive on April 9.

It started with British air and artillery bombardments that lasted eight hours. The effects were devastating, especially to the German 98th and 362nd Infantry Divisions. Even so, the Germans gave ground slowly, despite the overwhelming Allied air superiority. By nightfall, however, the British were across the Senio River, one of the innumerable small rivers flowing off the Apennine Mountains.

Two British divisions mauled the 42nd Jaeger Division, and the II Polish Corps joined the offensive but quickly bogged down in front of Major General Viktor Linnarz's 26th Panzer Division. The retreat of the 98th and 362nd Infantry, however, exposed Linnarz's left flank, and the panzer division had to pull back. By noon on April 12, both the British

V and Polish II Corps had moved troops across the Santerno River against strong German resistance.

The battle now spilled over into an area known as the Argenta Gap, between the Reno River and Lake Comacchio. By this time, both Vietinghoff and Herr were convinced that the Allies did not intend to launch a major amphibious operation north of the Po, so they committed the 29th Panzer Grenadier Division to the battle for the gap. It did not arrive in time, however, to prevent the British from capturing the critical Bastia Bridge over the Reno River before the remnants of the 42nd Jaeger could blow it up. General von Vietinghoff saw his front collapsing and signaled OKW that to counter the Allied advance he needed to adopt a mobile defense. Without waiting for a reply from Berlin, he ordered the I Parachute Corps to abandon an increasingly dangerous salient and pull back to the Genghis Khan Line. General Herr, meanwhile, committed the entire 29th Panzer Grenadier to the defense of the town of Argenta; transferred the 278th Volksgrenadier Division from the I Parachute Corps to plug the gap in the east left by the burned-out 98th Infantry Division; and withdrew the 26th Panzer Division, which was fighting the Poles, into a reserve position behind the Reno.[8]

Despite Herr's astute tactics, Lieutenant General Charles F. Keightley's British V Corps, broke through the German lines east of Argenta on April 17, endangering the Reno River line, with the combined Allied thrust threatening to overwhelm Army Group C. Vietinghoff then received a remarkable signal from General Jodl—although it undoubtedly originated with Hitler:

> All further proposals for a change in the present war strategy will be discontinued. I wish to point out particularly that under no circumstances must troops or commanders be allowed to waver or to adopt a defeatist attitude as a result of such ideals apparently held by your headquarters. Where any such danger is likely, the sharpest countermeasures must be employed. The Fuehrer expects now, as before, the utmost steadfastness in the

fulfillment of your present mission, to defend every inch of the north Italian areas entrusted to your command. I desire to point out the serious consequences for all those higher commanders, unit commanders, or staff officers who do not carry out the Fuehrer's orders to the last word.[9]

More than threatening letters would be needed, however, to halt the Allied offensive. The British steadily advanced against the battered 10th Army with its 1st Parachute Division and 278th Infantry Division bearing the brunt of the fighting. Further west, the Americans advanced. At 8:30 a.m. on April 14, Lemelsen's 14th Army was hit by hundreds of heavy bombers dropping tens of thousands of high explosive and napalm bombs. Then, at 9:10 a.m., more than two thousand guns blasted German positions. After this barrage, the American infantry jumped off: eight divisions (two of them armored) under the U.S. II and IV Corps. They were opposed by LI Mountain Corps (commanded by Lieutenant General Friedrich-Wilhelm Hauck) and Senger's XIV Panzer Corps, which deployed (from left to right) the 114th Jaeger, 334th Volksgrenadier, 94th Infantry, 8th Mountain, and 65th Infantry Divisions, with about two-thirds of the 90th Panzer Grenadier Division in reserve.

The Roffeno Massif—the key terrain feature in the 14th Army's sector—was defended by Lieutenant General Hellmuth Boehlke's 334th Volksgrenadier Division and Lieutenant General Bernhard Steinmetz's 94th Infantry Division, which had been crushed south of Rome the year before. Each now had only three understrength regiments of two battalions each, and neither had any significant reserves. By nightfall of April 14, the American mountaineers had forced a serious gap between the divisions of Boehlke and Steinmetz. The following morning, Allied air forces dropped 1,500 tons of bombs on the German front and 800 tons in its rear. By nightfall, Steinmetz, facing encirclement, requested permission to pull back. Senger refused to authorize voluntary withdrawals. By the following afternoon the Americans had cut every road in Steinmetz's sector, and the 94th Infantry had to abandon most of its vehicles and heavy equipment in a cross-country retreat. Vietinghoff committed his last reserves—the 90th Panzer Grenadier Division—to a counterattack against the left flank of the American advance but was repulsed. By nightfall on April 18, the U.S. 10th Mountain Division, overcoming the terrain and the grenadiers, reached the edge of the mountains and could see Highway 9 and the Lombardy Plain below.

General Boehlke was a solid commander. When World War I began, he joined the 2nd Pomeranian Jaegers; by war's end, he was a battlefield-commissioned lieutenant commanding a company. He then served in the *Freikorps* during "the war after the war," as the civil unrest of 1918–1923 was called.[10] Not selected for the Reichsheer, he joined the police and rose to the rank of major. He rejoined the army in 1935 and in 1937 was commanding a battalion in the 21st Infantry Regiment, which he led in Poland. Promoted to colonel, he directed a replacement-training regiment, and then a line regiment in central Russia. Here he contracted a liver and biliary disease from which he suffered the rest of his life. For his service at Rzhev, Boehlke received the Knight's Cross. A tour of duty as commander of the 9th Army's Training School followed. Marked for higher command, Boehlke attended a division commanders' course in Germany, was promoted to major general on January 1, 1944, and assumed command of the 334th Infantry (later Volksgrenadier) Division a month later. He was twice praised in Wehrmacht dispatches for his courage and leadership (at Cassino and in the heavy fighting north of Florence), which noted that his excellence had been "proven." Meanwhile, he was promoted to lieutenant general and was awarded the Oak Leaves to the Knight's Cross. His excellent record, high decorations, unquestionable courage, and the fact that he had made no major mistakes in April 1945 could not save him; a scapegoat was needed for Germany's latest defeat, and Boehlke was selected. On April 16, 1945, he was relieved of his command and sent back to the Fatherland in disgrace. (He could not go home because it was under Soviet occupation.) He was never reemployed.[11]

While the U.S. IV Corps gained ground fairly rapidly in the center of the American attack, Major General Martin Strahammer's 114th

Jaeger Division limited the I Brazilian Corps on the Allied left to purely local gains, and Senger's XIV Panzer Corps stalled the advance of the U.S. II Corps south of Bologna. By April 19, the German line resembled an inverted V, making it a longer front, and Lemelsen's depleted units could not fill all the gaps.

On April 19, two U.S. divisions attacked the *Michelstellung* (the Michel position), the last German line south of the Po Valley. It was discontinuous and centered on inadequately fortified strongpoints; nevertheless, its defenders put up fierce resistance.

This, however, was the last hurrah for Army Group C. At noon on April 20, the American mountain troops captured Monte San Michele, and the German front collapsed. Realizing that the 14th Army was routed, the brilliant General Lucian Truscott sent the U.S. 1st Armored Division in pursuit of the retreating Germans. Lemelsen countered by throwing in his last reserve: the 190th Panzer Battalion of the 90th Panzer Grenadier Division, a rebuilt "Afrika Korps" unit with a pitiful handful of worn-out tanks.[12] It temporarily halted the American armored division and bought the fleeing infantry a few hours. But Truscott now committed three divisions to the pursuit.

A German rearguard put up a desperate fight in the village of Pradalbino and had to be crushed, but again it offered the fleeing Germans only a temporary respite. Around 3:00 p.m., the U.S. 10th Mountain cut Highway 9, ten miles northwest of Bologna, forcing General Senger to abandon the city later that night. General von Vietinghoff, meanwhile, withdrew Major General Friedrich von Schellwitz's 305th Infantry Division from southeast of Bologna and ordered it to plug a gap that was threatening the XIV Panzer Corps to the west. But the maneuver did not work: the Americans were moving too rapidly. After nightfall on April 20, Vietinghoff, without contacting Hitler or OKW, ordered that Operation "Autumn Mist"—the withdrawal to the Po—be put into effect immediately. Had he been given permission to withdraw on April 14, as he requested, this veteran East Prussian general would probably have escaped with his command intact. But by April 20 it was too late.

General of Panzer Troops Fridolin von Senger und Etterlin (1891–1963), commander of the XIV Panzer Corps, in the field. His son, Ferdinand, later became a Bundeswehr (West German) general. *U.S. Army Military History Institute*

The XIV Panzer Corps was the first to be smashed. During the night of April 21/22, Senger ordered General Steinmetz to form a blocking position at Mirandola, about halfway between Modena and the Po River, and to hold it until the rest of the corps could retreat past that point. When the 94th Infantry reached Mirandola, however, they found the U.S. 88th Infantry Division was already there. Thus cut off, Steinmetz ordered his men to break into small detachments and sneak across the Po. The general made good his escape, but most of his division did not, and its vehicles and heavy weapons were lost.

Early on the morning of April 23, Senger disbanded his corps and ordered his men to reassemble at Legnano across the Po and on the Adige River. Only two thousand men made it, and four more German divisions essentially ceased to exist.

Lieutenant General Paul Schricker's 8th Mountain Division (formerly the 157th Reserve Mountain Division) and Lieutenant General Hellmuth Pfeiffer's 65th Infantry Division were also trapped south of the Po. General Pfeiffer was killed in action on April 22; most of his and Schricker's troops surrendered.

The loss of the XIV Panzer Corps left General Lemelsen's 14th Army with one intact corps: General of Artillery Friedrich-Wilhelm Hauck's LI Mountain. It had three intact divisions—the 148th Infantry, the 232nd Infantry, and the 114th Jaeger—but was separated from the rest of Army Group C by the advancing Americans. Hauck pulled back as rapidly as possible to the northwest, hoping to outmarch American tanks and trucks and get behind German lines. General Truscott did not pursue the LI Mountain too closely because he wanted to eliminate the elite 1st and 4th Parachute divisions of the I Parachute Corps.

Late in the evening of April 23, the U.S. 88th Infantry Division reached the Po River and cut off Major General Alois Weber's 362nd Infantry Division of the I Parachute Corps. The Americans bagged 11,000 prisoners over the next two days, including Generals Weber and von Schellwitz. On the U.S. II Corps's right wing, the U.S. 91st Infantry and 6th South African Armoured Divisions were checked by the 1st and 4th Parachute, which made a determined stand on the small Panaro River.

To the east, the British 6th Armoured Division had been committed to the Battle of the Argenta Gap with the mission of cutting off the retreat of the I Parachute Corps. On April 21, it smashed Lieutenant General Harry Hoppe's 278th Infantry Division, which had been holding the escape corridor for the rest of the I Parachute. Two days later, the British 6th linked up with the South African Armored Division at the village of Finale, encircling the I Parachute Corps. The corps commander, General of Paratroopers Richard Heidrich, and the survivors of the 1st and 4th Parachute Divisions, swam the river Po and reformed, but without artillery, anti-tank guns, or even heavy machine guns. They were no longer any match for the rapidly advancing Allies and were finished off by the Americans at Verona on April 26. Among the prisoners were Major General Karl-Lothar Schultz, commander of the 1st Parachute, and Major General Heinrich Trettner, the commander of the 4th Parachute Division, General Kurt Student's former chief of staff and one of the principle architects of the German parachute branch. General Heidrich was not captured until May 3.[13]

The destruction of the I Parachute Corps at Finale on April 23 left General Count von Schwerin's LXXVI Panzer Corps as the only more or less intact German force south of the Po, and it was also under heavy British attack. The next day Lieutenant General Walter Jost, commander of the depleted 42nd Jaeger Division, was killed at Villadosa, and elements of two British corps reached the river. With no way to successfully extricate his corps, General Schwerin ordered his remaining divisions—the 98th

Infantry, 162nd Infantry, 26th Panzer, and 29th Panzer Grenadier—to abandon their vehicles, artillery, and heavy equipment, and swim across the river. Knowing that Hitler would want him shot, he did not cross the river but surrendered to the British on April 25.

The Battle of the Po was over. Of the twenty-three German divisions in Italy, nineteen were engaged in the battle; only one emerged roughly intact and only the 90th Panzer Grenadier could still function as a mobile unit. Army Group C had made it across the Po, but it lacked vehicles, tanks, or heavy weapons to reach and defend the Adige or Venetian lines.

Thanks to Hitler's interference, the strongest remaining German army group had been destroyed in a battle lasting sixteen days. The war in Italy was lost.

By April 25, Italian partisans controlled Milan, Genoa, and Turin. On April 26, Lieutenant General Max Pemsel, chief of staff of the Ligurian Army (the Axis rear command), surrounded by partisans, surrendered to the Americans. On April 28, the Allies closed the last escape route through the Alpine passes when they captured its defenders, Lieutenant General Doctor Fritz Polack and his staff and the remnants of the 29th Panzer Grenadier Division. With collapse facing him everywhere, the rear area commander, General of the SS Karl Wolff, secretly arranged for a separate surrender of Army Group C (with General Vietinghoff's implied approval). The surrender was signed on April 29, the day after partisans captured and killed Mussolini.[14]

Kesselring, however, as OB West (and in charge of Army Groups A, G, C, Ostmark, and E, in eastern Germany/Czechoslovakia, southern Germany, Italy, Austria, and the Balkans, respectively), did not approve the idea of a separate surrender for Army Group C. He believed that Vietinghoff had deceived him, retreated precipitously, and deliberately failed to coordinate his movements with Army Group E. He relieved Vietinghoff of his command, placed him under house arrest in Innsbruck, repudiated the surrender, and sacked General of Panzer Troops Hans Roettiger, the army group chief of staff. Vietinghoff and Roettiger were replaced by General of Infantry Friedrich Schulz, the commander-in-chief of Army

Group G, and Lieutenant General Fritz Wentzel.[15] (Schulz also remained in command of Army Group G.) Kesselring ordered Schulz and Wentzel to Italy immediately to ensure that Army Group C continued to fight. But at 7:00 a.m. on May 1, General Roettiger arrested Schulz and Wentzel, and a co-conspirator, Major General Siegfried Kempf, the chief signal officer of Army Group C, cut communications between Army Group C Headquarters and the rest of the Reich. General Roettiger and General Ritter Maximilian von Pohl, the Luftwaffe commander in Italy, then tried to persuade Generals Lemelsen and Herr, commanders of the 14th and 10th armies, to agree to the surrender terms. They refused to consider such an action while General Schulz was under arrest. At this impasse, SS General Wolff worked out a compromise with Schulz and Wentzel. The arrested officers refused to enter negotiations while they were captives but did agree to hold a general conference after their release to determine what should be done. Wolff then freed them, and the conference began at Army Group C Headquarters at 6:00 p.m. with General Schulz acting as chairman. Wolff, Wentzel, Pohl, Roettiger, Lemelsen, and Herr were also present. Herr opened the discussion by reporting that 10th Army was virtually destroyed. Everyone except Wentzel urged Schulz to surrender within twenty-four hours. Schulz and Wentzel conceded that surrender was the rational decision but refused to authorize it without Kesselring's approval. Wolff called Kesslring's headquarters and was connected to the OB West chief of staff, General of Cavalry Siegfried Westphal. He was sympathetic and promised that Kesselring would call Wolff at 10:00 p.m.

Shortly after 10:30 p.m., with no call from Kesselring, General Traugott Herr decided to act. He turned to his adjutant and issued orders for the men of the 10th Army to lay down their arms, beginning at 2:00 p.m. on May 2. Lemelsen then issued surrender orders for the remnants of the LI Mountain, I Parachute, and XIV Panzer Corps.[16] At 11:00 p.m., the generals received word that Adolf Hitler was dead. The conference principles—except for Schulz and his chief of staff—adjourned to Wolff's command post, where the SS general had prudently posted 350 troops loyal to him, along with seven panzers. At 1:15 a.m., news arrived that the

Luftwaffe High Command had ordered the arrest of General von Pohl. A few minutes later, a message arrived from Kesselring's headquarters, ordering the arrest of Vietinghoff, Roettiger, Colonel Victor von Schweinitz (the General Staff officer who had signed the surrender document), and Major General Kempf, the chief signal officer of Army Group C. The conspirators thought Schulz had betrayed them. In fact, Schulz had betrayed no one; the arrest orders were ignored, and at 4:30 a.m. on May 2, after much agonizing, General Schulz finally sanctioned the surrender of Army Group C. Kesselring later gave his belated and begrudging approval.

Two days later, on May 4, General Frido von Senger und Etterlin arrived at Mark Clark's headquarters at Florence as liaison officer in charge of arranging the details of the German capitulation. "It was," Senger noted in his war diary, "a tragic moment, the complete defeat and the imminent surrender after a fight lasting six years, tragic even for those who had foreseen it for a long time."[17] The agony of Army Group C was over.

SS General Karl Wolff (right) inspecting Mauthausen-Gusen concentration camp with Heinrich Himmler (left) and camp commandant SS Major Franz Ziereis (center). Wolff's efforts to arrange an early surrender in Italy may have saved his life. Karl Wolff was an enthusiastic participant in the Holocaust and was found guilty of deporting 300,000 Jews to the Treblinka extermination camp. He was sentenced to fifteen years imprisonment but was released in 1971. Born in Darmstadt in 1900, Wolff died in 1984. *Bundesarchiv Bild 192-139/CC-BY-SA 3.0*

CHAPTER XI

ON THE EDGE

By the end of March 1945, it was clear that Nazi Germany was doomed. Adolf Hitler, however, refused to admit it. Hundreds of officers who injudiciously expressed their disagreement (one Luftwaffe officer merely noted in his diary that the war was lost) were hauled before a special court or a "flying court-martial" and hanged.

Hitler was convinced (or at least pretended to be convinced) that the Allied coalition would fall apart, and the Third Reich would emerge triumphant. Rationalization, self-deception, and a belief that willpower could triumph over superior battalions were widespread at Fuehrer Headquarters in 1945. Hitler had lost none of his hypnotic powers of personal persuasion. He was even able to convince intelligent men like General of Infantry Wilhelm Burgdorf and Luftwaffe Field Marshal Robert Ritter von Greim that the war could yet be won.

In making his decision to prosecute the war until "final victory," Hitler told his Gauleiters in August 1944 that if "the German people" were "to be the conquered in this struggle," then they "had been too weak to face the test of history," and were "fit only for destruction."[1]

This notion had become a familiar theme around Fuehrer Headquarters: Would the German people prove "worthy" of the Fuehrer?

By 1945, however, Hitler's own physical deterioration was obvious to everyone. Years of taking Dr. Theodor Morrell's drugs had taken a serious toll on him physically, just as the assassination attempt of July 20, 1944, had affected him both physically and psychologically. His left arm trembled to the point that it was useless; he dragged his left foot when he walked; he had developed a pronounced stoop; he worked incessantly but monotonously. The once sociable Fuehrer was now practically a recluse, living in complete isolation except for his entourage. This, too, had changed and shrunken considerably since 1939. It now consisted of his secretaries, his mistress (Eva Braun), his doctor the quack, a few generals who still pandered to him, and Nazi Party leader Martin Bormann. As defeat approached, Hitler himself grew increasingly miserable and frustrated. More and more he dreamed of retirement at Linz and devoted himself to his only remaining amusement: architectural planning. Playing with Albert Speer's old models in his underground bunker, he did not have to face the present, where fate was closing in on him.

When Hitler announced that superior willpower could triumph over superior numbers of battalions, he was dismissing a great many battalions, for Stalin was already within sixty miles of Berlin and was massing his forces for the final onslaught. Three full fronts (army groups) were earmarked for the drive on the German capital: 2,500,000 men, 6,250 tanks, 41,600 pieces of artillery and mortars, 3,255 multiple-tube rocket launchers, and nearly 100,000 motorized vehicles. To meet this mammoth threat, Heinrici's Army Group Vistula had perhaps 700,000 men, 750 tanks, and 400 to 500 guns (excluding anti-aircraft guns). It was supported by Ritter von Greim's 6th Air Fleet, which had only 300 operational airplanes. In addition, the Germans were critically short of ammunition.

Stalin placed Zhukov in charge of the last offensive. From north to south, he deployed Rokossovsky's 2nd Belorussian Front, General Vasili D. Sokolovosky's 1st Belorussian Front, and Konez's 1st Ukrainian Front.

The battle plan called for the 1st Belorussian to launch the main attack against the German 9th Army. Konev's 1st Ukrainian Front was to crush the 4th Panzer Army (on the left flank of Army Group Center) and, in conjunction with the 1st Belorussian Front, encircle the 9th Army and Berlin from the south. The 2nd Belorussian Front was to push the 3rd Panzer Army toward the coast (away from the capital) and encircle Berlin from the north. Simultaneously, south of the main combat zone, the 4th, 2nd, and 3rd Ukrainian Fronts were to pin down Army Groups Center and South to prevent them from reinforcing the Berlin sector.[2]

The odds against General Heinrici's Army Group Vistula were overwhelming. As of April 1, General of Infantry Theodor Busse's 9th Army had seventeen badly understrength divisions. The 32nd SS Panzer Grenadier Division, for example, had only 2,846 men, while the Panzer Division Muencheberg had only 2,867. The Berlin (309th) Infantry Division was apparently the largest in the army (5,889 men), while the 25th Panzer Grenadier Division had 5,196 soldiers, the Panzer Grenadier Division "Kurmark" had 2,375, and the 712th Infantry Division could muster only 3,699 troops. The other divisions of the 9th Army were in equally miserable shape.[3] Busse's depleted legions opposed the 1st Belorussian Front, which had eighteen armies—more armies than 9th Army had divisions. In all, the 1st Belorussian had seventy-seven rifle divisions, eight artillery divisions, seven tank or mechanized corps, plus dozens of independent brigades and regiments. They outnumbered Busse 3,155 to 512 in tanks and assault guns and 16,934 to 344 in artillery pieces (excluding about 350 anti-aircraft guns). Baron von Manteuffel's 3rd Panzer Army had eleven divisions, all understrength and none of which were panzer. Opposing him, Rokossovsky's 2nd Belorussian Front had eight armies, controlling thirty-three rifle divisions, three artillery divisions, and four tank or mechanized corps. They had 951 tanks and assault guns against Manteuffel's 242; they outnumbered him in artillery by a margin of at least 10 to 1. On Zhukov's left flank, Konev's front outnumbered General Fritz-Hubert Graeser's 4th Panzer Army by a similar margin.[4]

Many of Heinrici's divisions were recently created units and came from the Replacement Army or were ad hoc formations of regimental size and divisions in name only, including SS units made up of foreign "volunteers," and "marine" formations, consisting of sailors converted into infantry. They were in no way comparable to United States Marines. On March 26, in what amounted to a declaration of military bankruptcy, the Home Army was dissolved. In the so-called "March of the Goths," its cadre units were formed into divisions (numbered 402 to 490) and were sent to the front, providing 70,000 men as reinforcements for the Oder sector and 45,000 for OB West. Table 11.1 shows the Order of Battle of Army Group Vistula on March 31, 1945. Table 11.2 shows the Order of Battle of the German Army on the eve of its final campaign.

Order of Battle, Army Group Vistula March 31, 1945		
3rd Panzer Army:		
	Swinemuende Garrison:	
		3rd Marine Infantry Division
		KG Schmidt
	III SS Corps:	
		Group Klosseck
	XXXII Corps:	
		1st Marine Infantry Division
		281st Security Division
		Fortress Stettin
		549th Volksgrenadier Division
	Corps Oder:	
		Division Staff 610 z.b.V.
		547th Volksgrenadier Division
	Army Reserve:	

		5th Jaeger Division
		28th SS Volunteer Grenadier Division "Wallonien"
		11th SS Volunteer Panzer Grenadier Division "Nordland"
		23rd SS Volunteer Panzer Grenadier Division "Nederland"
		27th SS Volunteer Grenadier Division "Langemarck"
9th Army:		
	CI Corps:	
		Infantry Division "Gross Berlin"
		Division Staff 606 z.b.V.
	XXXIX Panzer Corps:	
		(303rd) Infantry Division "Doeberitz"
		20th Panzer Grenadier Division
		9th Parachute Division
	XII SS Corps:	
		712th Infantry Division
		Panzer Grenadier Division "Kurmark"
		169th Infantry Division
	V SS Mountain Corps:	
		Division Staff 391 z.b.V.
		32nd SS Panzer Grenadier Division "30. Januar"
		Division Staff Raegener (1)

		Remnants, 433rd Infantry Division +
		463rd Infantry Division
		Fortress Frankfurt
	Army Reserves:	
		600th (Russian) Infantry Division
		25th Panzer Division (2)
		25th Panzer Grenadier Division
		Fuehrer Grenadier Division (2)
		Panzer Division "Muencheberg"
		10th SS Panzer Division "Hohenstaufen" (3)
	Army Group Vistula Reserves:	
		Headquarters, Group Steiner
		4th SS Panzer Grenadier Division "Polizei"
		Panzer Verbaende "Ostsee"
		156th Field Training Division (4)
		Headquarters, LVI Panzer Corps
		Staff, 20th Luftwaffe Field Division (4)
		299th Infantry Division (4)
		541st Volksgrenadier Division (5)

NOTES:

(1) Later redesignated 286th Infantry Division.
(2) Transferred to Army Group South, April 2–3.
(3) Transferred to Army Group Center, April 2.
(4) In transit.
(5) Employed as a supply delivery unit.
SOURCES: Mehner, *Geheimentagesberichte*, Volume 12, 436; Stauffenberg MS.

Table 11.1

Order of Battle of the German Army, March 31, 1945

OKH:	
Army Group South:	
	2nd Panzer Army
	6th Army
	6th SS Panzer Army
	8th Army
Army Group Center:	
	1st Panzer Army
	17th Army
	4th Panzer Army
Army Group Vistula:	
	9th Army
	3rd Panzer Army
	Group Steiner (1)
Army Group North:	
	2nd Army
	4th Army
	Army Detachment Samland
Army Group Courland:	

	18th Army	
	16th Army	
OKW:		
20th Mountain Army		
Wehrmacht Command Denmark		
OB West:		
	Army Group H (2):	
		25th Army
		1st Parachute Army
	Army Group B:	
		15th Army
		5th Panzer Army
	11th Army	
	12th Army	
	Army Group G:	
		7th Army
		1st Army
		19th Army
	Marine Command West	
OB Southwest (Army Group C):		
	Ligurian Army	
	14th Army	
	10th Army	
Army Group E		
	2nd Panzer Army	
NOTES:		
(1) Upgraded to Army Detachment Steiner in April 1945.		
(2) Redesignated OB Northwest, April 6.		

Table 11.2

In such impossible circumstances, Army Group Vistula was fortunate to
have one of Germany's most gifted and experienced commanders—Gotthard

Heinrici was a tough, solid, tactically brilliant, tested, and respected East Prussian officer and gentleman.

When Heinrici took command of Army Group Vistula from Heinrich Himmler, he knew he had inherited a likely hopeless situation. Hitler made his job harder by insisting that the Soviets' main objective would be Prague, not Berlin. On April 2 and 3, Hitler, overruling Heinrici's objections, transferred almost half of Heinrici's armor to the south.

Heinrici and his operations officer, Colonel Georg Eismann, met with Hitler at the Fuehrer Bunker in Berlin during the afternoon of April 4. Also present were Admiral Doenitz, Bormann, Jodl, Krebs (now chief of the General Staff and *de facto* head of OKH), Himmler, and Goering. To partially compensate for the loss of his armor, Heinrici wanted permission to abandon "Fortress Frankfurt" (Frankfurt-on-the-Oder), which would give him eighteen additional battalions to deploy. Hitler's reaction was bizarre—at first a lengthy silence, then a quiet acquiescence, followed by an outburst of fury. Screaming that no one understood him, he commanded that Frankfurt be held, while authorizing Heinrici to withdraw six battalions. Hitler asked who commanded the fortress.

"Colonel Biehler," said Heinrici.

"Is he a Gneisenau?" Hitler demanded, referring to a Prussian hero of the Napoleonic Wars.

Heinrici said he thought so.

He returned to the issue of the six battalions, telling Hitler that his divisions would probably lose a battalion a day against a major Soviet offensive. He needed at least 100,000 replacements.

Goering, Doenitz, and Himmler promised that they could provide one hundred thousand people.

"There!" Hitler exclaimed. "There are your people."

Heinrici said he did not need "people," he needed trained divisions. But Hitler was now carried away by the prospect of another 100,000 troops, and ordered Heinrici to place them in his second line of defense. "They'll simply annihilate the Russians who break through!" he exclaimed.

Heinrici said he already had too many inexperienced soldiers and if they were not reinforced with battle-hardened divisions, then "I can't guarantee they'll withstand the coming Russian attack. And the lack of proper reserves dangerously lessens my chance of holding off the Russian attack."

"You have your 100,000 new men," the dictator said quietly. "As for holding the line, it's up to you to back up the troops with morale and confidence, and the battle will be won." That was the end of their discussion.[5]

General Heinrici, incidentally, received about thirty thousand of the one hundred thousand reinforcements he was promised.

Colonel Ernst Biehler, the commandant of Fortress Frankfurt/Oder, had just recovered from wounds suffered on the Eastern Front, where he had served as acting commander of the 205th Infantry Division. He was selected to defend the fortress because he was familiar with the city and had a family of four children who were available for reprisals if he surrendered too quickly. When he took command on January 25, 1945, he had about 5,000 men, most of whom were artillery trainees. The rest were convalescents, stragglers, and Volkssturm. By the second week of April, he had 30,000 men; half of them positioned east of the Oder and half in training camps on the western side. He had about one hundred guns (captured French and Soviet pieces), a few German mortars, and about forty Panthers and assault guns. When he met with Hitler in the Fuehrer Bunker on April 6, the Soviets had advanced north and south of the city, and he advocated withdrawing from Frankfurt and consolidating his forces to the west.

Hitler insisted that Frankfurt remain a German fortress. "That is a direct command," he announced.

"No, my Fuehrer," said Biehler. The Fuehrer's entourage was shocked and Hitler jumped to his feet. "Get out of here!" he roared, pointing to the door.

Biehler picked up his maps and papers and walked out through the emergency exit to the Chancellery garden. General Krebs followed him, relieved him of his command, and ordered him to report to General Busse. Biehler eventually telephoned Heinrici to tell him what happened.

The salty East Prussian told him to return to Frankfurt and resume his command. (Some senior officers called Heinrici "the poisonous dwarf" because he was both short and unyielding.) Unknown to Biehler, General Burghoff, the chief of the Army Personnel Office, had already informed Heinrici that Biehler had been relieved. Heinrici demanded that the order be rescinded, and when Burghoff said it was impossible because it was a direct order from the Fuehrer, Heinrici repeated his demand, saying it was ridiculous to relieve Biehler, and also demanded that the colonel be awarded the Knight's Cross.

When Burghoff again cried that it was impossible, Heinrici said that either Biehler stayed or he quit—and hung up.[6]

Ernst Friedrich Biehler was reinstated as commandant of Fortress Frankfurt, decorated with the Knight's Cross, and promoted to major general on April 20, 1945—Adolf Hitler's fifty-sixth birthday.

Heinrici made his final defensive preparations, planning to make his main stand in the Seelow Heights area, in the zone of 9th Army, about forty-five miles from Fuehrer Headquarters. To defend this vital sector, Heinrici selected Major General Georg Scholze's 20th Panzer Grenadier Division, a tough, veteran formation and one of the best units left in Army Group Vistula, along with the 9th Parachute Division—an inexperienced unit of young men and boys with about two weeks of training. Its commander was Luftwaffe Major General Bruno Brauer. Brauer had distinguished himself as a parachute commander early in the war but was now an exhausted, worn-out, and dispirited man who had apparently been given this command because of a falling out with Goering. Heinrici placed the 20th Panzer Grenadier Division and the 9th Parachute Division under the command of the LVI Panzer Corps led by the tough and experienced General of Artillery Helmuth Weidling, who had led the XXXXI Panzer Corps on the Eastern Front since 1943 and the 86th Infantry Division before that. He sacked Brauer and replaced him

Lieutenant General Hellmuth Reymann (1892–1986). A tough Silesian, he was educated in the cadet schools and commissioned in the infantry. Not selected for the Reichswehr after World War I, he joined the police but returned to the army as a major in 1935. He commanded the 212th Infantry, 13th Luftwaffe Field, and 11th Infantry Divisions on the Eastern Front before being named commandant of Berlin on March 6, 1945. He was relieved of this position on April 23 and given command of Armee Gruppe Spree, an ad hoc formation with the strength of a division. Reymann escaped to Allied lines, along with most of his men. *Wikimedia Commons*

with Colonel Harry Herrmann, a much younger and more vigorous parachute officer.[7]

Heinrici's plans included a strategic retreat a few miles to the rear, once he knew where the Soviet would strike. His hope was to avoid a massive, preliminary Soviet artillery bombardment. If the Soviets proved unstoppable, he planned to maneuver his armies to the west and surrender to the British or the Americans; he did not want to surrender his men to the Russians and he did not want Berlin to become a battlefield. On April 14, he met with Speer and Lieutenant General Hellmuth Reymann, the commandant of Berlin since March 6, and told them his plan. With Hitler's permission, Heinrici had already stripped combat units from the capital, except for ninety-two battalions of Volkssturm, two battalions of guard troops, and a few Alarm battalions, made up of cooks and clerks. Heinrici had even designated which bridges Reymann could blow up (none of them carried water pipelines, gas mains, or electric cables that civilians would need after the war).

Joseph Stalin desperately wanted the Red Army to capture Berlin. He saw it as vital to his postwar goal of advancing Soviet power and influence. His western allies seemed willing to accommodate him. On March 28, U.S. Major General John R. Deane, the chief of the American Military Mission to Moscow, handed Stalin a telegram from

General Eisenhower. It was a remarkable document. Without consulting the Combined Chiefs of Staff, Eisenhower had decided that Berlin had lost its previous strategic significance and estimated that to capture the city would cost him one hundred thousand men; he therefore informed Stalin that, after reducing the Ruhr Pocket, the Anglo-American forces would advance to the southeast, toward Erfurt, Leipzig, and Dresden. He also intended to advance into the Regensberg-Linz area to prevent the Nazis from occupying their Alpine Redoubt in Bavaria and Austria. The capture of Berlin he therefore left to the Soviets.

Both Prime Minister Winston Churchill and Field Marshal Bernard Montgomery were surprised when they learned of Eisenhower's telegram. Both objected to it, and Churchill suggested that the general may have overstepped his bounds by assigning himself his own military and political objectives. Neither Sir Winston nor Monty, however, could do anything about it because the British were now definitely the junior partners in the Western Alliance and both President Franklin Roosevelt and General George Marshall supported Eisenhower, even though Marshall considered the Alpine Redoubt threat to be a minor one. "The remarkable aspect of this sudden change of strategic aim," military historian Albert Seaton noted, "is that Roosevelt and the United States Chiefs of Staff should have left this final stage of the war to the discretion of a single individual who, although a soldier of distinction, may at that time have been lacking in political acumen and an understanding of the aims and methods of the Soviet Union. Military objectives should of necessity have been related to post-war political strategy."[8]

Stalin signaled Eisenhower that he generally agreed with his conclusions—especially about Berlin no longer being strategically significant—and his proposals. Stalin said he intended to make his main offensive in the direction of Dresden and Leipzig, and that it would be launched in the second half of May. This, however, was misdirection on Stalin's part. He did not believe that his Anglo-American allies intended to hand him Berlin, and he was determined to get there before them. Three days later, on the afternoon of Easter Sunday, April 1, he ordered Zhukov and Konez to be ready to attack on April 16. The Anglo-Americans would not be informed of the date of the offensive until April 15. Until then, Stalin could only watch in alarm as the British and Americans overran western and central Germany.

DISINTEGRATION IN THE WEST

On March 28, the day Eisenhower sent his dispatch to Stalin, Patton's 3rd Army crossed the Rhine at Mainz, and the next day the French 1st Army stormed across the river near Germersheim. The northern wing of General Hans von Obstfelder's 7th Army was now on the verge of disintegration. General of Infantry Gustav Hoehne's LXXXIX Corps was overrun. Smilo von Luettwitz's LXXXV Corps escaped the rapidly moving U.S. armored columns but was practically worthless as a combat formation. General of Infantry Walter Hahm's LXXXII Corps was the only intact corps in the 7th Army, but its three divisional units could not contain the Allied advance through Hanau and Aschaffenburg.

Obstfelder tried to restore his line by upgrading General of Artillery Herbert Osterkamp's Wehrkreis XII to XII Provisional Corps and ordering it to hold a thirty-five-mile-long front in the center of 7th Army's line. He tried to organize a counterattack, but panzers he hoped to use were dispersed by the U.S. 4th Armored Division.

Disaster overtook OB West all along the line. On March 30, Heidelberg fell, and the U.S. 6th Armored Division dashed toward Kassel. The next day, two U.S. armored divisions pushed into Fulda, which was defended by elements of the 166th Reserve Division (which managed to hold until April 2), and the Wehrmacht began its withdrawal from the western Netherlands. On April 1, Army Group B was encircled in the Ruhr Pocket, and by the morning of April 3, American units had driven the troops of Wehrkreis VI (Westphalia and Rhineland) from the streets of Muenster.

On all fronts, the litany of disaster continued. On April 3, the Russians took Wiener Neustadt, an Austrian manufacturing center (a major producer of Messerschmitt airplane engines) south of Vienna. On April

4, Bratislava fell to the Red Army; the U.S. 4th Armored Division took Gotha without opposition; the U.S. 80th Infantry Division won the battle for Kassel; the French captured Karlsruhe; the U.S. 4th Armored Division seized Ohrdruf, the headquarters of OB West (Field Marshal Kesselring and his staff escaped just ahead of the American tanks); and the U.S. 90th Infantry Division cleared the town of Merkers of German troops.

The Americans would soon make a discovery in Merkers. Two American military policemen spotted a woman out after curfew and running down a street. She told them that it was an emergency—she needed to find a midwife. The two MPs—to her obvious surprise— helped her rather than arresting her. In thanks, she pointed them to the Merkers Salt Mine and said: "That's where the bullion is hidden." Before long, 2,100 feet below the surface, the Americans discovered the sealed vaults of the Reichsbank, which contained more than $1,000,000,000 in paper money and an estimated $200,000,000 worth of gold. The vault also contained priceless art works, including those evacuated from the Kaiser Friedrich Museum in Berlin.

On April 5, the U.S. 6th Armored Division took Mulhouse, the U.S. 30th Infantry Division took Hameln on the Wesel (the legendary home of the Pied Piper), and the French 1st Army began attacking German fortified positions in the Black Forest. The next day, the U.S. 84th Infantry and 2nd Armored Divisions broke the Weser River line near Minden, while Yugo-slav partisans seized control of Sarajevo. In the north, the Allied advance severed General Johannes Blaskowitz's Army Group H from OB West. OKW therefore removed Army Group H (1st Parachute Army and a few miscellaneous forces) from Kesselring's control, redesignated it OB North-west (*Oberbefehlshaber Nordwest*), and placed it under the command of Field Marshal Ernst Busch, a veteran Nazi most famous for his mishan-dling of Army Group Center during the Battle of White Russia (1944). Blaskowitz was named commander of OB Netherlands and placed under the command of Busch—a definite demotion.

Busch created the ad hoc Army Blumentritt—incorporating Weh-rkreis VI and XI, plus a few naval battalions in the Bremen sector—to

The heavy cruiser ("pocket battle-ship") *Admiral Scheer*, docked at Gilbraltar, circa 1936. It was sunk by British bombers on April 9, 1945, and went down with most of its crew. *U.S. Navy*

defend a line along the Weser from Hameln to the coast. But it could not hold out for long—indeed, the line was breached before it was even established.

On April 7, the Americans took Goettingen; on April 8, they reached Schweinfurt. On April 9, the Anglo-Americans began their final push in Italy and British bombers sank the German cruiser *Admiral Scheer* at Kiel, destroying most of what was left of the German surface fleet.[9]

The Americans pushed east, beyond the Ruhr, into Middle Franconia. Resistance were spotty, and more than ever Nazi Germany turned against itself. More than 26,000 members of the Wehrmacht were sentenced to death for desertion or undermining the war effort, although many were sent to penal battalions instead. From January until May 1945, 4,000 people were executed, and "flying court-martials" executed seven thousand more.[10]

April 7 was a day of cold rain. The Allies approached the town of Aub, about ten miles south of Ochsenfurt. While desperate and exhausted German troops tried to stop them, the mayor of a nearby village asked Private Alfred Eck, a thirty-five-year-old deserter, to help him contact the Americans. Eck, in civilian clothes and carrying a white flag, reached U.S. lines and was brought to a senior commander. He gave the Americans the location of German units and the location of a minefield. The American commander promised Eck that the village—and the town of Aub—would not be destroyed if the German troops withdrew and every house flew a white flag. (The Nazis had already decreed that any residents who flew a white flag would be shot.) Private Eck tried to reach Aub but German soldiers intercepted him.

Aub was smoldering. It had been pounded by Jabos the day before. It was now under the command of Captain August Busse. Busse was born in 1914. His father had been killed in action in 1915, and his mother died three years later. He grew up in an orphanage. By 1933, he was a fervent member of the Hitler Youth. He served a year in the RAD (Reich Labor Service) and entered the army in June 1935. He underwent officers' training, earned his commission, and fought in Poland, France, and Russia. After being seriously wounded in April 1942, he recovered by spending two years as a training officer at an infantry school. In May 1944, Busse returned to the Eastern Front. He was seriously wounded again in December 1944 and evacuated to the Reich. After three months in the hospital, he was posted to Troop Maneuver Area Grafenwoehr, near Nuremberg. Finally, he was attached to the 79th Volksgrenadier Division, which gave him command of Aub. He had about six hundred men—mostly Fahnenjunkers and second lieutenants. Like Busse, they had been in action for several days and were nearly exhausted, but most believed in Hitler's promised "miracle weapons" and still believed Germany could win the war.

When Eck was hauled before Busse, the angry captain struck him in the face. He accused Eck of sabotage and treason. The captain quickly formed a court-martial (consisting of himself, his adjutant, and a nearby lance corporal) and accused Eck of approaching American lines without authorization for the purpose of surrendering the village of Baldersheim, and giving away German positions, which had come under enemy fire. They quickly found Eck guilty and sentenced him to death by hanging.

Busse allowed a priest to visit Eck while the captain inspected nearby positions. Someone told Busse that he had seen Eck in uniform several days before. Busse returned to his headquarters and confronted Eck, who confessed that he had burned his military papers. The captain reconvened the court-martial and added desertion to Eck's list of crimes. The private asked either to be shot or to be sent to a penal battalion at the front instead of being hanged. Busse rejected the penal battalion request and the other members of the court-martial indignantly declared that shooting was too good for Eck—he wasn't worth the bullets.

Interrupted only by occasional American artillery fire, gallows were hastily constructed in the town square. Eck was hanged about 1:00 p.m.—and Busse ordered that his body remain hanging for twenty-four hours, as a warning to others.

A few days later, the Americans captured Aub. Captain Busse escaped with about fifty men. They traveled fifteen miles at night, through forests and fields, without food or water. They collapsed in a haystack, where they were surprised by a U.S. patrol. Busse was wounded and captured. He was sent to a prisoner-of-war compound in France, from which he was released in May 1946.

After the war, Busse made the mistake of visiting old friends in Aub. Eck's brother had him arrested and brought murder charges against him. Busse was convicted of having set up an illegal court-martial, and he was sentenced to two and a half years' imprisonment. Busse, who considered himself a career officer and a decent man, never believed that he had done anything wrong and died embittered over the incident.[11]

On April 10, the Americans took Hanover (in Lower Saxony) and Brunswick (Braunschweig), capturing the huge Hermann Goering Steel Works, along with sixty-seven large anti-aircraft guns. Coburg fell on April 11, as did Erfurt and Weimar, the hometown of Schiller, Liszt, and Goethe. In the hills above the city, the Americans liberated the infamous Buchenwald concentration camp, along with 21,000 inmates.[12] In the eight years of its existence, 56,000 of its inmates had been liquidated.[13]

The Nordhausen concentration camp was also liberated on April 11. For the Americans, it was an unbelievably grisly experience. A sergeant from the 329th Medical Battalion reported:

> Rows upon rows of skin-covered skeletons met our eyes. Men
> lay as they had starved, discolored, and lying in indescribable
> human filth. Their striped coats and prison numbers hung to

their frames as a last token or symbol of those who enslaved and killed them.... One girl in particular I noticed; I would say she was about 17 years old. She lay there where she had fallen, gangrened and naked. In my own thoughts I choked up—couldn't quite understand how and why war could do these things.... We went downstairs into a filth indescribable, accompanied by a horrible dead-rot stench. There in beds of crude wood I saw men too weak to move dead comrades from their side. One hunched-down French boy was huddled up against a dead comrade, as if to keep warm.... There were others, in dark cellar rooms, lying in disease and filth, being eaten away by diarrhea and malnutrition. It was like stepping into the Dark Ages to walk into one of these cellar-cells and seek out the living.[14]

A few miles away, men of the U.S. 104th Infantry Division discovered a large underground factory, which had been used to manufacture Werner von Braun's V-2 rockets. Production had only stopped the day before, when SS General Hans Kammler, the special commissioner of the V-weapons program, fled southward to Oberammergau, along with five hundred of his specialists. American scientific teams sent about one hundred of the rockets back to the United States for study.

Near the factory they found a slave labor camp which had a capacity of 30,000 prisoners. It was obvious that the Germans intended that none of the laborers would ever leave the factory alive. The crematory ovens could and had handled up to 150 bodies a day.

The German defeats continued on April 12, when Sangerhausen fell, Jena was bypassed, U.S. armored divisions reached the Elbe at Wittenberg, Werben, and Sandau, and the Canadian Army began its push on Arnhem. The most important event of the day, however, occurred half a world away, at Warm Springs, Georgia. Here, at the Little White House, President Franklin D. Roosevelt suffered a cerebral hemorrhage

at 1:15 p.m. He died at 4:35 p.m. Eastern Standard Time. He was succeeded by Vice President Harry S. Truman.

Hitler saw FDR's death as the turning point. It was the miracle he
had been waiting for. For some time, Hitler had seen himself as a sort of
reincarnation of Frederick the Great. During the Seven Years' War, as
the Fuehrer had been telling everyone for months, Prussia seemed
defeated by the Allied coalition. Then the Czarina died, the coalition fell
apart, and Frederick and Prussia survived. Now, Hitler and Goebbels
declared, history was repeating itself. The death of Roosevelt, they
believed, signaled the being of the turning point for Nazi Germany.

Paul Joseph Goebbels was the first to return to reality. On April
13, he noticed that Roosevelt's death had no impact on the enemy's
operations. The Red Army took Vienna that day; U.S. General Simpson's 9th Army continued to advance on a wide front, pushing into the
rear of the German 11th and 12th Armies; the Ruhr Pocket was obviously collapsing; Patton—unchecked—continued his rampage across
central and southern Germany; Sandy Patch's U.S. 7th Army made
unaccountable headway in Bavaria; and Germany's last powder factory
had been lost, leaving the Wehrmacht with no more than a month's
worth of ammunition.

"Perhaps fate has again been cruel and made fools of us," Goebbels
told members of his staff that evening. "Perhaps we counted our chickens
before they were hatched."[15]

Goebbels's view was confirmed over the next two days. On April 14,
the Ruhr Pocket was split in two, Patton captured Chemnitz, and the
U.S. 3rd Armored Division advanced twenty-three miles against weak
opposition. That same day Bayreuth was captured by the Americans.
The "battle" consisted of one Hitler Youth member firing a Panzerfaust
at an American Sherman. He missed the tank and hit the side of a house.
There were no casualties.

The next day, April 15, the British 49th Infantry Division finally
took Arnhem, and the 5th Canadian Armoured Division drove toward
the Zuider Zee (IJsselmeer) to split the German forces in the Netherlands

in two. The French 1st Army took Kehl in the Black Forest, the Americans captured the huge I. G. Farben chemical plant at Leverkusen, and the British liberated the Belsen concentration camp and freed 40,000 prisoners. They also found 10,000 unburied bodies and the world was again shocked by fresh evidence of the Nazi brutality. Nuremberg, the site of infamous party rallies, fell to the Americans on April 20, Hitler's last birthday.

April was a disastrous month for the German Officer Corps. Casualties among its leadership included:

- Lieutenant General Anton Rathke, Battle Commander of Halle, captured.
- Major of the General Staff Baerwinkel, chief of operations, 131st Infantry Division, missing in action at the beginning of April.
- Lieutenant Colonel of the General Staff Karl Daub, chief of operations, 61st Volksgrenadier Division, killed in action, Heiligenbeil, Eastern Front, beginning of April.
- Lieutenant General Doctor Johannes Mayer, commander, II Corps, Courland, relieved of his command and promoted to general of infantry the same day, April 1, 1945. He was not reemployed.
- Lieutenant General Franz Sensfuss, commander, 212th Infantry, Western Front, relieved of his command, April 1, 1945.
- Major General Walter Schade, killed in action, Glogau, Eastern Front, April 2.
- Major General Johannes Erxlehen, commandant of Kassel, captured by the Americans, April 4.
- Lieutenant General Karl Wintergerst, commanding general, Harko 304 (304th Higher Artillery Command), supporting 17th Army on the Eastern Front, missing in action on April 8 and never found.

- Major of the General Staff Hans-Guenther Stotten, Id (chief training officer), Army Group South, captured at Wolfgraben near Vienna, April 4. He was shot and killed the next day by Soviet guards during an escape attempt. Stotten had earned the Knight's Cross as a second lieutenant in France (1940) and the Oak Leaves as commander of the I/8th Panzer Regiment of the Afrika Korps in Tunisia, 1943.
- Colonel General Walter Weiss, commander-in-chief, Army Group North, relieved of his command, April 5.
- Major General of Medical Services Doctor Arthur Zimmer, chief medical officer, Wehrkreis XVII, committed suicide.
- Colonel of the General Staff Heinrich Borgmann, OKW adjutant to the Fuehrer, killed by a low-flying air attack in the Magdeburg sector, April 6.
- Lieutenant General Bernhard von Clear, commander, Special Purposes Staff von Clear, wounded in action, Western Front. Captured by the Americans, April 29.
- Major General Doctor Karl Koske, commander, 212th Infantry Division, killed in a bombing attack on Vienna, April 8.
- Lieutenant General Karl Loewrick, commander, 542nd Volksgrenadier Division, killed in action near Pillau, Eastern Front.
- Lieutenant General Hans Mikosch, Battle Group Commander and Deputy Commandant of Koenigsburg, Eastern Front captured, April 8.
- Major Guenther Sempert, commander, 1st Parachute Anti-Tank Battalion, wounded in action, Italy, April 8. He was captured by the Americans on May 2.
- Lieutenant General Karl von Beeren, commander, Division 526, captured by the British, April 9.

- Major General Doctor Walter Kuehn, commander, 246th Volksgrenadier Division, captured near Pillau, Eastern Front, April 9.
- Major General Eugen-Alexander Lobach, commander, Division Hela East, reported sick on April 9 and evacuated to the West.
- Lieutenant General Johann Mickl, commander, 392nd (Croatian) Infantry Division, shot in the head in a skirmish against partisans in Yugoslavia, April 9. He died in the hospital at Rijeka the next day.
- Major General Guenter Hoffmann-Schoenborn, commander, 5th Panzer Division, wounded in action, Eastern Front, April 10. He was evacuated from East Prussia by ship on April 15.
- Lieutenant General Rudolf Sperl, commander, 61st Infantry Division, captured on the Eastern Front, April 10.
- General of Infantry Ernst Haase, retired, committed suicide in Potsdam, April 11.
- Major General Erich Seidel, commander, 257th Volksgrenadier Division, killed in action near Dobein, Bavaria, in a skirmish against the French, April 11.
- General of Artillery Curt Gallenkamp, former commander of the LXXX Corps, captured by the Russians, April 12.
- General of Infantry Karl Kriebel, commander, Wehrkreis VII, transferred to Fuehrer Reserve, April 12.
- Major General Karl Meltzer, Higher Artillery Commander I, captured on the Eastern Front, April 12.
- Lieutenant General Richard Wirtz, General of Engineers, Army Group B, captured, April 12.
- Private Gerhard Kegler, who had been a major general before he ran afoul of the Nazis and was court-martialed and demoted, critically wounded, April 12. He spent the next year in various hospitals.

- Lieutenant General Ernst Hammer, commander, Division 190, captured by U.S. forces, April 13.
- Lieutenant General Curt Siewert, commander, 58th Infantry Division, severely wounded, Hela peninsula, East Prussia, April 13.
- Major General August Hagl, commandant of Bayreuth, captured by the Americans, April 14.
- Lieutenant Colonel of the General Staff Karl-Ludwig von Rittberg, chief of intelligence, Army Group South, found guilty of being a defeatist by a drumhead court-martial and executed, April 14.
- Lieutenant General Kurt Roeder von Diersburg, Wehrmacht Replacement Inspector, Cologne, captured by the Americans, April 13, 1945.
- Major General Karl Arnold, retired, died from wounds suffered in an air attack on Vienna, April 15.
- Major General Hans-Joachim Ehlert, commander, 114th Jaeger Division, captured in northern Italy, April 15.
- Major General Wolf Ewert, commander, 338th Infantry Division, captured by the Americans, April 15.
- Major General Maximilian Jais, former commandant of Luxembourg and now commanding a sector on the West Wall, captured, April 15.
- Major of the General Staff Alfred Dippold, quartermaster, 75th Infantry Division, transferred to Fuehrer Reserve due to wounds suffered in Upper Silesia, Eastern Front, April 15.
- Lieutenant General Walter Botsch, commander, LVII Panzer Corps, captured in the Ruhr, April 16.
- Lieutenant General Eduard Crasemann, commander, XII SS Corps, captured on the Western Front, April 16. Promoted to general of artillery, April 20.
- Lieutenant General Hellmuth Boehlke, commander, 334th Volksgrenadier Division, Italy, sacked April 16.

- General of Infantry Carl Puechler, commander, LXXIV Corps, captured in the Ruhr, Western Front, April 16.
- Colonel General Karl Adolf Hollidt, formerly, former commander, 6th Army, and now military advisor to the Gauleiter of the Rhineland-Westphalia, surrendered to U.S. troops, April 17.
- Colonel General Joseph Harpe, commander, 15th Army, surrendered to U.S. troops in the Ruhr Pocket, April 17.
- Lieutenant General Karl Burdach, commander, 320th Higher Artillery Command, captured by U.S. forces in the Ruhr, April 17.
- Major General Alois Weber, commander, 362nd Infantry Division, captured in Italy, April 17.
- General of Infantry Kurt von der Chevallerie, former commander of the 1st Army, missing in the vicinity of Kolberg, East Prussia, April 18. Chevallerie had been sacked by Hitler on September 5, 1944. He was presumed killed by Soviet aircraft that attacked a refugee column he was in.
- Major General Georg Haus, commander, 50th Infantry Division, killed on the Eastern Front, April 18.
- Lieutenant General Hans Kaellner, acting commander, XXIV Panzer Corps, killed in action near Sokoinica, southeast of Brunn, on the Eastern Front, April 18.
- Major General Ernst von Kurnatowski, retired, a former staff officer at OKH, arrested by the Russians on April 18 and never seen again.
- Major General Karl von Dewitz, former commander of the 137th Infantry Division, executed by the Nazis, April 19. Members of the Hitler Youth did the shooting.
- General of Infantry Otto Hitzfeld, commander of the 11th Army, captured by Americans in the Harz Mountains, April 19.
- Major General Heinrich Buercky, commander, 159th Infantry Division, captured on the Western Front, April 20.

- Lieutenant General Martin Dehmel, General of Engineers and Leader, Engineer Staff North Coast, captured, April 20.
- General of Infantry Sigismund von Foerster, commander, LXXII Corps, captured, Western Front, April 20.
- General of Infantry Joachim von Kortzfleisch, commander, Rhine Bridgehead of Army Group B (between Koblenz and Duesseldorf), killed in action by U.S. forces, April 20.
- Major General Walter Nagel, chief of staff of the Ligurian Army, relieved, April 20.
- Major General Peter-Paul Peterson, chief inspector of Motor Pool Troops at OKH, killed in an air attack on Straubing, April 20.
- General of Mountain Troops Kurt Versock, commander of the XXXXIII Corps, placed in Fuehrer Reserve, April 20.
- Major General Kurt Forster, commandant of Colmar, captured on the Western Front, April 21.
- General of Panzer Troops Karl Decker, commander of the XXXIX Panzer Corps, committed suicide near Gross Brunsrode, Brunswick, April 21.
- Lieutenant General Hermann Floerke, commander, LXVI Corps, captured by the Americans in the Harz Mountains, April 21.
- Lieutenant General Gustav Hundt, commander, 1st Ski Division, missing in action at Pfaffenhofen, Upper Palatinate (near Troppau, now Opava in the Czech Republic), April 21. Declared dead, 1950.
- Field Marshal Walter Model, commander-in-chief, Army Group B, committed suicide near Duisburg, April 21.
- Major General Alfred Heisig, commander, Battle Command Deutsch Eylau, killed in action, Eastern Front, April 22.
- Major General Friedrich von Schellwitz, commander, 305th Infantry Division, captured south of the Po, Italian Front, April 23.

- Lieutenant General Ralf Sodan, commandant of Cottbus, a university city seventy-eight miles southeast of Berlin, committed suicide, April 23, near the Eastern Front.
- Luftwaffe Lieutenant General Alfred Sturm, former chief of motorization at OKW, now commander, Division Sturm, captured at Thale in the Harz Mountains.
- Lieutenant General Ernst-Guenther Baade, acting commanding general, LXXXI Corps, wounded by a British fighter-bomber near his estate at Neverstade, Holstein. He died in the hospital at Bad Segeberg on May 8.
- Lieutenant General Walter Jost, commander, 42nd Jaeger Division, killed in action, Villadosa, Italy, April 24.
- Colonel Alexander Moeckel, commander, 16th Volksgrenadier Division, killed in action near Karlsruhe, April 24.
- Major General Georg Scholze, commander, 20th Panzer Grenadier Division, committed suicide in Berlin, April 24. Scholze's wife and children had been killed in an Allied bombing attack a few days before. He had been promoted to major general on April 20.
- Lieutenant General Otto Butze, Inspector of Wehrmacht Ersatz Troops, Linz, severely wounded.
- Former Major General (now Private) Wolfgang von Holwede, surrendered to the French on April 25. He had been demoted for his part in the Conspiracy of July 20.
- General of Panzer Troops Count Gerhard von Schwerin, commander, LXXVI Panzer Corps, surrendered in Italy, April 25.
- Major General Marian von Wessely, chief of the Army Archives in Vienna, killed in Vienna, April 25.
- Lieutenant General Oskar Blumm, commanding general, Division 407, captured on the Western Front, April 26.
- Lieutenant General Hanskurt Hoecker, former commander of the 167th Volksgrenadier Division and now

commander, Korpsgruppe Hoecker, captured on the Western Front, April 26.

- Lieutenant General Henning von Thadden, commander, 1st Infantry Division, mortally wounded near Fischhausen, East Prussia, April 26. He died on May 18 in a field hospital near Vordingborg, Denmark.
- Major General of Reserves Maximilian Wengler, commander, 83rd Infantry Division, killed at Pillau, Eastern Front, April 26.
- Lieutenant Colonel Walter Paul Liebing, commander, 23rd Parachute Regiment, 2nd Parachute Division, captured by the Americans at Hagen, Westphalia, April 26.
- SS Colonel Ruediger Pipkorn, commander, 35th SS Police Grenadier Division, killed in action, Berlin, April 26.
- Lieutenant General Fritz Becker, commandant of Bremen, surrendered to the British, April 27.
- Major General Carl Henke, commander, 290th Infantry Division, killed in action, Eastern Front, April 27.
- Professor Doctor Zeiss, Army Sanitation Inspector and former chief of the Military Medical Academy, killed in action, Battle of Berlin.
- Lieutenant General Werner von Bercken, commander, 558th Volksgrenadier Division, captured on the Eastern Front.
- Major General Ernst Friedrich Biehler, commandant of Fortress Frankurt/Oder, captured, April 28.
- Major General Kurt Domansky, commander, 50th Infantry Division, killed in action, Stutthof, Frische Nehrung, East Prussia, April 28.
- Major General Dr. Erwin Kaschner, commander, 326th Volksgrenadier Division, captured by U.S. forces, April 28.
- Major General Rudolf Sieckenius, commander, 391st Security Division, killed in action, Berlin, April 28.[16]

- Major General of Reserves Rudolf von Oppen, commander, 352nd Volksgrenadier Division, captured, April 29.
- General of Mountain Troops Valentin Feurstein, Inspector of Tyrolian Troops and Commandant of the Alpine Front and former commander of the LI Mountain Corps, captured, April 29.
- Colonel General Heinrich von Vietinghoff, commander-in-chief, Army Group C and OB Southwest, relieved of duty and arrested, April 29.
- Major General Gustav-Adolf von Wulffen, commandant of Potsdam and commander, Infantry Division Potsdam, mortally wounded, April 29, and died near Beelitz, May 4. Wulffen was a holder of the *Pour le Merite*.

German infantry in the street fighting in Wollin, March 1945. Wollin was both a city and an island in the Baltic Sea and was part of Western Pomerania. It was transferred to Poland after the war and is now called Wolin. *Bundesarchiv Bild 183-H26409/Unknown/CC-BY-SA 3.0*

- Major General Johannes Hoelz, chief of staff, 9th Army, killed in an Allied air attack near Ruckzug on the Elbe, April 29.
- Lieutenant General Hans Schmidt, commander, 275th Infantry Division, captured at Halbe on the Eastern Front.
- Major General Heinrich Gaede, commander, 719th Infantry Division, captured by U.S. forces, April 30.
- Major General of Medical Services Doctor Karl Holm, Chief Medical Officer of Wehrkreis II, committed suicide, Schwerin, Eastern Front.
- Lieutenant General Werner Marcks, commander, 21st Panzer Division, captured on the Eastern Front, end of April 1945.
- Major of the General Staff Gert Dickore, quartermaster, 50th Infantry Division, wounded in action, end of April 1945.

The Wehrmacht was dying—and its last battle was imminent.

CHAPTER XII

GOETTERDAEMMERUNG

On April 12, the Red Army launched probes against Army Group Vistula and the 4th Panzer Army (on the left wing of Army Group Center). On April 14, the 20th Panzer Grenadier Division prevented five Soviet divisions, supported by two hundred tanks, from storming Seelow Heights west of Kuestrin, and inflicted heavy losses on the Soviets. But the probes continued. Then, on April 16, Zhukov launched his main blow, pounding what he assumed to be the German frontline with tens of thousands of guns, howitzers, cannons, mortars, airplanes, and multiple-tube rocket launchers. Zhukov had so concentrated his batteries that in some areas there were three hundred to four hundred guns per mile. What Zhukov didn't know was that Heinrici had retracted the German frontline by an average of a mile or two during the night.[1] The Red barrage struck thin air.

After a three-hour bombardment, and still under cover of darkness, the Russian assault divisions advanced—into soggy earth that had been plowed by artillery fire. Heinrici's new battleline was completely intact. It cut down wave after wave of Soviet assault troops, and the entire Red

A Soviet artillery battalion bombarding German positions on Seelow Heights. *Bundesarchiv Bild 183-E0406-0022-012/CC-BY-SA 3.0*

offensive degenerated into a mass of blood, confusion, death, and disorganization.

With the Soviet offensive was stalled, Stalin could not resist meddling and ordered General Vasilii Sokolovsky, the chief of staff of the 1st Ukrainian Front, to commit the 1st and 2nd Guards Tank Armies to the attack, which added to the tangled mess, as Red tanks maneuvered through mud and disorganized infantry.

April 17 was another frustrating day for Stalin, Stavka (the Russian High Command), Zhukov, and Sokolovsky. They committed the 47th Army of the 1st Belorussian Front's reserve near Seelow, close to where the 1st and 2nd Guards Tank Armies had been committed, but Heinrici and Busse brought up two of their mobile reserve divisions—the 18th Panzer Grenadier and Panzer Division Muencheberg—just in time. The Soviets captured Seelow Heights—after the 20th Panzer Grenadier ran out of ammunition and much of the division was slaughtered—but the German second line of defense held, and the Reds were kept to minor gains. The young men of the 9th Parachute Division not only held their line but knocked out forty Soviet tanks, despite suffering 30 percent casualties.

On April 18, Zhukov again tried—and failed—to break through. Soviet casualties were so heavy that by the end of the day, supply and service troops were thrown into the battle. Zhukov threatened that any soldier failing to advance would be executed.

South of Army Group Vistula, however, the Soviets found more success.

On April 16, Konev's 1st Ukrainian Front attacked General Fritz-Hubert Graeser's 4th Panzer Army. By nightfall, the Soviets had thirty-seven fixed and pontoon bridges and were operating ferries for infantry across the Neisse River. On April 17, Konev moved the tanks of the 3rd and 4th Guards Tank Armies across the river, and on April 18 advanced to the German strongpoints of Spremberg and Cottbus. He bypassed Spremberg, and severed connections between Army Groups Center and Vistula, which German counterattacks could not restore.

April 18 was a day of optimism at Fuehrer Headquarters. Hitler believed that the Soviet offensive had "substantially" run its course; however, most of this optimism was based on Field Marshal Keitel's dubious rule of thumb that offensives stalled if they did not achieve a major break-through within three days.[2] On April 19, however, the 1st Belorussian Front pushed as far as Muencheberg; the 2nd Guards Tank Army broke through west of Wriezen and separated the German 9th Army from the 3rd Panzer Army; and the Soviet 3rd and 4th Guards Tank Armies pushed towards Zossen and Potsdam. Map 12.1 shows the Battle of Berlin.

Heinrici, with Hitler's permission, moved Berlin's battleworthy formations to the 9th Army's front. By now, however, the 3rd Guards Tank Army was across the Spree and advancing on Berlin. Field Marshal Ferdinand Schoerner, meanwhile, reinforced the 4th Panzer with four divisions and signaled Berlin that he hoped to halt the Soviets' southern thrust at Bautzen, about a hundred miles south of Berlin.[3]

During the night of April 19/20, after a day of very hard fighting, two armies of the 1st Belorussian Front broke through Heinrici's third line of defense and the 2nd Guards Tank Army reached open country. The offensive was far behind schedule, but Zhukov had at last achieved his breakthrough. The Soviets had been surprised by the tenacity of the defense and had been especially surprised by the courage and stubbornness of the Volkssturm. In the West, these formations were a joke. In the East, however, they were defending their families against the Red Terror, which they knew meant the rape and perhaps the murder of their women, forced deportations to Siberia, and slavery or death. Cold, frightened, and lonely in their foxholes, trenches, or bunkers, these civilians-in-uniform—old men and boys—were tenacious defenders against Soviet infantry and armored units. Grandfathers often occupied the same foxholes as their grandsons. Instead of running away or surrendering, as in the West, they clung to their Panzerfausts (the one weapon they had in abundance), let the Russian tanks rumble to within easy range of their positions, and then knocked them out—by the hundred.

Despite the resistance of the Volkssturm, the 9th Army had no more mobile reserves, and Zhukov pushed into the northern outskirts of Berlin, reaching Ladeburg and Zepernick by daylight. Konev had done a much better job of controlling his forces than had Zhukov, and, on April 20, his 3rd and 4th Guards Tank Armies pulled away from the left flank of Army Group Center. By the end of the day, he had pushed north of Jueterbog (where he captured probably the largest remaining ammunition depot the Wehrmacht had left) and was closing in on a new German line, ten miles south of Zossen. This line was hastily organized by General Reymann (who had been relieved as commandant of Berlin), but it amounted to no more than a screen and certainly would not hold for long.

The twin breakthroughs of Zhukov and Konev isolated 9th Army, as Map 12.1 shows. On the morning of April 20, General Busse reported that the only way he could maintain a solid line east of Berlin was to pull back from the Oder and the area south of Frankfurt. Hitler, however, refused to allow it. Heinrici therefore moved SS General Felix Steiner's ad hoc command ("Group Steiner") north of Berlin to take command of the weak units on the exposed southern flank of General Manteuffel's 3rd Panzer Army. Three Soviet armies heavily attacked the 3rd Panzer Army in the Mecklenburg sector but were turned back.

Map 12.1: The Battle of Berlin, April 16–May 2, 1945.

On April 20, 1945, Hitler celebrated his 56th birthday. At the Fuehrer conference that day, General of Fliers Karl Koller, the chief of the General Staff of the Luftwaffe, announced that anyone intending to leave Berlin for Bavaria would have to depart soon, as the city's roads south would soon be in enemy hands. Admiral Doenitz, to whom Hitler had given command of the Reich's northern forces, could not decide whether to leave Berlin. "How can I call upon the troops to undertake the decisive battle for Berlin if at the same moment I withdraw myself to safety?" he asked Hermann Goering. "I shall leave it to fate whether I die in the capital or fly to Obersalzberg at the last moment."[4]

By the end of the conference, according to Speer, Goering seemed "utterly distraught," announcing that he and General Koller had to leave Berlin urgently to deal with matters in the south. Hitler stared at him absently and told him he could leave, but General Koller needed to remain at Fuehrer Headquarters. The two shook hands in icy silence and the Fat One departed; they never saw each other again.

Himmler also left, heading for Hohenlychen in northern Germany, and Grand Admiral Doenitz left for Ploen in Schleswig-Holstein late that night, leaving Vice Admiral Hans-Erich Voss as his liaison officer with Fuehrer Headquarters. Doenitz was joined two days later by General of Infantry Eberhard Kinzel, the newly appointed chief of staff of OKW Command Staff North and an experienced General Staff officer. Kinzel was succeeded as chief of staff of Army Group Vistula by Major General Ivo-Thilo von Trotha, the chief of the Operations Branch of OKH since late March. Jodl's deputy, Lieutenant General August Winter, who was to be chief of staff of OKW Command Staff B (the southern command post) also departed for Bavaria on April 20, along with most of the essential members of the OKW Operations Staff and the Operations Branch of OKH. Field Marshal Kesselring, the OB West, was placed in charge of all forces south of Berlin.

That night, the 3rd Guards Tank Army captured Zossen—the Headquarters of the High Command of the Army since August 1939—the 4th Guards Tank Army advanced west into the area of Luckenwalde, and Konev, with much of the Soviet army still pinned down in heavy fighting at Spremberg and Cottbus, brought up another army, the 28th, to cover gaps in the Soviet offensive. The first Russian artillery shells landed in Berlin on April 21.

Hitler, meanwhile, found a new source of hope: Group Steiner. Although it only had about 15,000 men, the Fuehrer quickly magnified it in his imagination into an army-sized command and ordered it to take charge of the 25th Panzer Grenadier, 5th Jaeger, and 4th SS Panzer

Grenadier Divisions (all north of the Finow Canal) and the LVI Panzer Corps (east of Berlin, near Werneuchen). He upgraded Group Steiner to Army Detachment Steiner, took it from Army Group Vistula, and placed it directly under the command of OKW (which meant himself), and ordered that it fight its way to the LVI Panzer Corps to seal the gap exploited by Zhukov's forces. To Steiner's orders he added a personal note: "Officers who do not accept this order without reservation are to be arrested and shot instantly. You yourself I make responsible with your head for its execution."[5]

Hitler had ordered Steiner to attack with four divisions, but the SS general had only one he could deploy: the weak 4th SS Panzer Grenadier, which had lost most of its heavy equipment in the Battle of Danzig. He had been assigned the 3rd Marine Division (made up of sailors with little training in ground combat), but it had not yet arrived from the coast to relieve the 5th Jaeger and 25th Panzer Grenadier. Since he only had one division for the attack, Steiner wisely decided not to move at all.

Fourth Panzer Army did advance on April 21. It was a purely local counterattack northwest of Goerlitz, and it made some progress, but Hitler quickly saw in it the beginnings of a major thrust that would close the gap between Army Groups Center and Vistula—a chasm now forty miles wide. He ordered 4th Panzer to continue with the counterattack and instructed 9th Army to attack as well, eliminating the gap between them and cutting off most of the 1st Ukrainian Front in the process.

In Berlin, Adolf Hitler was oscillating violently between optimism and reality. When Keitel and Jodl visited the Fuehrer Bunker that afternoon, they found Hitler in despair. He told his longtime OKW cronies that he now intended to remain in Berlin until the end; if there had to be any negotiating with the enemy, Goering was better suited to do it than he. This time neither general was able to lift the spirits of the dictator. The Red Army was already in the eastern suburbs of Berlin. Zhukov had crossed the main autobahn ring north of the city with three armies, and the 3rd Guards Tank Army had reached Koenigswusterhausen, well in the rear of Busse's 9th Army. Still, the 8th Guards and 1st Tank Armies were checked east of Berlin and had suffered heavy losses, especially in tanks, in attacks against the Volkssturm. Local counterattacks from regular German infantry units had driven Soviet casualties even higher. Meanwhile, Major General Biehler, the commandant of "Fortress Frankfurt," had fully justified Heinrici's confidence in him and had pinned down two Soviet armies, while the Russian 61st and Polish 1st (Communist) Armies (on the northern flank of 1st Belorussian Army) had gained nothing in attacks against Army Detachment Steiner.

Jodl told General Koller what Hitler had said about Goering as a negotiator—and Koller immediately assumed that Goering would soon be negotiating peace with the Allies. Tremendously excited, he telephoned Goering at Berchtesgaden and, over a scratchy line, told him this latest development. A few minutes later Colonel Berndt von Brauchitsch, Goering's chief adjutant, instructed Koller to personally report to the Reichsmarschall. Koller drove to Gatow Airfield and, that night, flew out of the impending encirclement of Berlin, along with several other members of the Fuehrer's entourage, heading for Bavaria.

On April 22, Hitler again assumed personal command of Berlin's defenses. He named General of Engineers Walter Kuntze and Colonel Ernst Kaether (the National Socialist Leadership Officer at OKH) as his deputies.

While Zhukov's right wing crossed the Havel at Hennigsdorf and moved south against Potsdam to complete the encirclement of Berlin, Hitler waited impatiently for a report on the progress of the Steiner offensive. During the afternoon situation conference, he learned that the SS general had not attacked. Adolf Hitler snapped, and in a crying rage, he (for the first time) declared that the war was lost—a fact he blamed exclusively on his generals. He intended to remain in Berlin until the end, he declared, and would commit suicide at the last possible moment; he would not let the Russians take him alive. Anyone who wanted to leave for Obersalzberg could do so, he shouted, but he was staying here, in Berlin. Keitel and Jodl pledged to stand by him until the last.

Others were more pragmatic. Julius Schaub, his longtime personal adjutant, elected to depart, as did Hitler's two stenographers, two of his five secretaries, Admiral von Puttkamer, Major General Eckard Christian (the chief of operations of the Luftwaffe), and quite a few others. Among those to leave was Doctor Theodor Morell, his personal physician. "I don't need drugs to see me through," were Hitler's last words to Morell.

Hitler's depression was short-lived, after all. Jodl noted that the 12th Army, facing west on a line southeast of Magdeburg, was not yet fully engaged with the Americans. Hitler saw another glimmer of hope and demanded that the 12th Army be brought to Berlin. He would stand or fall in the city. "I will never leave Berlin—*never!*" he shouted at Keitel and Bormann later that afternoon. As if to emphasize his decision, Hitler sent for his personal papers, sorted them, and decided which ones to destroy. His personal adjutant Schaub took them into the Chancellery garden, burned them, and then left for Gatow airfield. Hitler also asked Joseph and Magda Goebbels to move into the Fuehrer Bunker, along with their six children. They occupied the rooms just vacated by Doctor Morell.

The Reds continued to advance. The 2nd Belorussian Front, against tough opposition from Manteuffel's 3rd Panzer Army, established a bridgehead ten miles long above Stettin. To the south, Konev's armies finally took Cottbus and smashed the 9th Army's front south of Frankfurt.

When Krebs talked with Heinrici on the telephone at 9:00 p.m., the chief of the general staff was full of optimism that General Walther Wenck's 12th Army would reach Berlin and save the Reich. Heinrici, however, disagreed and was instead looking to preserve the Wehrmacht's strength. He asked permission to pull 9th Army back at least twenty miles to the west. Three hours later, Hitler authorized Heinrici to withdraw the 9th Army to a line stretching from north of Cottbus to Liebe-rose, Beeskow, and the Spree, a position that he thought would assist his plans for the 12th Army.

When Hitler made the decision to order 12th Army to relieve Berlin, Keitel volunteered to hand deliver the order to Wenck. Jodl left at the same time to set up a new OKW command post at Krampnitz. Krebs remained behind as Hitler's principle military advisor.

Early in the morning of April 23, Keitel turned up at Wenck's head-quarters and ordered the astonished general to leave the Elbe, turn his army around 180 degrees, and head east, toward Jueterbog and Potsdam. This order could have been issued several hours earlier had Keitel remained in Berlin and used the telephone. In any case, Wenck turned his back on General Simpson's U.S. 9th Army and marched east, toward Potsdam and Berlin.

Meanwhile, General of Infantry Theodor Busse, commanding the German 9th Army, signaled General of Artillery Helmuth Weidling to use his LVI Panzer Corps to retreat to a line from Koenigswusterhausen to Rangsdorf, about twelve miles south of Berlin, to protect the 9th Army's left flank as it tried to escape the Soviet juggernaut. But when Hitler learned of the order, he cancelled it.

At approximately the same time in Bavaria, Karl Koller arrived at Hermann Goering's house at Berchtesgaden and told the Reichsmarschall that it was time to negotiate with the Allies. Goering was uncertain. "Bormann is my deadly enemy," he said. "He is only waiting to get me. If I act, he will call me a traitor. If I don't, he will accuse me of having failed at the most difficult hour."[6] After some vacillation, he, Hans Lammers (the chief of Hitler's Presidential Chancellery), and Koller wrote a dispatch which they sent to Berlin. It read:

> Mein Fuehrer, since you are determined to remain at your post in Fortress Berlin, do you agree that I as your deputy in accordance with your decree of 29 June 1941 assume imme-diately total leadership of the Reich with complete freedom of action at home and abroad? If by 10 p.m. no answer is forthcoming, I shall assume that you have been deprived of your freedom of action. I will then consider the terms of your

decree to have come into force and act accordingly for the good of the Volk and the Fatherland. You must realize what I feel for you in these most difficult hours of my life, and I am quite unable to find words to express it. God bless you and grant you may come here after all as soon as possible. Your most loyal Hermann Goering.

When the telegram arrived, it was handed to Martin Bormann, who immediately tried to distort and falsify its meaning. "Goering's engaged in treason!" he shouted. Hitler, however, was in one of his apathetic moods, and Bormann could not arouse his anger. It took some time, but Bormann succeeded in convincing Hitler that Goering was attempting a coup d'état when word arrived that Goering had ordered von Ribbentrop to report to Berchtesgaden (if Hitler did not answer Goering's original message by midnight). Hitler threw off his lethargy and, Speer recalled,

An outburst of wild fury followed in which feelings of bitterness, helplessness, self-pity and despair mingled. With flushed face and staring eyes, Hitler ranted... "I've known it all along. I know Goering is lazy. He let the Luftwaffe go to pot. He was corrupt. His example made corruption possible in our state. Besides, he's been a drug addict for years, I've known it all along."

Then, suddenly, like a deflated balloon, he slumped back into a chair. "Well, all right," he said, returning to apathy. "Let Goering negotiate the surrender. If the war is lost, it doesn't matter who does it."[7]

Bormann, however, pressed Hitler and before 10:00 p.m., Hitler forbade Goering from negotiating a surrender, charged him with high treason, and dismissed him from his offices. Bormann wanted Goering executed, but Hitler spared him in view of his previous services to the Reich. The next morning, April 24, Radio Hamburg announced:

"Reichsmarschall Hermann Goering is suffering from heart disease which has now reached an acute stage. He has therefore asked to be relieved of the command of the Luftwaffe" and resigned all of his offices.[8] The broadcast announced that the Fuehrer had named Robert Ritter von Greim as his successor and had promoted him to the rank of field marshal.

On April 24, at the headquarters of the 6th Air Fleet in the Ober-foehring-Freimann section of Munich, Ritter von Greim received an order instructing him to report to the Fuehrer Bunker. At Berchtesgaden, General Koller (now released from SS custody) received a similar tele-gram. Koller refused to go. He believed it was suicidal to fly to Berlin. Greim, on the other hand, was a devoted Nazi. He and Hanna Reitsch, a daredevil test pilot and one of the few women to hold the Iron Cross, flew to Berlin on April 26. En route, with Greim at the controls, they flew over embattled Grunewald. A Russian bullet tore through the floor-board of the airplane and struck Greim's right foot, shattering it. Reitsch then took the controls and landed on a street near the Brandenberger Tor and the Chancellery. They quickly commandeered a passing car and took Greim to the Bunker, where he was rushed into surgery.

While SS Colonel Doctor Ludwig Stumpfegger dressed Greim's wound, Hitler came into the room and asked the colonel general if he knew why he had been summoned. When Greim said he did not know, Hitler answered: "Because Hermann Goering has betrayed both me and his Fatherland! Behind my back he has established connections with the enemy. His action was a mark of cowardice!" He went on to repeat the entire story and handed the offending telegram to Greim, calling it "a crass ultimatum." As Greim read the telegram, Hitler threw another fit. "Nothing now remains!" he screamed. "Nothing is spared me! No loy-alty is kept, no honor observed; there is no bitterness, no betrayal that has not been heaped upon me; and now this! It is the end. No injury has been left undone!"[9] After a pause, Hitler regained his composure and informed the astonished Greim that he had called him to Berlin to appoint him commander-in-chief of the Luftwaffe and promote him to the rank of field marshal! This message, of course, could have easily been sent to him by radio, and then he would not have been lying on his back with a severe wound in doomed Berlin.

On the afternoon of April 24, Hitler summoned General Weidling, commander of the LVI Panzer Corps to the Fuehrer Bunker. He greeted him with the words: "Weidling, I will have you shot!" He then launched into a vicious tirade against the general, who, he said, had retreated without permission. Weidling said he had been following General Busse's orders to withdraw. Hitler—who had not been aware of Busse's orders—calmed down, even became friendly, and, a short time later, named Weidling commandant of Berlin. When General Krebs told him of his appointment, the tough veteran of the Eastern Front replied that he wished they had shot him instead. "What bastards Krebs and Burgdorf are!" Weidling snapped to his operations officer. "They did not warn me that Hitler was threatening to have me shot… " Busse and Burgdorf were brothers-in-law and close friends, which is possibly why Krebs and Burgdorf did not inform Hitler of Busse's order.[10]

General Weidling said he would accept the command on one condition: he must be the sole commander; he would not tolerate any interference from Doctor Goebbels, the Gauleiter of Berlin. "It was a courageous thing for Weldling to do," his chief of operations recalled, "because generals simply did not impose conditions on the acceptance of an order from Hitler. But Hitler probably realized that Goebbels would otherwise be a problem for Weidling, and he accepted the condition."[11]

He was Berlin's fifth commandant in 1945. The next one would be General Alexander Gorbatov—a Russian.

Just after nightfall on April 24, the LVI Panzer Corps fell back to the east—into Berlin—in accordance with Hitler's orders, which virtually ensured that General Busse's 9th Army would be encircled. That night, Busse told Heinrici that he had no ammunition for his artillery, but that using small arms, his men would attempt a breakout to the west.

On April 24, the LVI Panzer Corps included the remnants of the Panzer Division "Muencheberg," the 18th Panzer Grenadier Division, the 11th SS Panzer Grenadier Division "Nordland," and elements of the 9th Parachute Division. It was also supposed to include the 20th SS Volunteer Grenadier Division "Estonia # 1" and the 20th Panzer Grenadier Division, but the former had gone missing, and the latter had been virtually annihilated. Its commander, Major General Georg Scholze, had committed suicide after learning that his wife and children had been killed in an air raid.[12] Already preparing for the defense of Berlin were the 1st Flak Division (which also manned the huge flak towers in the Tiergarten, the Humboldthain, and the Friedrichshain), a naval battalion, part of Himmler's personal bodyguard, Oberfuehrer Wilhelm Mohnke's SS guards, two police battalions, about thirty Volkssturm battalions, and a few labor and Hitler Youth detachments.

"I was shocked when I found the prepared defense ring around Berlin," Major Knappe wrote later.

> It was empty foxholes and trenches and roadblocks—completely unmanned! Disgustedly, I realized that it was no more than a line on a map. It had been Goebbels's responsibility, as defense commissar for Berlin, to prepare these defenses, but it was painfully obvious that he had no idea how to do it. So much for Goebbels's ability to assume military command.[13]

General Heinrici, however, had planned for his armies to escape to the west all along—not to be trapped in Berlin. The 3rd Panzer Army did in fact bypass the city to the north, as did the 11th Army, but the 9th Army had been decisively engaged by the Soviets in the Halbe sector and most of it was not able to skirt the city to the south, as Heinrici had hoped. "So be it" was Heinrici's attitude. He was out to save what he could.

Heinrici and OKW pursued mutually exclusive objectives. Heinrici, realizing Berlin was doomed, concentrated on evacuating German soldiers and refugees to the West. Jodl and Keitel, however, blindly determined to defend Berlin, as the Fuehrer willed.

Early on the morning of April 25, Weidling took over the Headquarters of Wehrkreis III at Hohenzollerndamm in Wilmersdorf (a southwestern suburb of Berlin). The chief of staff of the military district, Lieutenant Colonel Hans Refior, was a General Staff officer and an old friend of Weidling's, an officer who knew his way around the political jungle of Berlin and a man who "knew how to get things done." Weidling decided to keep both his chiefs of staff: Refior for political matters and Lieutenant Colonel Theodor von Dufving, the chief of staff of the LVI Panzer Corps, for the actual fighting. He was less impressed with Major Sprotte, the Wehrkreis operations officer, so he dispatched him to Potsdam. This was perfectly fine with Sprotte, who wanted to get out of Berlin as quickly as possible. "To turn everything over to me in an orderly manner would have taken several days," Weidling's operations officer recalled, "so he showed me his maps and drawings with a sweep of his hand and promptly disappeared."[14]

Inside the city, SA and SS commandos and military police had set up "flying courts-martial." Some were members of General Wilhelm Mohnke's SS command, while others seem to have been self-appointed. They grabbed soldiers who were away from the front without proper authorization and, operating on the principle of "better hang one too many than one too few," hanged or shot them with no regard for justice. Major General of Reserves Werner Mummert, the commander of Panzer Division Muencheberg, turned on these self-anointed executioners and threatened to shoot any of them who dared enter his area of operation.

Late on the afternoon of the 24th, Konev and Zhukov linked their forces northwest of Potsdam. Berlin was now surrounded. On April 25, the Reds completed the encirclement of the German 9th Army and the Soviet 5th Guards Army met patrols of the U.S. 1st Army near the town of Torgau on the Elbe, fifty miles below Dresden. Germany was now cut in two (see Map 12.2).

That afternoon, General Busse summoned Colonel Baron Hans von Luck, the commander of the 125th Panzer Grenadier Regiment of the veteran 21st Panzer Division, and ordered him to prepare to break out. During the night of April 25/26, Luck was to strike westward across the Dresden-Berlin highway, with the objective of reaching the Luckenwalde area on the Berlin-Leipzig autobahn.

Map 12.2

At first, Luck made good progress; then he ran into Stalin tanks and anti-tank units. Despite assistance from elements of the 35th SS Police Grenadier Division, he was unable to make any further progress and was quickly pinned down by vastly superior Soviet forces. On the morning of April 27, practically out of ammunition, the 125th Panzer Grenadier was forced to surrender. This was the fate that overtook most of the regiments of the 9th Army over the next several days.

Southwest of Berlin, near the Havel, Soviet artillery and fighter-bombers had finally rendered the Gatow Airfield unusable. Hitler's capital could now be reached via emergency airstrips only. To the north, the 2nd Belorussian Front finally managed to break through the 3rd Panzer Army, and drove towards Prenzlau despite Baron von Manteuffel's desperate efforts to stop it.

Senior OKW officers still made strenuous efforts to relieve Berlin and rescue the Fuehrer. As military historian Earl Ziemke noted, "In Jodl and Keitel, Hitler had ideal collaborators in futility."[15] During the night of April 24/25, Hitler signed an order consolidating his general staffs, with OKW absorbing OKH. Jodl had finally achieved the goal he had pursued for ten years—a unified command of the German ground forces. But it was too late to matter now.

For Hitler, the war had narrowed to the Battle for Berlin. That evening, he signaled the new OKW Command Post at Neu Roffen and ordered it to launch the "fastest execution of all relief attacks, without regard for flanks and neighbors." Jodl issued a series of utterly unrealistic orders that, simplified, had the 9th and 12th Armies advancing to Ferch, south of Potsdam, where they would join forces and drive to Berlin to rescue the Fuehrer. Army Detachment Steiner was to attack toward Berlin with the 25th Panzer Grenadier, 3rd Marine, and 7th Panzer Divisions. Manteuffel's 3rd Panzer Army was ordered to prevent the Soviets from expanding their Oder bridgehead.

On the Western Front, many divisions simply quit fighting. In the West, between April 1 and April 16, more than 755,000 German troops surrendered.

On April 16, R.A.F. bombers sank the pocket battleship *Luetzow* at Swinemuende (part of which is now Swinoujscie, Poland), and the U.S. 1st Army occupied Halle. The next day, the U.S. 30th Infantry Division took Magdeburg; the U.S. 7th Army began closing in on Nuremberg, the symbolic heart of Nazi Germany; the French 1st Army cut General Erich Brandenberger's 19th Army in two; and the U.S. VI Corps raced for the Swiss border to block any possible German escape from the Black Forest. Organized resistance in the Ruhr Pocket ended on April 18: the same day that Nuremberg was surrounded, an American patrol entered Czechoslovakia, and the Canadians reached the Zuider Zee, cutting Field Marshal Ernst Busch's OB Northwest in two and isolating most of its combat forces in eastern Holland.

April 19 saw the British reach the Elbe and two U.S. infantry divisions took Leipzig. Nuremberg fell on April 20 and French troops entered Stuttgart, the home of Mercedes-Benz and the administrative heart of the Saar. Many towns and smaller cities surrendered before the Allies even arrived. The Allied commander would simply learn the name of the Burgermeister of the next community, call him on the telephone, and arrange for a quick capitulation. By nightfall on April 23, the British had entered Bremen, the French had reached Lake Constance, Patch's U.S. 7th Army was sweeping along the Danube, and elements of Simpson's 9th U.S. Army had overrun the headquarters of the German 11 Army near Blankenburg and captured General Walther Lucht.[16] Potsdam, the garrison town of Frederick the Great, was besieged by the Russians on April 24, while the U.S. 1st Armored Division took Ulm and the U.S. 7th Army crossed the Danube at Dilligen.

On April 25, Eisenhower ordered the Allied armies not to advance beyond the Elbe and Mulde Rivers, effectively taking dozens of Allied divisions out of the battle for Berlin. The last strategic bombing raids of the war in Europe were flown against Pilsen, Wangerooge, Kiel, and Munich, while the former Italian naval base of La Spezia on the Ligurian coast was captured by the Allies. Brandenberger's forces in the Black Forest launched a desperate breakout attempt toward the Bavarian Alps on April 25 but were checked by April 27. On April 26, Marshal Petain of France was arrested as a collaborator, the last resistance in Bremen ended, and the Red Army captured Stettin and Brno (the capital of Moravia). On April 27, Hitler signaled Mussolini: "The struggle for our survival is at its height. Employing great masses and materials, Bolshevism and the armies of Jewry allied themselves to join their malignant forces in Europe in order to precipitate chaos in our continent."[17] This was to be the last message between the two. Mussolini was captured and shot by Italian partisans the next day; Hitler learned of his death via a Radio Stockholm broadcast.

The U.S. 7th Army took Ulm on April 27 and Augsburg on April 28, and reached Munich the same day. Hitler, however, hardly took notice of these events. He was too engrossed in the Battle of Berlin, and with good reason: by that time, the Russians were within a mile of the Reich Chancellery and the Fuehrer Bunker.

East and south of the city, Busse's 9th Army moved from the Spreewald due west to Luckenwalde, suffering heavy losses to Soviet air attacks along the way because the roads were thick with soldiers and refugees. Field Marshal Schoerner's southern offensive could not help the 9th Army because it had stalled after six days, forty miles south of its objective.[18]

To the north, the 25th Panzer Grenadier Division of Group Steiner had crossed the Havel west of Oranienburg and the 3rd Marine Division was strung out on the railroads between Oranienburg and the coast. The 7th Panzer Division, which had fought in the Battle of Danzig and had been brought to Swinemuende by sea only a few days before, had left its heavy equipment behind, did not have a single tank, and was now stuck in its assembly areas west of Neubrandenburg.

Jodl ordered Lieutenant General Rudolf Holste's XXXXI Panzer Corps of the 12th Army to assist Group Steiner by attacking northeast from Belzig while covering the Elbe River line and defending Brandenburg (to hold open the corridor between the Americans and the Russians). This was clearly asking too much of one weak corps that was too far west to help Steiner, but it took Jodl twenty-four hours to figure that out. Meanwhile General of Cavalry Karl-Erik Koehler's XX Corps, earmarked to relieve Berlin, was forced to defend the Brandenburg-Belzig-Wittenberg line to protect its staging areas.

The Fuehrer Bunker, shortly before it was demolished in 1947, as seen from the Chancellery garden. The opening at the left is the main emergency exit. The guard tower is in the center of the photograph. The large building to the rear is the Foreign Ministry. The building on the right is the reception hall of the Old Reich Chancellery. *Bundesarchiv Bild 183-V04744/CC-BY-SA 3.0*

The 2nd Belorussian Front broke through the 3rd Panzer Army (which had committed its last reserves) late on the afternoon of April 26 and pushed west; that evening, the telephone line connecting OKW with Berlin went dead. Communications were now dependent on a line-of-sight short wave that received and transmitted messages via a balloon, run up near OKW's command post.

The Russians contracted their ring around Berlin. They neared the Wehrkreis III building and from their office windows Weidling's staff officers could see hand-to-hand fighting in the gardens to the south. Weidling prudently moved his headquarters to the Bendlerstrasse—or at least to what was left of it.[19]

By now, the Red Army was subjecting Berlin to almost constant shelling. Major Knappe recalled how it "seemed as if the whole world were exploding around us." Artillery fire, he declared, was much worse in a city than in open terrain, because there was much more flying debris, which could be just as fatal as shrapnel.[20]

Fuehrer Headquarters meeting, 1945. Left to right: Lieutenant General Wilhelm Berlin, general of artillery at OKW; Field Marshal Ritter Robert von Greim, commander of the 6th Air Fleet; Luftwaffe Major General Franz Reuss, commander of the 4th Air Division; General of Flak Artillery Job Odebrecht, commander of the II Motorized Flak Corps; and General of Infantry Theodor Busse, commander of the 9th Army. *Bundesarchiv Bild 146-1971-033-33/CC-BY-SA 3.0*

On April 27, after a week's hard fighting, the armies of Rokossovsky's 2nd Belorussian Front were threatening to cut Manteuffel's 3rd Panzer Army in half. Heinrici ordered Manteuffel to withdraw from the exposed coastal area around Swinemuende and sent him the 25th Panzer Grenadier Division and part of the 7th Panzer Division.

Keitel was horrified to discover that Heinrici was conducting an orderly withdrawal without the permission of the Fuehrer or himself. He echoed Hitler's order that the 9th and 12th Armies should unite and relieve Berlin in the battle that would be "the decisive turning point of the war." To this, Keitel added: "History and the German people will despise everyone who does not do his utmost to save the situation and the Fuehrer."[21]

On April 27, with Rokossovsky's 2nd Belorussian Front threatening the vital communications center of Prenzlau, OKW activated the Headquarters of the 21st Army to come to Prenzalu's defense. But the headquarters, under the command of General of Infantry Kurt von Tippelskirch, consisted of only two regiments and the former staff of the 4th Army, and could do nothing to stop Rokossovsky's breakthrough.

With Berlin's defenses crumbling, General Weidling presented Hitler with a plan to break out of city. Hitler rejected it out of hand. A young General Staff officer, who had not seen Hitler in years, remarked:

> I was shocked by his appearance. He was stooped, and his left arm was bent and shaking. Half of his face drooped, as if he'd had a stroke, and his facial muscles on that side no longer worked. Both of his hands shook, and one eye was swollen. He looked like a very old man, at least twenty years older than his fifty-six years.
>
> . . . It occurred to me then that Hitler was still the living symbol of Germany—but Germany as it was now. In the same six years, the flourishing, aspiring country had become a flaming pile of debris and ruin.[22]

The Fuehrer was now suspicious of the SS and had lost faith in Steiner as a commander. He ordered that General Holste, the commander of the XXXXI Panzer Corps, assume command of the offensive (which Holste was in no position to do).

Hitler's suspicions then turned to Gruppenfuehrer Hermann Fegelein, the SS liaison officer to Fuehrer Headquarters. Hitler suddenly realized he had not seen him for some time. Fegelein was an arrogant, selfish opportunist and a womanizer—typical of the type of man who rose to prominence during the Nazi era. Born in Munich in 1906, he became a groom and then a jockey, working for Christian Weber, a notoriously corrupt friend of Hitler and one of his earliest cronies. By dealing in fraud and horse racing (and sometimes combining the two),

Weber amassed a fortune after 1933 and helped his friend Fegelein rise in the world. Weber arranged for him to enter the SS in 1935 and helped him advance, first in the "Death's Head" SS Cavalry *Standarte* and then in the SS Cavalry Brigade, which he commanded on the Eastern Front in 1941 and 1942. (Physical courage seems to have been Fegelein's only positive character trait.) Later, as an SS lieutenant general, he became Himmler's liaison officer to Fuehrer Headquarters. Shortly thereafter, in June 1944, he married Gretl Braun, the sister of Hitler's mistress, thus solidifying his position in the Fuehrer's court. Fegelein then joined forces with Bormann and Burgdorf and began betraying his chief, Himmler, to Hitler on a routine basis. According to SS Major General Friedrich Schellenberg, it was Fegelein who advised Hitler to publicly dishonor the SS divisions that had failed in the Lake Balaton offensive.[23] He also routinely cheated on Gretl. By April 1945, however, he realized that the end was near, and, showing an instinct for survival, quietly disappeared from the Fuehrer Bunker on April 26. Hitler did not miss him until late in the afternoon of April 27. Enquiries were made at once, and one of Hitler's former bodyguards, SS Lieutenant Colonel Peter Hoegl of the Reich Security Service, was ordered to find Fegelein. Hoegl, accompanied by an armed detachment of SS, tracked Fegelein to his home in Charlottenburg, quietly resting on his bed, in civilian clothes and very drunk.

Fegelein told Hoegl that he chose survival over death and tried to persuade the SS lieutenant colonel to join him in flying out of Berlin. Though Hoegl had a wife and family in Bavaria, he refused. Unruffled, Fegelein picked up the telephone, called Eva Braun, and asked her to smooth things over with the Fuehrer. This Eva apparently tried to do, until she learned that Fegelein was planning to abandon Gretl and escape with one of his mistresses. When Hoegl returned Fegelein to the Fuehrer Bunker, Hitler stripped Fegelein of his decorations, demoted him to the rank of SS private, and had him locked in a servant's room under armed guard.

At 10:30 p.m., Baron von Manteuffel reported to Heinrici that half of his divisions and his flak artillery (which constituted almost all his

General of Panzer Troops Baron Hasso von Manteuffel. *U.S. National Archives*

remaining guns) had quit fighting, and one hundred thousand men were streaming to the West to surrender. He had never seen anything like it, he said, not even in 1918. He then categorically stated that the war was over; the soldiers had "spoken." Heinrici did not correct him.[24]

By nightfall, Berlin was a sea of flames. The Russians had succeeded in surrounding Reymann's forces in Potsdam and had pushed Weidling's defenders into a pocket 9.5 miles long (east to west) and 1–3 miles wide.

On the morning of April 28, Field Marshal Wilhelm Keitel set out for the front. To his consternation and dismay, Heinrici was apparently not following orders. Keitel found the 5th Jaeger Division was backed onto a defensive line on the Havel River at Zehdenick—twenty miles west of where it should have been.

That afternoon, Keitel met with Heinrici and Manteuffel. By now, Jodl had spoken to Heinrici and threatened him with the "ultimate consequences" if he did not execute his orders. Keitel ordered Army Group Vistula to counterattack southeast of Neustrelitz. Heinrici returned to his headquarters—it took him three hours to cover twenty miles because the roads were so clogged with refugees and retreating soldiers—knowing that his orders were impossible. The troops, he observed, were "marching home in columns."[25]

To the south, in what became known as the Battle of the Halbe Pocket, 9th Army's breakout attempt failed. Busse signaled that his army was too depleted to make another attempt and could not hold out much longer. Weidling's forces were in no better shape. During the day, LVI

The Brandenburg Gate, more than a month after the fighting ended. *Bundesarchiv B 145-Bild-P054320/Weinrother, Carol/CC-BY-SA 3.0*

Panzer Corps was forced to retreat across the Spree (from the southeastern suburbs).

Miliary historian Earl Ziemke has noted that the battle for Berlin was fought mostly outside the city, and "What went on in the capital was hardly more than a contested mop-up. The fortress [of Berlin] had never come into existence."[26] This is true, but the Russians nevertheless suffered very heavy losses inside Berlin. Taking advantage of their knowledge of Berlin's streets, alleyways, byways, sewers, and interconnected basements, enterprising defenders (mostly Hitler Youth) kept appearing behind the Soviets, firing Panzerfaust rounds at nearly point-blank range at the back of Russian tanks where the armor was weakest, and then disappearing only to repeat the performance on another street. Konev's divisions alone lost eight hundred tanks to these tactics, and Zhukov's tank losses must have easily exceeded one thousand. Many Soviet soldiers were already drunk, which added to the casualty lists—on both sides.

The Red Army committed countless atrocities against the civilian population of Berlin, including untold numbers of rapes and murders. It was later estimated that four out of every ten women in Soviet-occupied Germany were raped, and many contracted venereal diseases as a result.[27]

On April 28, the Propaganda Ministry informed Hitler of a Reuters report that Himmler wanted to negotiate with the Western powers using Count Bernadotte of Sweden as an intermediary. Hitler grew even more furious at the SS and the world in general. "He raged like a madman," Hanna Reitsch recalled.[28] To Hitler, this was the last straw. Even *der treue Heinrich*—the faithful Heinrich Himmler, leader of the SS—had deserted him. Surely the end had come. That night, he expelled Himmler from the Nazi party and abolished Himmler's claim to be the Fuehrer's successor. Hitler was now convinced that the failure of the Steiner offensive and Himmler's treachery were connected. Since he could not take his revenge on the absent Reichsfuehrer, he decided to take it on Fegelein. Hitler quickly set up a tribunal to try Fegelein and any other Himmler co-conspirator he might discover. The members of the court included SS Oberfuehrer Wilhelm Mohnke, the commandant of the Reich Chancellery, SS Lieutenant General Johann Rattenhuber, chief of the Reich Security Service (Hitler's personal security forces), Krebs, and Burgdorf. Fegelein was condemned in record time. His sentence: death by SS firing squad in the Chancellery garden.

With Fegelein dead, Hitler ordered Ritter von Greim and Hanna Reitsch to fly out of the Fuehrer Bunker. Greim was to arrest Himmler and arrange maximum air support for General Walther Wenck's 12th Army to come to the relief of Berlin. Above all, they were to ensure that Himmler did not take control of the country. "A traitor must never succeed me as Fuehrer!" he cried to Greim and Reitsch. "You must get out to ensure that he will not."[29]

After Greim and Reitsch left the Bunker, sometime between 1:00 and 3:00 a.m. on April 29, Hitler rewarded Eva Braun for her years of loyalty by marrying her.[30] Bride and groom knew that their marriage would last only a few hours.

Following the wedding, Hitler dictated his last will and testament. He again denounced the Jews, exhorted the German people "not to give up the struggle," and told them that while National Socialism was temporarily defeated, "the seed has been sown that will grow one day ... into the glorious rebirth of the National Socialist movement in a truly united nation."

He appointed Grand Admiral Karl Doenitz president of the Reich and supreme commander of the armed forces and appointed his ministers for him—thus continuing his interference in military affairs from beyond the grave.

Field Marshal Ferdinand Schoerner (right), the last commander-in-chief of the army. This photograph was taken in Greece in 1941. *U.S. National Archives*

Among them was Ferdinand Schoerner, who was promoted to field marshal and named commander-in-chief of the army. Hitler urged Doenitz to "uphold the racial laws to the limit and to resist mercilessly the poisoner of all nations, international Jewry."[31] It was now after 4:00 a.m. on April 29, the last Sunday of his life. He went to bed with the Russians less than six hundred yards from the Reich Chancellery.

Shortly after midnight on April 29, General Heinrici again spoke to Keitel on the telephone. Heinrici had been sternly forbidden to retreat, but he made it clear that he had no intention of obeying such an irrational command; the retreat was going to continue, he said. Keitel immediately relieved both Heinrici and his chief of staff, von Trotha, of their posts, but it took Keitel and Jodl all day to find a replacement for Heinrici.[32] His permanent successor, Colonel General Kurt Student, was in the Netherlands and could not arrive before May 1 at the earliest. Keitel ordered Heinrici to have Manteuffel assume command, but Manteuffel refused to accept it even when ordered by Keitel himself. Keitel then offered General of Infantry Kurt von Tippleskirch the command, but he likewise refused until confronted with a direct order. Thus, Tippelskirch became the commander of Army Group Vistula on the afternoon of April 29. This formality had no effect on the battlefield. Communications with the 9th Army and the LVI Panzer Corps had been irrevocably severed, and, for all practical purposes, Army Group Vistula consisted of only the 3rd Panzer Army and two regiments of the 21st Army. Moreover, the Fuehrer Bunker had temporarily lost contact with OKW, Jodl, and Keitel after the Soviets spotted the communications balloon connecting the OKW command post to Berlin and shot it down.

Wenck's 12th Army, meanwhile, made surprising progress on April 29. In the morning, General of Cavalry Karl-Erik Koehler's XX Corps struck Russian lines near Beelitz. They took the Russians by surprise and quickly smashed the 5th Guards Mechanized Corps. Koehler recaptured Beelitz, freed more than three thousand wounded German soldiers who had been taken prisoner, and by afternoon, the Clausewitz, Scharnhorst, and Theodor Koerner divisions of XX Corps had surged forward fifteen miles and reached the tip of Schwielow Lake southwest of Potsdam. Wenck, however, realized that to continue the advance to Berlin—twenty miles away—was clearly impossible, so he called a halt to the drive. That night, General Reymann led the Potsdam garrison out of the pocket, crossing Lake Schwielow by rowboat. During the breakout Major General Gustav-Adolf von Wulffen—the city commandant since 1939 and a *Pour le Merite* holder from the First World War—was mortally wounded.[33]

Swarms of Soviet fighter-bombers kept the 9th Army from moving during the daylight hours of April 29. That night, guided by radio transmissions from XX Corps, several elements of the army infiltrated through weak spots in the Soviet lines and reached the 12th Army and safety, though they brought with them no guns, not a single tank, and some had even thrown away their rifles because they were out of ammunition. Those who did not make it out on the night of April 29/30 lay low in the forests the following day and tried to infiltrate to the west during the night of April 30/May 1. In all, 30,000 soldiers escaped, along with an unknown number of refugees. Counting the wounded who had already been evacuated, perhaps forty thousand of the 9th Army's 200,000 men escaped. General Busse was among those to get away, but his chief of staff, Major General Johannes Hoelz, was killed, as was SS Colonel Ruediger Pipkorn, the commander of the 35th SS Police Grenadier Division.[34] Except for LVI Panzer Corps, which was hopelessly surrounded in Berlin, the 9th Army had ceased to exist.

Shortly before midnight on April 29, Hitler dispatched his last message, which consisted of five short questions: 1) Where are Wenck's spearheads? 2) When will they attack again? 3) Where is the 9th Army? 4) Where is it breaking through? 5) Where are Holste's spearheads?

Keitel signaled that: 1) Wenck was stopped south of Schwielow Lake and facing strong Soviet attacks along his whole eastern flank; 2) 12th Army could not fight its way to Berlin; 3) 9th Army was encircled; 4) One of its panzer groups had broken out to the west, but its location was unknown; 5) Holste had been forced onto the defensive from Brandenburg to Kremmen. In short, no attack was progressing toward Berlin at any point. There would be no miracle. Berlin was doomed—and so was the Fuehrer.

THE DEATH OF A DICTATOR

Hitler's last military conference began at 10:00 p.m. on the night of April 29. Present were Hitler, Goebbels, Bormann, Krebs, Burghof, Ambassador Walter Hewel (Ribbentrop's liaison officer to Fuehrer Headquarters), Admiral Voss, and General Weidling. Weidling gave a briefing on the military situation. The Russians had advanced almost as far as the ruins of the Air Ministry. They would be in the Chancellery by May 1 at the latest. Now, he said, was the last possible moment for the LVI Panzer Corps, the last remaining military unit defending Berlin, to break out of the city. Hitler, however, stated that this was already impossible. As usual, there was no argument.

After the conference, Hitler ordered that no one in the Bunker was to go to sleep until further word from him. This was taken to mean that

LEFT: Hellmuth Weidling, commander of the LVI Panzer Corps; RIGHT: SS Major General Wilhelm Mohnke, commandant of the Fuehrer Bunker. Unpopular and considered unpleasant even by the officers of the SS, Mohnke lost a foot in the Balkans campaign of 1941 but went on to command the 1st SS Panzer Division until February 1945, when he was wounded in an air raid. After he recovered, Hitler personally named Mohnke commandant to the Central (Government) Sector of Berlin. Captured on May 2, he was a Soviet prisoner until 1955. He died in a suburb of Hamburg in 2001 at age ninety. *Bundesarchiv Bild 146-1983-028-05/CC-BY-SA 3.0; H. Hoffman Photo Archive*

the time for farewells was at hand. He instructed his secretary "Traudl" Junge to destroy the papers remaining in his files. He retired to his private quarters until about 2:30 a.m. on April 30, when he walked into the central dining passage, where about twenty people (mostly women) were assembled. Accompanied by Bormann, he shook hands with each person but said nothing or else mumbled inaudibly. Some present suggested that he was drugged, and that was probably the case. According to all accounts, there was a certain far away, misty look in his eyes as he approached the edge of eternity.

After Hitler returned to his quarters, the tension broke; the staff members went into the canteen in the servants' bunker to smoke, drink, play loud music, and dance. The music grew so loud that a messenger from the Fuehrer Bunker arrived to ask them to turn it down; he was ignored. Class distinctions melted away. SS General Rattenhuber, the chief of the SS guards, was seen cordially slapping a tailor on the back and treating him like an old friend. They danced and frolicked until well after dawn.

Meanwhile, the Russians had reached the eastern end of the Tiergarten and had pushed into the Potsdamerplatz. They were only one block away. By noon on April 30, the Soviets had captured the underground railway tunnel in the Friedrichstrasse, part of the Vossstrasse (which was very near the Chancellery), and the entire Tiergarten and had reached the Weidendammer Bridge over the Spree.

Hitler received these reports without displaying emotion. At 2:00 p.m., he had lunch. Frau Hitler apparently had no appetite, so Adolf ate his usual two fried eggs and mashed potatoes with two of his secretaries and his cook, as was his custom when not accompanied by Eva. The dictator was unusually quiet, but there was nothing unusual about the conversation. Hitler said nothing to indicate that it was his last meal.

He finished his lunch about 2:30 p.m., went into his suite and emerged one last time with Eva Braun. They said their goodbyes to Burgdorf, Krebs, and the rest of the entourage. The Fuehrer and his wife returned to their rooms. A few moments later, a revolver shot rang out. Everyone expected a second shot, but none came. After waiting several minutes, they entered Hitler's quarters. They found Hitler's body sprawled on the sofa, dripping blood. He had shot himself through the mouth. Eva Braun lay at his side. She had swallowed poison and had not used her pistol. It was 3:30 p.m. on Monday, April 30.

Hitler's body and that of his wife were soaked in gasoline and burned in a shell crater in the Chancellery garden. The mourners, headed by Goebbels and Bormann, retired to the shelter of the emergency exit, stood at attention, and raised their right hands in a farewell Nazi salute as the flames consumed the bodies. The ceremony was cut short by a Soviet artillery barrage. The Red Army had stormed the Reichstag and were about a quarter of a mile from the Fuehrer Bunker.

Grand Admiral Doenitz, who was in command of all armed forces in northern Germany, received a telegram from Martin Bormann that Hitler had appointed Doenitz his successor (though he did not tell him Hitler was dead). Doenitz was flabbergasted by this completely unexpected development; he had expected Himmler to be the successor; in fact, only two days before, he had visited the Reichsfuehrer-SS and offered him his support. Doenitz had absolutely no desire to succeed the Nazi dictator, but orders were orders. Thinking that Hitler was still alive, he sent him a message of acceptance and pledged his unconditional loyalty.

Bormann had hoped to escape Berlin and reach Doenitz's headquarters at Ploen. But now he and Goebbels hit upon another idea: they would negotiate with the Russians. On hand was the perfect representative, General Hans Krebs, the former military attaché to Moscow and a man who spoke fluent Russian.

At 1:00 a.m. on May 1, Krebs, accompanied by Colonel Theodor von Dufving, the chief of staff of the LVI Panzer Corps, and a Russian-speaking Latvian lieutenant, appeared at General Vasily Chuikov's headquarters under a flag of truce. Krebs did not return to the Bunker until noon. He reported that no agreement had been reached. The Soviets demanded a complete capitulation and would not grant an armistice but would allow Doenitz to return to Berlin and assemble his government.

At 3:15 p.m. on May 1, Goebbels belatedly informed Grand Admiral Doenitz that Hitler was dead. That evening, the Goebbelses sent their children to bed early, and after they fell asleep, Magda murdered all six of them via fatal injection. After helping his wife kill their children, Goebbels shot himself, and Magda bit a poison capsule. An SS guard then pumped a "make sure" bullet into each body, and SS men doused the corpses with gasoline. The Goebbels family were hastily and poorly burned. The Russians later found and identified the bodies without difficulty.

After the death of Hitler and Goebbels, Wilhelm Mohnke became the real power in the Fuehrer Bunker. He had already ordered that

Bormann be shot if he created the slightest difficulty. (He didn't.) It was Mohnke who planned and led an unsuccessful breakout during the night of May 1/2 that ended with Mohnke, SS Major Otto Guensche (Hitler's SS adjutant), Ambassador Walter Hewel, and a wounded Hans Baur (Hitler's pilot) hiding in a cellar with four women. The Soviets soon found them and forced them to surrender. Baur was taken to a hospital, where his leg was amputated. Hewell committed suicide, but Baur, Mohnke, and Guensche were imprisoned by the Soviets. Baur and Mohnke were finally released in October 1955 and Guensche in May 1956.

Sometime around 2:00 a.m. on May 2, Martin Bormann and SS Dr. Ludwig Stumpfegger committed suicide on the Invalidenstrasse Bridge. SS Lieutenant Colonel Peter Hoegl, who arrested Fegelein and helped burn Hitler's body, died on May 2 after he was shot and mortally wounded on the Weidendammer Bridge. The Soviets captured most of the rest of Hitler's entourage with a few notable exceptions.

Generals Krebs and Burgdorf committed suicide. On April 8, about three weeks before his death, Burgdorf told Krebs: "Ever since I took on this job, nearly a year ago, I've put all my energy and idealism into it. I've tried every way I know to bring the army and party closer together. . . . In the end they accused me in the forces of being a traitor to the German officer class, and now I can see that those recriminations were justified, that my work was in vain, my idealism wrong—not only wrong but naive and stupid."

Krebs and Burgdorf probably shot themselves in the servants' bunker below the New Chancellery on May 1, 1945. Their bodies were lost in the confusion accompanying the fall of Berlin, and their final resting places are unknown. Major General Erich Baerenfaenger, the thirty-year-old commander of Defense Sector B, also committed suicide. He was a holder of the Knight's Cross with Oak Leaves and Swords.

Just after midnight on May 2, the Soviets received a Russian language radio message from the LVI Panzer Corps, asking for a ceasefire to negotiate a surrender. Permission was quickly granted. At 5:00 a.m.

that morning, Helmuth Weidling crossed the Landwehr Canal on a rope suspension bridge and officially surrendered Berlin and its garrison. About 70,000 exhausted defenders were taken prisoner. Fighting in the city, however, did not end completely until May 4.

Like many of his men, General Weidling spent the rest of his life in captivity. He died in Vladimir Prison southeast of Moscow in 1955.

The Red Army raises the flag over the Reichstag Building in Berlin. *U.S. Army Military History Institute*

CHAPTER XIII

THE SURRENDERS

Grand Admiral Karl Doenitz, now the president of Nazi Germany, set up his government (the "Flensburg Government") at the naval base at Flensburg on May 1. His only goal was to play for time diplomatically and continue the war against the Soviet Union so that as many German soldiers and refugees as possible could escape to the West. He instructed the Wehrmacht to resist British and American forces only when they interfered with this objective. On May 2, Doenitz decided to avoid a general unconditional surrender by negotiating piecemeal army group-level surrenders. As a first step, he dispatched *Generaladmiral* Hans-Georg von Friedeburg (who had succeeded him as commander-in-chief of the navy) to negotiate an armistice with Field Marshal Montgomery. Among other things, Friedeburg was instructed to ensure that Hamburg was spared from further Allied attacks.[1]

On April 30, the day Hitler died, Munich fell to the Americans, the nearby concentration camp at Dachau was liberated, and 32,000 prisoners were released. On May 1, Field Marshal Gerd von Rundstedt was captured at Bad Toelz. On May 2, the war in Italy ended; elements of the British 2nd Army reached the Baltic coast at Luebeck

285

Grand Admiral Karl Doenitz. *Bundesarchiv Bild 146-1976-127-06A*

and Wismar (German General Guenther Blumentritt, who commanded that sector, ordered no resistance to the British); General Kurt von Tippelskirch surrendered his 21st Army to the Americans; and elements of the U.S. 9th Army pushed east to Ludwigslust and Schwerin, where they captured Headquarters, Army Group Vistula. General Student, who had just assumed command, escaped but surrendered a few days later.

On May 3 and 4, the litany of Allied advances continued: the British captured Hamburg and the Americans took Berchtesgaden, Bavaria, and Innsbruck, Austria, and reached the Brenner Pass on the Austro-Italian border. General Hasso von Manteuffel surrendered his 3rd Panzer Army to the British on May 3.

On the morning of May 3, Admiral von Friedeburg was escorted to Field Marshal Montgomery's headquarters on Luenburger Heide (Heath), about thirty miles southeast of Hamburg, accompanied by General Eberhard Kinzel, chief of staff of OKW Command Staff North. After a rather sharp greeting from Montgomery, Friedeburg read him a letter from Field Marshal Keitel, offering to surrender Army Group Vistula (which was currently engaged with the Russians). Montgomery saw through Friedeburg's game and quickly responded that German troops fighting the Red Army should surrender to the Russians. Of course, he added, any German soldiers who approached his lines with their hands raised would automatically be taken prisoner.

Friedeburg did not realize that Monty had thrown him a diplomatic lifeline. Instead, he replied that it was unthinkable to surrender to the

Russians. Montgomery retorted that he should have thought of that before June 1941.

Montgomery then demanded that Friedeburg surrender all of the German forces in northern Germany, the Netherlands, Friesland, the Frisian Islands, Heligoland, Schleswig-Holstein, and Denmark.

The admiral said he lacked the authority to comply with this request, but he was sure that Grand Admiral Doenitz would agree to it. Montgomery sent Friedeburg back to Karl Doenitz with the stipulation that the German surrender must be unconditional, as the Allied powers had agreed in their Casablanca Declaration.

Joining Doenitz in Flensburg were Speer, Keitel, Jodl, and—to his embarrassment—Himmler. The Reichsfuehrer-SS had a large entourage and still commanded forces in northern Germany, so Doenitz tolerated him. But he did not have to tolerate Dr. Arthur Seyss-Inquart, the *Reickskommissionar* of the Netherlands. Ignoring Hitler's appointment of Seyss-Inquart as foreign minister, Doenitz appointed the Reich Minister of Finance, Count Lutz Schwerin von Krosigk, in his place. Schwerin von Krosigk was a gentleman, a Rhodes scholar, and had a reputation for conservative, Christian leanings. He was certainly better suited than was Seyss-Inquart, a Nazi politician, to deal with the Allies.

Doenitz, of course, had no choice except to agree to Montgomery's demands. He instructed Friedeburg to sign the tactical surrender for northern Germany, Holland, and Denmark; and then to meet with General Eisenhower at Rheims and discuss the separate surrender of all German forces on the Western Front.

When Friedeburg and four of his officers arrived on the Lueneburg Heath late on the afternoon of May 4, Montgomery let them wait outside his command trailer in the rain, while he prepared the surrender documents. Just before 6:00 p.m., Monty had the dejected admiral escorted into his presence and asked him if he was prepared to sign the surrender. Friedeburg nodded. He and Kinzel were taken to a tent, which had been set up for the ceremony. The instrument of surrender was signed at 6:20 p.m. Under its terms, the roughly 1,000,000 German soldiers in the

Netherlands, northwestern Germany, and Denmark were to lay down their arms at 8:00 a.m. the next day.

Elsewhere, the mass surrenders continued. On May 4, the U.S. 3rd Infantry Division occupied Salzburg. On May 5, the Russians captured Swinemuende and Peenemuende on the Baltic Sea coast; the U.S. 3rd Army took Linz and closed in on the Czechoslovakian border; General of Infantry Friedrich Schulz surrendered Army Group G (Hermann Foertsch's 1st and Hans von Obstfelder's 7th Armies) to the Americans at Haar in Bavaria;[2] General Erich Brandenberger surrendered the German 19th Army to the American VI Corps; and U.S. troops captured Hans Frank, the former governor general of Poland, and liberated a V.I.P. prisoner column in Austria. Among those freed were former French Premiers Edouard Daladier, Leon Blum, and Paul Reynaud, French Generals Maurice Gamelin and Maxime Weygang, Dr. Kurt Schuschnigg, the former Austrian chancellor, and the Reverend Martin Niemoeller, the anti-Nazi Protestant church leader and World War I U-boat ace.

Even with the war nearing its end, the casualty rate for German generals remained high. The casualties included:

- Major General Joachim von Siegroth, commander of the 712th Infantry Division, missing in action in the Halbe Pocket, May 2.
- Major General Konrad Barde, commander of the 198th Infantry Division in the Palatinate, Western Front, committed suicide, May 4.
- Field Marshal Fedor von Bock, killed in his automobile near Oldenburg by a British fighter-bomber, along with his wife and daughter.
- Major General of Medical Services Dr. Johannes Lieschke, Chief Medical Officer, 9th Army, suicide at Schwerin on the Eastern Front.
- General of Mountain Troops Ludwig Kuebler, commander of the LXXXVII Corps, was trying to get his corps out of

Yugoslavia on May 6 when a partisan grenade tore up the right side of his face. He was captured the next day in the hospital. The Communists hanged him in Belgrade 1947.

- General of Infantry Wilhelm Haase, commander of the 17th Army, was apparently shot after he surrendered on May 8. He died of his wounds on May 21.
- Lieutenant General Gerhard Poel, commandant of Bruenn, Czechoslovakia, surrendered in May, sentenced to death by the Soviets, and presumed executed in 1947.
- Major General Robert Bader, the commander of the 97th Jaeger Division, missing in action near Deutsch-Brod on the Eastern Front, May 9.
- Major General Fritz Kistner, commander of Rear Area Command 534 (Korueck 534), mortally wounded on May 10. He died in Klingenthal, Saxony, on May 19.

Four German generals were murdered by Yugoslav partisans on June 5:

- General of Panzer Troops Gustav Fehn, commander of the XV Corps and former commander of the Afrika Korps.
- Lieutenant General Friedrich Stephan, commander of the 104th Jaeger Division.
- General of Infantry Werner von Erdmannsdorf, commander of the LXXXXI Corps.
- Major General Heinz Kattner, the commandant of Sarajevo.

While in the West, mass surrenders were the norm, in the East matters could be more desperate. In Prague, on May 4, Czech partisans revolted against the German occupation and were joined by General

Andrei Vlasov's Russian Liberation Army—a force of 50,000 men who, ironically, had once been German collaborators. The weak German forces in the city (an SS replacement-training battalion, a few Luftwaffe detachments, and Lieutenant General Richard Baltzer's 182nd Infantry [formerly Reserve] Division) were no match for them. General Baltzer was killed in the fighting, and most of the German survivors were soon surrounded near the Hradschin Palace or the Prague-Rusin airfield. SS Lieutenant Colonel Otto Weidinger, the commander of the 4th SS Panzer Grenadier Regiment "Der Fuehrer" (part of the 2nd SS Panzer Division) fought his way to the airfield and rescued the garrison there, but on May 9, before Weidinger could push on to the palace, General of Infantry Rudolf Toussaint, the commander of Wehrkreis Bohemia and Moravia and the military commandant of Prague, surrendered. Most of his men were subsequently murdered by the partisans. The general himself died in a Czechoslovakian prison in 1968. The Soviets did not care that Andrei Vlasov's Russian Liberation Army had returned to the anti-Nazi fold; they were judged traitors. Vlasov and his men—even those who reached American lines—were rounded up by the Soviets; Vlasov was hanged, and his men were sent to slave labor camps or executed.

For the German civilians still in Czechoslovakia, the end was horrible. Many were raped, tortured, and murdered by the partisans; others were beaten and robbed; and nearly every German was driven from the country, forced to join unarmed refugee columns that were frequently attacked by Czech partisans. One man, a Sudeten German whose family had farmed the land near Saaz since the 16th Century, recalled the behavior of the partisans:

> If we moved while standing in line we were beaten with sticks or gun butts. Sometimes we were beaten for no reason at all. . . . The girls were taken out and then stripped. Then the rapes began.
>
> Not just by one man of one girl but the multiple rape of one girl by a whole group of men. There were also some of

the rapists who had abnormal desires. When the attacks began we rushed forward to show the partisans that we were determined to protect our women. Bursts of machine gun fire over our heads caused only a slight hesitation and as we ran on the Czechs opened fire with machine pistols and killed or wounded about 40 of our group. We were flogged back with whips and clubs and some of the wounded were bayoneted. It was a humiliating experience to be so helpless and to be able to do nothing to help the poor girls . . . even now [it] makes me burn with a sense of outrage and shame.[3]

Another German recalled:

We were told by loudspeaker that as German swine we were not wanted in Czechoslovakia and that we were to leave the Republic within 24 hours. We were allowed to take nothing with us except what clothes we stood up in. . . . There would be no transport for German swine. Anyone who was left behind by the side of the road would be shot. Anyone found on Czech soil after 24 hours had elapsed would be shot. . . .

We were beaten constantly during the trek. . . . When we reached the frontier there was a whole mass of Czechs waiting. They fell on us like locusts, stealing whatever was left. Lots of them subjected our women to what they termed "body searches," to see if they had any jewels concealed—you can guess the nature of those searches. . . .[4]

Doenitz wanted to convince Eisenhower that Germans in the East should not be abandoned to Communism, and that a simultaneous surrender of all fronts was not possible. He asked Jodl to present a new set of proposals to the SHAEF commander, which aimed for separate surrenders, but held open the possibility of simultaneous surrenders.

As part of this diplomatic offensive, Doenitz distanced his government from the Nazis and their crimes. He dismissed Heinrich Himmler and Joseph Goebbels from their government posts (not knowing that Goebbels had already committed suicide). Himmler returned to his headquarters in good humor after being sacked (apparently he had been expecting it) and gave his staff its last order: "Dive for cover in the Wehrmacht."[5] This they did. Rudolf Hoess, the infamous Commandant of the Auschwitz extermination camp, took on the identity of a boatswain's mate at the Naval Intelligence School on the island of Sylt. Adolf Eichmann assumed the identity of a Luftwaffe corporal and peacefully surrendered to a U.S. unit. Later, he became SS Lieutenant Otto Eckmann. In 1946, he escaped from prison and ended up in South America, where Israeli intelligence finally unearthed him in 1960. Himmler himself changed his name, put on an army uniform, shaved off his mustache, put a patch over one eye, and disappeared. Two weeks later he was captured by the British. On May 23, he committed suicide, biting down on a cyanide capsule.

Albert Jodl landed in Rheims on the afternoon of May 6 and was ushered into the presence of U.S. Lieutenant General Walter Bedell Smith, chief of staff of SHAEF, who handled the discussions for Eisenhower. The OKW operations' officer quickly realized that the Americans had liberated too many concentration camps to have much sympathy for Germans in the East, and General Smith categorically rejected the idea of separate peace in the West while the Germans fought on against the Soviets. Smith ended the conference with an ultimatum: either Jodl signed the instrument of unconditional surrender that day or negotiations would be broken off, bombing would resume, and Western Allied lines would be closed to German refugees and troops hoping to surrender to the British or the Americans. He gave Jodl thirty minutes to decide.

Jodl insisted on one concession: a forty-eight-hour delay between the signing of the instrument of surrender and the termination of hostilities. That would allow German forces and refugees in the East two days to make good their escape. Major General Kenneth Strong, Eisenhower's chief of intelligence, advised Ike to give Jodl the grace period he demanded. Eisenhower agreed: he would give Jodl forty-eight hours from midnight that night— hostilities would end at midnight on May 8/9.

General Jodl signaled Doenitz who denounced the terms as "sheer extortion." Jodl, a former firm opponent of unconditional surrender, recommended signing, which convinced Doenitz there was no alternative. At 1:30 a.m. on May 7, Doenitz signaled Jodl authorization to sign the capitulation, ordered an end to all hostilities against the Western Allies at once, and instructed Generals Schoerner, Rendulic, and Loehr, to rush their army groups to the west.[6]

The surrender ceremony took place at 2:30 a.m. on May 7 in the recreation hall of the Ecole Professionnelle et Technique de Garcons, a modern, three-story, red brick schoolhouse in Rheims. Jodl signed for the Reich, and Smith signed for the Americans. Generaladmiral Friede-burg represented the navy, and Jodl's Luftwaffe adjutant, Major Wilhelm Oxenius signed for the air force. The ceremony ended at 2:41 a.m. The

Jodl signing the surrender document. Left to right: Luftwaffe Major Wilhelm Oxenius, Jodl, and Admiral (Generaladmiral) Hans-Georg von Friedeburg. *Franklin D. Roosevelt Library*

Field Marshal Keitel signing the instrument of surrender. *U.S. National Archives*

forty-eight hours Jodl gained during the Rheims negotiations enabled tens of thousands of Germans to escape the Soviets.

Typically, the Soviets insisted upon their own surrender ceremony. This took place in Berlin at 12:28 on the morning of May 8, in the Headquarters of the 1st Belorussian Front. Zhukov signed for the Russians. The senior German delegate was Field Marshal Keitel. Admiral Friedeburg represented the navy, and Colonel General Horst Stumpff, the commander of Air Fleet Reich, signed for the Luftwaffe.

Carl Hilpert's Army Group Courland, of course, did not have the option of surrendering to the Anglo-Americans. Doenitz and Friedeburg sent Hilpert every ship that could be spared and evacuated most of the 14th Panzer and 11th Infantry Divisions, the wounded, and up to 125 men (mostly family men) from each division of the 16th and 18th Armies. About 200,000 men (including SS and Luftwaffe personnel) were surrendered to the Soviets on May 9. Many of them—like their commander Colonel General Hilpert and Luftwaffe Colonel General Kurt Pflugbeil, whose Luftwaffe Command Courland (formerly 1st Air Fleet) had supported the army group since 1941—never made it home, dying in Soviet prisons.[7]

Knowing that surrender to the Soviets could be a death sentence, some tried to escape to Sweden by sea and drowned in the Baltic or were captured and given to the Soviets. Some committed suicide rather than face a presumed future of slave labor. Others tried to reach Germany overland but were captured or killed in the Baltic states, like General of Waffen-SS Walter Krueger, the commander of

The German emissaries opening surrender negotiations in Breslau, May 6, 1945. *Public Domain, Poland*

the VI (Latvian) SS Volunteer Corps and a holder of the Knight's Cross with Oak Leaves and Swords, who was killed by Soviet soldiers on May 22, 1945. Most of the Latvian, Estonian, and Lithuanian volunteers who joined the Wehrmacht were executed by the Communists after they surrendered.

In Poland, as elsewhere, the Soviets exacted a horrible vengeance. The Gauleiter of Breslau, Karl Hanke, had refused to surrender, even though the garrison troops were woefully short of food and ammunition. On May 4, however, he learned that Hitler had named him Reichsfuehrer-SS and chief of the German Police, and flew out of the city in an experimental helicopter to join an SS unit in Czechoslovakia.[8]

Though he had orders from Field Marshal Schoerner to fight on, the Breslau fortress commander, General of Infantry Hermann Niehoff, took advantage of Hanke's departure to surrender at 2:00 p.m. on May 5. If he had hoped for fair treatment, he was to be bitterly disappointed. The Red Army entered the city that same day, bent on revenge, including a vicious campaign of rape. It was "as if we women were being punished for Breslau having resisted for so long," one woman recalled.[9]

General Niehoff spent the next ten years in solitary confinement in a Soviet prison.[10] His men were sent to prisoner-of-war or slave labor camps in Siberia. Breslau's women worked clearing rubble for the Russians. The beautiful churches of St. Barbara and Mary Magdalene were razed to the ground. Communist Poland renamed the city Wroclaw, and Germans who had not already been sent to Siberia were expelled.

The isolated remnants of the Army of East Prussia (formerly the 2nd Army) had no chance of escaping Russian captivity. General of Panzer Troops Dietrich von Saucken surrendered its 100,000 men on May 9. Saucken and many of his men spent the next ten and a half years in captivity—in Saucken's case, much of it in solitary confinement. Here he was tortured so badly by the Communists that he spent the rest of his life in a wheelchair.[11]

On May 7, Field Marshal Ferdinand Schoerner ordered the commanders of Army Group Center to bring their men west and escape, if they could. Then, dressed in a traditional Bavarian costume, he packed his briefcase with money and flew off to the Bavarian Alps. Absent his leadership, the Soviets captured much of Army Group Center—consisting of Fritz Hubert Graeser's 4th Panzer Army, Wilhelm Hasse's 17th Army, and Walter Nehring's 1st Panzer Army—and many of its men were massacred by Czech partisans.

Schoerner's chief of staff, Lieutenant General Oldwig von Natzmer, later testified that Schoerner's courage deserted him and that while he had appealed to Schoerner not to flee, the field marshal thought only of himself and sacrificed Army Group Center. Lieutenant Helmut Dirning, Schoerner's aide-de-camp, told an entirely different story to my friend, the late Theodor-Friedrich von Stauffenberg. According to Dirning, Hitler had not only named Schoerner Commander-in-Chief of the Army but had wanted him to assume command of the "National Redoubt" in the Bavarian Alps, where he would organize the last stand of Nazi Germany.[12]

In either case, Schoerner never made it to Bavaria. His small airplane crashed in eastern Austria. He surived, but only to be captured later by the Americans and handed over to the Russians who imprisoned him as a war criminal. Released in 1955, he returned to his hometown of Munich. He died in 1973.

On May 7, Field Marshal Kesselring, commanding the German forces in the south, met with Colonel General Dr. Rendulic, Colonel General Loehr, Major General Heinz Gaedcke (chief of staff of the 6th Army), and other senior officers of Army Group Ostmark (formerly South) at the headquarters of General of Mountain Troops Julius Ringel, the commander of Wehrkreis XVIII and the ad hoc Corps Ringel. Also present was Gauleiter Siegfried Ueberreiter of Graz.

Kesselring informed his commanders that a ceasefire with the Americans would take effect at 8:00 a.m. on May 7. The Enns River (separating Upper and Lower Austria) had been approved as the demarcation line between the U.S. and Red Armies. Units hoping to escape Soviet captivity, Kesselring said, would have to cross the Enns by 9:00 a.m. on May 9. The commanders of Rendulic's four armies (the 8th, 6th, 6th SS Panzer, and 2nd Panzer) were to disengage their forces from the Soviets on the evening of May 7.

Army Group Ostmark was fortunate not to have been involved in heavy fighting since the Battle of Vienna and to have had time to prepare its escape (some units were already thinning their lines). Every army commander's plan was, of course, heavily influenced by local terrain, road networks, and the position and reaction of the Red Army. Most of Rendulic's 430,000 men escaped. General of Artillery Maximilian de Angelis, for example, the commander of Rendulic's 2nd Panzer Army, moved west under a screen of artillery that blasted Soviet lines. It was almost twenty-four hours before the Russians realized that it had left.

In Balck's 6th Army the mobility of the IV SS Panzer and III Panzer Corps helped them escape, despite poor roads in their sector, but the rearguard—the 1st Mountain and 9th Mountain Divisions—were sacrificed. About half of the 8th Army (in northern Austria and the Budweis area of Moravia) fell into Soviet hands, but the bulk of Sepp Dietrich's 6th SS Panzer Army reached American lines. Only the Fuehrer Grenadier Division and parts of the 3rd SS Panzer and 10th Parachute Divisions were captured by the Russians.[13]

The 180,000 men of Loehr's Army Group E had faced a Yugoslavian partisan offensive since April. As Marshal Josip Broz Tito's partisan forces entered Trieste, Gorizia, and Tolmein on May 1, Loehr tried to pull his units back but was hampered by the mountainous terrain, bad weather, poor roads, and lack of fuel that forced him to abandon 70 percent of his vehicles. The inexperienced LXXXXVII Corps, led by General of Mountain Troops Ludwig Kuebler, tried to adopt a "moving pocket" strategy to avoid being pinned down but was finally forced to surrender on May 6.

Yugoslav partisans surrounded one surrendered German regiment, and even before the regiment was fully disarmed, the partisan murder squads began shooting its officers. The regiment closed ranks and resumed the battle. Eventually it was able to fight its way across the Mur River and into Austria.[14]

When the German surrender took effect on May 9, the vast majority of Army Group E was still south of the Mur and had to surrender to the Yugoslavians. They were then subjected to what has been called the "murder march," or the "starvation march," or the "march of hate." They were forced to trek more than 1,300 miles. Every possession they had was stolen from them. They were attacked by thugs, and the guards were brutal. The death march lasted two months, and more than 60 percent of the Germans subjected to it died before 1945 was out.[15]

The Communist partisans were equally brutal toward supporters of the independent Croatian government that had allied with the Germans and fielded three divisions for the Wehrmacht. By the end of May, the Communists had murdered at least 110,000 Croatians, and as many as 200,000 might have been murdered by the end of 1945.

On May 3, the parliament of Slovenia (which had been occupied by Axis forces) met in Ljubljana, declared its independence, and asked King

Peter to return from exile. Slovenia's defense force, however, totalled only 12,000 men. Tito sent in fourteen partisan divisions to deal with the new republic, which was promptly overwhelmed. Fifteen hundred people were slaughtered in a single atrocity.[16]

Colonel General Loehr was subjected to what one officer called a "flimsy trial" and was hanged on February 16, 1947. General of Fliers Heinrich Danckelmann, the Military Commander in Serbia in 1941, was hanged on October 30, 1947, and General of Fliers Martin Fiebig, the Luftwaffe Commander, Southeast, was hanged a few days later. General Kuebler was also executed. General of Panzer Troops Gustav Fehn, former commander of the Afrika Korps, was simply murdered, as were several others.

In the West, surrendering Germans felt reasonably confident that they would be well-treated, but there were some exceptions, especially when it came to looting. The Germans, in fact, joked that USA stood for *Uhren stehlen's auch* (watches also stolen).[17]

Seyss-Inquart was arrested in Hamburg on May 7. On May 8, Goering was captured near Fischhorn, Austria. Also on May 8, Crown Prince Olaf of Norway, accompanied by British representatives, landed in Oslo to accept the surrender of the German forces in Norway. This involved mainly Franz Boehme's 20th Mountain Army, which still controlled five corps, the equivalent of 14 divisions, and 400,000 men.[18] Shortly thereafter, Reichskommissar Dr. Joseph Treboven went to his command bunker. Inside was the corpse of General of SS Wilhelm Rediess, who had shot himself; Treboven committed suicide by exploding dynamite. Vidkun Quisling, the puppet prime minister, surrendered to the Norwegian police on May 9 and was executed by a firing squad on October 24. General Boehme committed suicide in the Nuremberg prison in May 1947.

The war in Europe officially ended at one minute after midnight on May 9, 1945, although some isolated German units in Czechoslovakia continued to resist for several more days. On May 9, after contemplating suicide, Kesselring finally surrendered, and Major General Rudolf Wulf surrendered the Channel Islands and his isolated 319th Infantry Division, which had been trapped behind enemy lines since the Allied invasion of Normandy. Other isolated garrisons at Lorient, St. Nazaire, la Rochelle, and Dunkirk also surrendered.

The last German warship, the heavy cruiser *Prinz Eugen*, docked at Copenhagen on May 9 and surrendered. It was the only major German warship to survive the war. Launched in 1938, it had seen as much action as any ship in the fleet. It had been bombed, torpedoed, struck with a mine, fought alongside the *Bismarck*, escaped, and took part in the Channel Dash and in the Baltic evacuations. It was later used as a target ship in the American atomic bomb tests and was finally destroyed near Bikini.

The German forces on the Aegean Islands surrendered on May 11, and the Crete garrison capitulated the next day. Sepp Dietrich was captured on May 12, and Field Marshal Keitel was arrested at Flensburg on May 13. He was succeeded as commander-in-chief of OKW by Alfred Jodl. The Allies needed Admiral Doenitz's government only so long as German forces remained at large and it could help with surrenders and in the distribution of food. By the middle of May, its usefulness was coming to an end. During its existence, as many as two million soldiers and refugees had escaped from the East to the West.

Jold and Doenitz tried to extend their usefulness by condemning Nazi concentration and extermination camps. On May 15, Jodl issued a directive in the name of the High Command of the Armed Forces denouncing the camps, and Doenitz decreed that German courts would try camp guards and administrators who had violated basic morality and justice. Schwerin von Krosigk sent a copy of the decree to Eisenhower, along with a cover letter asking him to let the Reich courts proceed. Ike did not reply.

On the afternoon of May 22, the Allied Control Commission telephoned Flensburg and instructed Doenitz, Jodl, and Friedeberg to report to the liner *Patria* to meet with U.S. Major General Lowell W. Rooks, the chief of the commission, at 9:45 the following morning. Doenitz knew what this order meant and curtly ordered his people to pack their bags.

Members of the Flensburg government following their arrest. Right to left are Admiral Doenitz, Albert Speer, and Alfred Jodl. *Imperial War Museum*

He was right. The meeting was very brief. Rooks told them that Eisenhower had instructed him "to call you before me this morning to tell you that he has decided, in concert with the Soviet High Command, that today the acting German government and the German High Command, with the several of its members, shall be taken into custody as prisoners of war. Thereby the acting German government is dissolved . . ."[19]

The Germans returned to their quarters to fetch one suitcase of personal belongings for their trip into captivity. Among those arrested were Schwerin von Krosigk and Albert Speer. Two officers did not join them. General Kinzel, the chief of staff of OKW Command Staff North, and Generaladmiral Friedeburg, the commander-in-chief of the German navy, committed suicide.

Meanwhile, history turned a page. The Third Reich passed into what was. The War Crimes trials were about to begin.

APPENDIX I

<table>
<tr><th colspan="2">TABLE OF COMPARATIVE RANKS</th></tr>
<tr><th>U.S. Army</th><th>German Army and Luftwaffe</th></tr>
<tr><td>—</td><td>Reichsmarschall (Luftwaffe only) *</td></tr>
<tr><td>General of the Army</td><td>Field Marshal (Generalfeldmarschall)</td></tr>
<tr><td>General</td><td>Colonel General (Generaloberst)</td></tr>
<tr><td>Lieutenant General</td><td>General of (Infantry, Panzer Troops, etc.)</td></tr>
<tr><td>Major General</td><td>Lieutenant General (Generalleutnant)</td></tr>
<tr><td>Brigadier General **</td><td>Major General (Generalmajor)</td></tr>
<tr><td>Colonel</td><td>Colonel (Oberst)</td></tr>
<tr><td>Lieutenant Colonel</td><td>Lieutenant Colonel (Oberstleutnant)</td></tr>
<tr><td>Major</td><td>Major (Major)</td></tr>
<tr><td>Captain</td><td>Captain (Hauptmann)</td></tr>
</table>

First Lieutenant	First Lieutenant (Oberleutnant)
Second Lieutenant	Second Lieutenant (Leutnant)
	Senior Officer Cadet or Ensign (Faehnrich)
Officer Candidate	Officer-Cadet (Fahnenjunker)
Master Sergeant	Sergeant Major (Stabsfeldwebel)
First Sergeant	
Technical Sergeant	Technical Sergeant (Oberfeldwebel)
Staff Sergeant	Staff Sergeant (Feldwebel)
Sergeant	Sergeant (Unterfeldwebel)
Corporal	Corporal (Unteroffizier)
	Lance Corporal (Gefreiter)
Private First Class	Private First Class (Obersoldat)
Private	Private (Soldat, Grenadier, Jaeger, etc.)
* Held only by Hermann Goering (July 19, 1940–April 23, 1945). ** Brigadier in British Army.	

U.S. Army	Waffen-SS
General of the Army	Reichsfuehrer-SS
General	SS Colonel General (SS-Oberstgruppenfuehrer)
Lieutenant General	SS General (SS-Obergruppenfuehrer)
Major General	SS Lieutenant General (SS-Gruppenfuehrer)
Brigadier General	SS Major General (SS-Brigadefuehrer)
	SS Oberfuehrer (SS-Oberfuehrer)
Colonel	SS Colonel (SS-Standartenfuehrer)

Lieutenant Colonel	SS Lieutenant Colonel (SS-Obersturmbannfuehrer)
Major	SS Major (SS-Sturmbannfuehrer)
Captain	SS Captain (SS-Hauptsturmfuehrer)
First Lieutenant	SS First Lieutenant (SS-Obersturmfuehrer)
Second Lieutenant	SS Second Lieutenant (SS-Untersturmfuehrer)
Officer Candidate	SS Officer-Cadet (SS Fahnenjunker)
Master Sergeant	SS Sergeant Major (SS-Sturmscharfuehrer)
First Sergeant	SS First Sergeant (SS-Hauptscharfuehrer)
Technical Sergeant	SS Technical Sergeant (SS-Oberscharfuehrer)
Staff Sergeant	SS Staff Sergeant (SS-Scharfuehrer)
Sergeant	SS Sergeant (SS-Unterscharfuehrer)
Corporal	SS Corporal (SS-Rottenfuehrer)
Private First Class	SS Private First Class (SS Sturmann)
Private	SS Private (SS-Mann)
	SS Aspirant (SS-Anwaerter)

German Army/Luftwaffe	German Navy (Officer Ranks Only)
Reichsmarschall (Luftwaffe only)	Grand Admiral (Grossadmiral)

Field Marshal (Generalfeldmarschall)	—
Colonel General (Generaloberst)	General Admiral (Generaladmiral)
General (General der . . .)	Admiral (Admiral)
Lieutenant General (Generalleutnant)	Vice Admiral (Vizeadmiral)
Major General (Generalmajor)	Rear Admiral (Konteradmiral)
Colonel (Oberst)	Captain (Kapitaen zur See)
Lieutenant Colonel (Oberstleutnant)	Commander (Fregattenkapitaen)
Major (Major)	Lieutenant Commander (Korventtenkapitaen)
Captain (Hauptmann)	Lieutenant (Kapitaenleutnant)
First Lieutenant (Oberleutnant)	Leutnant *
Second Lieutenant (Leutnant)	Leutnant zur See **
Officer-Cadet (Fahnenjunker)	Seekadett
* Equivalent to lieutenant (j.g.) in U.S. Navy **Equivalent to ensign in the U.S. Navy	

APPENDIX 2

GERMAN STAFF POSITIONS

Chief of Staff (Not present below the corps level)

Ia — Chief of Operations

Ib — Quartermaster (Chief Supply Officer)

Ic — Staff Officer, Intelligence (subordinate to Ia)

Id — Director of Training (Not usually present below army level)

IIa — Chief Personnel Officer (Adjutant)

IIb — Second Personnel Officer (subordinate to IIa)

III — Chief Judge Advocate (subordinate to IIa)

IVa — Chief Administrative Officer (subordinate to Ib)

IVb — Chief Medical Officer (subordinate to Ib)

IVc — Chief Veterinary Officer (subordinate to Ib)

IVd — Chaplain (subordinate to IIa)

V — Motor Transport Officer (subordinate to Ib)

National Socialist Guidance Officer (added 1944)

Special Staff Officers (Chief of Artillery, Chief of Projectors [Rocket Launchers], Chief Signal Officer, etc.)

NOTE: The Ia was referred to as the *Generalstabsoffizier* 1 (1st General Staff Officer or GSO 1); the Ib was the *Generalstabsoffizier* 2; the Ic was the *Generalstabsoffizier* 3; and the Id was the *Generalstabsoffizier* 4.

APPENDIX 3

GERMAN UNITS, RANKS, AND STRENGTHS		
Unit	Rank of Commander*	Strength
Army Group	Field Marshal	2 or more armies
Army	Colonel General	2 or more corps
Army Detachment	General	1 or more corps plus independent divisions
Corps	General	2 or more divisions
Division	Lieutenant General/Major General	10,000–18,000 men ** 200–350 tanks (if panzer)

Brigade ***	Major General/ Colonel	2 or more regiments
Regiment	Colonel	2–7 battalions
Battalion	Lieutenant Colonel/ Major/Captain	2 or more companies (approximately 500 men per infantry battalion; usually 50–80 tanks per panzer battalion)
Company ****	Captain/ Lieutenant	3–5 platoons
Platoon	Lieutenant/ Sergeant Major	Infantry: 30–40 men Panzer: 4 or 5 tanks
Section	Warrant Officer/ Sergeant Major	2 squads (more or less)
Squad	Sergeant	Infantry: 7–10 men Armor: 1 tank

* Frequently, units were commanded by lower-ranking men as the war went on.

** As the war progressed, the number of men and tanks in most units declined. SS units usually had more men and tanks than Army units.

*** Brigade Headquarters were rarely used in the German Army after 1942.

**** Called batteries in the artillery (4 or 5 guns per battery).

APPENDIX 4

CHARACTERISTICS OF SELECTED GERMAN AND ALLIED TANKS OF WORLD WAR II					
Model	Weight (in tons)	Speed (mph)	Range (miles)	Main Armament	Crew
BRITISH					
Mark IV "Churchill"	43.1	15	120	16-pounder	5
Mark VI "Crusader"	22.1	27	200	12-pounder	5
Mark VIII Cromwell	30.8	38	174	175mm	5
AMERICAN (2)					
M3A1 "Stuart" (3)	14.3	36	60	137mm	4
M4A3 "Sherman"	37.1	30	120	176mm	5
GERMAN					
PzKw II	9.3	25	118	120mm	3
PzKw III	24.5	25	160	150mm	5

PzKw IV	19.7	26	125	175mm	5
PzKw V "Panther"	49.3	25	125	175mm	5
PzKw VI "Tiger"	62.0	23	73	188mm	5
RUSSIAN					
T34/Model 76	29.7	32	250	176mm	4
T34/Model 85	34.4	32	250	185mm	5
KV 1	52	25	208	176.2mm	5
JSII "Joseph Stalin"	45.5	23	150	122mm	4

(1) Characteristics of each tank varied somewhat from model to model
(2) All American tanks were also in the British inventory. The British
Shermans were sometimes outfitted with a heavier main battle gun.
These Shermans were called "Fireflies."

APPENDIX 5

LUFTWAFFE AVIATION UNITS, STRENGTHS, AND RANK OF COMMANDERS		
Unit	Composition	Rank of Commander
OKL	All Luftwaffe Units	Reichsmarschall
Air Fleet	Air Corps and Air and Flak Division	General to Field Marshal
Air Corps	Air and Flak Divisions plus various miscellaneous units	Major General to General
Air Division	2 or more wings	Colonel to Major General

Wings	2 or more groups	Major to Colonel Rarely Major General
Group	2 or more squadrons 30 to 36 aircraft	Major to Lieutenant Colonel
Squadrons	2 or more sections 9 to 12 aircraft	Lieutenant to Captain
Section	3 or 4 aircraft	Lieutenant

BIBLIOGRAPHY

Absolon, Rudolf, comp. *Rangliste der Generale der deutschen Luftwaffe Nach dem Stand vom 20 April 1945*. Friedberg, Germany: Podzun, 1984.

Air University Archives.

Air University Files SRGG 1106 (c).

Angolia, John R. *On the Field of Honor*. San Jose, California: Bender Publishing, 1981.

Assmann, Karl. "Hitler and the German Officer Corps." United States Naval Institute *Proceedings* 82 (May 1956): 508–20.

Bacque, James. *Other Losses*. North York, Canada: Stoddart Publishing, 1989.

Balck, Hermann, and F. W. von Mellenthin, "Generals Balck and von Mellenthin on Tactics: Implications for NATO Military Doctrine, Dec. 19, 1980." United States Army Command and General Staff College publication M-313-5. 1981.

Bannister, Sybil. *I Lived Under Hitler*. London: Rockliff Books, 1957.

Barnett, Correlli, ed. *Hitler's Generals*. New York: Grove Press, 1989.

Baumbach, Werner. *The Life and Death of the Luftwaffe*. New York: Coward, 1960.

Beck, Earl R. *Under the Bombs*. Lexington, Kentucky: University Press of Kentucky, 1986.

Bekker, Cajus. *The Luftwaffe War Diaries*. London: Corgi, 1969.

Benary, Albert. *Die Berliner 257. Baeran-Division*. Friedberg, Germany: Bad Nauheim and H. H. Podzun, 1957.

Boehmer, Rudolf and Werner Haupt. *Fallschirmjaeger*. New Malden, United Kingdom: Almark Publishing, 1979.

Boldt, Gerhard. *Hitler's Last Days*. Translated by Sandra Bance. Revised edition. London: Sphere Publishing, 1973.

Boucsein, Heinrich. *Halten oder Sterben: Die hessisch-thueringische 129. Infanterie-Division in Russlandfeldzug und Ostpreussen, 1941–1945*. Gilching, Germany: Vowinckel, 1999.

Bradley, Dermot, Karl-Friedrich Hildebrand, and Markus Roevekamp. *Die Generale des Heeres, 1921–1945*. 7 volumes to date. Columbus, Ohio: Biblio Publishing, 1993–2006.

Buchner, Alex. *Ostfront, 1944*. Translated by David Johnston. Reprint. Atglen, Pennsylvania: Schiffer Publishing, 1991.

Bullock, Alan J. *Hitler: A Study in Tyranny*. Revised edition. New York: Harper Torchbooks, 1964.

Carell, Paul. *Verbrannte Erde: Schlacht zwischen Wolga und Weichsel*. Leinfelden-Echterdingen, Germany: Eduard Kaiser Verlag, 1966.

Carlson, Verner R. "Portrait of a German General Staff Officer." *Military Review* 70, no. 4 (April 1990): 69–81.

Carter, Kit C., and Robert Mueller, comp. *The Army Air Force in World War II: A Combat Chronology, 1941–1945*. Washington, D.C.: U.S. Government Printing Office, 1973.

Chant, Christopher, et al. *The Marshall Cavendish Illustrated History of World War II*. 25 volumes. Singapore: Marshall Cavendish Corporation, 1979.

Charman, Terry C. *The German Home Front, 1939–45*. London: Barrie and Jenkins, 1989.

Clark, Alan. *Barbarossa: The Russian-German Conflict, 1941–45.* New York: William Morrow and Company, 1965.

Constable, Trevor J., and Raymond F. Toliver. *Horrido!* New York: Macmillan Publishers, 1968.

Cooper, Matthew. *The German Air Force.* New York: Stein and Day, Inc., 1978.

_____. *The German Army, 1933–1945.* New York: Stein and Day, Inc., 1978.

Craig, William. *Politics of the Prussian Army.* Oxford: Oxford University Press, 1956.

Deist, Wilhelm, ed. *The German Military in the Age of Total War.* Dover, New Hampshire: Berg, 1985.

Denzel, Egon. *Die Luftwaffen-Felddivisionen, 1942–1945.* 3rd edition, Gilching, Germany: Neckargemuend, Vowinckel, 1976.

Detlev von Plato, Anton. *Die Geschichte der 5. Panzer-Division, 1939–1945.* Regensburg, Germany: Walhalla U. Praetoria Verlag KG Georg Zwickenpflug, 1978.

Doenitz, Karl. *Ten Years and Twenty Days.* New York: Leisure Books, 1959.

Dulles, Allen W. and Peter Hoffmann. *Germany's Underground.* New York: Macmillan, 1947.

Dupuy, T. N. *A Genius for War.* Denver, Colorado: Hero Publishing, 1984.

Elstob, Peter. *Battle of the Reichswald.* New York: Ballantine Books, 1970.

Eisenhower, Dwight D. *Crusade in Europe.* New York: Doubleday and Company, 1949.

Eisenhower, John S. D. *The Bitter Woods.* New York: Putnam, 1969.

Fisher, Ernest F., Jr. *Cassino to the Alps.* Office of the Chief of Military History, U.S. Department of the Army. 1977.

Foerster, Juergen E. "The Dynamics of Volkegemeinschaft: The Effectiveness of German Military Establishment in the Second World War," in *The Second World War.* Vol. 3 of *Military Effectiveness,* edited by Alan R. Millet and Williamson Murray. Cambridge: Cambridge University Press, 1988.

Frankland, Noble. *Bomber Offensive: The Devastation of Europe.* New York: Ballantine Books, 1970.

Fretter-Pico, Maximilian. *Missbrauchte Infanterie.* Koenigsberg, Germany: Wehrwesen Bernard & Graefe, 1957.

Friessner, Hans, *Verratene Schlachten.* Kiel, Germany: Holsten, 1956.

Frischauer, Willi. *Reichsmarschall Hermann Goering.* London: Odhams Press, 1951.

Fuerbringer, Herbert. *9. SS-Panzer-Division "Hohenstaufen."* Bayeux, France: Heimdal, 1984.

Galland, Adolf. *The First and the Last.* 1954. Reprint, New York: Bantam Books, 1987.

Goerlitz, Walter. *The German General Staff, 1657–1945.* 1953. Reprint, New York: Praeger Publishers, 1957.

———. *Walter Model: Strategie der Defensives.* 2nd edition. Lime, 1975.

Goodspeed, D. J. *The German Wars, 1914–1945.* Boston: Houghton Mifflin, 1977.

Goolrick, William K., Ogden Tanner, and the editors of Time-Life Books. *The Battle of the Bulge.* New York: Time Life Books, 1979.

Goralski, Robert. *World War II Almanac, 1931–1945.* New York: Putnam, 1981.

Greiner, Heinz. *Kampf um Rom–Inferno am Po: Der Weg der 362. Infanterie-Division, 1944–45.* Neckargemuend: K. Vowinckel, 1968.

Grunberger, Richard. *The 12-Year Reich.* Boston: Da Capo Press, 1971.

Guderian, Heinz. *Panzer Leader.* Translated by Constantine Fitzgibbon. 1957. Reprint, New York: Ballantine Books, 1972.

Guingand, Francis de. *Operation Victory.* New York: C. Scribner's Sons, 1947.

Hake, Friedrich von. *Der Schicksalsweg der 13. Panzer-Division, 1939–1945.* Friedberg, Germany: Podzun-Verlag, 1971.

Halder, Franz. *The Halder Diaries.* Edited by Arnold Lissance. 2 volumes. 1948. Reprint, Washington, D.C.: Office of the Chief of

Counsel for War Crimes, Office of the Military Government, U.S., 1976.

_____. *The Halder War Diary, 1939–1942*. Edited by Charles Burdick and Hans-Adolf Jacobsen. Novato, California: Presidio Press, 1988.

Hastings, Max. *Das Reich*. New York: Holt Rinehart and Winston, 1981.

Haupt, Werner. *Das Buch der Panzertruppe, 1916–1945*. Friedberg, Germany: Podzun-Pallas, 1989.

_____. *Heeresgruppe Nord, 1941–1945*. Friedberg, Germany: Podzun-Pallas, 1966.

Hechler, Ken. *The Battle of Remagen*. New York: Ballantine Books, 1957.

Hildebrand, Hans H. and Ernst Henriot. *Deutschland Admirale, 1849–1945*. 3 volumes. Osnabrueck, Germany: Biblio Verlag, 1990.

Hildebrand, Hans-Friedrich. *Die Generale der deutschen Luftwaffe, 1935–1945*. 3 volumes. Osnabrueck, Germany: Biblio, 1990–1992.

Hoehne, Heinz. *The Order of the Death's Head*. Translated by Richard Berry. London: Penguin Books, 1971.

Hoppe, Harry. *Die 278. Infanterie-Division in Italien, 1944–45*. Bad Nauheim, Germany: H. H. Podzun, 1953.

International Military Tribunal. *Trial of the Major War Criminals Before the International Military Tribunal. 1946–1948*. 42 volumes. Nuremberg, Germany: The International Military Tribunal, 1947.

Irving, David. *The Destruction of Dresden*. 1964. Reprint, New York: Ballantine Books, 1965.

_____. *Hitler's War*. 2 volumes. New York: Viking Books, 1977.

Jackson, W. G. F. *The Battle for Italy*. New York: Harper and Row, 1975.

Jacobsen, Hans-Adolf, and J. Rohwer, eds. *Decisive Battles of World War II*. Translated by Edward Fitzgerald. New York: Putnam, 1965.

Jenner, Martin. *Die 216/272. niedersaechsische Infanterie-Division, 1939–1945*. Eggolsheim, Germany: Podzun, 1964.

Kameradschaftsdienst *35. Infanterie-Division. Die 35. Infanterie-Division, 1935–1945*. Eggolsheim, Germany: Podzun-Pallas-Verlag, 1980.

Kardorff, Ursula von. *Diary of a Nightmare: Berlin, 1942–1945*. Translated by Ewan Butler. 1965. Reprint, London: Rupert Hart-Davis, 1966.

Keegan, John. *Waffen SS: The Asphalt Soldiers*. New York: Ballantine Books, 1970.

Keilig, Wolf. *Die Generale des Heeres*. 1983.

Keitel, Wilhelm. *In the Service of the Reich*. Edited by Walter Goerlitz. Eggolsheim, Germany: Podzun-Pallas, 1966.

Kesselring, Albert. *A Soldier's Record*. New York: William Morrow and Company, 1954.

Kessler, Leo. *The Battle for the Ruhr Pocket*. Archdale, North Carolina: Scarborough House, 1989.

Knappe, Siegfried. "At What Cost!" Manuscript in possession of the author.

_____. *Soldat*. New York: Dell Publishing, 1992.

Koch, Horst-Adalbert. *Die Geschichte der deutschen Flakartillerie, 1935–1945*. Eggolsheim, Germany: Podzun-Pallas, 1955.

Kriegstagebuch des Oberkommandos der Wehrmacht (Wehrmachtfuehungsstab). 4 volumes. Frankfurt: Bernard and Graefe, 1961.

Kurowski, Frank. *Panzer Aces*. Translated by David Johnston. Winnipeg, Canada: J. J. Fedorowicz Publishing, 1992.

Kursietis, Andris J. *The Royal Hungarian Armed Forces, 1919–1945*. Warsaw: Aspekt Publishers, 1996.

_____. *The Royal Hungarian Army and Its Leadership in World War II*. London: Axis Europa, 1996.

_____. *Wehrmacht at War, 1939–1945*. Warsaw: Aspekt Publishing, 1998.

Landwehr, Richard. "Budapest: The Stalingrad of the Waffen-SS." *Siegrunen*, no. 37. 1985.

_____. *Charlemagne's Legionnaires: French Volunteers of the Waffen SS, 1943–1945*. Silver Spring, Maryland: Bibliophile Legion Books, 1989.

Lang, Joachim von. *Bormann: The Man Who Manipulated Hitler*. Translated by Christa Armstrong and Peter White. 1979. Reprint, Athens, Ohio: Ohio University Press, 1981.

Lanz, Hubert. *Gebirgsjaeger Die 1. Gebirgsdivision, 1935–1945*. Bad Nauheim, Germany: Podzun, 1954.

Lehmann, Rudolf. *The Leibstandarte*. 4 volumes. Translated by Nick Olcott. Winnipeg, Canada: J. J. Fedorowicz Publishing, 1987–1998.

Lemelsen, Joachim. *29. Division*. Falke-Verb, 1955.

Linklater, Eric. *The Campaign in Italy*. London: His Majesty's Stationery Office, 1951.

Lucas, James. *Alpine Elite: German Mountain Troops in World War II*. New York: Jane's Publishing Co., 1980.

_____. *Hitler's Enforcers*. London: Arms & Armour, 1996.

_____. *The Last Days of the Third Reich*. New York: William Morow and Company, 1986.

Luck, Hans von. *Panzer Commander*. New York: Praeger, 1989.

MacDonald, Charles B. *The Last Offensive*. Washington, D.C.: Center of Military History, United States Army, 1973.

Macksey, Kenneth. *Kesselring*. Philadelphia: D. McKay Company, 1978.

MacLean, French L. "German General Officer Casualties in World War II: Lessons for Future War." *Military Review* 70 (April 1990): 45–56.

Manstein, Erich von. *Lost Victories*. London: Methuen, 1958.

Manteuffel, Hasso von. "The Battle of the Ardennes, 1944–45" in *Decisive Battles of World War II: The German View*. Edited by H. A. Jacobsen and J. Rohwer. 1965. 217–53.

Manvell, Roger, and Heinrich Fraenkel. *Himmler*. 1965. Reprint, New York: Warner Books, 1968.

March, Cyril, ed. *The Rise and Fall of the German Air Force, 1933–1945*. 1948. Reprint, London: Public Record Office, 1983.

McTaggart, Pat. "Budapest '45." In *Command, Hitler's War: The Evolution and Structure of the German Armed Forces*. Conshohocken, Pennsylvania: Combined Books, 1995. 343–74.

Mehner, Kurt, ed. *Die Geheimen Tagesberichte der deutschen Wehrmachtfuehrung im Zweiten Weltkrieg, 1939–1945*. 12 volumes. Osnabureck, Germany: Biblio Verlag, 1984–95.

Mellenthin, F. W. von. *Panzer Battles*. Norman, Oklahoma: Oklahoma University, 1956.

Military Intelligence Division, U.S. War Department. "The German Replacement Army (Ersatzheer)." 1945. On file at the U.S. Army War College, Carlisle Barracks, Pennsylvania.

Milward, Alan S. *The German Economy at War*. London: University of London Athlone Press, 1965.

Mitcham, Samuel W., Jr. *Order of Battle of the German Army in World War II*. 3 volumes. Harrisburg, Pennsylvania: Stackpole Books, 2007.

_____. *Panzer Legions*. Boston: Greenwood Publishing Group, 2001.

Moll, Otto E. *Die deutschen Generalfeldmarshaelle, 1939–1945*. Rastatt, Germany: Erich Pabel, 1961.

Montgomery, Bernard Law, The Viscount of Alamein. *Normandy to the Baltic*. London: Hutchinson of London, 1958.

Mosley, Leonard, and the editors of Time Life Books. *The Reich Marshal*. New York: Time Life Books, 1974.

Musciano, Walter A. *Messerschmitt Aces*. Austell, Georgia: Arco Publishing, 1982.

Mueller-Hillebrand, Burkhart. *Germany and Its Allies*. Lanham, Maryland: University Press of America, 1980.

_____. *Das Heer*. 3 volumes. Berlin: E. S. Mittler, 1954–1969.

Munoz, Tony. *Obscure Combat Formations of the Waffen-SS*. Boulder, Colorado: Paladin Press, 1988.

Munzel, Oskar. *Die deutschen Panzer Truppen bis 1945*. Herford, Germany: Maximillian-Verlag, 1965.

Murray, Williamson. *Strategy for Defeat: The Luftwaffe, 1933–1945*. Montgomery, Alabama: Air University Press, 1983.

Nafziger, George F. *The German Order of Battle, Panzers and Artillery in World War II.* London: Greenhill Books, 1999.

_____. *The German Order of Battle, Infantry in World War II.* London: Greenhill Books, 2000.

Neumann, Peter. *The Black March.* New York: Bantam Books, 1960.

Overy, R. J. *The Air War, 1939–1945.* Philadelphia: Taylor & Francis Group, 1980.

Padfield, Peter. *Doenitz: The Last Fuehrer.* New York: Harper and Row, 1984.

Parker, Danny S. "War's Last Eruption." *World War II 5,* no. 1 (May 1990): 42–49.

Perrett, Bryan. *Knights of the Black Cross: The Panzerwaffe and Its Leaders.* New York: St. Martin's Press, 1986.

Pierik, Perry. *Hungary, 1944–1945.* Warsaw: Aspekt Publishers, 1996.

Pitt, Barrie, and the editors of Time Life Books. *The Battle of the Atlantic.* New York: Time Life Books, 1980.

Pohlmann, Hartwig. *Geschichte der 96. Infanterie-Division, 1939–1945.* Egglesheim, Germany: Podzun, 1959.

Praeger, Robert Payne. *The Life and Death of Adolf Hitler.* New York: Brick Tower Press, 1973.

Preradovich, Nikolaus von. *Die Generale der Waffen-SS.* Gilching, Germany: Vowinckel-Verlag, 1985.

Quarrie, Bruce. *Panzer-Grenadier-Division "Grossdeutschland."* Oxford: Osprey Publishing, 1977.

Rebentisch, Ernst. *Zum Kaukasus und zu den Tauern: Die Geschichte der 23. Panzer-Division, 1941–1945.* Esslingen, Germany: Association of the Former Relatives of the 23 Panzer-Division, 1963.

Reck-Malleczewen, Friedrich. *Diary of a Man in Despair.* New York: Macmillan, 1970.

Reitlinger, Gerald. *The SS: Alibi of a Nation, 1922–1945.* Boston: Da Capo Press, 1968.

Rendulic, Lothar. *Gekaempft, Gesiegt, Gechlagen.* Garding, Germany: Welsermuehl Verlag, 1957.

Riebenstahl, Horst. *The 1st Panzer Division*. Translated by Edward Force. Atglen, Pennsylvania: Schiffer Publishing, 1990.

Ritgen, Helmut. *Die Geschichte der Panzer-Lehr-Division im Westen, 1944–1945*. Stuttgart, Germany: Motorbuch-Verlag, 1979.

_____. *The 6th Panzer Division, 1937–45*. 1982. Reprint, Bloomsbury, United Kingdom: Bloomsbury Publishing Place, 1985.

Rudel, Hans Ulrich. *Stuka Pilot*. 1958. Reprint, New York: Random House, 1979.

Ryan, Cornelius. *The Last Battle*. New York: Simon and Schuster, 1966.

Sajer, Guy. *The Forgotten Soldier*. Translated by Lily Emmet Sajer. New York: Harper and Row, 1965.

Scheibert, Horst. *Bildband der 6. Panzer-Division, 1939–1945*. Berlin: Hans-henning Podzun, 1958.

Schellenberg, Walter. *The Labyrinth*. New York: Harper, 1956.

_____. *Die Traeger des deutschen Kreuzes in Gold*. Eggolsheim, Germany: Podzun-Pallas-Verlag, 1984.

Schick, Albert. *Die Geschichte der 10. Panzer-Division, 1939–1943*. Winnipeg, Canada: J. J. Fedorowicz, 1993.

Schmitz, Peter, et al. *Die deutschen Divisionen, 1939–1945*. 3 volumes. Osnabrueck, Germany: Biblio, 1993–1997.

Seaton, Albert. *The Fall of Fortress Europe, 1943–1945*. London: Batsford, 1981.

_____. *The German Army, 1933–1945*. 1981. Reprint, London: Weidenfeld and Nicolson, 1982.

_____. *The Russo-German War, 1941–45*. Westport, Connecticut: Praeger Publishers, 1970.

Seemen, Gerhard von. *Die Ritterkreuztraeger, 1939–1945*. Osnabrueck, Germany: Podzun-Pallas-Verlag, 1976.

Senger und Etterlin, Frido von. *Neither Fear Nor Hope*. Translated by George Malcolm. 1963. Reprint, Novato, California: Presidio Press, 1989.

_____. "War Diary of the Italian Campaign." Foreign Military Studies MS # C-095. 1947.

Shaw, John, and the editors of Time Life Books. *Red Army Resurgent.* New York: Time Life Books 1979.

Shirer, William L. *The Rise and Fall of the Third Reich.* Delran, New Jersey: Simon and Schuster, 1960.

Smith, Bradley F. and Elena Agarossi. *Operation Sunrise.* New York: Basic Books, 1979.

Snyder, Louis L. *Encyclopedia of the Third Reich.* New York: McGraw Hill, 1976.

Snydor, Charles W., Jr. *Soldiers of Destruction: The SS Death's Head Division, 1939–1945.* Princeton, New Jersey: Princeton University Press, 1977.

Speer, Albert. *Inside the Third Reich.* Delran, New Jersey: Simon and Schuster, 1970.

Stahlberg, Alexander. *Bounden Duty.* Translated by Patricia Crampton. London: Brassey's, 1990.

Staiger, Georg. *26. Panzer-Division: Ihr Werden und Einsatz, 1942– 1945.* Bad Nauheim: H. H. Podzun, 1957.

Stauffenberg, Friedrich von. Personal communications, 1985–1989.

_____. "Papers." Unpublished papers in the possession of the author.

Stein, George. *Waffen-SS.* Ithaca, New York: Cornell University Press, 1966.

Steinhoff, Johannes, et al. *Voices from the Third Reich.* Washington, D.C.: Regnery Publishing, 1989.

Stoeber, Hans. *Die Eiserne Faust–Bildband der 17. SS-Panzergrenadier-Division "Goetz von Berlichingen."* Osnabrueck, Germany: Vowinckel Verlag, 1966.

Stoves, Rolf O. G. *Die Gepanzerten und Motorisierten deutschen Gross-verbaende (Divisionen und selbstaendige Brigaden 1935–1945.* Osnabrueck, Germany: Podzun-Pallas-Verlag, 1986.

_____. *Die 1. Panzerdivision, 1935–1945: Die deutschen Panzerdivision im Bild.* Yorktown, Virginia: Battleground Books, 1976.

_____. *Die 22. Panzer-Division, 25. Panzer-Division, 27. Panzer-Division und 233. Reserve-Panzer-Division.* Osnabrueck, Germany: Podzun-Pallas-Verlag, 1985.

Strassner, Peter. *Europaeische Freiwillige: Die Geschichte der 5. SS-Panzer-Division "Wiking."* Osnabrueck, Germany: Munin-Verlag GmbH, 1968.

Studnitz, Hans-Georg von. *While Berlin Burns.* Upper Saddle River, New Jersey: Prentice Hall, 1964.

Tessin, Georg. *Verbaende und Truppen der deutschen Wehrmacht und Waffen-SS im Zweiten Weltkrieg, 1939–1945.* 16 volumes. Frankfurt: Verlag E. S. Mittler and Sohn, 1973–1981.

Thomas, Franz. *Die Eichenlaubtraeger, 1940–1945.* 2 volumes. Osnabrueck, Germany: Biblio, 1997–98.

Thorwald, Juergen. *Defeat in the East.* 1951. Reprint, New York: Ballantine Books, 1980.

Thumm, Helmut. *Der Weg der 5. Infanterie-und-Jaeger Division, 1921–1945.* Eggolsheim, Germany: Podzun-Pallas-Verlag, 1976.

Toland, John. *Adolf Hitler.* 1976. Reprint New York: Doubleday, 1977.

_____. *The Last 100 Days.* 1966. Reprint, New York: Bantam Books, 1967.

Trevor-Roper, Hugh R. *The Last Days of Hitler.* 1947. Reprint, London: Macmillan, 1973.

United Kingdom C.S.D.I.C. G.G. Interrogation Reports.

U.S. Army Office of Military History. *Command Decisions.* Washington, D.C.: 1959.

United States Chief Counsel for the Prosecution of Axis Criminality. *Nazi Conspiracy and Aggression.* 7 volumes. Nuremberg, Germany: Office of the United States Chief of Counsel for Prosecution of Axis Criminality, 1946.

United States Military Intelligence Service. "Order of Battle of the German Army, 1945." 1945.

United States War Department. Technical Manual *TM-E 30-451,* "Handbook on German Military Forces." Washington, D.C.: War Department, 1945.

Vassiltchikov, Marie. *The Berlin Diaries, 1940–1945.* 1985. Reprint, New York: Knopf, 1987.

Voss, Klaus, and Paul Kehlenbeck. *Letzte Divisionen–Die Panzerdivision Clausewitz und die Infanteriedivision Schill.* Schleusingen: AMUN-Verlag, 2000.

Wallace, Robert, and the editors of Time Life Books. *The Italian Campaign.* New York: Time Life Books, 1981.

Warlimont, Walter. *Inside Hitler's Headquarters.* Translated by R. H. Barry. New York: Praeger, 1964.

Webster, Charles and Noble Frankland. *The Strategic Air Offensive against Germany, 1939–1945.* 4 volumes. London: Her Majesty's Stationery Office, 1961.

Weidinger, Otto. *Division Das Reich: Der Weg der 2. SS-Panzer-Division "Das Reich."* 5 volumes. Osnabrueck, Germany: Munin Verlag, 1967–1982.

_____. *Division Das Reich im Bild.* Osnabrueck, Germany: Munin Verlag, 1981.

Westphal, Siegfried, et al. "Feldzug in Italien." Foreign Military Studies MS # T-1a. 1947. A copy of this manuscript is available at the library of the U.S. Army War College, Carlisle Barracks, Pennsylvania.

Westphal, Siegfried. *The German Army in the West.* London: Cassell, 1951.

Wheeler-Bennett, John W. *The Nemesis of Power: The German Army in Politics, 1918–1945.* 1964. Reprint, London: Macmillan, 1967.

Whiting, Charles. *Battle of the Ruhr Pocket.* New York: Ballantine Books, 1970.

Williamson, Gordon. *Infantry Aces of the Third Reich.* London: Arms and Armour, 1991.

Wilmot, Chester. *The Struggle for Europe.* 1981.

Windrow, Martin. *The Panzer Divisions.* New York: Hippocrene Books, 1985.

Wistrich, Robert. *Who's Who in Nazi Germany.* London: Macmillan, 1982.

Yerger, Mark C. *Waffen-SS Commanders: The Army, Corps and Divisional Leaders of a Legend.* Volumes 1–2. Atglen, Pennsylvania: Schiffer Publishing, 1997–1999.

Young, Peter, ed. *The Marshall Cavendish Illustrated Encyclopedia of World War Two*. 20 volumes. Singapore: Marshall Cavendish Corporation, 1981.

Zeitzler, Kurt. "Men and Space in War: A German Problem in World War II. *Military Review* 42. (April 1962).

Ziemke, Earl F. *Stalingrad to Berlin: The German Defeat in the East*. Washington, D.C.: Office of the Chief of Military History, U.S. Department of the Army. 1966.

Zweng, Christian. *Die Dienstlaufbahnen der Offiziere des Generalstabes des deutschen Heeres, 1935–1945*. 2 volumes. Osnabrueck, Germany: Biblio, 1995.

INTERNET SOURCES:

Andres, Wladyslaw, and Antonio Munoz. "Russian Volunteers in the German Wehrmacht in World War II." www.feldgrau.com/rvol. html.

Axis History Forum. www.forum.axishistory.com.

"Das Ritterkreuz des Eisernen Kreuzes." http://www.dieritterkreuztraeger.de/Ritterkreuz%20des%20EKEinleitung.htm.

Denniston, Peter, and Patrick Kiser. "Die Gebirgstruppen." www. gebirgsjaeger.4mg.com.

Die deutsche Wehrmacht: To the Bitter End. wwii.info.net.

"Divisionen und Verbände der deutschen Wehrmacht und Waffen-SS 1933–1945." www.diedeutschewehrmacht.de.

Eötvös Loránd Tudományegyetem, Bölcsészettudományi Kar Filozófia Intézet. http://philosophy.elte.hu/.

Feldgrau German Armed Forces Research 1918–45. www.feldgrau.com.

"Koszalin." http://en.wikipedia.org/wiki/Koszalin.

Miller, Michael D., and Gareth Collins. "Kreigsmarine." http://www. geocities.ws/orion47.geo/WEHRMACHT/KRIEGSMARINE/ Kriegsmarine.html.

www.lexikon.com.

www.ritterkreuztraeger-1939-45.de.

Notes

Chapter I: Setting the Stage

1. Wilhelm Keitel (1882–1946) was an artillery officer. He joined the Imperial Army as a Fahnenjunker in 1901, served in World War I as a battery commander and a regimental adjutant, and attended an abbreviated General Staff course during the war. He was Ia (chief of operations) of the German Marine Corps in Flanders at the time of the Armistice. He was selected for the Reichsheer and was chief of the Organization's Office of the Reichswehr (1935–38), where he proved to be a talented organizer.

2. Like Keitel, Alfred Jodl (1890–1946) was an artillery officer. He attended the Cadet School at Munich and joined the 4th Bavarian Field Artillery Regiment as a *Faehnrich* (senior officer cadet) in 1910. He fought on the Western Front in World War I and emerged as a first lieutenant and General Staff officer in 1918. He alternated between artillery and General Staff assignments thereafter. He was chief of the operations branch of OKW (1938) and commander, 44th Artillery Command (Arko 44), 1938–39. He returned to Berlin for a second tour as chief of operations at OKW when World War II began and remained in this post throughout the war.

3. The chiefs of the General Staff in World War II were: Franz Halder (September 1, 1939–September 24, 1942); Kurt Zeitzler (September 24, 1942–July 21, 1944); Heinz Guderian (July 21, 1944–March 28, 1945); and Hans Krebs (March 28, 1945–May 1, 1945).

4. Rommel was seriously wounded by a fighter-bomber on July 17, 1944, and he was later forced to commit suicide because of his involvement in the Stauffenberg plot. His replacement, Field Marshal Guenther von Kluge, was replaced by Model on August 16. When he was summoned to Berlin, Kluge—who was also peripherally involved in the July 20 conspiracy—knew what that meant. On August 19, on the way to the capital, he stopped near Metz and took a poison capsule.

5. The elite 78th Sturm Division was destroyed along with most of Army Group Center in July 1944. Only a tiny remnant, consisting of wounded men or troops who were in training schools or on leave when the Soviet offensive struck, survived. They were incorporated into the 78th Volksgrenadier Division, which was redesignated 78th Volks-Sturm-Division on October 9, 1944. It was not significantly different from any other Volksgrenadier division.

Chapter II: Defeat in the Ardennes
1. Meinrad von Lauchert (1905–1987) was born in Potsdam, joined the Reichsheer as a *Fahnenjunker* (officer-cadet) in 1924, and was commissioned second lieutenant in the 5th Cavalry Regiment in 1931. He became a company commander in the 35th Panzer Regiment in late 1938. During World War II, he commanded I Battalion, 35th Panzer Regiment (abbreviated I/35th Panzer) (1939–43), Panzer Regiment Grafenwoehr (1943), and 15th Panzer Regiment (1943–44). Apparently he was wounded on August 1, 1944; in any case, he was an excess officer on the staff of the 5th Panzer Army on the eve of the Battle of the Bulge. Meanwhile, General of Panzer Troops Heinrich von Luettwitz, commander of the XXXXVII Panzer Corps, inspected the 2nd Panzer Division and sacked its commander. He and the 5th Panzer Army commander, Baron Hasso von Manteuffel, quickly decided that Lauchert was the best available replacement. Lauchert assumed command of the division on December 15—the day before the offensive began. He did not even have time to meet some of his principle subordinates before

the battle began. In spite of heavy casualties, the 2nd Panzer pushed farther forward than any other German division.

2.   Baron Heinrich von Luettwitz (1896–1969) was an East Prussian. Upon the outbreak of World War I, his father refused to allow him to enter the service, so he ran away from home and joined the army as a private. He excelled in trench warfare on the Western Front, and his mother, a member of the von Unruh military family, secured a commission for him at age seventeen. Accepted into the Reichsheer, he was a cavalry officer and in 1936, led the German Olympic Equestrian Team. They did not win the gold medal, and Luettwitz paid the price, being condemned to backwater posts for years. But heavy losses on the Eastern Front in 1942 meant he was finally given his chance, and he distinguished himself as the commander of a rifle brigade and the 20th and 2nd Panzer Divisions. He assumed command of the XXXXVII Panzer Corps in September 1944. Luettwitz was a better division leader than corps commander.

3.   Most American armored divisions in late 1944 had three combat commands: CCA, CCB, and CCR (Combat Command Reserve).

4.   Ernst von Cochenhausen was born in Bad Freienwalde, on the Alte Oder, an old branch of the Oder River in eastern Germany, in 1910. He joined the army as a fahnenjunker in the 15th (Prussian) Cavalry Regiment at Paderborn. Commissioned in 1934, he was assigned to the 3rd Motorcycle Battalion of the 3rd Panzer Division in 1935. He commanded a company in the 3rd Motorcycle in Poland (1939), France (1940), and on the Eastern Front (1941–42). He became battalion commander and was promoted to major on July 1, 1942. He led the 3rd Motorcycle until May 1943, when he was apparently wounded. In any case, he returned to duty on August 1, 1943, as commander of the 122nd Panzer Reconnaissance Battalion on the Eastern Front. In early 1944, he enrolled in the Regimental Commanders' Course. He was sent to the Western Front and General von Luettwitz promoted him to the command of the 304th Panzer Grenadier Regiment of the 2nd Panzer Division in December 1944. He held this position until the end of the war. Cochenhausen was promoted to lieutenant colonel on March 1, 1945, and surrendered to the Americans in May 1945. He held the Wounded Badge in Gold, meaning that he was wounded at least five times during World War II. He died in 1998.

5. SHAEF, the Supreme Headquarters, Allied Expeditionary Force, was commanded by U.S. General Dwight D. Eisenhower.

6. John S. D. Eisenhower, *The Bitter Woods* (New York: Putnam, 1969), 342.

7. Eisenhower, *Bitter Woods*, 425.

8. Adolf Galland, *The First and the Last* (1954; repr., New York: Bantam, 1987), 249.

9. Colonel Langhäuser was an acting commander only. Major General Gerhard Engel, the permanent commander of the division and Hitler's former army adjutant (1937–43), had been seriously wounded on January 1. He did not return to duty until February. Although he owed his appointment to his connection with the Fuehrer, Engel nevertheless turned out to be a very good divisional commander.

10. Stephen H. Newton, *Hitler's Commander: Field Marshal Walther Model—Hitler's Favorite General* (Boston: Da Capo Press, 2006), 345. Model was one of the few army generals who showed no reluctance to sack SS generals.

11. Eisenhower, *Bitter Woods*, 425.

12. Richard D. Law and Craig W. H. Luther, *Rommel* (San Jose, California: Bender Publishing, 1980), 239–40.

13. The term "OB West" is the abbreviation for Oberbefehlshaber West, which referred to the commander-in-chief, West, or his headquarters. In late 1944, the OB West controlled (north to south) Army Groups H, B, and G. Army Group B was by far the strongest. It controlled the 5th Panzer, 6th Panzer, and 7th Army, all of which fought in the Battle of Bulge. It also controlled the 15th Army, which was positioned north of the Ardennes.

14. Eisenhower, *Bitter Woods*, 153; William H. Goolrick et al, *The Battle of the Bulge* (New York: Time Life Education, 1979), 53. Also see Hugh M. Cole, *The Ardennes: The Battle of the Bulge* (Washington, D.C.: Center of Military History, 1965).

15. Juergen E. Foerster, "The Dynamics of Volkegemeinschaft: The Effectiveness of German Military Establishment in the Second World War," in *Military Effectiveness*. Volume III, *The Second World War*, eds. Alan R. Millet and Williamson Murray (Boston: Allen and Unwin, 1988), 206.

16. Hasso von Manteuffel, "The Battle of the Ardennes, 1944–45" in *Decisive Battles of World War II: The German View*, eds. H. A. Jacobsen and J. Rohwer (New York: Putnam Publishing Group, 1965), 417.

17. See Samuel W. Mitcham Jr., *The Panzer Legions: A Guide to the German Army Tank Divisions of World War II and Their Commanders* (Boston: Greenwood, 2001).

18. Most of the motorized infantry divisions were designated panzer grenadier divisions in the fall of 1942.

19. By 1945, the panzer grenadier divisions also had a tank battalion; in fact, during the last weeks of the war, the TO&E (Table of Organization and Equipment) of the new panzer grenadier and panzer divisions was the same.

Chapter III: Operation Northwind and the Battle of the Colmar Pocket

1. Chester Wilmot, *The Struggle for Europe* (New York City: Harper and Brothers, 1981), 606.

2. An *Oberbefehlshaber*, abbreviated OB, was a supreme headquarters, which normally controlled two or more army groups. Himmler's was the smallest and controlled only the 19th Army and a few odds and ends. OB West, on the other hand, controlled several armies and at one point directed Army Groups H, B and G, which included the 25th, 15th, 6th Panzer, 5th Panzer, 7th, 1st, and 19th Armies (north to south), as well as the Armed Forces Netherlands, a special headquarters.

3. General of SS Erich von dem Bach-Zelewski (1899–1972), the son of a Pomeranian Junker, fought in World War I (where he was wounded twice), served in the Freikorps, joined the Reichswehr, and transferred to the border guards (*Grenzschutz*) in 1924. He joined the *Nationalsozialistische Deutsche Arbeiterpartei* (NSDAP or Nazi Party) in 1930 and the SS in 1931. He rose rapidly and was an SS major general by late 1933. By 1937, he was higher SS and police leader (HSSPF) in Silesia and was involved in the setting up of concentration camps, including Auschwitz, in May 1940. He became HSSPF Center (behind Army Group Center) in June 1941. The police

and security units under his command murdered 200,000 people in a purge of Jews from eastern Poland and White Russia. After Reinhard Heydrich was assassinated in 1942, Hitler recommend Bach as acting reich protector of Bohemia and Moravia, but Himmler chose Kurt Daluege instead. Meanwhile, Bach became known as an "expert" on anti-partisan operations. His methods, however, always involved slaughtering thousands of innocent, unarmed civilians. In early August 1944, he was placed in charge of suppressing the Warsaw Uprising, which he did with his usual ruthless brutality, and 200,000 Polish civilians were killed. He later led the XIV SS Corps (succeeding Heinz Reinefarth in December 1944). This corps was redesignated X SS in January 1945. Bach was in U.S. custody from 1945 until 1949 but was never tried as a war criminal. The West German government, however, prosecuted him for the murders of political opponents, and he went to jail in 1958. He died in a Munich prison in 1972. Heinz Reinefarth (1903–1979), who became HSSPF Warthegau (formerly part of Poland) was never held responsible for his war crimes which included persecuting Jews and Poles. After World War II, he was elected mayor of the town of Westerland (on the North Sea island of Sylt) and was elected to the *Landtag* (provincial legislature) of Schleswig-Holstein. Polish demands for his extradition were ignored by the West German government which awarded him a general's pension instead.

4.   Walter Wiese was born in Nordhastedt, Schleswig-Holstein, in 1892 and joined the army as a war volunteer in 1914. He earned a reserve commission in the 147th Infantry Regiment on the Eastern Front in 1915. Later, he served on the Western Front as well, commanded an infantry platoon and a machine gun company, and was wounded at least once. Discharged in 1919, he joined the Hamburg police but rejoined the army as a major in 1935 when Hitler began his military expansion. He commanded the I Battalion/116th Infantry Regiment (1936–late 1940), the 39th Infantry Regiment (1940–1942), the 26th Infantry Division (April 15, 1942 to August 5, 1943) and XXXV Corps (August 5, 1943–late May 1944). In the process, he fought on the Saar, in Luxembourg, Belgium, and France, and on the central sector of the Russian Front, including the battles of Kalinin and the Rzhev salient. He succeeded Georg von Sodenstern as commander of the 19th Army on June 1, 1944. Wiese was promoted to general of infantry on October 1, 1943.

5. Wiese also had the 654th Heavy Panzer Battalion—a Tiger unit—in army reserve.

6. Gerald Reitlinger, *The SS: Alibi of a Nation, 1922–1945* (New York: Viking Press, 1968), 393, 398–99.

7. General Wiese died in Giessen, Hesse, in 1975.

8. Siegfried Rasp was born in Munich in 1898. He joined the 1st Bavarian Infantry Regiment as a Fahnenjunker in 1915 and fought on the Western Front in World War I, where he was a battalion and then regimental adjutant and where he was wounded. He spent most of the Weimar years (1919–1933) in the infantry and began General Staff training in 1927. He became a tactics instructor at the War Academy in 1934. During World War II, he was Ia (chief of operations) of the 17th Infantry Division (from November 1, 1938), Ia of the 1st Army (October 19, 1939), course commander at the Dresden War School (January 1, 1940), chief of staff of XXIII Corps (May 15, 1942), acting commander of the 3rd Mountain Division (August 26, 1943), commander of the 335th Infantry Division (September 10, 1943), commander of the 78th Assault Division (July 12, 1944) and chief of staff to the commander of the North Coast (September 23, 1944). See Wolf Keilig, *Die Generale des Heeres* (Eggolsheim, Germany: Podzun-Pallas, 1983), 268.

9. The capable Botsch (1897–1969) was not unemployed for long. He was named commander of the 18th Volksgrenadier Division on February 2, 1945, and was acting commander of the LVIII Corps from March 25–April 16, 1945, when he was captured in the Ruhr Pocket. He previously served as chief of operations and then chief of staff of the XXX Corps (1939–1943) and Army Detachment Felber, which was upgraded to 19th Army in 1943. He was from Wuerttemberg. Botsch was succeeded by Colonel Kurt Brandstaedter, who was chief of staff of the 19th Army until it surrendered.

10. Robert Manvell and Heinrich Fraenkel, *Himmler* (1965; repr., Eugene, Oregon: Stock, 1968), 219–20.

11. Werner Ostendorff was born in Koenigsberg on August 15, 1903, and joined the Freikorps at age fifteen, helping put down Communist insurrections in his native East Prussia. He joined the East Prussian 1st Infantry Regiment as a private in 1925 and earned a promotion to second lieutenant in 1930. He transferred to the Luftwaffe as a first

lieutenant in 1934 and trained as a pilot and aerial observer. He transferred again—this time to the SS—in 1935 and was an instructor (mainly in aerial photo interpretation) until 1938. He then commanded a company in the SS Regiment "Der Fuehrer" and became the commander of the SS-VT's anti-aircraft battalion during the Polish campaign of 1939. In the meantime, he impressed Paul Hausser, who made him the first Ia of the SS Division "Das Reich" (later 2nd SS Panzer) in October 1939. He held this position in the French and Russian campaigns (1940–1942) and became chief of staff of the SS Panzer Corps (again under Hausser) in June 1942. This unit was redesignated II SS Panzer Corps in June 1943. He distinguished himself in the Battle of Kharkov in March 1943 and, as a result, Ostendorff was given command of the 17th SS Panzer Grenadier Division "Goetz von Berlichingen" in January 1944. He led this command in the Battle of Normandy from D-Day to June 15, when he was seriously wounded near Carentan. He returned to duty on October 21 but left again in December to become chief of staff of Himmler's Army Group Upper Rhine. Ostendorff assumed command of the 2nd SS Panzer Division on the Eastern Front on February 10, 1945, and led it until March 9, when he was critically wounded by an incendiary shell during the fighting in Hungary. He died in the hospital at Bad Aussee on May 4, 1945. Ostendorff, who was a highly capable and well-liked officer, was one of the few SS officers to refuse to renounce his Christian faith. He was promoted to SS captain (1936), major (1939), lieutenant colonel (late 1940), colonel (1942), Oberfuehrer (April 20, 1943), major general (April 20, 1944) and lieutenant general (December 1, 1944). He left behind a wife, a son, and a daughter. The SS rank of Oberfuehrer has no exact English equivalent, as it was between colonel and major general. It will therefore remain untranslated in this book.

12. According to Peter Young, ed., *The Marshall Cavendish Illustrated Encyclopedia of World War Two,* Vol. 15, (Singapore: Marshall Cavendish Corporation, 1981), 2045.

13. Danny S. Parker, "War's Last Eruption," *World War II*, Vol. 5, no. 1 (May 1990): 45.

14. Lattre de Tassigny (1889–1952) formerly commanded the French 14th Infantry Division (1940) and was GOC-in-C (General Officer Commander-in-Chief), Tunisia (1941–1942).

15. Augustin-Leion Guillaume (1895–1983) had previously commanded the 2nd Algerian Division in Italy (1943–1944). He was later French Military Attaché to the Soviet Union, Commander-in-Chief of French Forces in Occupied Germany, and Commander in Chief of Allied Land Forces under NATO. Promoted to full general, he ended his career as Chief of Staff of the French Armed Forces and President of NATO's Chief of Staffs' Committee (1954–1956).

16. Hellmuth Thumm (1895–1977) joined the Wuerttemberg Army as a war volunteer in the 125th (7th Wuerttemberg) Infantry Regiment in 1914. Commissioned in 1915, he fought on the Western Front in World War I, where he was captured by the British in August 1918. Released in 1919, he served in infantry and machine gun units the Reichswehr and during World War II commanded the I/75th Infantry Regiment (1938–1940), the 56th Infantry Regiment of the 5th Infantry (later Jaeger) Division (June 1940–January 1943), the division itself (January 3–October 31, 1944), and the LXIV Corps (November 1, 1944–January 20, 1945). Never reemployed, he died in his native Wuerttemberg. His career was unusual in that he was virtually always in infantry command positions—he never held a significant staff position except in 1936, when he was an instructor at the War School at Munich. He wrote a history of the 5th Jaeger Division after the war.

17. Both Leclerc (1902–1947) and Lattre de Tassigny (1889–1952) became marshals of France—the latter posthumously. After the war, Leclerc later became commander-in-chief Indochina (1940–1946) and inspector general of forces in French North Africa. He was killed in an airplane crash. Lattre later became chief of the army general staff (1945–1947); commander-in-chief, West European Union Forces (1948–1950); and commander-in-chief, Far East (1950–1951), where he won three major battles over Vietnamese communists. He contracted cancer and retired in 1951.

18. Bethouart (1889–1982) commanded the 1st Light Chasseurs Division and the French Expeditionary Forces in Norway (1940) and was head of the French Military Mission to the United States (1942–1943). Later he was general officer commander-in-chief of French troops in Austria (1945–1950). He was promoted to full general in 1948.

19. Rasp was recalled to active duty as commander of Korps Ems (the LXXXI Corps) on April 2, 1945. He surrendered to the Western

Allies at the end of the war. Released from the POW camps in 1948, he died in Garmisch-Partenkirchen, an old Bavarian garrison town, in 1968; Hermann Foertsch was born in the Deutsch Krone area (now Walcz, Poland) in 1885. He joined the army as an infantry Fahnenjunker in 1913, fought in World War I, served in the Reichsheer, and was press chief for the defense ministry from 1932–1936. He was named chief of staff of the VIII Corps when the war began. Later, he was chief of staff of 12th Army, Army Group E, and Army Group F/OB Southeast, all in the Balkans (1941–1944). He was sent to the northern sector of the Eastern Front in September 1944, where he commanded the X Corps before being recalled to assume command of the 19th Army. Later, he commanded the 1st Army from March 26, 1945, until it surrendered on May 6. An American POW, he was released in 1948 and settled in Munich, where he died in 1961.

Chapter IV: The Battle for Hungary

1. Alfred Seaton, *The Russo-German War, 1941–45* (Novato, California: Presidio Press, 1970), 494.

2. Seaton, *The Russo-German War,* 494. Joseph Radowitz was born in Frankfurt/Main in 1899. He joined the army as a Fahnenjunker in the 20th Dragoons in 1917, fought in World War I, and was discharged in 1919. He joined the Reichswehr as a second lieutenant in 1924 and was adjutant of the III Corps (later III Panzer Corps) when the Second World War began. He joined the staff of the 2nd Panzer Army in early 1942 and assumed command of the 28th Panzer Grenadier Regiment in 1943. He took charge of the 23rd Panzer Division on June 9, 1944, and led it for the rest of the war. Promoted to major general on September 1, he surrendered to the British in May 1945. Radowitz joined the West German army as a major general in 1955 but died in Bad Wiesee, Bavaria, in 1956.

3. Johannes Friessner, *Verratene Schlachten* (Holstein, 1956), 151.

4. The descendent of an old Calvinist noble family, Miklos Horthy was born in 1868, joined the Austro-Hungarian navy in 1896 and became the last commander-in-chief of the Austro-Hungarian Fleet in 1918. He became regent of Hungary in 1920 following the collapse of a Communist rebellion. Under Nazi pressure, he instituted relatively

mild anti-Semitic laws and tried to protect the Hungarian Jews from the Holocaust. Following his capture by the Germans, he lived in house arrest in Bavaria. He was an American prisoner from May to December 1945, moved to Portugal in 1949, and died there in 1957. His remains were returned to Hungary in 1993.

5. Earl F. Ziemke, *Stalingrad to Berlin* (Washington, D.C.: Government Printing Office, 1968), 363.

6. Voeroes died in 1958. Miklos served as prime minister of the Provisional Government (1944–1945). Verres was a German prisoner until 1945. He was named minister of defense and chief of the general staff under the Provisional Government, but was arrested as an American spy by the Communists. He was sentenced to life imprisonment in 1950 but was released during the Revolution of 1956. Remarkably, after the Soviets crushed the revolution, they did not rearrest Verres, who lived peacefully in Balatonfuered, where he died in 1976. General Heszlenyi committed suicide on May 15, 1945, to avoid capture by the Russians. Also see Andris J. Kursietis, *The Royal Hungarian Armed Forces, 1919–1945* (Warsaw: Aspekt Publishers, 1996); Andris J. Kursietis, *The Royal Hungarian Army and Its Leadership in World War II* (Oldbury, United Kingdom: Axis Europa, Inc., 1996); and Leo W. G. Niehorster, *The Royal Hungarian Army, 1920–1945* (Oldbury, united Kingdom: Axis Europa, Inc., 1998).

7. Volksdeutsche were ethnic Germans living outside the borders of the Reich. Many did not even speak German.

8. Friessner, *Verratene Schlachten*, 194–95.

9. Otto Woehler was born in Gross Burgwedel, Hanover, in 1894 and joined the army as a Fahnenjunker in the 167th Infantry Regiment in 1913. He fought in World War I (where he was wounded at least three times), was accepted into the Reichswehr, and was a captain commanding a company in the 6th Infantry Regiment in Eutin, eastern Holstein, in 1939. A War Academy graduate, he was named Ia of the 14th Army when Germany mobilized on August 26, 1939. After serving in Poland, he became chief of staff of XVII Corps in France, and was chief of staff of the 11th Army in Russia (late 1940–1942). He was named commander of the I Corps on April 1, 1943, and assumed command of the 8th Army on August 15, 1943. General

Friessner was born in Chemnitz on March 23, 1892. He joined the army as a Fahnenjunker in 1911 and served in the infantry until 1916, when he underwent General Staff training. During World War II, he commanded the 102nd Infantry Division (1942–1943), XXIII Corps (1943), Army Detachment Narva (1944), Army Group North (1944) and Army Group South Ukraine (later South) (1944). He surrendered to the U.S. Army in May 1945 and was a POW until November 1947. He died in Bad Reichenhall, Upper Bavaria, in 1971, at the age of seventy-nine.

10. Ziemke, *Stalingrad to Berlin*, 385.

11. Hermann Breith was born in Pirmasens in the Rhineland in 1892. He joined the Imperial Army as an officer-cadet in 1910, fought in World War I as an infantry officer (where he was wounded at least three times) and joined the Reichswehr in 1919. He assumed command of the 36th Panzer Regiment in late 1938. Breith was promoted rapidly during the Nazi years, to lieutenant colonel (1936), colonel (1938), major general (1941), lieutenant general (1942) and general of panzer troops (March 1, 1943). He led the 36th Panzer until February 1940, when he assumed command of the 5th Panzer Brigade. He led it until May 22, 1940, when he was severely wounded during the Battle of France. He resumed command after he recovered. In July 1941, he became the General of Mobile Troops at OKH, but on October 2, 1941, returned to the front as commander of the 3rd Panzer Division. He assumed command of the III Panzer Corps on January 3, 1943, and led it for the rest of the war. He was considered a capable and solid commander but not a brilliant one. Breith, however, was considered an exceptionally brave man. He held the Knight's Cross with Oak Leaves and Swords. He managed to surrender to the Western Allies at the end of the war. A POW until May 1947, he settled in Pech (near Bad Godesberg in his native Rhineland) and died there in 1964.

12. Richard Landwehr, "Budapest: The Stalingrad of the Waffen-SS," *Siegrunen*, No. 37 (1985): 6.

13. They had left most of their horses behind outside the city.

14. Gerhard Schmidhuber (1894–1945) was an excellent commander of armored formations and a forceful human being. It was reportedly Schmidhuber who ended the Holocaust in Budapest. A Saxon, he had

enlisted in the army in 1914 and was discharged as a reserve second lieutenant in 1920. He returned to active duty as a captain in 1934 and was a company commander (2/103rd Infantry Regiment) in 1938. Later he commanded II/103rd Infantry Regiment (1939–1942) and 304th Panzer Grenadier Regiment (1943–1944), was deputy commander of the 7th Panzer Division (1944) and commander of the 13th. He was promoted to major general on October 1, 1944.

15. Guenter Pape was born in Duesseldorf in 1907. He joined the Reichsheer as a Fahnenjunker in the 15th (Prussian) Cavalry Regiment in Paderborn in 1927. He rose rapidly, fighting in Poland and France. He led the 3rd Motorcycle Battalion of the 3rd Panzer Division in Russia (1941–1942). He then commanded the 394th Panzer Grenadier Regiment (1942–1944). He assumed command of Panzer Division Feldherrnhalle on July 8, 1944 and was promoted to major general in December 1944. He surrendered his division to the Americans in May 1945. Released in 1947, he joined the Bundeswehr (West German Armed Forces) as a brigade-general and retired as a major general in 1966. He died in the city of his birth in 1986.

16. Pfeffer was born in Kalkberge, Brandenburg, (about fifteen miles east of Berlin) in 1888. He joined the 22nd Field Artillery Regiment as a Fahnenjunker in 1907 and was commissioned the following year. He fought in World War I as a battery commander and a regimental adjutant. He then underwent an abbreviated General Staff training program and was sent to Baghdad as a general staff officer with the Turkish Army. He then served as Ia (chief of operations) to the German military mission in Constantinople. Pfeffer-Wildenbruch returned to the Western Front in late 1917 and served as a general staff officer with the 11th Infantry Division, LV Corps z.b.V. ("for special purposes") and the XXIV Reserve Corps. Not retained by General von Seeckt's Reichsheer in 1920, he joined the Order Police and worked in the Reich Ministry of the Interior. From 1928 to 1933, he was in Santiago, Chile, as chief of the Carabinieros. He returned to Germany in 1933, as a lieutenant colonel of police, and was assigned to the National Police Regiment at Frankfurt/Oder. He and his unit were soon absorbed into the SS, and Pfeffer became inspector of police schools. He was promoted to major general of police in 1937 and became a member of Himmler's staff in the spring of 1939. Promoted to lieutenant general of police in late 1939, he had led the

SS Motorized Division "Polizei" (which later became the 4th SS Panzer Grenadier Division "Police") on the Western Front in 1940. The following year he was named chief of the Colonial Police Bureau of the Interior Ministry, which oversaw police operations in the occupied territories. On September 27, 1943, he was named commander of the the VI (Latvian) Volunteer SS Corps, which he led on the northern sector of the Eastern Front, until he was named commander in chief of Waffen-SS forces in Hungary. He was promoted to SS-Obergruppenfuehrer und General der Waffen-SS in the fall of 1943.

17. Landwehr, "Budapest," 13.

18. Ziemke, *Stalingrad to Berlin*, 433.

19. The Heinkel He-111 was a two-engine bomber which could carry a ton of supplies in an emergency. The Junkers Ju-52 was a tri-engine transport which could carry 1.5 tons.

20. Landwehr, "Budapest," 13.

21. Herbert Otto Gille was born on March 8, 1897, in Gandersheim, Lower Saxony. He attended the Prussian cadet schools and joined the army as a second lieutenant in the 55th Field Artillery Regiment in 1910. He later served in the 30th Field Artillery Regiment and was seriously wounded in World War I. He was discharged as a first lieutenant in 1919 and became an estate manager and a car dealer for the next fifteen years. He joined the SS-Verfuegungstruppe (the forerunner of the Waffen-SS) in 1934 and was an SS major by 1937. After attending the battalion commanders' course at the army's Doeberitz Infantry School, he became commander of the II Battalion/SS Motorized Regiment "Der Fuehrer." He commanded the I Battalion/5th SS Artillery Regiment in Poland and France. Promoted to SS colonel on January 30, 1941, he led the artillery regiment of the SS Division "Viking" in Operation Barbarossa. He was promoted to SS-Oberfuehrer on October 1, 1941, and assumed command of the 5th SS Panzer Division "Viking" on May 1, 1943. He was promoted to SS major general on November 9. Remaining on the Eastern Front, he was appointed commander of the IV SS Panzer Corps on August 6, 1944, and was promoted to general of Waffen-SS on November 9. An apolitical soldier and an excellent divisional commander, he was less successful and less impressive at the corps level. After the war,

Gille worked for a newspaper, owned a small bookstore, and founded "Wiking Ruf," an SS veterans' magazine. He died of a heart attack on December 26, 1966, in Stemmen, near Hanover. His grave no longer exists. Gille was married in 1935. His wife gave birth to their only child, a daughter, nine months and six days later.

22. Landwehr, "Budapest," 21.

23. Seaton, *Russo-German War*, 501.

24. Landwehr, "Budapest," 26.

25. Ibid., 27.

26. Ibid., 20.

27. Peter Neumann, *The Black March* (New York: Bantam Books, 1990), 266.

Chapter V: Stalin's January Offensive

1. Friedrich Hossbach (1894–1980) was born in Unna, North Rhineland-Westphalia, educated in the cadet schools, and joined the Imperial Army in 1913. He fought in World War I, served in the Reichswehr, successfully completed his general staff training, and became armed forces adjutant to Adolf Hitler in 1934. The Fuehrer fired him in February 1938 for deliberately disobeying an order. (Hitler was preparing to fire Colonel General Baron Werner von Fritsch, the commander-in-chief of the army, for alledged homosexual offenses and instructed Hossbach not to tell Fritsch. Hossbach told him anyway.) Hossbach nevertheless rose to the rank of general of infantry. During World War II, he commanded the 82nd Infantry Regiment (1939–1942), the 31st and 82nd Infantry Divisions (1942–1943), the LVI Panzer Corps (1943–1944) and the 4th Army (July 19, 1944–January 28, 1945). He was a POW from 1945–1947.

2. Heinz Guderian, *Panzer Leader,* Constantine Fitzgibbon, trans. (1957, repr. New York: Ballantine Books, 1972), 309.

3. Seaton, *The Russo-German War*, 527.

4. Guderian, *Panzer Leader,* 309.

5. Seaton, *Russo-German War*, 527–28.

6. Siegfried Knappe, "At What Cost!" manuscript in the possession of the author. Later published as *Soldat* by Siegfried Knappe and Ted Brusaw (1992).

7. Ziemke, *Stalingrad to Berlin,* 417. These figures exclude the relatively weak 1st Panzer Army, which was defending the Carpathians against the 4th Ukrainian Front.

8. Ziemke, *Stalingrad to Berlin,* 418.

9. Juergen Thorwald, *Defeat in the East,* 4th ed. (1951; repr., New York: Bantam Books, 1980), 16.

10. John Toland, *The Last 100 Days,* 4th ed. (1966; repr., New York: Bantam Books, 1967), 27.

11. Ibid., 172.

12. *Reichsfreiherr* (Reichsbaron) Maximilian von Edelsheim was born in Berlin in 1897. He entered the service as a Fahnenjunker in the 2nd Guards Uhlan Regiment when World War I broke out. Commissioned the following year, he served in the Reichsheer and later commanded the 1st Bicycle Battalion (1938–1941), the 22nd Cavalry Regiment (1941–1942), the 26th Panzer Grenadier Regiment (1942) and 20th Panzer Brigade (1942). The fact that he held his last appointment for less than a month and was unassigned for more than four months thereafter suggests that he was wounded in the Eastern Front. In any case, he rebuilt the 24th Panzer Division (1943–1944) and led the XXXXVIII Panzer Corps from September 21, 1944, until the end of the war. A highly capable panzer officer, Reichsbaron von Edelsheim was promoted to major general on June 1, 1943, to lieutenant general on March 1, 1944, and to general of panzer troops on December 1, 1944. He held the Knight's Cross with Oak Leaves and Swords. Hermann Recknagel was born in Strauchmuehle, Hesse, on July 18, 1892, and joined the Imperial Army as a Fahnenjunker in the infantry in 1913. He fought on both the Western and Eastern Fronts during World War I and was a major commanding the II Battalion/54th Infantry Regiment at Glogau, Lower Silesia (now Glogow, Poland) in late 1934. He assumed command of the regiment itself when World War II began and led it in Poland, France, and southern Russia. He assumed command of the Lower Saxon 111th Infantry Division on January 1, 1942, and led it brilliantly until November 15, 1943. Cut off by a Soviet advance south of Rostov in

early 1943, Recknagel led the 111th to safety by retreating across ice covering the Sea of Azov. After directing a special staff at OKH, he assumed command of the XXXXII Corps on June 15, 1944, and was promoted to general of infantry on July 1. He held the Knight's Cross with Oak Leaves and Swords.

13. Walter Nehring (pronounced NAIR-ring) was born in Stretzin, West Prussia, in 1892. He joined the army as an infantry *Fahnenjunker* in 1911. Commissioned in the 152nd Infantry (his father's regiment), he fought on both the Eastern and Western Fronts, and was severely wounded three times. He also had a one-week career as an aerial observer, which ended in a crash and a broken jaw. He fought with the Freikorps in 1919 and was accepted into the Reichswehr in 1920. An early convert to the panzer branch, he commanded the 5th Panzer Regiment (1937–1939), was Guderian's chief of staff at XIX Motorized (later Panzer) Corps (1939–1940), and was chief of staff of Panzer Group Guderian (1940) before assuming command of the 18th Panzer Division. Nehring was promoted to lieutenant general on February 1, 1942, and to general of panzer troops on July 1, 1942— only five months later. He then left Russia to command the Afrika Korps (1942) until he was seriously wounded by an Allied fighter-bomber on the night of August 31/September 1, 1942, during the advance on Alma Halfa Ridge. Returning to duty in November, he was commander of the newly formed XC Corps during the initial American drive on Tunis, whose capture he prevented. He earned Goebbels's censure and fell out with the Nazis when he argued that Tunisia could not be held. The fact that subsequent events proved him right and the Fuehrer wrong meant nothing—he was permanently barred from promotion. From February 1943 to March 1945, he was commander of the XXIV Panzer Corps on the Eastern Front. As a result, Nehring was given command of the 1st Panzer Army in Czechoslovakia on March 22, 1945—but without a promotion. He surrendered his Staff to the Americans on May 9, 1945. In my opinion, Nehring was the best all-round panzer commander in World War II. He lived in an apartment in Duesseldorf after the war and died on April 20, 1983.

14. Fritz-Hubert Graeser (1888–1968) was born in Frankfurt/Oder, attended cadet schools, and joined the army as an infantry Faehnich in 1907. He fought in World War I but was discharged from the

service in 1920. He rejoined the army in 1933 and commanded the 8th Machine Gun Battalion (1935–1939) and the 29th Infantry Regiment (1939–1941) in Poland, Luxembourg, Belgium, France, and Russia. On July 11, 1941, he was so severely wounded in the right knee that he could not return to active duty until March 1, 1943, when he assumed command of the 3rd Panzer Grenadier Division. He later served as acting commander of the XXIV Panzer Corps in Russia (July 1944) and commander of the XXXXVIII Panzer Corps (August 5, 1944), before assuming command of the 4th Panzer Army on September 21, 1944. He was promoted to general of panzer troops on September 1. From May 1945 to June 1947 he was an American POW. Graeser lived in Goettingen, Lower Saxony, after the war.

15. Baron Smilo von Luettwitz (1895–1975) was born in Strassburg, Alsace (now Strasbourg, France), and was promoted to major general on September 1, 1942, to lieutenant general on October 1, 1943, and to general of panzer troops on September 1, 1944. During World War II, he served as adjutant, XV Motorized Corps (1938–1940); commander, 12th Rifle Regiment (1940–1942); commander, 4th Rifle Brigade (1942); commander, 26th Panzer Division (1942–1944) in Italy; and commander, XXXXVI Panzer Corps (1944). He commanded the 9th Army on the Eastern Front from September 1, 1944 to January 17, 1945, when he was relieved of his command by Field Marshal Schoerner. Luettwitz began his military career as an infantry Fahnenjunker in 1914 and was wounded at least three times in World War I.

16. Smilo von Luettwitz was given command of the LXXXV Corps on the Western Front on March 31, 1945, and led it until the end of the war. In the late 1950s, he was a lieutenant general and commander of the III Corps of the West German Army. He retired in 1961 and died in 1975. Smilo von Luettwitz was one of the better panzer officers in World War II, yet he is virtually unknown today, because most of his service was in the East. His more famous cousin Heinrich commanded the 2nd Panzer Division and XXXXVII Panzer Corps in Normandy and on the Western Front during World War II.

17. Theodor Busse (1897–1986) was born in Frankfurt an der Oder and joined the army as a Fahnenjunker in 1916. He nevertheless ended the war as a company commander, and was wounded. He served in infantry and general staff positions during the Reichswehr years and

was on the staff of OKH when World War II began. He was chief of operations of 11th Army (1940–1942) and Army Group Don (later South) (1942–1944), before assuming command of the 121st Infantry Division on July 10, 1944. He led the I Corps on the Eastern Front from September 1, 1944, to January 9, 1945, when he took charge of the 9th Army. Busse was not captured by the Western Allies until July 1945. A POW until December 1947, he was director of West German Civil Defense after the war. He was promoted to general of infantry on November 1, 1944.

18. Guderian, *Panzer Leader,* 326.

19. Fries was tried at Torgau Prison, with General of Artillery Maximilian Fretter-Pico serving as chief judge, General of Infantry Kurt von Tippelskirck acting as chief prosecutor, and General of Panzer Troops Otto von Knobelsdorff serving as chief defense attorney. He was acquitted on March 24, 1945, and was taken prisoner by the Allies on May 8, 1945. He was released in June 1947 and retired to Weilburg, Hesse, where he died on August 6, 1982, at the age of ninety. Born in 1894, he had lost an arm and a leg in the Rzhev Salient in 1942 and commanded the 29th Panzer Grenadier Division from March 1, 1943 to August 31, 1944.

20. Guderian, *Panzer Leader,* 326.

21. Ernst Gonell was born in Koenigsberg, East Prussia, on November 24, 1902. He joined the army as a Fahnenjunker in 1922 and was commissioned second lieutenant in the 2nd Infantry Regiment at Allenstein in 1925. A major by 1938, he assumed command of the III/234 Infantry Regiment when Germany mobilized on August 26, 1939. He served in the Polish campaign, commanded a battalion in the 164th Infantry Division (1940–1941) and fought in Greece. In September 1941, he took charge of the III/17th Infantry Regiment and fought on the central sector of the Eastern Front. He assumed command of the Officer Training School at Posen in January 1943. He was named fortress commander of Posen and was promoted to major general on January 30, 1945.

22. Thorwald, *Defeat in the East,* 37–44.

23. Kurt Mehner, *Die Geheimen Tagesberichte der deutschen Wehrmachtfuehrung im Zweiten Weltkrieg, 1939–1945* Vol. 12, (Osnabrueck, Germany: Biblio Verlag, 1984–1995), 421. The term

"kampfgruppe" was used to refer to a regimental sized battle group or a division which had been so burned out by casualties that it had the combat value of a regiment.

24. American troops found the Hindenburgs' caskets in an abandoned salt mine on April 27, 1945. They were reburied in the Elisabeth Church at Marburg, where they still rest. The surprised American soldiers also found a coffin marked "Hitler." Naturally, they opened it. It was empty.

25. Guderian, *Panzer Leader,* 350.

26. Oskar Kummetz (1891–1980) was a native of Illowo, East Prussia. He joined the navy as a *Seekadett* in 1910 and served on battleships until 1916, when he transferred to torpedo boats. Eventually he became commander of torpedo boats (1934–1937), before becoming chief of staff of the Baltic Sea Naval Station (1937–1938) and chief of staff of the High Seas Fleet (1938–1939). As a rear admiral, he commanded a naval group during the invasion of Norway, where his flagship, the heavy cruiser *Bluecher,* was sunk by Norwegian coastal batteries, and Kummetz was briefly a POW. After he was freed, Kummetz became inspector of torpedo affairs (1939–1942), commander of cruisers (1942–1943) and battle groups commander (1943). He became commander-in-chief of the Baltic Sea Command (formerly the Baltic Sea Naval Station) on March 1, 1944. He went into Allied captivity on July 23, 1945, but was released in late 1946. After the war, he initially lived by selling vegetables. Later, he ran a casino in Bad Duerkheim. He died at Neustadt an der Weinstrasse in the Rhineland-Palatinate.

27. Rogge (1899–1982) was promoted to vice admiral on March 1, 1945.

28. Although he was the senior military officer aboard, Commander Zahn lacked the legal authority to give orders to the merchant marine captain.

29. Ironically, the Soviets' S-class submarines had been designed by the Germans, collaborating with the Russians to circumvent the Treaty of Versailles's naval restrictions on Germany.

30. Wilhelm Zahn faded into civilian life after the war and died in 1976 at the age of sixty-six.

31. Hering and *T-36* would rescue many more people before the war ended, but on May 4, 1945, five days after Hitler committed suicide, she was hit by aircraft bombs off Swinemuend, ran into a mine, and sank.

32. Thomale (1900–1978) previously commanded the 27th Panzer Regiment of the 19th Panzer Division on the Eastern Front before joining the staff of the Replacement Army in the spring of 1942. He became chief of staff of the Panzer Inspectorate on March 1, 1943, and was promoted to major general (February 1, 1944) and lieutenant general (March 1, 1945).

33. Ziemke, *Stalingrad to Berlin*, 446. German locomotives were now being forced to use lignite instead of bituminous coal, cutting their efficiency by 60 percent.

34. Walter Wenck was born in Wittenberg, Saxony-Anhalt, in 1900. He joined Freikorps von Oven as a Fahnenjunker in 1919 and was commissioned in the elite 9th Infantry Regiment at Potsdam in 1923. An early convert to the blitzkrieg idea, he held a number of important posts in World War II, including chief of operations, 1st Panzer Division (1939–1942), and chief of staff of the LVII Panzer Corps (1942), 3rd Romanian Army (1942), Army Detachment Hollidt (later 6th Army) (1942–1943), 1st Panzer Army (1943–1944) and Army Group South Ukraine (1944). He became deputy chief of the general staff and chief of operations of OKH on July 22, 1944. A major when the war began, he was promoted to general of panzer troops on April 1, 1945. General Wenck was killed in an automobile accident in Austria in 1982. He was eighty-one years old.

35. Erhard Raus (1889–1956) was born in Wolframitz, Moravia. He attended cadet schools and was commissioned in the Austro-Hungarian Army. During World War I, he fought in southern Poland and northern Italy. He commanded a bicycle jaeger platoon, was a battalion adjutant, and a company commander. Raus was retained in the Austrian Bundesheer in the interwar period and was absorbed into the German Army as a colonel in 1938. During World War II, he successively led the 4th Rifle Regiment, 8th Rifle Brigade, 6th Panzer Division, XI Corps, XXXXVII Panzer Corps, 4th Panzer Army, 1st Panzer Army, and 3rd Panzer Army. He excelled at every level.

36. Hans Krebs was born in Helmstedt, Brunswick, in 1898. He was a Fahnenjunker in the Kaiser's Army when World War I started. He commanded infantry and machine gun units on the Western Front, where he was wounded. Remaining in the Reichsheer, he had a variety of assignments during the Reichswehr period, including commanding a mortar company and a cavalry squadron. He spent all of World War II in staff positions of increasing responsibility, including chief of staff of a corps, an army, and an army group.

37. Toland, The *Last 100 Days*, 30.

38. Seaton, *The Russo-German War*, 544.

39. Ibid, 543–46.

40. Bradley F. Smith and Elena Agarossi, *Operation Sunrise* (New York: Basic Books, 1979), 24.

41. Division Woldenberg was created in January 1945 from the commander and men of the Greifswald Army Anti-Aircraft School.

42. See "Edgar Feuchtinger," Lexikon der Wehrmacht, http://www.lexikon-der-wehrmacht.de/Personenregister/F/FeuchtingerEdgar-R.htm.

Chapter VI: The Russians Close In

1. Seaton, *The Russo-German War*, 351–52.

2. Otto Lasch was born on June 25, 1893, in Pless, Upper Silesia, the son of a forrester. He joined the army as a Fahnenjunker in 1913 and was commissioned second lieutenant the following year. He became a company commander in the West Prussian 2nd Jaeger Battalion shortly thereafter and was wounded in 1915. After he recovered, Lasch became an aerial observer. He remained in aviation for the rest of the war and was adjutant to the air commander, 19th Army, in 1918. Not accepted into the Reichswehr, he was a police officer from 1920 to 1935, when he returned to duty as a major and commander of the III Battalion/3rd Infantry Regiment at Osterode. He fought in Poland, after which he became commander of the 43rd Infantry Regiment (1st Infantry Division), which he led in Belgium, France, and on the northern sector of the Eastern Front, including the battles for Riga, Narva, and Leningrad. In September 1942, he became commander of the 217th Infantry Division, which he led in the Siege

of Leningrad and in the Battle of Kiev. He was sent to France in November 1943, where he helped form the 349th Infantry Division, which he led on the Eastern Front, including the Battle of Brody. On August 5, 1944, Lasch assumed command of the LXIV Corps, then forming in Alsace. He led it in the battles of the Upper Rhine before he was named commander of Wehrkreis I on November 1, 1944—the day he was promoted to general of infantry. He was named commandant of Fortress Koenigsberg on January 28, 1945, and faced 36 Soviet divisions with the equivalent of three German divisions. He was a POW from 1945 to 1955 and spent eight years in a labor camp. He died at Bad Godesberg, near Bonn, on April 29, 1971.

3. General Weiss was never re-employed. He surrendered to the Americans in May 1945 and was a POW until March 1948. His native Tilsit was incorporated into Russia after the war, so he settled in Aschaffenburg am Main, Bavaria. He died on December 21, 1967.

4. Lasch's wife and daughters were arrested, as was his son-in-law, who was commanding a battalion at the front. Due to the rapid collapse of the Third Reich, however, they were not executed.

5. Seaton, *The Russo-German War*, 554.

6. Stephen Fritz, *Endkampf* (Lexington, Kentucky: University Press of Kentucky, 2004), 40.

7. Steinhoff was born in Bottendorf, Thuringia, in 1913, the son of a mill worker. He died in 1994 at the age of 80.

8. Rudel (1916–1982), the son of a Lutheran pastor in Silesia, flew 2,530 combat missions during the war (a record) and was the only holder of the Knight's Cross with Golden Oak Leaves, Swords, and Diamonds. He also shot down nine enemy airplanes and rose from second lieutenant in 1939 to colonel in 1945. Germany's most decorated soldier, he was a successful businessman after the war.

9. Snyder, *Encyclopedia of the Third Reich*, 66.

10. Gottlob Berger, the son of a sawmill owner and carpenter, was born in Gerstetten, Wuerttemberg, in 1896. He fought in World War I, rose to the rank of first lieutenant, and was partially disabled. He joined the NSDAP in 1922, became one of Himmler's principle lieutenants, and was chief of the SS Main Leadership Office from April 1, 1940, until the end of the war. Here he was primarily

responsible for building the Waffen-SS to a strength of thirty-eight divisions, mainly using Volksdeutsche and foreign personnel. He was also chief of staff of the Volkssturm from September 1944. Sentenced to twenty-five years imprisonment in 1949, he was released in late 1951 and died in the town of his birth in 1975.

11. Ziemke, *Stalingrad to Berlin*, 453–54.

12. Forty-five thousand Hungarians surrendered to the Russians on March 30 and 31 alone (Seaton, *The Russo-German War*, 557).

13. Robert Goraliski, *World War II Almanac, 1931–1945* (New York: Random House, 1981), 397.

14. Ernst-Guenther Kraetschmer, *Die Ritterkreuztraeger der Waffen-SS* (Pour Le Merite, 1982), 49.

15. Speer, *Inside the Third Reich*, 440.

16. Tessin, *Verbaende und Truppen der deutschen Wehrmacht*, Vol. 1, 100–1.

17. The staff of the former 299th Infantry Division (from 2nd Army in West Prussia) became Staff, Infantry Division "Schlageter;" Headquarters, 251st Infantry Division (also from 2nd Army) became the HQ of the Friedrich Ludwig Jahn Division. The 215th Infantry Division staff took charge of the Theodor Koerner Division and the staffs of the 131st and 562nd Volksgrenadier Divisions became HQ, Ferdinand von Schill Infantry Division.

18. Gotthard Heinrici was born in Gumbinnen, East Prussia, on December 21, 1886, the descendant of a military family which could trace its roots back to the 12th Century. He entered the service as a Fahnenjunker in 1905 in the 95th (6th Thuringian) Infantry Regiment. He served in World War I as a battalion and regimental adjutant, and took the General Staff course at Sedan in the fall of 1917. He was Ia of the 203rd Infantry Division during the last year of the war. He spent the Reichsheer years alternating between infantry and General Staff positions, and became commander of the 16th Infantry Division in 1937. Later he served as commander of the VII Corps (1940), the II Corps (1940), the XXXXIII Corps (1940–1942), and the 4th Army (1942–1944). He came down with hepatitis in May 1944 and did not return to duty until August 16, 1944, when he assumed command of the 1st Panzer Army. He led it until March 19,

1945, when he became commander-in-chief of Army Group Vistula. Meanwhile, he developed a well-earned reputation as a defensive expert.

19. Guderian surrendered to the Americans in Tyrol on May 10, 1945. Released in June 1948, he wrote the armor classic, *Panzer Leader*, in retirement. This book should be handled with care by historians because General Guderian is not always entirely candid. He died in Schwangau, Bavaria, on May 14, 1954.

Chapter VII: Back across the Rhine

1. Karl Assman, "Hitler and the German Officer Corps," *United States Naval Institute Proceedings* 82 (May 1956): 518.

2. Charles B. MacDonald, *The Last Offensive* (Washington, D.C.: Office of the Chief of Military History, 1973), 6–7, 14.

3. Ibid.

4. Young, *The Marshall Cavendish Illustrated Encyclopedia*, vol. 15, 2046.

5. The U.S. 9th Army was part of Montgomery's 21st Army Group for most of the Western campaign of 1944–1945. Peter Elstob, *Battle of the Reichswald* (New York: Ballantine Books, 1970), 100–3.

6. Koenig was born in Trier on September 19, 1896, entered the service as a war volunteer in 1915 and earned a battlefield commission in the infantry in 1917. Discharged in 1920 as a second lieutenant of reserves, he returned to active duty as a first lieutenant of reserves in 1936. Nine years later he was a lieutenant general. During World War, he served as a regimental adjutant, battalion commander, adjutant of the 246th Infantry Regiment, commander of the 352nd Infantry Regiment, and commander of Division Group 251 (the remnants of the 251st Infantry Division). He attended the four-week division commanders' course in the early summer of 1944 and became commander of the 91st Air Landing Division after its original commander was killed in action on D-Day. Koenig did well and was promoted to major general on September 1, 1944. After the 91st suffered so many casualties that it had to be disbanded, he was named commander of the 272nd Volksgrenadier on December 13, 1944—the very day the American offensive against the division

began. An able and effective commander, Koenig was promoted to lieutenant general on March 1, 1945. He surrendered to the Americans on April 18. A POW until 1948, he settled in Bitburg after the war and died in 1985.

7. Stauffenberg papers.

8. MacDonald, *The Last Offensive*, 137.

9. Gustav-Adolf von Zangen was born in Darmstadt in 1892. He entered the Imperial Army as an officer-cadet in 1910 and was commissioned in the infantry. After World War I, he was discharged from the army, so he joined the police. Zangen reentered the army as a lieutenant colonel in 1935 and rose rapidly, commanding the 88th Infantry Regiment (1938–1941), the 17th Infantry Division (1941–1943), LXXXIV Corps (1943), LXXXVII Corps (1943), Army Detachment von Zangen in northern Italy (1943–1943), and 15th Army. Zangen was promoted to colonel (1938), major general (1942), lieutenant general (1943), and general of infantry (1944). A talented commander, he surrendered 15th Army to the Americans at the end of the Battle of the Ruhr Pocket on April 18, 1945. He lived in Hanau/Main after the war and died there in 1964.

10. MacDonald, *The Last Offensive*, 168.

11. Ibid., 183–84.

12. Gersdorff was a lucky man. On March 21, 1943, he tried to assassinate Hitler with a concealed bomb at a captured weapons inspection, but when Hitler cut the inspection short, Gersdorff had to rush to a restroom to detach the bomb from himself before it went off. The was a line at the restroom, but a chuckling Walter Model, thinking Gersdorff was in pain, let him go first, and Gersdorff was able to disable the bomb just in time. After the Stauffenberg plot failed, the Gestapo missed rounding up Gersdorff who was one of the conspirators. Later, when the British overran the headquarters of the 5th Panzer Army, Gersdorff was the only one who escaped. He was, however, struck by lightning almost as soon as he reached German lines.

13. To his everlasting credit, General Hodges forbade his artillery from firing on the church. The German military commanders and Nazi civilian authorities used the church as a hospital, so it was not a legitimate military target.

14. Baron von Elverfeldt was posthumously promoted to lieutenant general. Colonel Helmut Zollenkopf became acting commander of the division and led it until April 26, when it was dissolved. Zollenkopf had earlier been acting commander of the 21st Panzer Division (January 25–February 12, 1945).

15. Koechling survived the war and did not die until 1970.

16. John R. Angolia, *On the Field of Honor,* vol. 1 (San Jose, California: Bender Publishing, 1981), 101–2.

17. MacDonald, *The Last Offensive*, 204.

18. Ibid.

19. Wilhelm Viebig was born in 1899 and entered the service as a Fahnenjunker. Commissioned *Lieutnant* in the artillery in 1917, he fought in World War I, served in the Reichsheer, and was a major commanding the II/23rd Artillery Regiment in 1937. His subsequent career was not particularly distinguished. He was named commander of the 257th Artillery Regiment when World War II broke out but was not promoted to lieutenant colonel until the spring of 1940 and did not become a colonel until 1942. In the meantime, he served on Manstein's artillery staff (something of a demotion), commanded the 23rd Artillery Regiment on the Eastern Front (1941–1942), and led the 93rd Panzer Artillery Regiment (1942–1944). He assumed command of the 277th Volksgrenadier Division on August 10, 1944, but was not promoted to major general until January 1, 1945. He was captured by the Americans on March 7, 1945. He was released from prison in May 1948. Later that year he became a riding instructor with the British Army of Occupation, a job he held until 1952, when he became a trainer for the riders of the German Olympic Team. He was a stable director in Warendorf after that. He died in 1982.

Chapter VIII: Remagen

1. For the best account of the Battle of the Remagen Bridge, see Ken Hechler, *The Bridge at Remagen* (New York: Ballantine Books, 1957). The foundations of the bridge, incidently, are still visible.

2. Krueger (1892–1973) assumed command of Wehrkreis IV at Dresden on April 10.

3. MacDonald, *The Last Offensive*, 232. North to south, the Remagen bridgehead covering force included the LIII, LXXIV and LXVII Corps.

4. Lauchert was promoted to major general on March 1, 1945. He was later incarcerated by the French, who held him as a POW until 1948. He died in Stuttgart in late 1987 at the age of eighty-two. Major General Oskar Munzel assumed command what was left of the 2nd Panzer shortly thereafter, followed by Major Waldemar von Gazen (April 3, 1945) and Colonel Karl Stollbrock (April 4, 1945, until the capitulation).

5. Herbert Osterkamp was born in Hamm, a city in the northeastern Ruhr, in 1894. He joined the Imperial Army as a Fahnenjunker in the 7th Westphalian Foot Artillery Regiment but was a company commander in the 51st (4th Lower Silesian) Infantry Regiment at the armistice. He fought in the *Freikorps* until he was selected for the one-hundred-thousand-man army Germany was allowed under the Versailles Treaty. Osterkamp began his General Staff training in 1930 and worked in the General Army Office of the Defense Ministry in the 1930s. He became chief of the Army Administrative Office in 1939 and stayed there until November 1, 1944, when he assumed command of Wehrkreis XII. He was promoted to general of artillery on August 1, 1943. General Osterkamp surrendered to the Americans at the end of the war. He died in Dortmund on March 17, 1970.

6. MacDonald, *The Last Offensive*, 301.

7. Infantry Division Hamburg was cobbled together from an assortment of odds and ends on March 10, 1945. Its headquarters was the former Division Staff z.b.V. ("for special purposes") 618, which was formed on March 4, 1945. It included Grenadier Regiments "Hamburg 1" and "Hamburg 2," each of which had two battalions from the 558th and 559th Grenadier Regiments. Its artillery (one battalion and one battery) was provided by the 324th Artillery Regiment of the 180th Infantry Division. Other elements were contributed by the 84th Infantry Division, the 149th Infantry Division, and Wehrkreis X replacement and training units. It was commanded by Major General Walter Steinmueller, a veteran of the Eastern Front.

8. The prison that held General Schneider was taken by the Americans; he remained a prisoner of war until 1947. He died at Wiesbaden in

1980. He had previously commanded the 4th Panzer Division on the Eastern Front.

9.   Schlemm died in Ahlten near Hanover in 1986. He was born in 1894.

10. Colonel Groeschke later made his way back to German lines and was given command of the 5th Parachute Division on April 4, 1945.

11. Major Eller was probably in Muenster when he was killed.

Chapter IX: The Battle of the Ruhr Pocket

1.   Albert Kesselring, *Kesselring: A Soldier's Record* (Westport, Connecticut: Greenwood Press, 1970), 305, 312.

2.   Marcel Stein, *A Flawed Genius: Field Marshal Walter Model*, (Solihull, United Kingdom: Helion & Company, Ltd., 2010), 39.

3.   Herta Model died in 1985.

4.   Hans Roettiger (1896–1960) was later chief of staff of Army Group C in Italy. Born in Hamburg, the son of a reserve major, he joined the 45th Field Artillery Regiment as a *Fahnenjunker* when World War I began. He spent the war on the Western Front and did well. Selected for the *Reichsheer*, he remained in artillery units until 1930, when he underwent General Staff training. He served as Ia of the VI Corps in the Western Campaign of 1940, where he was wounded. He left the XXXXI Corps in the spring of 1942 to become chief of staff of the 4th Army and was later chief of staff of Army Group A on the Eastern Front before being sent to Italy.

5.   Paul Carell, *Hitler Moves East, 1941–1943* (New York: Ballantine Books, 1964), 398.

6.   Model assumed command on August 17. Field Marshal von Kluge committed suicide near Metz on August 19.

7.   Charles Whiting, *Battle of the Ruhr Pocket* (New York: Ballantine Books, 1970), 46.

8.   After the war, the Americans did not look for the SS man who killed General Rose. They did not believe they would convict him of a crime.

9.   Kesselring, *A Soldier's Record*, 297.

10. Zanger and the entire headquarters of 15th Army hid in the forest and escaped to German lines. The HQ, however, was not functional again until April 1.

11. A fine divisional commander, Luettwitz was a mediocre corps leader. He embarrassed himself badly when he demanded the surrender of the American commander at Bastogne. The American called his bluff and replied "Nuts." His army commander, Baron von Manteuffel, would have fired him, except the next senior officer in the corps was Fritz Bayerlein, whom Manteuffel considered even less effective than Luettwitz.

12. Walter Lucht was a Berliner, born in 1882. He entered the Imperial Army as a *Fahnenjunker* in the 1st Foot Artillery Regiment in 1901. During World War I, he commanded an artillery battery, an artillery battalion, and was a General Staff officer, ending the conflict as the chief of operations of an infantry division. He retired as a colonel in 1932 but returned to duty in 1937 and was artillery commander for the Condor Legion in Spain. During World War II, he successively commanded the 215th Artillery Regiment (1939-40), Arko 44 (1940–1941), Harko 310 (1942), 87th Infantry Division (1942), 336th Infantry Division, the Kerch Straits (1943), and the LXVI Corps (1943–1945), mostly on the Eastern Front.

13. Wehrkreis IX was commanded by General of Artillery Maximilian Fretter-Pico, who had previously commanded 6th Army on the Eastern Front until he was sacked in December 1944. He was unemployed until March 1945, when he assumed command of the military district.

14. Whiting, *Battle of the Ruhr Pocket*, 85.

15. Becher did not surrender until May 5. A POW until 1947, he settled in Theerbude, where he died in 1957.

16. Whiting, *Battle of the Ruhr Pocket*, 85.

17. *Die deutsche Wehrmacht: To the Bitter End*, wwii-info.net.

18. Whiting, *Battle of the Ruhr Pocket*, 135.

19. Heinrich Luettwitz surrendered on April 16. He was released from prison in 1946 and retired to Neuberg, Bavaria, where he acquired a small stable from funds saved from his old East Prussian estates, which were then lost. He died in 1969 at the age of seventy-three.

20. Whiting, *Battle of the Ruhr Pocket*, 146.

21. The location of Model's body was kept secret because the Allies were cremating the bodies of dead German leaders and scattering their ashes at undisclosed locations. The bodies of Goering, Keitel, Jodl, Himmler, Kaltenbrunner (all executed in 1946) and others met this fate. After this danger subsided, the field marshal's body was reinterred by his son, Hans-Georg, who later became a general in the West German Army.

22. Leo Kessler, *The Battle of the Ruhr Pocket: April 1945* (Chelsea, Michigan: Scarborough House, 1989), 203–4.

23. James Bacque, *Other Losses* (Toronto, Ontario: Stoddart Publishing Company, 1989).

Chapter X: Defeat in Italy

1. W. G. F. Jackson, *The Battle for Italy* (New York: Harper and Row, 1967), 275–78.

2. Kesselring, *Kesselring: A Soldier's Record*, 264–65.

3. Ernest F. Fisher, *Cassino to the Alps* (Washington, D.C.: Center of Military History, United States Army, 1977), 387.

4. Ibid., 458.

5. Heinrich von Vietinghoff (1887–1952) was a tough, solid East Prussian soldier—extremely capable but not brilliant. After attending cadet schools, he spent most of his career in the infantry, entering the service as a *Faehnrich* (senior officer cadet—sometimes translated as "ensign") in the 2nd Guards Grenadier Regiment in 1906. A better infantry than armored commander, Vietinghoff did not earn any special laurels commanding the 5th Panzer in Poland in 1939. He later led XIII Corps in the West (1939–1940), XXXXVI Panzer Corps in the Balkans and Russia (1940–1942), 9th Army in Russia (September–December 1942), and 15th Army in France (late 1942– September 1943) before being sent to Italy. He fought his most famous battles here as commander of the 10th Army (September 1943–January 1945) or as acting commander-in-chief of Army Group C (October–December 1944). He was named commander of Army Group Courland in January 1945 but returned to Italy as OB Southwest (Supreme Commander, Southwest)—this time on a

permanent basis—in March 1945. He was promoted to general of panzer troops in 1940 and to colonel general in September 1943. An excellent commander at all levels, General von Vietinghoff is best known for his very skillful retreats before the Americans and British in Italy (1943–1944).

6. Anton Dostler was born in Munich, Bavaria, on May 10, 1891. He joined the army as a *Fahnenjunker* in the 6th Bavarian Infantry Regiment and fought on the Western Front in World War I, where he became a company commander. During the Reichswehr years he qualified for the General Staff, and served in a variety of assignments, including infantry, cavalry, and artillery positions. He was later chief of operations of the 8th Infantry Division (1935–1937), chief of operations of Army Group 4 (1937–1939), Ia of the 7th Army (1939), chief of staff of the XXI Corps (1939–1941), (where he played a major role in conquering Norway); commander of the 57th Infantry Division on the southern sector of the Russian Front (1941–1942), commander of the 163rd Infantry Division in Lapland (1942), and commander of the XXXXII, LXXV and LXXII Corps (1943–1945). He was promoted to general of infantry on August 1, 1943. General Dostler obeyed Hitler's orders to execute commandos. As a result, he faced a firing squad on December 1, 1945.

7. Count Gerhard von Schwerin, a holder of the Knight's Cross with Oak Leaves and Swords, was born in Hanover in 1899. He joined the army as a *Faehnrich* (senior officer cadet) in the elite 2nd Guard Regiment of Foot when World War I broke out and fought on the Western and Eastern Fronts. He was not initially selected for the Reichswehr and was discharged as a lieutenant in 1920. He re-entered the service in 1922 as a lieutenant in the East Prussian 1st Infantry Regiment and was on the staff of OKH when the next world war began. Count von Schwerin commanded the I Battalion of the elite Grossdeutschland Motorized Infantry Regiment, the 86th Rifle Regiment, the Grossdeutschland Regiment itself, and the 200th Special Purposes Regiment (1939–1941), which he led in North Africa, until the Desert Fox sent him home. He was then given command of the 76th Infantry Regiment (1941–1942) on the Eastern Front. After briefly serving as acting commander of the 254th Infantry Division (April–May 1942), he was acting commander of the 8th Jaeger Division (summer 1942) and commander of the 16th

Panzer Grenadier Division (November 13, 1942–August 23, 1944), which was upgraded to the 116th Panzer Division in the spring of 1944. Sacked during the Battle of Aachen, he was labeled a defeatist by the Nazis in the fall of 1944, and they considered court-martialing him for his attempt to evacuate Aachen without permission. (The Nazis, for once, were right: there was no need to abandon the city at that time, and the 116th Panzer was not under any pressure to do so from the Americans.) Possibly because he held the Knight's Cross with Oak Leaves and Swords, however, they decided not to do so. His friends at OKH even succeeded in obtaining another command for Schwerin, who took over the 90th Panzer Grenadier Division in Italy on December 1, 1944. From April 1 to April 25, 1945, Schwerin commanded the LXXVI Panzer Corps in Italy and surrendered it to the Western Allies, which earned him Kesselring's censure. He was promoted to major general on October 1, 1942, to lieutenant general on June 1, 1943, and to general of panzer troops on April 1, 1945. He lived in Bonn for a time but died in Rottach-Egern, Upper Bavaria, in 1980, at the age of eighty-one.

8. Traugott Herr (1890–1976) joined the Imperial Army as an officer-cadet in the 35th Fuesilier Regiment in 1911. He fought in World War I, mainly as a battalion adjutant and as a machine gun company commander, and was wounded twice. He commanded the III/33rd Infantry Regiment (1937–1939), the 13th Replacement and Training Regiment (1939), the 66th Rifle (or Motorized Infantry) Regiment of the 13th Motorized Division (1939–1940), the 13th Motorized Infantry Brigade (1940–1941), and 13th Panzer Division on the Eastern Front (1941–1942). He was promoted to major general on April 1, 1942, and to lieutenant general on December 1, 1942. Herr was wounded in the head on November 1, 1942, and saw no further service until June 25, 1943, when he assumed command of the LXXVI Panzer Corps in Italy (1943–1945). He had to take an extended medical leave to undergo a brain operation. A general of panzer troops from September 1, 1943, he was acting commander of the 14th Army in Italy (November–December 1944) and commander of 10th Army (1945), which he surrendered to the Western Allies at the end of the war in Italy. A holder of the Knight's Cross with Oak Leaves and Swords, General Herr was an excellent panzer commander.

9. Fisher, *Cassino to the Alps*, 469.

10. The *Freikorps* (free corps) were loosely organized, right-wing paramilitary formations.

11. General Boehlke surrendered to the Americans in late April 1945 and was released in 1947. He died in Munich in 1956. Boehlke was born in Lubahn, West Prussia, in 1893.

12. See Georg Tessin, *Verbaende und Truppen der Deutschen Wehrmacht und Waffen-SS im Zweiten Weltkrieg, 1939–1945*, vol. 6, *Die Landstreitkraefte* (Osnabrueck: Biblio-Verlag, 1979).

13. John Angolia, *Field of Honor*, vol. 1, (San Jose, California: Bender, 1979), 160–61. Trettner later served in the West German Air Force. He died on September 18, 2006—one day before his ninety-ninth birthday. He was a true gentleman and the last of the Wehrmacht's generals to die.

14. Jackson, *The Battle for Italy*, 315.

15. Karl Friedrich Wilhelm Schulz (1897–1976) was born in Nettkow, Silesia. He joined the army as a war volunteer in the 54th Field Artillery Regiment in 1914 but earned a commission in the 58th Infantry Regiment in 1916. He spent the war on the Western Front, was selected for the Reichsheer, and successfully completed general staff training. He was on the staff of OKW when World War II began. Later, he was chief of staff of General Heinrici's XXXXIII Corps (1940–1942), and chief of staff of Manstein's 11th Army (1942) and Army Group Don (later South) (1942–1943). He then commanded the 28th Jaeger Division in Russia (1943–1944) and served as acting commander of the III Panzer Corps (late 1943) and the LIX Corps (early 1944). He assumed command of the XXXXVI Panzer Corps on the Eastern Front on March 22, 1944, this time as permanent commander. He led the 17th Army from July 25, 1944 to March 30, 1945, when he was named commander of Army Group South. He arrived in Italy on April 2. A prisoner of war until 1948, Schulz died in Freudenstadt, in the Black Forest, at the age of seventy-nine; Fritz Wentzel was born at Kassel in 1899 and died in Bad Nauheim in 1948, shortly before his 49th birthday. He joined the army as a Fahnenjunker in the 17th Field Artillery Regiment in 1917 and fought in the last battles of World War I. He was accepted into the Reichswehr and became a second lieutenant in 1919. He was

commanding the I Battalion/2nd Artillery Regiment when Germany mobilized, but he was immediately named chief of operations of the 257th Infantry Division in the Saar. He became chief of operations of the 17th Army in late 1940 and served in this post (mainly on the Eastern Front) until mid-1943. He became chief of staff of Vietinghoff's 10th Army in August 1943 and served until November 30, 1944. He took a divisional commanders' course in early 1945 but was not given a command; instead, he became chief of staff of Army Group G on April 2, 1945. He was promoted to major general on March 1, 1944, and to lieutenant general on April 20, 1945.

16. Joachim Lemelsen was born in Berlin in 1888 and entered the service as an artillery Fahnenjunker in 1907. Commissioned the following year, he served in World War I as a General Staff officer in infantry and artillery units. He was commander of the Artillery Lehr (Demonstration) Regiment in 1934 and later was a course commandant at the Infantry School at Dresden (1935–1938), and commander of the 29th Motorized Infantry Division (1938–1940). Named commander of the 5th Panzer Division in the last days of the French campaign (in part because he was close at hand), he was promoted to general of artillery on August 1, 1940. (Later, on June 4, 1941, he changed his branch affiliation and became a general of panzer troops.) Lemelsen only commanded the 5th Panzer for two weeks. He led XXXXVI Panzer Corps (1940–1943) in Russia, was acting commander of the 10th Army in Italy (October–December 1943), and commanded 1st Army in France (May–June 5, 1944) and 14th Army in Italy (1944). Lemelsen held the Knights Cross with Oak Leaves. A pro-Nazi, Lemelsen was an excellent motorized divisional commander and did well leading panzers in Russia. He was less successful as an army commander in Italy. A British prisoner of war until 1948, Lemelsen died in Goettingen in 1954.

17. Frido von Senger und Etterlin, *War Diary of the Italian Campaign (1943–45),* (Foreign Military Studies MS # C-095, 1951–53). Fridolin von Senger und Etterlin was born in the medieval town of Waldshut, Baden, (on the Upper Rhine) in 1891. He grew up in an aristocratic family of wealth and prestige and was very well educated. During World War I, he served mainly with the 76th Field Artillery Regiment. After the war, he transferred to the cavalry, and spent much of his career (1920–1933) with the 18th Cavalry Regiment at

Stuttgart-Cannstatt. He also served in the 1st Cavalry Division, about which he later wrote a book. After leaving the 18th Cavalry, he was chief of staff of the Cavalry Inspectorate (1934–1938), and commanded the 3rd Cavalry Regiment (1938–1939), the 22nd Cavalry Regiment (1939–1940), and the 2nd Rifle Brigade (1940) before becoming a German delegate to the Italian-French Armistice Commission (1941–1942). He briefly commanded the 10th Panzer Grenadier Regiment in occupied France (July–September 1942), before becoming the commander of the 17th Panzer Division (October 10, 1942–June 1943). After leaving the 17th Panzer, Senger, who possessed considerable diplomatic ability, was briefly Wehrmacht Commander in Sicily (1943) and German liaison officer to the Italian 6th Army. He did a brilliant job of evacuating Sardinia and Corsica, which led to his promotion to the command of the XIV Panzer Corps on October 23, 1943. He led on the Italian Front for the rest of the war. He was promoted to lieutenant general on May 1, 1943, and to general of panzer troops effective January 1, 1944. He also briefly commanded the 14th Army in Italy in October 1944. An American prisoner of war until May 1948, he became the headmaster of a private school near Lake Constance, a writer, and a military journalist after the war. His son, who lost an arm when he was run over by a tank on the Eastern Front, became a West German general and an author in his own right. General Frido von Senger died at Freiburg in Breisgau in January 1963.

Chapter XI: On the Edge

1. Hugh R. Trever-Roper, *The Last Days of Hitler* (1947; reprint ed., 1973), 111.

2. Army Group South was renamed Army Group Ostmark in April 1945.

3. Anthony J. Munoz, *Forgotten Legions: Obscure Combat Formations of the Waffen-SS* (Boulder, Colorado: Paladin Press, 1988), 376. Figures are as of March 17, 1945.

4. Ziemke, *Satlingrad to Berlin*, 470–71; Seaton, *The Russo-German War*, 566–67; Mehner, *Geheimen Tagesberichte* 12: 436.

5. Toland, *The Last 100 Days*, 379–81.

6. Toland, *The Last 100 Days,* 378–83. Ernst Biehler was born in Ulm in 1903. He joined the *Reichsheer* as a private in the infantry in 1923 and was commissioned second lieutenant in the Wuerttemburger 13th Infantry Regiment at Ludwigsburg in 1928. He underwent General Staff training and was the adjutant of his regiment in 1939, when World War II began. He served on the Saar Front (1939–1940), on the staff of the XXV Corps in France (1940), and was chief supply officer (Ib) of the 24th Infantry Division from late 1940 to January 1942, when he became its chief of operations (Ia). Ironically, this position had been held by Hans Krebs in the 1930s. He fought on the southern sector of the Eastern Front, including the drive on Kiev, and in the Crimea, before being sent north, where he participated in the Siege of Leningrad. In late 1943, he was named chief of operations of the 9th Luftwaffe Field Division, and in early 1944 became a lecturer at the War Academy. He briefly served as chief of staff of the XXVII Corps (July–August 1944) on the Eastern Front before assuming command of the 358th Infantry Regiment in Russia on September 20, 1944. Biehler became acting commander of the 205th Infantry Division (of which the 358th was a part) on October 20, but was seriously wounded in action on November 15. He returned to duty in Frankfurt/Oder in January 1945; General Biehler was a Soviet prisoner until 1955. He lived in Clausthal-Zellerfeld, in the Harz Mountains, after the war, and died in 1997, less than two weeks before his ninety-fourth birthday.

7. Siegfried Knappe, "At What Cost?" manuscript in possession of the author. Brauer was executed by the Greeks after the war as a war criminal.

8. Seaton, *The Russo-German War,* 563.

9. The last major German battleship, the *Tirpitz*—the sister of the *Bismarck*—had been sunk at anchor in a fjord near Tromso, Norway, by the RAF on the night of November 11/12, 1943. Some 900 of her 1,500-man crew went down with her.

10. Stephen G. Fritz, *Endkampf* (Lexington, Kentucky: University of Kentucky Press, 2004), 117.

11. Ibid., 213–16

12. Recent evacuations had lowered the camp's prison population by nearly fifty thousand people.

13. Toland, *The Last 100 Days*, 402–3.

14. MacDonald, *The Last Offensive*, 390.

15. Toland, *The Last 100 Days*, 420.

16. Sieckenius had previously commanded the 16th Panzer Division. He was made the scapegoat for the German defeat at Salerno, Italy.

Chapter XII: Goetterdaemmerung

1. Heinrici had pulled off this exact same maneuver several times before on Germany's Eastern Front.

2. Ziemke, *Stalingrad to Berlin,* 475.

3. Ibid., 476.

4. Leonard Mosley, *The Reich Marshal* (New York: Dell Publishing, 1974), 376.

5. Ziemke, *Stalingrad to Berlin,* 478.

6. Mosley, *The Reich Marshal*, 378.

7. Ibid., 379–80.

8. Ibid., 383.

9. Hugh R. Trevor-Roper, *The Last Days of Hitler,* (1947; repr., New York: Berkley, 1973), 211.

10. Knappe manuscript.

11. Ibid.

12. Ibid.

13. Ibid.

14. Ibid.

15. Ziemke, *Stalingrad to Berlin,* 483.

16. Lucht was a POW until 1948. He was killed in an automobile accident near Heilbronn on March 18, 1949.

17. Robert Goralski, *World War II Almanac, 1931–1945,* (New York: Putnam 1977), 400.

18. Seaton, *The Russo-German War,* 579.

19. The Bendlerstrasse was the German equivalent of the Pentagon. It was the former seat of the War (later Defense) Ministry and, during World War II, was the headquarters of the Home Army. It had been heavily damaged by Anglo-American bombers.

20. Knappe manuscript.

21. Ziemke, *Stalingrad to Berlin* 486.

22. Knappe manuscript.

23. Schellenberg (1910–1952) was a high-ranking officer in the SD (*Sicherheitsdienst* or Security Service) and head of foreign intelligence for Nazi Germany.

24. Ziemke, *Stalingrad to Berlin,* 486–87.

25. Ibid., 488.

26. Ibid., 488.

27. Johannes Steinhoff et al, *Voices from the Third Reich* (Washington, D.C.: Regnery Gateway, 1989), 488.

28. William L. Shirer, *The Rise and Fall of the Third Reich* (Delran, New Jersey: Simon and Schuster, 1960), 1122.

29. Ibid.

30. His repeatedly stated reason for not marrying her earlier was that it would interfere with his dedication to his political mission.

31. International Military Tribunal, *Nazi Conspiracy and Aggression* (Nuremberg, Germany: Office of the United States Chief of Counsel for Prosecution of Axis Criminality, 1946), vol. 6, 259–63.

32. Heinrici was captured by the British on May 28, 1945, and was not released until May 19, 1948. He spent much of his time as a POW with his cousin, Field Marshal Gerd von Rundstedt. He died on December 13, 1971, in Waiblingen, Wuerttemberg. Strangely enough, General von Trotha was reemployed. On May 10, he was named a special advisor to Reich Minister Speer. He died in Heidelberg in 1998 at the age of ninety-two.

33. Keilig, *Die Generale des Heeres*, 378.

34. Ruediger Pipkorn, a veteran General Staff officer, had been transferred to the Waffen-SS against his will. He was killed by a Stalin tank on April 26.

Chapter XIII: The Surrenders

1. Ziemke, *Stalingrad to Berlin*, 495.

2. Hermann Foertsch (1885–1961) was an East Prussian who had been chief of staff of the 12th Army and Army Groups E and F in the Balkans and commander of the 21st Infantry Division and X Corps on the Eastern Front. He was named commander of the 1st Army on March 26, 1945, succeeding Obstfelder. He was an American POW until 1948.

3. James Lucas, *Last Days of the Third Reich* (New York: William Morrow and Company, 1986), 63.

4. Ibid., 63–64

5. Peter Padfield, *Doenitz: The Last Fuehrer* (New York: Harper and Row, 1984), 423.

6. Ziemke, *Stalingrad to Berlin*, 497.

7. Hilpert died in Moscow in 1946. Pflugbeil died in May 1955.

8. On May 6, he was captured by Czech partisans. He was killed during an escape attempt in June 1945.

9. Lucas, *Last Days of the Third Reich*, 112.

10. He died in Upper Bavaria in 1980.

11. Dietrich von Saucken was born in Fischhausen, East Prussia (now Primorsk, Russia), in 1892, the son of an administrative official. He entered the service as a Fahnenjunker in the 2nd East Prussian Grenadier Regiment in 1910 and was commissioned Leutnant in 1912. He fought on the Eastern Front (including the Battle of Tannenberg), the Western Front (including Verdun), in Romania, the Western Front again, and then the Baltic sector. He joined the Freikorps after the war, transferred to the cavalry in 1921 and was on special assignment to the Soviet Union in the 1920s. He assumed command of the 2nd (Prussian) Cavalry Regiment in 1937 and was promoted to colonel in 1939. He led horse soldiers in Poland and France, and was transferred to the mobile branch in the fall of 1940. He successively commanded the 4th Rifle Brigade, the 4th Panzer Division, the III Panzer Corps (acting commander only), XXXIX Panzer Corps, and the Grossdeutschland Panzer Corps, all on the Eastern Front. He was the 27th and last soldier to receive the Knights'

Cross with Oak Leaves, Swords, and Diamonds. He died in Bavaria in 1980.

12. Friedrich von Stauffenberg, personal communication, 1984.

13. One group that did not benefit from surrendering to the Americans was the *SS-Totenkopfverbaende*. The men of these "Death's Head" units were former concentration camp guards. They were often shot or turned over to the Soviets.

14. Lucas, *Last Days of the Third Reich*, 112.

15. Ibid., 119–24.

16. Ibid., 121–24.

17. Fritz, *Endkampf*, 48.

18. Young, *The Marshall Cavendish Illustrated Encyclopedia*, vol. 16, 2178.

19. Padfield, *Doenitz*, 433.

Index